THE STUDY OF ECONOMIC HISTORY

THE STUDY OF ECONOMIC HISTORY

Collected Inaugural Lectures
1893-1970

Edited, and with an introduction by

N. B. HARTE

Lecturer in Economic History, University College, London

FRANK CASS : LONDON

First published in 1971 by
FRANK CASS AND COMPANY LIMITED
67 Great Russell Street, London, WC1B 3BT

Distributed in the United States by
International Scholarly Book Services, Inc.
Beaverton, Oregon 97005

Library of Congress Catalog Card Number 74-177972

ISBN 0 7146 2905 7

Printed in Great Britain by
Clarke, Doble & Brendon Ltd.,
Plymouth

CONTENTS

	Preface		vii
	Introduction	: THE MAKING OF ECONOMIC HISTORY	xi
1	W. J. Ashley	: ON THE STUDY OF ECONOMIC HISTORY (*Harvard, 1893*)	1
2	L. L. Price	: THE POSITION AND PROSPECTS OF THE STUDY OF ECONOMIC HISTORY (*Oxford, 1908*)	19
3	George Unwin	: THE AIMS OF ECONOMIC HISTORY (*Edinburgh, 1908*)	37
4	J. H. Clapham	: THE STUDY OF ECONOMIC HISTORY (*Cambridge, 1929*)	55
5	G. N. Clark	: THE STUDY OF ECONOMIC HISTORY (*Oxford, 1932*)	71
6	R. H. Tawney	: THE STUDY OF ECONOMIC HISTORY (*L.S.E., 1932*)	87
7	Eileen Power	: ON MEDIEVAL HISTORY AS A SOCIAL STUDY (*L.S.E., 1933*)	109
8	M. M. Postan	: THE HISTORICAL METHOD IN SOCIAL SCIENCE (*Cambridge, 1939*)	127
9	W. K. Hancock	: ECONOMIC HISTORY AT OXFORD (*Oxford, 1946*)	143
10	T. S. Ashton	: THE RELATION OF ECONOMIC HISTORY TO ECONOMIC THEORY (*L.S.E., 1946*)	161
11	F. J. Fisher	: THE SIXTEENTH AND SEVENTEENTH CENTURIES: THE DARK AGES IN ENGLISH ECONOMIC HISTORY? (*L.S.E., 1956*)	181
12	W. Ashworth	: THE STUDY OF MODERN ECONOMIC HISTORY (*Bristol, 1958*)	201
13	A. J. Youngson	: PROGRESS AND THE INDIVIDUAL IN ECONOMIC HISTORY (*Edinburgh, 1959*)	219

v

14 **J. D. Chambers** : THE PLACE OF ECONOMIC HISTORY IN HISTORICAL STUDIES (*Nottingham, 1960*)   231

15 **M. W. Beresford** : TIME AND PLACE (*Leeds, 1960*)   253

16 **S. G. E. Lythe** : THE HISTORIAN'S PROFESSION (*Strathclyde, 1963*)   273

17 **Sidney Pollard** : ECONOMIC HISTORY—A SCIENCE OF SOCIETY? (*Sheffield, 1964*)   289

18 **Ralph Davis** : HISTORY AND THE SOCIAL SCIENCES (*Leicester, 1965*)   313

19 **A. W. Coats** : ECONOMIC GROWTH: THE ECONOMIC AND SOCIAL HISTORIAN'S DILEMMA (*Nottingham, 1966*)   329

20 **W. A. Cole** : ECONOMIC HISTORY AS A SOCIAL SCIENCE (*Swansea, 1967*)   349

21 **Peter Mathias** : LIVING WITH THE NEIGHBOURS: THE ROLE OF ECONOMIC HISTORY (*Oxford, 1970*)   367

Index   385

PREFACE

THIS volume collects together the twenty-one inaugural lectures in economic history, eighteen of them delivered by professors of the subject in British universities between 1929 and 1970. To these, three earlier lectures have been appropriately added. The first is that delivered in 1893 by the Englishman who inaugurated at Harvard the first chair anywhere in the subject and the second and third, while not professorial inaugural lectures, are of the same nature; they were given by two of the first lecturers in economic history before chairs in the subject had been established in Britain. Although there is no statutory obligation to deliver an inaugural, many scholars appointed to chairs have either taken or been encouraged to take the opportunity of making a statement about the nature, scope or practice of their subject. Most such lectures however were originally published in rather fugitive form and are not readily available to students of the subject today; it is hoped that collecting them all together in a single volume might itself make a contribution to the study of economic history.

Two of the lectures, those by Professor W. Ashworth and Professor S. G. E. Lythe, are published here for the first time. The others have been reprinted in full from the original published versions, in some cases with minor textual amendments by the author or minor corrections by the editor. In two cases short additional postscripts have been added. The editor and the publishers are grateful to the following for permission to reprint these lectures: for that by W. J. Ashley, originally published in the *Quarterly Journal of Economics*, VII, 2, 1893, pp. 115–136, to the Editor of that journal; for the lecture by L. L. Price to the Clarendon Press, Oxford; for the lecture by George Unwin, originally published in R. H. Tawney (ed.), *Studies in Economic History: The Collected Papers of George Unwin* (London, 1927) to Frank Cass & Co.; for the lecture by J. H. Clapham to Mr. Michael Clapham, the Trustees of the late Sir John Clapham and the Cambridge University Press; for the lecture by G. N. Clark, originally published in *History*, N.S., XVII, 66, 1932, pp. 97–110, to Sir George Clark and the Editor of *History*; for the lecture by R. H. Tawney, originally published in *Economica*, XIII, 39, 1933, pp. 1–21, to Mr. J. M. K. Vyvyan and the Editor of

vii

Economica; for the lecture by Eileen Power, originally published in *Economica*, NS, I, 1934, pp. 13–29, to Professor M. M. Postan and the Editor of *Economica*; for the lecture by M. M. Postan to Professor Postan and the Cambridge University Press; for the lecture by W. K. Hancock to Sir Keith Hancock and the Clarendon Press, Oxford; for the lecture by T. S. Ashton, originally published in *Economica*, NS, XIII, 50, 1946, pp. 81–96, to Mrs. T. S. Ashton and the Editor of *Economica*; for the lecture by F. J. Fisher, originally published in *Economica*, NS, XXIV, 93, 1957, pp. 2–18, to Professor Fisher and the Editor of *Economica*; for the lecture by A. J. Youngson, originally published by the University of Edinburgh, to Professor Youngson; for the lecture by J. D. Chambers, originally published by the University of Nottingham, to the late Professor Chambers—it must sadly be recorded that to give this volume his blessing was one of Professor Chambers' last acts; for the lecture by M. W. Beresford, originally published by the Leeds University Press, to Professor Beresford; for the lecture by Sidney Pollard, originally published by the University of Sheffield (a slightly altered version of which appeared in *Past and Present*, 30, 1965, pp. 3–22) to Professor Pollard; for the lecture by Ralph Davis, originally published by Leicester University Press, to Professor Davis; for the lecture by A. W. Coats, originally published by the University of Nottingham, to Professor Coats; for the lecture by W. A. Cole, originally published by the University College of Swansea, to Professor Cole and the Registrar of the College, and for the lecture by Peter Mathias, to the Clarendon Press, Oxford, and to Professor Mathias.

In the introduction I have not presumed to provide a summary of these lectures, much less anything in the nature of a further inaugural lecture; I have merely tried to clarify some of the background to the twenty-one lectures themselves and to bring out a few factors involved in the making of the subject, some of them well-known, some of them rather overlooked. The lectures themselves should need no further introducing. Anyway, in 1970, while the volume was being compiled, at least two brief introductory surveys of the subject were published—Harold Perkin, 'Social and Economic History' in H. Perkin (ed.), *History: An Introduction for the Intending Student* and Peter Mathias, 'Economic History—Direct and Oblique' in Martin Ballard (ed.), *New Movements in the Study and Teaching of History* and a third was reprinted as 'What is Economic History?' in W. H. B. Court, *Scarcity and Choice in History*. Furthermore, a small volume entitled *Research in Economic and Social History*, a modest but invaluable guide to current activity in the subject, is to be published by the Social Science Research Council early in 1971.

Of those who encouraged me in the task of putting this volume together I would like to record my gratitude for the kindnesses shown by the late Professor David Joslin, whose sudden and saddening death occurred as the volume was going to press. I am also indebted to a number of friends for their generous help, particularly to R. S. Craig, D. J. Tierney, R. J. Bullen, Dr. W. H. Chaloner and especially to Professor A. W. Coats. I am indebted to Eva Harte, my wife, for helping me face the unexpected rigours of editorship.

University College London   N. B. HARTE
1971

INTRODUCTION

The Making of Economic History

THE effective emergence of economic history has been one of the significant academic achievements of the last hundred years. What was virtually uncultivated territory a century ago, barely explored even, has become one of the most productive fields on the academic map. Before the last quarter of the nineteenth century economic history was not a recognized field of interest in any acknowledged sense at all, much less a subject or an academic discipline. In 1970 it is established in practically every British university; there are nearly 30 professors of the subject and almost as many separate departments offering teaching for degrees in it. It is the only branch of history to have attained this independent status. There are textbooks galore and ever-growing series of 'readings' and reprints of one kind or another to cater for expanding numbers of students devoting some of their time to the study of the subject in the universities, technical colleges, colleges of education and schools of all sorts. There are nearly 200 specialist teachers of the subject in the universities alone. The Economic History Society has a membership of over 3,000 and the *Economic History Review* has a circulation of almost 5,000. It is an interesting historical problem to account for the growth of the subject on this scale, quite apart from the historiographical question as to what it was that went into the making of the subject. The history of economic history has yet to be written.[1] Until it is, the inaugural lectures of the distinguished economic historians collected in this volume ought to provide some guide to an understanding of the scope of the subject and its development. This introduction does not attempt to deal comprehensively with the nature of the subject; it is intended to provide a sketch towards explaining its origin and its institutionalization as a university discipline, as a gloss on the twenty-one lectures that follow.

There is a sense of course in which the subject is more than a century old. The rising body of writing on economic subjects in the seventeenth century contained much in the way of historical treatment of certain economic problems, and especially when this was combined with the sort of treatment of macro-economic issues

created by the fashion for 'political arithmetic', something towards a
definite tradition of 'economic history' was established before 1700.
To the works of Petty, Graunt, Temple, Houghton and others, the
eighteenth century added a number of historical compendiums of
economic information—industrial, like John Smith's *Memoirs of
Wool* (1747); commercial like Adam Anderson's *Historical and
Chronological Deductions of the Origin of Commerce* (1764); financial,
like John Sinclair's *History of the Public Revenue of the British
Empire* (1784), or social, like Frederick Eden's *State of the Poor*
(1797). In the nineteenth century this tradition was further augmented
by works drawing on the rapid increase in output of governmental
statistics, such as G. R. Porter's *Progress of the Nation* (1836–43),
as well as by a number of volumes that owed their origin to a sense
of pride in British industrial achievements, like Edward Baines'
History of the Cotton Manufacture (1835) or J. Bischoff's *Comprehensive History of the Woollen and Worsted Manufactures* (1842).
All this was clearly 'economic history' in a sense, and the subject as
we know it today certainly owes something to this tradition.[2] But it
did not add up to a 'subject'. Economic history as a discipline taught
and studied in universities and schools today is an achievement of late
Victorian and Edwardian society. The annalists gave way to analysis.
In two or three decades what had merely been an interest of a
handful of diverse individuals for antiquarian or practical purposes
was woven into a discipline, characterized by its distinctive core of
problems, its method of answering them, its text-books, its examinations and its specialist university teachers. These developments took
place neither suddenly nor all at once, but they happened with
sufficient rapidity for a crucial period of growth that might be called
'take-off' to be identified between about 1882 and 1904.[3] Half of the
lectures gathered together in this volume illustrate the subject's
subsequent drive to maturity and half what might almost be regarded
as its age of mass consumption. It is therefore perhaps worth looking
at the factors that led to the 'take-off' itself and at the intellectual and
institutional pre-conditions for the growth of the subject in the later
nineteenth century.

Economic history as a line of inquiry was notably backward
relative to economics itself in the nineteenth century. Since Adam
Smith, economics had made important strides, while the historical
aspects of the subject during a period of enormous structural change
in the economy were left, by and large, to a handful of non-academic
Victorian worthies. Why was the genesis of economic history so long
delayed in a country and in a period which presents so much of
crucial importance to the economic historian today? The simple
answer is that economics as understood by the classical economists

of the nineteenth century was an a-historical subject, not to say an anti-historical one, while history was not conceived as being concerned with things economic. The method adopted by what became known as 'the dismal science' was that of logic and deduction from abstract principles, rather than that of empirical investigation and historical inquiry. The ample historical digressions employed by Smith in *The Wealth of Nations* (1776) conspicuously did not relieve the pages of David Ricardo's *Principles of Political Economy* (1817), and it was the approach laid down by Ricardo which dominated classical political economy in England. John Stuart Mill's *Principles of Political Economy* (1848), though concerned to some extent with what he called 'applications' as well as with the 'principles' themselves, followed Ricardo in treating economics in a basically non-historical manner. Economic thought in England in the generations dominated by Ricardo, Mill and the Benthamite distaste for the study of the past is to be contrasted with the line of development taking place at the same time in Germany. While Mill's system of economic principles became entrenched in English thought, the approach to economics in Germany was radically altered during the 1840s and after by the so-called 'historical school' of economists. The most influential of these was Wilhelm Roscher whose *Grundriss zu Vorlesungen über die Staatswirtschaft nach geschichtlicher Methode* was published in 1843, five years before Mill's *Principles* appeared. The 'historical method' was clearly outside the Ricardian framework of classical economics and the approach outlined by Roscher and by Friedrich List, Bruno Hildebrand and Karl Knies provided a quite different approach to the subject. The German historical economists later in the century, notably Gustav Schmoller, went some way towards realising the rather sweeping historical research programme propounded by the founders of the school. Economics in Germany but not in England became concerned with the investigation and study of economic activities and institutions in the past as well as in the present. Before the end of the century the fruits of much research into 'economic history' had been published, much of it relating to England and virtually none of it ever translated into English. English economics was however not unaffected by these developments and 'economic history' when it came to be recognized as a respectable line of inquiry in England was very much influenced by the German example.

It was not however a straightforward import from Germany. W. J. Ashley, beginning to talk about Schmoller to his friends in the early 1880s, found that his work was so unknown that he suspected they supposed he had invented him.[4] Although some of the best work in economic history in the mid-twentieth century has been done

by historians describing themselves as 'Marxist', the influence of
Karl Marx on the development of the subject in the late nineteenth
century was only marginal. It was not until after the First World
War, and especially after the great inter-war depression, that a
Marxist influence came to be felt so powerfully.[5] Economic history in
England was largely—though not exclusively—home-grown. There
were in fact political economists in England who stressed the
relativity of economic 'laws' despite the dominating influence of
Ricardo and Mill and who had rather more in common with the
school of thought dominant in Germany. In the 1850s Richard
Jones, who taught political economy at Haileybury and who is too
often dismissed as an isolated forerunner of the historical approach,
was urging that greater attention should be paid to the particular
historical context in which economic activity took place. In the
next generation, J. K. Ingram and T. E. Cliffe Leslie, both Irishmen,
were distinguished advocates of a more historical approach to
economics.[6] By the 1870s political economy came to be deeply
divided by what later generations were to regard as a futile methodological debate about whether economics should be inductivist or
deductivist, whether the efforts of economists should be devoted
towards developing theories or gathering facts. Consequently in the
1870s and 1880s economics as a subject reached a very low ebb.
Writing on the occasion of the centenary of *The Wealth of Nations*
in 1876, Walter Bagehot understated its position when he noted that
it lay 'rather dead in the public mind'.[7] This was partly a result of the
debilitating *Methodenstreit* among the economists themselves, and
partly the result of what was by the 1870s a yawning credibility gap
between them and the public as a whole. The whole tendency of
legislation since the days of Ricardo had been increasingly contrary
to the 'laws' of doctrinaire economics, with the only important
exception of Free Trade. Trade Unions were recognized despite the
wage-fund theory, more and more factory legislation was passed
inhibiting the making of 'free' bargains between employers and
employees, education became a matter for public provision, local
government activity was revolutionized in a number of fields, and
so on. As 'laissez-faire' fell more and more into discredit, so did the
standing of orthodox economics, divided and apparently increasingly
out of touch with the reality of events and the exigencies of a changing
society.[8]

It was in this situation that a new economic history began to take
root. The aftermath of the methodological controversy made the
ground fertile for it. One of the most powerful influences making for
a less inflexible approach to economics flowed from changes in the
structure and international position of the British economy itself,

changes that contemporaries labelled 'the Great Depression', an inaccurate but useful umbrella characterization that historians today are discarding. 'Perhaps the most effective of the influences which gave a new direction to economic study', wrote Foxwell in 1887:

> 'was that exercised by the rough but inexorable logic of events when in 1874 the easy flow of prosperity was checked by the demonetization of silver, the glamour cast by this prosperity on the so-called "orthodox" doctrine passed away with it, and the authority of pure commercialism received a severe blow.'[9]

In the 1870s the interests of many people were drawn to economics because of the prolonged nature of the 'depression', and what they read about the subject they found wanting. One such person for example was W. A. S. Hewins, later to be a pioneering economic historian. The 'depression' of the 1870s led him to turn to the established works on economics, but he found that they did not help him understand the world he experienced around him. 'I disliked,' he later wrote:[10]

> 'their theoretical outlook, their materialism leavened with sentiment and their remoteness from real events as I saw them in South Staffordshire. The "economic man" made no appeal to me. There was little correspondence between the industrial system of the economics textbooks and the industry that was being carried on around me and the men actually engaged in it.'

The limitations of orthodox economics were obvious, and a clear realization of the nature of these limitations was the first way in which fresh life could be breathed into the subject. Bagehot, in his balanced way, explained these clearly in 1876:[11]

> 'The science of Political Economy as we have it in England may be defined as the science of business, *such as business is in large, productive and trading communities*. It is an analysis of that world so familiar to many Englishmen—the 'great commerce' by which England has become rich. It *assumes* the principal facts which make that commerce possible, and as is the way of an abstract science it isolates and simplifies them: *it detaches them from the confusion with which they are mixed in fact*. . . . It *assumes* that every man who makes anything, makes it for money, that he makes that which brings him in most at least cost, and that he will make it in the way that will produce most and spend least. . . . Of course we know that this is not so, that men are not like this; but we assume it for simplicity's sake, as an *hypothesis*.'

It was therefore quite wrong to imagine that the theoretical postulates of orthodox political economy as understood in England in the 1870s were:[12]

> applicable to *all* states of society, and to *all* equally, whereas [they are] only true of—and only proved as to—states of society in which commerce has largely developed, and where it has taken the form of development, or something near the form, which it has taken in England.

A proper understanding of the use and usefulness of hypothetical statements despite the limits of their applicability stimulated theoretical changes from within the subject. The possibilities of an enormous increase in precision yielded by Jevons' advocacy of mathematical analysis in the 1870s in particular began to clarify the role of the subject among the sciences, and opened up a very significant new approach.[13]

Besides theoretical precision, there were two other inter-related ways out of the doldrums, both of which were more immediately relevant to the emergence of economic history. Increased attention came to be given to the detailed investigation of economic and social problems on the one hand, while on the other greater weight came to be given to research with an historical dimension. To the well-established tradition of humanitarian criticism of the economic system as it was, the 1880s brought a new rigour to the investigation of the actual workings of industry and the conditions of the workers. Charles Booth's pioneering researches in east London in the 1880s and L. L. Price's work on wages in Newcastle for example were received with a more general enthusiasm than that given earlier to the comparable work of such bodies as the Manchester Statistical Society or the National Association for the Promotion of Social Science.[14] Price's notable work[15] was commissioned by the Toynbee Trustees whose activities commemorated the premature death of Arnold Toynbee, himself a central figure in this development. Toynbee, according to Marshall, was:[16]

> 'impelled in the first instance to economic studies by seeing with his own eyes, and hearing with his own ears, the results of that physical and moral degradation and suffering which are caused by poverty.'

Marshall indeed stated:[17]

> 'What had made men become economists, in three cases out of four, was the belief that in spite of our growing command over nature it is still things that are in the saddle, still the great mass of

mankind that is oppressed—oppressed by things. The desire to put mankind into the saddle is the mainspring of most economic activity.'

This 'mainspring' came to be a powerful one in the last quarter of the nineteenth century, and one of its effects was to add an historical dimension to economic inquiry in the effort to understand the origins of the 'things'. 'The historical method,' wrote Beatrice Webb, who assisted Booth in the largest contemporary social investigation, 'is imperative.'[18]

'Only by watching *the processes* of growth and decay during a period of time, can we understand even the contemporary facts at whatever may be their stage of development. . . .'

The idea of 'development' became the key concept of late Victorian social theory. From the middle of the nineteenth century the ideas generated by the explosion of what might be called the historical natural sciences, biology and geology, had a powerful impact on what were beginning to be called the social sciences. Indeed Marshall stated that:[19]

'Darwin's development of the laws of the struggle and survival gave perhaps a greater impetus to the careful and exact study of particular facts than any other event that has ever occurred.'

The concept of evolution as applied to society had wider origins than simply in Darwinism,[20] but as the pioneering economic historian W. J. Ashley said, it was:[21]

'an idea which, whether conceived, as by Hegel, as the progressive revelation of spirit, or, as by Comte, as the growth of humanity, or, as by Spencer, as the adaptation of the social organism to its environment, had equally the effect of opening to the economist undreamt-of perspectives of the past and the future.'

Out of the disputes and disrespect of the 1870s and 1880s therefore a number of developments took place that rendered economics less rigidly anti-historical. Three inter-related tendencies in particular can be seen as contributing to the making of economic history: 'political economy', less susceptible to the crude simplifications of a Miss Martineau, was becoming 'economics'; thorough investigation of social problems and their origins was put on a new footing and ideas of evolution were pervasive. At the same time, there were significant changes overtaking 'history' that were also necessary before economic history could emerge.

B

The quiet revolution which created 'history' in Britain as the professional discipline it is understood to be today is usually dated from the chance appointment (for non-academic reasons) of William Stubbs to the Regius Chair of Modern History at Oxford in 1866.[22] He was the first professional historian to occupy the post. At Oxford under Stubbs and his successor E. A. Freeman history was established as a university subject rather than as the popular literary genre that it had been in the hands of Macaulay, Carlyle and Froude. The transformation of history was two-fold. Firstly, it came to be based on a thorough examination of documents in order to provide hard evidence rather than merely decorative quotations, and secondly it came to be a subject that could be taught, studied and examined in universities. In both these respects history in England lagged behind continental practice. There was nothing like an English equivalent of the École des Chartes, founded in Paris in 1829 for the study of the use of archives, nor was there anything like the famous seminar conducted at Berlin after 1833 by Leopold von Ranke which provided a thorough technical training in history as a discipline. In the field of history, as well as in the separate field of historical economics, England was two generations behind Germany.[23] Gentlemanly leisure and an antiquarian or fraudulent turn of mind had combined with low printing costs from the 1830s onwards in England to result in the publication of archives of various kinds, but this was well ahead of any demand from professional historians.[24] It was not until the early 1870s that Oxford, closely followed by Cambridge, established courses of historical study leading to degrees in the subject.[25] Thereafter it established itself with some rapidity; at Cambridge for example there were twelve candidates for the History Tripos in 1876 rising to forty a year within a decade and to 200 a year on the eve of the First World War, by which time history had replaced the classics as the major subject studied at both Oxford and Cambridge.[26] After a time-lag, the same sort of development took place in London and the new provincial universities.[27]

The 'take-off' in history as an academic discipline contributed to the making of economic history as a separate discipline in two ways. In the first place it was within the final examinations in history that 'economic history' first found itself a place in a university syllabus, albeit initially in a minor and subordinate position. 'Political Science and Political Economy with Economic History' was the title of a paper in the School of Modern History at Oxford, and in the History Tripos at Cambridge Economic History was at first bracketed with Political Economy and became the subject of a separate paper in 1885.[28] It grew in importance and by the time G. M. Trevelyan went up to Cambridge in 1893 he found that the History School was 'based on Stubbs and on Economic History.'[29] Thus history mothered economic history as a university subject, as indeed it sponsored the subject's other parent study, economics, which was institutionally more backward.[30] In the second place, before the end of the century certain tendencies within history were contributing to the opening up of a field of economic history from a different direction than those within economics already touched upon. Hitherto history, as conceived by Stubbs and his followers was almost entirely political and constitutional. 'History,' stated Freeman, 'is past politics', and the Stubbsian core of the subject was the development of the English constitution from its Germanic beginnings to its Victorian climax. J. R. Green was one of the earliest historians to challenge this narrow conception of history by publishing a *Short History of the English People* in 1874 which deliberately eschewed what he dismissed as 'drum and trumpet history'. It was a much acclaimed book and it certainly directed attention to the social and economic aspects of history. More important, however, for the development of the subject was the work of a number of professional historians—a growing breed after the 1870s—who directed their research towards institutions which were not exclusively political. After 1884, F. W. Maitland devoted himself to the study of English legal history which he saw not in any narrow dry-as-dust sense, but as a study of a crucial aspect of social organisation. The pages of his *History of English Law* (1895) and of *Domesday Book and Beyond* (1897) and his many other writings amply demonstrate his claim that 'legal documents are the best, often the only evidence we have for social and economic history.'[31] Other work on medieval legal and manorial institutions besides Maitland's, such as that of F. Seebohm, whose *English Village Community* was published in 1883 or Paul Vinogradoff, whose *Villeinage in England* appeared in 1892, was doing much in the 1880s and 1890s to widen the scope of the new academic history, and to establish economic history as a significant field of interest in its own right.

Thus in history on the one hand as in economics on the other, the last quarter of the nineteenth century saw from different directions a quickening of interest in past economic activities and their organization. The way in which the field of inquiry thus opened up coalesced into a subject in its own right is associated in differing degrees with the names of four pioneers—J. E. Thorold Rogers (1823–1890), Arnold Toynbee (1852–1883), W. J. Ashley (1860–1927) and William Cunningham (1849–1919). Thorold Rogers was certainly a pioneer, but is perhaps better regarded as the forefather of economic history as a subject than as its father.[32] Although his name was sometimes invoked as an opponent of the postulates of classical economics, he was, as befitted the friend of both Cobden and Bright, a relatively orthodox economist. He was however one of the few orthodox (or rather quasi-orthodox) economists who engaged in historical research, and the seven volumes of his *History of Agriculture and Prices in England* (1866, 1882, 1887 and 1902) remain a massive quarry of useful data today.[33] Rogers became—in his own words—'an antiquary by accident' after 1860, when a suggestion made at the International Statistical Congress about 'ancient values' led him to the exploration of the rich archives of Oxford colleges.[34] Rather an antiquarian by nature, Rogers went on to produce two general books, both written with more vigour than coherence, *Six Centuries of Work and Wages*, published in 1884 and *The Economic Interpretation of History*, based on lectures given at Oxford in 1887. These were influential works, and were used by students of economic history for many years, though Rogers regarded economic history as 'the modest handmaid of economic theory',[35] as furnishing illustration for 'economic laws' arrived at independently. The first major piece of historical research by a recognized English economist dealt with the thoroughly 'classical' subject of prices and the records of individual bargains, isolated and collected for periods in which their context was not that of Victorian England. Though informed by wrong-headed preconceptions, Thorold Rogers' work was nevertheless important in correcting the neglect of 'social life and the distribution of wealth' that—to use his own words—rendered history 'imperfect' and economics 'a mere mental effort, perhaps a mischievous illusion.'[36]

Arnold Toynbee, by contrast, was strongly opposed to the teachings of classical economics, which he called 'the old political economy'[37] and, according to Ashley, who was strongly influenced by him, 'at a time when the study of political economy was sunk to its lowest ebb in England, he did perhaps more than any other man to create a new interest in it.'[38] Toynbee combined a committed interest in contemporary social and economic problems and a search for ways of solving them with the conviction that 'the historical method' was of vital importance to the illumination of the present as well as the past. He died young, an idealist who left behind 'a beautiful memory'.[39] One aspect of his work is commemorated by Toynbee Hall, and the other by his posthumously published *Lectures on the Industrial Revolution of the Eighteenth Century in England* given at Oxford in 1881 and 1882, which first popularized the phrase 'Industrial Revolution'.[40] Had he lived longer the subject might well have taken a different course; as it was the crucial roles in its growth to maturity were played by his Cambridge contemporary, William Cunningham, and by William Ashley, who had attended his lectures.

It was Cunningham who made himself perhaps the most important single figure in the growth of the subject in England because of his long insistence that 'Economic History must be dealt with as a separate branch of study, if it is to be properly treated at all.'[41] After graduating at both Edinburgh and Cambridge (where he was bracketed with Maitland at the top of the Moral Sciences Tripos in 1872) and being ordained in 1873, Cunningham became one of the first lecturers for the newly-created Cambridge extension system. After four years extension lecturing based in Liverpool, he returned in 1878 to Cambridge to assist in the organization of the extension scheme, the first of his many part-time jobs. The separate History Tripos was three years old and no-one had been found to teach for the paper on Political Economy and Economic History. Cunningham found an opening by adding these subjects to his previous interests in philosophy and theology and thus 'rather accidentally' began to devote himself to economic history.[42] He found that the greatest need was for a textbook, the *sine qua non* of any recognized subject, and in 1882 he published the first edition in one relatively small volume of *The Growth of English Industry and Commerce*. Cunningham's view of the subject was a comprehensive one. 'Economic history', he stated early in this book, 'is not so much the study of a special class of facts, as the study of all the facts of a nation's history from a special point of view.'[43] His seminal contribution to the development of the subject was twofold: he devoted much of the rest of his life firstly to advancing economic history in successive editions of his textbook—it grew through five editions into three fat volumes—and secondly to a vigorous campaign to achieve public and scholarly recognition for this 'special point of view'. In a number of lectures and articles throughout the 1890s he mounted an attack on the abstract economics of Ricardo and Mill in a way reminiscent of an otherwise dead *Methodenstreit*. Mill's assumptions of self-interest and free competition were too narrow a basis for economics, he told section F of the British Association in 1891, and went on:[44]

'. . . we do not alter the logical form or change the scientific character of our study if, instead of framing a single hypothesis in regard to human nature and society, and restricting our attention to such phenomena as can be conviently studied in connection with it, we are prepared to investigate all economic phenomena by making such assumptions in regard to men as are appropriate to the various ages with which we may have to deal.'

He devoted his inaugural lecture as Tooke Professor of Economic Science and Statistics at King's College London in the following year to insisting on 'the narrow limits of place and time within which generalizations about actual economic affairs hold good'[45] and elsewhere he stressed the historian's point of view, that of seeing 'important contrasts between things that are superficially similar.'[46] 'If there is any lesson that history teaches us', he wrote, 'it is that nothing is so well-known that we can assume it will always be well-known and does not need to be explained.'[47] He did not give up the attempt to make economics itself into an historical science, but while stirring this unfortunate controversy he diverted it into a more constructive channel, that of establishing economic history as a subject at once separate from, though complementary to, both economics and history.

Cunningham never received from his own University a full teaching appointment in the subject, much less a Chair. He was a candidate in 1885 for the Chair of Political Economy that went to Alfred Marshall, with whom his relations were not cordial. Marshall, in a manner Cunningham thought high-handed, prevented him from lecturing on economic history as he wished, and he published an attack on Marshall's approach to economics.[48] The antagonism of Marshall and Cunningham unnecessarily marred the development of the subject and in so far as it was not merely personal it was distinctly anachronistic by the 1890s.[49] It thus fell to W. J. Ashley, less of a controversialist, to occupy the first separate Chair of economic history in the world; this was created for him at Harvard in 1892.[50] The inaugural lecture he gave soon after taking up this appointment is the first lecture included in this volume. Ashley was a product of the Oxford History School whose interest in economic studies was inspired originally by Toynbee at Oxford and then by Schmoller at Berlin. In the early 1880s he made several visits to Germany, the first time with an introduction from Stubbs. In 1885 he left Oxford to become Professor of Political Economy and Constitutional History at the University of Toronto, dedicating his inaugural lecture there to Schmoller.[51] In the same year the first volume of his great work appeared, strikingly entitled *An Introduction to English Economic History and Theory*, and it was dedicated to the memory of Arnold Toynbee. The second volume followed in 1893, soon after he moved to Harvard. This work was both more scholarly than that of Cunningham in its use of original sources, and more original in its conception of the subject in that it did not follow the conventional approach to periodisation derived from political history. No further volumes appeared, since in his efforts to be—to use his own significant phrase—'an economist without ceasing to be an historian', Ashley cast the net of his interests wide.[52] In 1901 he returned to England to occupy the Chair of Commerce at Birmingham University and to establish there a 'Faculty of Commerce'. He became involved in Chamberlain's campaign for Tariff Reform, and in the first world war and after devoted more and more time to government committees besides university administration, and the advancement of economic history became no longer the main call on his time. Rogers in 1860 and Cunningham in 1878 both came to economic history by accident, and then devoted most of the rest of their lives to it; Ashley by contrast made economic history his first career but found that the activities that it lead on to became his main occupation.

The work of Thorold Rogers, Toynbee, Cunningham and Ashley combined to make economic history available as a valid subject. The way in which it entered the syllabuses of the universites old and new between the 1870s and the 1900s made it into a discipline. The demands of society as evidenced through the changing organization of its institutions of higher education and particularly the structure of its examinations form the neglected dimension to historiography, and indeed to the history of any modern subject. That there was a public demand for economic history before it was fully institutionalized into a subject is shown by the widespread attention given to it by the extension movement from the 1870s, and in the place it found in the examinations for the Home and the Indian Civil Service and the growing number of examinations demanded by late Victorian society and set by the Institute of Bankers, the Royal Society of Arts, Chambers of Commerce and other such bodies. Since it was capable of being both respectably academic and yet having distinct and obvious practical implications, the new subject of economic history was an ideal subject for such examinations. The demand for qualifications for professional or semi-professional purposes created a demand for examinations and thus a derived demand for subjects in which to be examined. Examinations necessitated syllabuses of study, textbooks and teaching posts, and these combined in the case of economic history to concentrate a growing field of interest into a subject and then to raise it to the status of a recognized discipline. In a society in which examinations were coming to play so central a part it was only by these means that a subject could become established as such.[53] The adoption of economic history as a subject for examination in the History Tripos at Cambridge in 1875 directly lead to Cunningham producing the first textbook for the subject in 1882. Others soon followed; besides Thorold Rogers' contributions, there was H. de B. Gibbins' *Industrial History of England* which appeared in 1890, the first of twenty-eight impressions, and in 1899 Townsend Warner's *Landmarks in English Industrial History* was published; 7,000 copies of this were printed before 1907 and a further 20,000 before 1913.[54] The number of textbooks—those provided by Price and Meredith followed in 1900 and 1908—and their popularity indicate the rapid growth of interest in the subject outside the universities. About half the classes established by the W.E.A. in the years after 1908 were devoted to 'industrial history' or to economics treated in an anti-orthodox historical manner. The demands of such courses and of the schemes of study developed in the new institutions of higher education established around the turn of the century were responsible for advancing the subject beyond the secondary role it played in the history syllabuses of the old universities. To a considerable extent the examination-orientated organization of the subject called forth its content. The main object of the Faculty of Commerce in the University of Birmingham was, Ashley stated, the education of 'those who . . . will ultimately guide the business activity of the country';[55] it followed that it had to be at once academic and practical.[56] Economic history found its feet in such new institutions. The most significant of these developments, as far as the future growth of the subject was concerned, took place at the London School of Economics.

The L.S.E., founded in 1895 to be the first institution in Britain to provide a centre for systematic training and research in economics and the related social sciences, was informed, not, despite its Fabian origins, by socialism, but by an opposition to the tenets of orthodox economics. Economic history was therefore from the start one of its major concerns. The Webbs appointed a young economic historian, W. A. S. Hewins, to be its first Director. After reading mathematics at Oxford, Hewins had turned to historical research, combining this after 1888 with lecturing in the north of England for the extension movement, that classical recruiting ground for economic historians.[57] In 1892 he published his *English Trade and Finance chiefly in the Seventeenth Century*, on the title page of which he is described as 'University Extension Lecturer on Economic History'. At the L.S.E. he established a number of courses in economic history as part of the aim of the School to study 'the concrete facts of industrial life and the actual working of economic and political relations, as they exist *or have existed*'.[58] The teaching at first was for already existing examinations, including those of the University of London, which in the 1890s began to include a paper on 'Outlines of English Economic History' as part of the Political Economy branch of the B.A. degree.[59] In 1900 the L.S.E. became part of the reorganized University of London and in 1901 the B.Sc. (Econ.) degree was instituted. For the first time in Britain economics was fully recognized as a university subject and it became possible for students to specialize in economic history.[60] The subject was mainly taught by Hewins himself with the aid of a number of part-time lecturers. The first of these in 1895 was Cunningham, who was brought in, as Sidney Webb explicitly said, 'to counteract Marshall'.[61] When Hewins resigned the Directorship of the School at the end of 1903 in order to devote his time to the Tariff Commission set up by Joseph Chamberlain, it became necessary to make a full-time appointment to continue the courses he taught in economic history. Lilian Tomn, a few months later to become Mrs. Knowles, was appointed and at the beginning of 1904 she became the first full-time lecturer in economic history in a British university.[62] It is curious to note that this significant innovation was therefore an indirect consequence of the Tariff Reform Campaign. Lilian Knowles had read history at Cambridge before going to the L.S.E. as a research student in the second year of its existence.[63] The most important influence on her life was Archdeacon Cunningham; he diverted her from her initial ambition of following a legal career and she assisted him with the growth of *The Growth of English Industry and Commerce*. She was destined to become a great teacher of a new but established subject, rather than a pioneer in its development. In 1907 she became the first Reader in the subject and a chair in it—by then the second in the country—was established for her at the L.S.E. in 1921.[64] With her original appointment in 1904 the period of 'take-off' for economic history was complete and the subject embarked on a new stage in its development. Its growth was now self-sustaining.

The second university appointment specifically in economic history that held by H. O. Meredith in the University of Manchester from 1905 to 1908. After graduating at Cambridge, Meredith was a research student at the L.S.E. from 1901 to 1903 and whilst there he had assisted Hewins in the expansion of the teaching of the subject at the School.[65] Meredith was unusual among his contemporaries in being both an economic historian and an opponent of Tariff Reform, and for three years he taught at Manchester under the direction of Professor S. J. Chapman, almost the only other historically-minded economist opposed to the Chamberlain campaign.[66] In 1908 he published a textbook, *Outlines of the Economic History of England*, which was based on the courses he had given at L.S.E. and in Manchester; it is a book which shows how much the outlines of the subject as it was first taught in the universities owed to the work of Cunningham. In 1908 Meredith left Manchester for Cambridge to occupy the lectureship in economics vacated by Pigou on his succession to Marshall's chair.[67] In the same year J. H. Clapham returned from Leeds to begin his famous course of lectures on British economic history in Cambridge and C. R. Fay, later holder of a Canadian chair and author of a number of brilliant and eccentric books also returned to Cambridge from the L.S.E.[69] The first examinations in the Economics Tripos had been held in 1905

(Part I) and 1906 (Part II) and the subject that Cunningham ceased to teach in 1906 was expanding.[69]

Despite this increased activity in the teaching of economic history at Cambridge, there was no university post established specifically in the subject, whereas a lectureship was established in 1907 at Oxford. This was created for L. L. Price and the lecture he gave on the 'position and prospects' of the subject in the first year of his appointment is the second lecture reprinted in this volume. After the research that Price had carried out in 1886 for the Toynbee Trustees he too was an extension lecturer and from 1888 a Fellow and Treasurer of Oriel College Oxford. In 1900 he wrote an introductory textbook on economic history, based on the work of both Cunningham and Ashley who, as he said, 'have created Economic History for English students'.[70] He did little teaching but was an important figure in the development of both economics and economic history, too easily overlooked since he was not a dogmatist like Cunningham. In 1909 he became Reader in Economic History at Oxford, a post he held until his retirement in 1921, though he did not die until 1950.[71] The fourth appointment in the subject was a lectureship established at Edinburgh in 1908 with the aid of funds from the Carnegie Trust and occupied by George Unwin.[72] The fifth was established in 1910 at Belfast, where a tradition of historical economics doubtless remained from Cliffe Leslie's long tenure of the chair of Jurisprudence and Political Economy there.[73]

More significant in 1910 was the creation of the first chair of economic history in Britain. This was instituted at Manchester at Tout's suggestion and Unwin was invited to occupy it.[74] Unwin did not give an inaugural lecture at Manchester—nor indeed did his two successors to the chair in the flourishing school of economic history he created there[75]—and the lecture printed as the third in this volume is consequently the lecture that he gave soon after taking up the appointment at Edinburgh in 1908 on 'The Aims of Economic History'. Unwin's dislike of 'the State' is evident in this lecture. It is this attitude (despite Unwin's having first developed his interest in economic history at the feet of the nationalistic Schmoller at Berlin in 1898)[76] that is crucial to the way in which the subject was to develop in his hands. For Unwin, 'what gave history its meaning', wrote Tawney,[77]

> 'was not the activities of the State, but the broadening and multiplication of human relations, economic, social and cultural, which States have more often impeded than assisted.'

History was not past politics for Unwin, since politics, in Tawney's phrase, were merely 'the squalid scaffolding of more serious matters'.[78]

Unwin therefore did not see economic history as subordinated in any way to political history and he did not look, as Cunningham had, to the periods and problems of political history to provide the framework for his approach to the subject. Unwin did not write a textbook; he did research. Economic history as established before the first world war in half-a-dozen universities was in fact prematurely consolidated in the sense that the organization and outlines of the subject had outstripped its content and substance. There were more appeals for further research to be done than actual research undertaken. Between 1882 and 1904 in terms of examinations, textbooks and university posts economic history had firmly established itself as a discipline while research had lagged behind. It was during Unwin's teaching career, and to a large extent under his guidance, that this imbalance began to be corrected. Economic history became launched, in Sir Frederick Rees' phrase, upon 'a period of monographs', a movement that Rees dated from the publication in 1904 of Unwin's first work, *Industrial Organization in the Sixteenth and Seventeenth Centuries*.[79] A number of such works were published prior to the first world war and before his death in 1919 Cunningham could write of the subject that 'the annual output of literature is so large that it is very difficult to keep up with it'.[80] The heyday of the monographs testing the generalizations generated by the pioneering economic historians was the 1920s. Many were concerned with particular industries or particular business enterprises, important works such as G. W. Daniels' *The Early English Cotton Industry* (1920), Unwin's own *Samuel Oldknow and the Arkwrights* (1924), T. S. Ashton's *Iron and Steel in the Industrial Revolution* (1924) and so on.[81] In these seminal works of research, generalization was kept to a strict minimum; theories of any sort, whether Jevonsian, Schmolleresque, Marxist, Weberite or whatever were virtually absent as the drive to research moved into a higher gear. The subject, while not totally losing ideological or system-building overtones, became characterized by a certain English empiricism. The massive work that typified so much about the subject at this stage was J. H. Clapham's three volumes on the *Economic History of Modern Britain*, the first of which appeared in 1926. Significantly it was dedicated jointly to the memory of Marshall and Cunningham, a perfectly appropriate linking of their names, but one which might have surprised them both. The climax of this phase of the subject's development, its drive to maturity, came in 1926 with the founding of the Economic History Society and the publication in 1927 of the first number of the *Economic History Review*.[82]

Such was the stage the subject had reached when three new professors—J. H. Clapham, G. N. Clark and R. H. Tawney—each gave an inaugural lecture entitled 'The Study of Economic History'.

In 1928 a chair in the subject was at last established in Cambridge and it was occupied by J. H. Clapham.[83] He was then, as he pointed out at the beginning of his lecture, the only occupant of a chair in the country since the first two holders of chairs had died—Unwin in 1925 and Mrs. Knowles in 1926. In 1931, three years after the creation of the Cambridge chair, two more chairs were established, one at Oxford, held by G. N. Clark, and another at the L.S.E., held by Eileen Power. Sir George Clark held the Chichele chair at Oxford for twelve years and is still very much alive.[84] Eileen Power however died suddenly in 1940, the year after delivering the Ford lectures at Oxford, published posthumously as *The Wool Trade in English Medieval History*.[85] She combined her historical interests with a striking aestheticism and a social conscience. She was deeply influenced by R. H. Tawney, for whom a personal chair in economic history was created at L.S.E. in the same year, 1931. Tawney was the most deceptively simple of this generation of economic historians; he has been linked with Namier as one of the two greatest British historians of the twentieth century.[86] Like Unwin he set economic history in a wider philosophical framework than was becoming normal in this lifetime. On the eve of the first world war he wrote in his private commonplace book:[87]

> 'Too much time is spent today upon *outworks*, by writers who pile up statistics and facts, but never get to the heart of the problem. That heart is not economic. It is a question of moral relationships. This is the citadel that must be attacked—the immoral philosophy which underlies much of modern industry.'

Tawney's research in economic and social history was concerned with exploring these 'moral relationships' and, as a socialist and a Christian, he was deeply concerned with contemporary political issues. In many respects therefore he placed himself outside the mainstream of economic history as it developed into a self-sustaining specialized subject, despite the importance of his contributions to it.

The following four lectures in this volume were given by the successors to the chairs in the three established centres of the subject, Cambridge, Oxford and L.S.E. In 1938 M. M. Postan succeeded Clapham on his retirement from the Cambridge chair.[88] Professor Postan was educated at the universities of Odessa, Petrograd, Kiev, Czernovitz and Berlin and came to Cambridge via the L.S.E. and University College London. He had married Eileen Power in 1937. In his inaugural lecture, 'The Historical Method in Social Science', Postan opened up discussion of the themes that were to occupy the next generation of economic historians in their inaugural lectures.

Earlier inaugurals had been concerned to establish the distinct identity of the subject; the dominant theme was now to be the subject's relations with neighbouring subjects. In 1944 W. K. Hancock was appointed to succeed G. N. Clark in the Chichele chair at Oxford.[89] Hancock had previously held chairs of history without adjectival qualification at Adelaide and Birmingham and was the supervisor of the official civil histories of the war in which Professor Postan was also involved. In 1944 T. S. Ashton was appointed at L.S.E. in succession to Eileen Power's chair. Ashton's work for many years had been in what had become the main tradition of the writing of English economic history, though he had previously held the Readership in Currency and Public Finance at Manchester.[90] His inaugural lecture was therefore appropriately entitled 'The Relation of Economic History to Economic Theory'. Ashton was succeeded on his retirement in 1954 by F. J. Fisher who had been a pupil of Tawney's and whose inaugural lecture in defence of the sixteenth and seventeenth centuries surveys the state of the subject on the eve of a further phase in its development. Outside the triumvirate of L.S.E., Cambridge and Oxford there were only two other chairs before the later 1950s, that at Manchester revived in 1945 for Arthur Redford[91] and the new chair created at Birmingham in 1947 for W. H. B. Court.[92] These were the five chairs in the subject before the number was doubled in the late 1950s.[93] In 1956 a chair of economic history was established at what was to become the University of Dundee and occupied by D. F. Macdonald[94] and in 1957 S. G. Checkland became the first professor of the subject at Glasgow.[95] In 1958 three more new chairs were established at Bristol, Edinburgh and Nottingham, held respectively by W. Ashworth,[96] A. J. Youngson,[97] and J. D. Chambers.[98] Each of them gave inaugural lectures which are included in this volume. In 1959 the University of Leeds created a chair in the subject for M. W. Beresford who gave the fifteenth of the lectures reprinted here.

In the course of the 1960s the number of chairs doubled again as the subject was increasingly taught in the provincial universities and in the new universities established in the wake of the Robbins Report. No longer were professors of the subject automatically to be included in *Who's Who*. By 1970 there were chairs at Aberdeen (P. L. Payne), Belfast (K. H. Connell), Durham (F. C. Spooner), East Anglia (R. H. Campbell), Exeter (W. E. Minchinton), Kent (T. C. Barker), Leicester (R. Davis), Sheffield (S. Pollard), Strathclyde (S. G. E. Lythe), Sussex (B. E. Supple), Swansea (A. W. Cole) and York (E. M. Sigsworth).[99] The scope for inaugural lectures having decreased somewhat, in this period of the subject in its full maturity only five were given—by Professor Lythe at Strathclyde in

1963, by Professor Pollard at Sheffield in 1964, by Professor Davis at Leicester in 1965, by Professor Coats at Nottingham in 1966 after having succeeded Professor Chambers there and by Professor Cole at the University College of Swansea in 1967.[100] Their discussions of the nature of the subject in the 1960s are included in this volume. The final lecture is that given in 1970 by Peter Mathias who was appointed to the Chichele chair at Oxford in 1968. His discussion of the subject brings the discussion of the study of economic history up to date.

The countervailing themes of these inaugural lectures are on the one hand the separate identity of economic history as a subject and on the other its intimate relations with the other social sciences and with history. They show that a mature subject is far from being a dead one. When the Economic History Society was being founded in 1926, Tawney said that economic historians had made three mistakes:[101]

'they had tended to treat economic history within the framework of political history, employing a ground plan of periods, etc., which were often inapplicable; they had been insufficiently analytical and too purely narrational; and in England at least they had treated the subject on purely national lines, which were too narrow.'

These criticisms still to some extent apply today, but since the 1920s the subject has become, as Tawney said it ought, more sociological, more analytical and more international. New questions prompted by contemporary economic problems have been asked, especially about prices and business fluctuations before the war and about economic growth since the war. New methods of dealing with them have been developed as economic and social theory has advanced, as more sophisticated statistical methods have been devised, as computers have been harnessed to the processing of historical data. To be sure, a subject conceived essentially in revolt against the orthodoxies of the nineteenth century has been attacked in some quarters for having itself established too constricting an orthodoxy.[102] The 1960s indeed saw the return of something in the nature of a *Methodenstreit* and the criticisms levelled by the protagonists of 'the new economic history', if more relevant in an American context, are not without a validity in Britain.[103] But the subject is a flourishing one.[104] The first stage in challenging received ideas is to understand their origins. Students of economic history can ensure the continued vigour of the subject by understanding something of the way in which it has developed.

N.B.H. 1971

NOTES

1   There are four useful short accounts of the growth of the subject: N. S. B. Gras, 'The Rise and Development of Economic History', *Economic History Review*, I, 1927–8, pp. 12–34; L. L. Price in chapter IX of the 14th and subsequent editions of *A Short History of Political Economy in England*, London, 1931; Sir John Clapham in the *Encylopaedia of the Social Sciences*, 1935 and Sir Frederick Rees, 'Recent Trends in Economic History', *History*, XXXIV, 1949, pp. 1–14, reprinted in *The Problem of Wales and Other Essays*, Cardiff, n.d. For the growth of the subject in America, not discussed here, see N.S.B. Gras in *Encyclopaedia of the Social Sciences* and Arthur H. Cole, 'Economic History in the United States: Formative Years of a Discipline', *Journal of Economic History*, XXVIII, 1968, pp. 556–589.

2   See the introduction to W. H. Chaloner, *People and Industries*, London, 1963.

3   That is to say between the appearance of the first edition of Cunningham's textbook and Mrs. Knowles' appointment at the London School of Economics as the first full-time university lecturer in the subject. Slightly different periods of growth can be identified; Gras singles out 1879–88 as the decade in which the subject reached 'its full manhood' (*op. cit.*, p, 20), while Rees sees 1882–93 as the crucial decade (*op. cit.*, p. 2). The dates preferred here are discussed below.

4   Quoted in Janet L. MacDonald, 'Sir William Ashley (1860–1927)' in Bernadotte E. Schmitt (ed.), *Some Historians of Modern Europe*, Chicago, 1942, p. 21.

5   There is unfortunately no study of the changing reaction to Marx in English thought or English historiography. 'Dr. Marx and the Victorian Critics' in E. J. Hobsbawm, *Labouring Men*, London, 1964, pp. 239–49, touches upon the reaction of a few early economic historians.

6   For Jones see Eric Roll, *A History of Economic Thought*, London, 1937, pp. 313–20, and L. G. Johnson, *Richard Jones Reconsidered*, privately published, 1955. J. K. Ingram's *History of Political Economy*, Edinburgh, 1888, chapter VI, contains a sympathetic discussion of the historical school in Germany, France and Italy as well as in England. See also T. W. Hutchison, *A Review of Economic Doctrines* 1870–1929, Oxford, 1953, pp. 18–22; A. W. Coats, 'The Historist Reaction in English Political Economy 1870–90', *Economica*, N. S., XXI, pp. 143–53 and V. W. Bladen, 'Mill to Marshall: The Conversion of the Economists', *Journal of Economic History*, I, Supplement, 1941, pp. 17–29.

7   Walter Bagehot, *The Postulates of English Political Economy*, London, 1885, p. 4. This essay was originally published in the *Fortnightly Review* in 1876.

8   See H. S. Foxwell, 'The Economic Movement in England', *Quarterly Journal of Economics*, II, 1887–8, pp. 84–103.

9   *Ibid.*, pp. 85–6.

10 W. A. S. Hewins, *The Apologia of an Imperialist*, London, 1929, I, p. 15.

11 Bagehot, *Postulates of Political Economy*, pp. 7–8. Italics added.

12 *Ibid.*, p. 9.

13 W. S. Jevons, *The Theory of Political Economy* was first published in 1871, though his 'Brief Account of a General Mathematical Theory of Political Economy' appeared in 1862. (See Jevons, *Theory of Political Economy*, 4th ed., 1911, pp. 303–14.)

14 For the Manchester Statistical Society's activities see T. S. Ashton, *Economic and Social Investigations in Manchester 1833–1933*, London, 1934. The multifarious activities of the National Association for the Promotion of Social Science, founded in 1857, lack a thorough examination.

15 L. L. Price, *Industrial Peace*, London, 1887. This was based on fifteen weeks research in 1886 by Price on wages and conciliation in the Newcastle coal trade.

16 *Ibid.*, preface by Alfred Marshall, p. vii.

17 Alfred Marshall, *The New Cambridge Curriculum in Economics*, London, 1903, p. 8.

18 Beatrice Webb, *My Apprenticeship*, London, 1926, p. 211. For her comments on the significance of Booth's work see *ibid.*, pp. 186 *et seq.*, and for an essay of hers written in 1886 entitled 'My Objections to a Self-contained, Separate, Abstract Political Economy', *ibid.*, pp. 373–8.

19 A. Marshall, 'The Old Generation of Economists and the New', *Quarterly Journal of Economics*, XI, 1897, p. 119.

20 See J. W. Burrow, *Evolution and Society*, Cambridge, 1966, which deals suggestively with the creation of social anthropology.

21 W. J. Ashley, *An Introduction to English Economic History and Theory*, London, 1888, pp. ix-x.

22 Stubbs, thoroughly Tory, was appointed for political reasons; N. J. Williams, 'Stubbs's Appointment as Regius Professor, 1866', *Bulletin of the Institute of Historical Research*, XXXIII, 1960, pp. 121–5.

23 For the development of historical scholarship in England see G. P. Gooch, *History and Historians in the Nineteenth Century*, London, 1913, especially chapter XVIII on the Oxford School and chapter XX on Acton and Maitland, and the two articles commemorating the centenary of the Royal Historical Society—M. D. Knowles, 'Some Trends in Scholarship, 1868–1968, in the Field of Medieval History', *Transactions of the Royal Historical Society*, 5th ser., 19, 1969, pp. 139–58 and H. Butterfield, 'Some Trends in Scholarship, 1868–1968, in the Field of Modern History', *ibid.*, pp. 159–84. Both these essays give a prominent place to the development of economic history. The foundation of the Royal Historical Society was, initially at least, quite unconnected with the revolution in the academic position of history; see R. A. Humphreys, *The Royal Historical Society 1868–1968*, London, 1969.

24 The Surtees Society was founded in 1834 and its publications provided a model for other local societies like the Chetham Society (1843) and the national Camden Society (1838). In the 1850s government publications began also to cater for the diverse market thus opened up. See F. J. Levy, 'The Founding of the Camden Society', *Victorian Studies*, VII, 1963–4, pp. 295–305 and David Knowles, 'The Rolls Series' in *Great Historical Enterprises*, London, 1963, pp. 100–34, and for the origins of the Historical Manuscripts Commission, founded in 1869, see R. H. Ellis, 'Origins and Transformations', *Journal of the Society of Archivists*, III, 9, 1969, pp. 441–52. For the opportunities for the pursuit of self-advancement rather than scholarship in such activities see R. A. Humphreys, *op. cit.*, and P. Morgan, 'George Harris of Rugby and the Prehistory of the Historical Manuscripts Commission', *Birmingham Archaeological Society Transactions and Proceedings*, 82, 1965, pp. 28–37.

25 See J. O. McLachlan, 'The Origin and Early Development of the Cambridge Historical Tripos', *Cambridge Historical Journal*, IX, 1, 1947, pp. 78–105.

See also the curious information about the teaching of history in British universities in 1884 given by a visiting Belgian professor; Paul Frédéricq, *The Study of History in England and Scotland*, Johns Hopkins University Studies in Historical and Political Science, 5th ser., X, Baltimore, 1887.

26 Frédéricq, *op. cit.*, p. 28; C. H. Firth, *The Study of Modern History in Britain*, read at the International Historical Congress in London in 1913, p. 4.

27 See A. F. Pollard, 'The University of London and the Study of History', a lecture given in 1904 and published in *Factors in Modern History*, 1907, and for some account of the development in one provincial university see A. J. Taylor's inaugural lecture *History in an Age of Growth*, Leeds, 1964.

28 McLachlan, *op. cit.*, p. 91.

29 G. M. Trevelyan, *An Autobiography and Other Essays*, London, 1949, p. 12.

30 For the backward state of the teaching of economics in British universities until the beginning of the twentieth century see 'Methods of Economic Teaching in this and other countries' in *Report of the 1894 Meeting of the British Association for the Advancement of Science*, London, 1894, pp. 365–91 and L. L. Price, *The Present Position of Economic Study at Oxford*, a letter to the Vice-Chancellor dated 14 Jan. 1902. For the growth of economics as a subject see two articles by S. G. Checkland, 'The Advent of Academic Economics in England', *Manchester School of Economic and Social Studies*, XIX, 1951, pp. 43–70 and 'Economic Opinion in England as Jevons found it', *ibid.*, pp. 143–69 and one by A. W. Coats, 'Sociological Aspects of British Economic Thought (ca. 1880–1930)', *Journal of Political Economy*, 75, 5, 1967, pp. 706–29.

31 Quoted from Maitland's inaugural lecture as Downing Professor of the Laws of England at Cambridge in 1888 by G. P. Gooch, *op. cit.*, p. 394.

32 For Thorold Rogers see W. J. Ashley, 'James E. Thorold Rogers', *Political Science Quarterly*, IV, 3, 1889, pp. 381–407 and, for a contrasted view, the obituary by H. de B. Gibbins in *Economic Review*, I, 1891, pp. 86–9; see also the articles by W. A. S. Hewins in the *D.N.B.* and A. W. Coats in the *International Encyclopaedia of the Social Sciences*.

33 The seventh volume was completed after Roger's death by his son, A. G. L. Rogers, and published in 1902. It brought the whole work up to the time at which Thomas Tooke and William Newmarch, *A History of Prices and of the State of the Currency from 1793*, 6 vols., London, 1838–57, began.

34 Rogers, *loc. cit.*, II, p. xi.

35 The phrase is Ashley's; *Political Science Quarterly*, *op. cit.*, p. 382.

36 Rogers, *Economic Interpretation of History*, pp. 1–2.

37 'Ricardo and the Old Political Economy', written in 1879, in Arnold Toynbee, *Lectures on the Industrial Revolution of the Eighteenth Century in England*, London, 1884, which is the posthumous collection of his writings. For Toynbee see the 'Memoir' by Benjamin Jowett in *ibid.*; F. C. Montague, *Arnold Toynbee*, Johns Hopkins University Studies in Historical and Political Science, 7th ser., I, Baltimore, 1889; Alfred Milner, *Arnold Toynbee: A Reminiscence*, London, 1895; Gertrude Toynbee, *Reminiscences and Letters of Joseph and Arnold Toynbee*, London, n.d.; W. J. Ashley, *Surveys Historic and Economic*, London, 1900, pp. 428–31 and L. L. Price, *Short History of Political Economy*, pp. 184–95.

38 Ashley, *Surveys Historic and Economic*, p. 429.

39 Ingram, *History of Political Economy*, p. 234.

40 See G. N. Clark, *The Idea of the Industrial Revolution*, Glasgow, 1953.

c

41 W. Cunningham, 'The Teaching of Economic History' in W. A. J. Archbold (ed.), *Essays on the Teaching of History*, Cambridge, 1901, p. 42. For Cunningham, see Audrey Cunningham, *William Cunningham: Teacher and Priest*, London, 1950 and the obituaries by W. R. Scott in *D. N. B. 1912–1921*, pp. 141–2, by H. S. Foxwell in *Economic Journal*, XXIX, 1919, pp. 382–90, by Lilian Knowles in *ibid.*, pp. 390–3. See also the chapter on him in Bernard Semmel, *Imperialism and Social Reform*, London, 1960, and the article by R. M. Hartwell in *International Encyclopaedia of the Social Sciences*, 1968. There is a bibliography of Cunningham's many writings on economic subjects in his *Progress of Capitalism in England*, 1916, pp. 136–42.

42 See Cunningham's letter quoted in N. S. B. Gras, 'The Present Condition of Economic History', *Quarterly Journal of Economics*, XXXIV, 1920, p. 211 and Audrey Cunningham, *op. cit.*, pp. 36, 52 *et seq.*

43 Cunningham, *The Growth of English Industry and Commerce*, Cambridge, 1882, p. 5.

44 Cunningham, 'Nationalism and Cosmopolitanism in Economics', *Report of the 1891 Meeting of the British Association for the Advancement of Science*, 1892, p. 729.

45 Cunningham, 'The Relativity of Economic Doctrine', *Economic Journal*, II, 1892, p.l. The Tooke chair was a part-time one; it was founded to commemorate the work of Thomas Tooke (1778–1858). Cunningham succeeded Thorold Rogers who was the first holder. A colleague of Rogers' at K.C.L. ought to be mentioned—Leone Levi, who held the chair of the principles and practice of commerce there from 1855 to 1888 and who published in 1872 his *History of British Commerce*. Levi might be regarded as bridging the gap between the earlier practical writers of economic history and its academic exponents. For the curious story of his appointment see F. J. C. Hearnshaw, *The Centenary History of Kings College London 1828–1928*, London, 1929, pp. 244–6.

46 Cunningham, 'A Plea for the Study of Economic History', *Economic Review*, IX, 1899, p. 69.

47 Cunningham, 'Nationalism and Cosmopolitanism in Economics', p. 733. For other writing in the same vein see his 'A Plea for Pure Theory', *Economic Review*, II, 1892, pp. 25–41; 'The Perversion of Economic History', *Economic Journal*, II, 1892, pp. 491–506 and 'Why had Roscher so little influence in England?', *Annals of the American Academy of Political and Social Science*, V, 1894, pp. 317–34.

48 Cunningham, 'The Perversion of Economic History', *op. cit.*, and Audrey Cunningham, *op. cit.*, pp. 63–5.

49 See Ashley's comments in his lecture, especially below p. 3, 7-8.

50 For Ashley see Anne Ashley, *William James Ashley: A Life*, London, 1932; Janet L. MacDonald, 'Sir William Ashley (1860–1927)' in Bernadotte E. Schmitt, *Some Historians of Modern Europe*, Chicago, 1942, pp. 20–44; the contribution by Bernard Semmel in *International Encyclopaedia of the Social Sciences* and the relevant chapter in the same writer's *Imperialism and Social Reform*, London, 1960 (also in *Economica*, N.S., XXIV, 96, 1957, pp. 343–53), and the obituaries by W. R. Scott in *Economic History Review*, I, 1927–8, pp. 319–21, by J. H. Clapham in *Economic Journal*, XXXVII, 1927, pp, 678–84 and J. F. Rees in *D.N.B. 1922–1930*, pp. 27–9.

51 W. J. Ashley, *What is Political Science?* Toronto, 1888.

52 This phrase is from the dedication, again to Schmoller, of a number of

Ashley's articles collected in *Surveys Historic and Economic*, London, 1900.

53   W. J. Ashley, 'The Present Position of Political Economy', *Economic Journal*, XVII, 1907, p. 484.

54   H. Heaton, *The Yorkshire Woollen and Worsted Industries*, 2nd ed., Oxford, 1965, p. viii.

55   W. J. Ashley, *The Faculty of Commerce in the University of Birmingham: its Purpose and Programme*, dated 23 April 1902, p.l.

56   See also W. J. Ashley (ed.), *British Industries*, London, 1903, preface.

57   Hewins, *Apologia of an Imperialist*, I, pp. 19–24.

58   The original prospectus of the School quoted in W. A. S. Hewins, 'The London School of Economics and Political Science', in *B.P.P.*, 1898, XXIV, p. 85. Italics added.

59   *Ibid.*, p. 81.

60   The first intermediate B.Sc. (Econ.) examination in economic history was set in 1903; see *University of London Calendar for 1903–04*, III, pp. cdlxxxiv-cdlxxxv. Perusal of this and other early examination papers is instructive. The questions, more simplistic perhaps than might be set today, do at least call for some analysis, while contemporary papers in history remained heavily descriptive.

61   F. A. Hayek, 'The London School of Economics 1895–1945', *Economica*, N.S., XIII, p. 5.

62   In 1901 Hewins was the first 'recognized teacher' in economic history in the University of London's new Faculty of Economics and Hubert Hall was a 'recognized teacher' first in Palaeography and then in the Sources of Early Economic History; *University of London Calendar for 1901–02*, II, p. 112 and *L.S.E. Calendar for 1903–04*. Both Hewins and Hall however were part-time teachers, Hewins being primarily Director of the School and Hall being at the Public Record Office. Other part-time teachers (including Ellen Macarthur in 1897–9 and W. J. Ashley in 1898–9) are listed in the *L.S.E. Register 1895–1932*, London, 1934, Appendix F. Mrs. Knowles became a 'recognized teacher' of the University in February 1904; unfortunately the records of the L.S.E. do not give the exact date on which she was appointed to the full-time staff of the School, but it is clear that it was in either December 1903 or January 1904.

63   For Lilian Knowles (1870–1926) see the memoirs of her by W. H. Beveridge and Graham Wallas in *Economica*, VI, 1926, pp. 119–22, by T. E. Gregory in *Economic Journal*, XXXVI, 1926, pp. 317–20 and *The Times* obituary, 27 April 1926.

64   Professor Knowles seems however not to have given an inaugural lecture. An undated typescript of her's in the British Library of Political and Economic Science, *How Economic History may best be taught*, is characteristically more practical than philosophical.

65   *L.S.E. Register 1895–1932*, p. 255; *L.S.E. Calendar for 1903–04*.

66   A. W. Coats, 'Political Economy and the Tariff Reform Campaign of 1903', *Journal of Law and Economics*, XI, 1968, pp. 224–5 and the same writer's 'The Role of Authority in the Development of British Economics' in the same journal, VII, 1964, pp. 99–103. Unwin too was a convinced Free Trader; Price, *Political Economy in England*, pp. 211–2.

67   R. F. Harrod, *The Life of J. M. Keynes*, London, 1951, pp. 94, 144. Meredith (b.1878) had been a Fellow of Kings College from 1903; in 1911 he left Cambridge to begin his long tenure of the Chair of Economics at Belfast. He died in 1964, publishing nothing more in economic history and

very little in economics. See the lecture he gave in 1952 printed in R. L. Smyth (ed.), *Essays in Modern Economic Development*, London, 1969, pp. 44–57.

68 J. H. Clapham, *A Concise Economic History of Britain to 1750*, Cambridge, 1949, p.v; C. R. Fay, 'Reminiscences' in A. C. Pigou (ed.), *Memorials of Alfred Marshall*, London, 1925, p. 75.

69 Audrey Cunningham, *op. cit.*, p. 107.

70 L. L. Price, *A Short History of English Commerce and Industry*, London, 1900, p. iii. The first chapter of this book, entitled 'Economic History: its Objectives and its Difficulties' is an early survey of the field as a subject.

71 For Price (1862–1950) see *Who was Who* and *The Times* obituary, 28 Feb. 1950.

72 This is the lectureship referred to below by Price; see p. 22. It appears to have been established in 1906 (*Edinburgh University Calendar for 1907–08*, p. 648), but it was not filled until Unwin was appointed in 1908 after the Carnegie money had arrived; *Edin. Univ. Cal. for 1909–10*, p. 723 and Youngson below p. 221; Margaret Lodge, *Sir Richard Lodge: A Biography*, Edinburgh, 1946, p. 108; *The Carnegie Trust for the Universities of Scotland: Seventh Annual Report (for 1907–08)*, pp. 112–3 and *Eighth Annual Report (for 1908–09)*, p. 31. For some years previously a course in economic history had been taught by Archibald B. Clark who in the *Calendar* for 1904–05, 1905–06, 1906–07 and 1907–08 was unaccountably described as 'Lecturer in Economic History' in respect of his post in 'Economics' instituted in 1901 (*Edin. Univ. Cal. for 1902–03*, p. 5); after 1908 Clark was described as 'Lecturer in Political Economy'. In 1910 Unwin was succeeded by James Eadie Todd who held the lectureship until 1912; see H. A. Cronne, T. W. Moody and D. B. Quinn (eds.), *Essays in British and Irish History in honour of J. E. Todd*, London, 1949, and J. E. Todd, 'The Apprenticeship of a Professor of History, 1903–1919', *History*, XLIV, 1959, pp. 124–33. I cannot trace a copy of the 'inaugural lecture' that Todd here states he had to deliver in 1910. The post was then held by J. B. Guild on an interim basis and in 1913 J. F. Rees was appointed; Rees became Reader in 1924, leaving the following year to succeed Ashley in the Chair of Commerce at Birmingham. See A. L. Turner (ed.), *History of the University of Edinburgh, 1833–1933*, Edinburgh, 1933, pp. 234, 373, 384, 402 and 412; David Williams, 'Foreword' in J. F. Rees, *The Problem of Wales and Other Essays*, Cardiff, n.d.

73 The Belfast lectureship was first held for less than a year by R. L. Jones and then appears not to have been filled until J. F. Rees was appointed in 1912. When Rees departed the following year for Edinburgh, he was succeeded by Conrad Gill, who held it until 1919 and then by Joseph Lemburger until 1948. I am grateful to Dr. L. A. Clarkson of the Queen's University of Belfast for information about this post.

74 H. B. Charlton, *Portrait of a University 1851-1951*, Manchester, 1951, pp. 89–90. There had been no successor to Meredith after 1908. For Unwin (1870–1925) see the obituary by R. H. Tawney in *Economic Journal*, XXXV, 1925, pp. 156–7; G. W. Daniels, *George Unwin: A Memorial Lecture*, Manchester University Lectures XXIV, 1926; 'Introductory Memoir' in R. H. Tawney (ed.), *Studies in Economic History: The Collected Papers of George Unwin*, London, 1927 and T. S. Ashton 'A Note on George Unwin' in Unwin, *Industrial Organisation in the Sixteenth and Seventeenth Centuries*, 2nd ed., London, 1957, pp. xi–xvi.

75 Arthur Redford (1896–1961) became Reader after Unwin's death in 1925

and Professor in 1945; see W. H. Chaloner, 'A Memoir' prefaced to the second edition of A. Redford, *Labour Migration in England 1800–1850*, Manchester, 1964, pp. xv–xviii. Redford was succeeded in 1961 by T. S. Willan.

76 Tawney, 'Introductory Memoir', pp. xxi–xxii and Unwin, *Industrial Organisation*, preface.

77 Tawney, *Economic Journal, op. cit.*, p. 157.

78 *Loc. cit.*

79 Rees in *History, op. cit.*, p. 5.

80 W. Cunningham, *Hints on the Study of English Economic History*, S.P.C.K. Helps for Students of History, 14, London, 1919, p. 14. For a list of some of these works see J. H. Clapham, *Bibliography of English Economic History*, Historical Association, London, 1913.

81 Some of the fruits of the 'period of monographs' are discussed in T. S. Ashton, 'Studies in Bibliography III: The Industrial Revolution', *Economic History Review*, V, 1, 1934, pp. 104–19.

82 For a survey of 'The Teaching of Economic History in Schools' at this stage by G. H. K. Marten see *Economic History Review*, I, 2, 1928, pp. 198–207 and of 'The Teaching of Economic History in Universities' by J. de L. Mann see *ibid.*, III, 2, 1931, pp. 197–218 and 325–345, especially for Britain pp. 334—42.

83 For Clapham (1873–1946) see the memoirs by G. N. Clark in *Proceedings of the British Academy*, 32, 1946, pp. 339–52; Herbert Butterfield in *Cambridge Historical Journal*, VIII, 3, 1946, pp. 115–6 (and the bibliography of his writings in *ibid.*, pp. 205–6); G. M. Trevelyan in *Economic Journal*, LVI, 1948, pp. 499–507 and in *An Autobiography and Other Essays*, London, 1949. See also A. P. Usher, 'Sir John Howard Clapham and the Empirical Reaction in Economic History', *Journal of Economic History*, XI, 2, 1951, pp. 148–53; W. H. B. Court, 'John H. Clapham' in J. T. Lambie (ed.), *Architects and Craftsmen in History: Festschrift für Abbott Payson Usher*, Tübingen, 1956, pp. 147–55 and in *Scarcity and Choice in History*, London, 1970; Peter Mathias in *International Encyclopaedia of the Social Sciences*, 1968.

84 Sir George Clark is the senior surviving economic historian, although his many writings indicate that he has never been constrained by the adjective. He resigned the Chichele Chair of Economic History at Oxford in 1943 to become Regius Professor of History at Cambridge and returned to his old university in 1947 as Provost of Oriel College.

85 See the obituary notices of Eileen Power (1889–1940) by R. H. Tawney in *Economic History Review*, X, 1939–40, pp. 92–4 and in *D.N.B. 1931–1940*, pp. 718–9; by J. H. Clapham in *Economica*, N. S., VII, 1940, pp. 351–9 and by C. K. Webster in *Economic Journal*, I, 1940, pp. 561–72.

86 For Tawney (1880–1962) see T. S. Ashton in *Proceedings of the British Academy*, XLVIII, pp. 461–82, which gives a bibliography of his main historical writings and the notable essay on him in W. H. B. Court's *Scarcity and Choice in History*, London, 1970, pp. 127–40. See also J. M. Winter, 'R. H. Tawney's 'Early Political Thought', *Past and Present*, 47, 1970, pp. 71–96. A biography of Tawney is long overdue.

87 An edition of the remarkable commonplace book that Tawney kept before the first world war has been prepared by Dr. Winter and the late Professor Joslin and is to appear as a supplement to the *Economic History Review*. This quotation, with their kind permission, is from the entry for 26 March 1913.

88   Postan retired from the chair in 1965; see the commemorative issue of the *Economic History Review*, 2nd ser., XVIII, 1, 1965. His successor, Professor D. M. Joslin (1925–1970) did not give an inaugural. 'I never did get round to one', he wrote, 'and quite a few of my contemporaries seem to regard it as a function of an earlier generation to state what a subject is all about.' (Personal communication, dated 19 August 1970).

89   Sir Keith Hancock has given an honest sketch of his unhappy tenure of this chair in *Country and Calling*, London, 1954, pp. 232–4. He resigned in 1949 and was succeeded by H. J. Habakkuk, who did not give an inaugural. Habakkuk resigned in 1967 to become Principal of Jesus College Oxford.

90   There is a bibliography in the *Festschrift* for Ashton, L. S. Pressnell (ed.), *Studies in the Industrial Revolution*, London, 1960, pp. 328–33. See also the obituary of Ashton (1889–1968) by A. H. John in *Economic History Review*, 2nd ser., XXI, 3, 1968.

91   See above pp. xxxvi–xxxvii.

92   It was not then the practice at Birmingham University to give inaugural lectures and Professor Court therefore did not give one. He informs me however that what he would have said was later written as the essay on 'Economic History' he contributed to H. P. R. Finberg (ed)., *Approaches to History*, London, 1962. This is reprinted as 'What is Economic History?' in *Scarcity and Choice in History*, London, 1970, where there is also a very interesting autobiographical essay, 'Growing up in an Age of Anxiety'.

93   Besides the five established chairs there was Tawney's personal chair at L.S.E. Between 1953 and 1965 E. M. Carus-Wilson also held a personal chair at L.S.E.

94   Professor Macdonald gave an inaugural lecture on 'Labour and the Community', but it was not published and Professor Macdonald informs me that it is not in a publishable form.

95   Professor Checkland did not give an inaugural lecture.

96   Professor Ashworth was the first graduate in economic history, as distinct from history, economics or classics, to hold a chair in the subject.

97   In 1963 Professor Youngson was translated to the chair of Political Economy and was succeeded in the chair of Economic History by S. B. Saul. Professor Saul gave an inaugural lecture but did not put it into publishable form.

98   Professor Chambers (1898–1970), Nottingham born and bred, had taught economic history extra-murally since 1924 and in the University since 1947; he retired from the chair in 1965. See his *Festschrift*, E. L. Jones and G. E. Mingay (eds.), *Land, Labour and Population in the Industrial Revolution*, London, 1967.

99   In the last decade the increasing specialization within the subject has also led to the appointments of R. H. Hilton as Professor of Medieval Social History at Birmingham, G. E. Mingay as Professor of Agrarian History at the University of Kent at Canterbury and of two Professor of Social History, H. J. Perkin at Lancaster and M. W. Flinn at Edinburgh. In the University of London two further professors were appointed at the L.S.E., A. H. John and D. C. Coleman, and in 1970 E. J. Hobsbawm became Professor of Economic and Social History at Birkbeck College. None of these gave inaugural lectures.

100   At Exeter Professor Minchinton gave an inaugural lecture but it was not put into publishable form. I understand that Professor Spooner has it in mind to give one at Durham.

101   In the report of the economic history section meeting of the Anglo-American

Conference of Historians, *Bulletin of the Institute of Historical Research*, IV, 1926–27, p. 110.

102 See for example the cogent strictures of E. P. Thompson in *The Making of the English Working Class*, London, 1964, pp. 204–5.

103 See R. W. Fogel, 'The New Economic History, its Findings and Methods', *Economic History Review*, 2nd ser., XIX, 1966, pp. 642–56 and the works discussed there. See also Professor Mathias' remarks below.

104 It is not intended to give the impression that this flourishing state has been produced only by those who hold or have held chairs in the subject. Any full explanation of the growth of the subject would of course have to take into account many other individuals: E. Lipson and H. L. Beales, for example, to mention only two influential economic historians who held Readerships; those who held chairs abroad, such as Herbert Heaton or C. R. Fay; people who made important contributions to the subject from outside academic life, such as the Hammonds or A. P. Wadsworth. And then there are many others who held chairs in other subjects: in economics, such as W. Smart, W. R. Scott, T. E. Gregory, Henry Hamilton, F. E. Hyde, R. S. Sayers and—above all—Alfred Marshall; in history, such as Charles Wilson and F. M. L. Thompson, or in local history, such as W. G. Hoskins and H. P. R. Finberg.

1

W. J. Ashley

ON THE STUDY OF ECONOMIC HISTORY
(Harvard, 1893)

This inaugural lecture was delivered at Harvard
University on the 4th January 1893.

ON THE STUDY OF ECONOMIC HISTORY

THE teacher in England or America who seeks to explain his attitude towards economic science does so at the present time under peculiarly favourable conditions. There reigns just now a spirit of tolerance and mutual charity among political economists such as has not always been found within their circle. It is not that we have returned to the confident dogmatism and unanimity of the last generation,—of the period which extended from the publication of John Stuart Mill's treatise to the sounding of the first note of revolt in Cliffe Leslie's essays. It is rather that, though there are still marked divergencies, the followers of one method no longer maintain that it is the *only* method of scientific investigation; that, on the other hand, the believers in induction now recognize more fully the value of deduction; that the most abstract sometimes refer to facts and the most concrete occasionally make use of abstraction; and, what is far more important, that they are inclined, whatever their own turn of thought may be, to let others alone who walk not with them, or even to cheer them on their way in the benevolent hope that they may arrive at something worth the getting. It has now become almost a commonplace even with economists of the older school that students may usefully be led to work in different ways, owing to 'varieties of mind, of temper, of training, and of opportunities.'[1] In England an association has at last been founded which includes among its members most of those writers and teachers who are seriously interested in economics, and a journal has been established which welcomes contributions from every side with admirable impartiality. In America an association, which has for some years been doing excellent work, but which has hitherto been a little one-sided in its membership, has just widened its borders, and brought in even those against whose teachings it was once its business to protest. The controversies which break the monotony of life for our German colleagues have now but a faint echo among English-speaking economists; the personal anatgonisms which separate French schools are altogether absent; and to most of us the recent exchange of hostilities between two distinguished English economists has seemed almost an anachronism. It is, therefore, with something of trepidation that I venture upon what may possibly look like a renewal of

3

old controversies. Yet it is encouraging to think that, even if one had something very 'extreme' to say, one might now count upon being heard with patience and urbanity.

It would be idle to deny that the hopes which were entertained by the younger men of the 'historical' or 'inductive' school in Germany some twenty years ago, and by Cliffe Leslie and more recently by Dr. Ingram among English writers, have not hitherto been realized. They looked for a complete and rapid transformation of economic science; and it needs only a glance at the most widely used text-books of to-day to see that no such complete transformation has taken place. Of this disappointment a partial explanation may be found in the fact that the historical economists were still so far under the spell of the old discipline as to continue to conceive of economics under the forms made familiar by the manuals. They still had before their eyes the customary rubrics of Production, Distribution, and Exchange; they still handled the sacred terms Value, Supply, Demand, Capital, Rent, and the rest,—terms which, to use Oliver Wendell Holmes's phrase, were just as much in need of *depolarization* as the terms of theology; they still looked forward to framing 'laws' similar in character, however different in content, to the 'laws' in possession of the field. Aiming, as they unconsciously did, at the construction of a body of general propositions dealing with just the same relations between individuals as the older school had given its attention to, it was natural that they should fall back on the use of that deductive method which is certainly of service for the analysis of modern competitive conditions, although they had begun by unnecessarily rejecting it. And thus the 'methodological' arguments of the orthodox may seem to have gained an easy victory.

I shall attempt to show later that this is not an adequate version of the matter; that during this period the historical movement has been slowly pushing its way towards it own true field of work. Even in its relation to current economic teaching, it has performed a work of vital importance. It has been no mere aberration, passing away and leaving no trace; nor is it quite a complete account of it to say that it has contributed useful elements which have been incorporated in the body of economic science. It has done more than this: it has changed the whole mental attitude of economists towards their own teaching. The acceptance of the two great principles,—which are but different forms of the same idea,—that economic conclusions are *relative* to given conditions, and that they possess only *hypothetical* validity, is at last a part of the mental habit of economists. The same is true of the conviction that economic considerations are not the only ones of which we must take account in judging of social phenomena, and that economic forces are not the only forces which move men. It need hardly be said that all this was recognized *in word* long ago; but it may be left to the verdict of those who are conversant with the literature of the last generation whether these convictions were really underlying and fruitful parts of daily thought, as they are now tending to be. The remark, indeed, is not out of place in passing that, although this salutary conversion may be discerned among professional economists, it has hardly taken place so completely as one could wish with the educated public, and that historical zealots may still do good service in insisting on these well-worn platitudes.

The altered mental attitude of the theoretic economists themselves towards their own doctrine is so much the most important result, from the point of view of current teaching, of the historical movement that it dwarfs its other effects in the same direction. But these other effects are well worth looking at; and they are evident enough, if we turn over the two most important of modern treatises, the *Principles* of Professor Marshall and the *Lehrbuch* of Professor Wagner. Professor Marshall so clearly realizes that the understanding of modern conditions is assisted by a consideration of their genesis that he introduces his work by two chapters on 'The Growth of Free Industry and Enterprise,' and by another chapter on 'The Growth of Economic Science.' So, again, his discussion of Population is preceded by a history of the doctrine, and a history of population itself in England. His treatment of Industrial Organization consists largely of historical reflections. The theory of Distribution is introduced by a sketch of its history, and the doctrine of Rent is considered in relation to early forms of land tenure. With Professor Wagner the influence of historical thought is even more marked. As every one is aware who has had occasion to consult the recent volumes of his *Finanzwissenschaft*, his accumulation of historical material has grown so fast that it is threatening to become unwieldy. A more convincing evidence of his familiarity with historical modes of thought is presented in many parts of his treatment of general theory; *e.g.*, in his acceptance of the position that 'capital,' as it is now understood, is an 'historical,' and not an eternally necessary 'category.' He even attempts to formulate an historical law,—a law of the course of economic evolution,—and that in a matter which touches modern problems very closely; to wit, his 'law of the increasing extension of public and state activity.' That Wagner should to-day be regarded, and should regard himself, as a champion of abstraction and deduction as against the 'extreme *Historismus*,'— though just enough in the main,—has in it something of the irony of circumstances. It reminds one of the observation of John Stuart Mill that the great advantage from the presence of extremists is that any course short of the extreme gains the charm of 'moderation.'

It need hardly be said with regard to the examples just given that, suggestive as such historical reflections and generalizations may be, they are not to be regarded as necessarily either accurate or desirable methods of using historical material. They illustrate, however,—and that is all I wish to show,—the influence, to a large extent the un-realized influence, of the *Zeitgeist* even over writers who wish to carry on the old traditions.

In the wider issue of the comparative merits of induction and deduction, it may be observed that conservative economists them-selves no longer employ the sweeping language in favour of deduc-tion which characterized their predecessors. They have discovered, like M. Jourdain with his prose, that in one very important field, that of Production, they have been inductive all along without knowing it.[2] It is further allowed by recognized authorities that 'within the province of *descriptive* and *classificatory* economics there is unlimited scope for valuable economic work.'[3] And, accordingly, we see a series of useful studies in modern industrial life,—studies largely historical,—appearing under the highest economic patronage.[4] Even the pages of the Harvard *Quarterly Journal of Economics*,—the peculiar home of theory,—furnish articles on the history of the tariff or of the currency; though it must be allowed that even the severest theorists have sometimes coquetted with facts when they approached these particular topics. It is true that we are cautioned that 'the knowledge of particular facts, which is thus afforded, does not in itself constitute the end and aim of economic science.'[5] But we will not be distressed by this if only the work of inquiry will go on. It marks the awakening,—or the reawakening,—in American and English economics of a sacred passion for the observation of real life, of which it has too long been devoid.

I have, however, already remarked that, while thus affecting the character of the teaching of economic theory, the historical move-ment has pursued its way, and is now settling down into a channel of its own. This is none other than the actual investigation of economic history itself. This may, perhaps, be a somewhat surprising remark. It may be asked, 'What, then, have the economists of that school been doing hitherto?' It will, however, I think be found that the creators of the school were rather men who had been touched by the historical thought around them, and inspired by its ideas, than original investigators. This was not to their discredit: it was the result of the situation. But to-day the leaders of the school are throwing them-selves into detailed research, and are feeling their way towards independent historical construction. We have only to look at the publications of Professor Schmoller, of Berlin, and of the body of

fellow-workers he has gathered around him, or at the large programme of inquiry into agrarian history which Professor Knapp, of
Strasburg, and his circle have put before themselves,[6] to discover how
strong is the current in this direction. And with this serious engage-
ment in historical inquiry has come a clearer perception of the nature
of the generalizations towards which that inquiry must work. It is
seen that these will not be mere corrections or amplifications of
current economic doctrines: they will rather be conclusions as to the
character and sequence of the stages in economic development. The
point of view is here no longer that of a bargain between individuals
in given social conditions, but of the life and movement of whole
industries and classes, of the creation and modification of social
mechanism, of the parallel progress and inter-action of economic
phenomena and economic thought. The studies of the school are no
longer individualist and psychological, but collectivist and institutional. To help out my meaning by two hackneyed but convenient
phrases, the 'laws' of which they think are 'dynamic' rather than
'static'; and they aim at presenting the 'philosophy' of economic
history. And, thus, their interest in any one period is not that they
may compare it with the present or any other period, but because
every period may furnish them with points from which they may determine the curve of economic evolution.

It has been inevitable that, with such an ideal before him, the leader
of this newer historical school, Gustav Schmoller, should sometimes
have spoken slightingly of the attempt to continue the old work of
deductive argumentation: it was inevitable that the theorists he has
in mind should retort with language of equal confidence in the
superior merits of their own methods. It is often hard for a man to
recognize that he pursues a particular line of thought chiefly because
his own mental gifts lie in that direction. It is very natural that he
should feel that the task towards which he is himself drawn is the
most urgent and beneficent of all tasks. But when Professor
Schmoller, instead of being submissive to the lessons read to him,
remarks that it is useless to expect progress from 'the further distilla-
tion of the already-a-hundred-times-distilled abstractions of the old
dogmatism,'[7] and declares very plainly that those who attempt the
process lack a wide philosophical training,[8] he uses language, which,
as Matthew Arnold said on a somewhat similar occasion, has
certainly 'too much vivacity,' and is sure to create soreness. And
when Professor Menger retorts by inventing for the labors of his
opponent the pleasing terms 'miniature-painting',[9] 'micrography.'[10]
and 'specialissima about some gilds or other,'[11] he can hardly be
acquitted of a certain acerbity.

It is surely time to cry a truce to controversy. Let it be acknow-

ledged that for a long time to come there are likely to be many honest
and hard-working and intelligent men who will be interested in
economic theory: let it be acknowledged, likewise, that there are
likely to be a number,—small, indeed, in America and England, but
still noticeable,—who also are honest and hard-working and not
altogether unintelligent, who will be interested in economic history.
Let us try for the next twenty years to leave one another severely
alone, and see what will come of it. If we have time, let us read one
another's books. Perhaps we shall be converted: perhaps we shall
only get a suggestion here and there; but, if we cannot agree, let us
be silent. We shall, at any rate, gain some little additional time for
our own inquiries; and meanwhile the general progress of human
thought may quietly bring a solution. And yet I would hardly be
supposed to imply that the controversy of the last few years has
been a waste of words. A good deal of fighting was necessary before
the right of the historical economist to a fair field was recognized in
England and America. I should not be surprised to hear that in
Germany some few years ago there was the opposite evil,—a too
complete exclusion of economic theorists from places of academic
influence. But now that an armistice can be signed on honourable
terms, it were well to do so. Harvard must receive the credit of having
been the first among universities to realize the altered situation. It has
been the first to see the wisdom of having both attitudes—the theoretical and the historical—represented in a great institution of
learning. Its action is the more commendable because it has been
determined upon at the instigation of teachers already in possession
of the territory, whose own intellectual sympathies are chiefly on the
side of theory. They have shown a confidence in free inquiry, and an
understanding of the true nature of a university, which are still rare.

But such a truce ought not certainly to prevent any of us from
frankly expressing his own private opinions to any student who cares
to ask for them. And the opportunity to make one's own position
plain upon assuming new duties in a new sphere is so rare that it
may fairly be brought within the same exception. It must be remembered that I shall be expressing only my own individual judgment; that I know full well that there are many able men who
absolutely differ from me; that is it probable enough that, having
heard what I may have to say, students may straightway go off and
work in another direction, and that they may be happy in doing so.
Still, what I should say to an able and properly prepared student of
mature mind who came to me for suggestions would be somewhat as
follows:
    'You have already, I understand, given some attention to Political

Economy. You are acquainted with the main outline of the theory as it is presented, for instance, by John Stuart Mill. You know something of the history of Political Economy from Adam Smith to Mill, and of the general character of the development since Mill's time. If, indeed, you have not already got this equipment, I would advise you to get it; the study will supply you with points of view which you will afterwards find convenient, and it will introduce you to an interesting chapter of modern thought. Moreover, as teaching is now arranged in the great universities, you will have little difficulty in making these preliminary studies. Six months' steady work will probably suffice. I can assume, you tell me, that you already have this knowledge; you are interested in the economic life of society; you would like to attempt a little independent work of your own; and you ask in what direction your efforts are likely to be most fruitful. I cannot say that the outlook in the field of theoretic discussion looks very hopeful. For years there has been a keen controversy going on upon the subject of Distribution; and economists, even economists of the first rank, seem as far from agreement as ever. According to President Walker, Wages are the Residual Share which falls to the laborer out of the joint produce of capitalist, employer, land-owner, and laborer, the three other shares being limited. For fifteen years he has maintained this in books of every size: it has been echoed in half the colleges of America and Great Britain; and yet I doubt whether you could discover another living economist of importance who agrees with him. Or take Profits. You will find equally competent writers who explain Profits as the Wages of management, as a reward for Risk, and as a species of gain governed by laws similar to those of Rent. I am aware that several of the younger American economists are accepting wholesale the new Austrian doctrine of "subjective value," and think they find in it the key to every problem. But I notice that, in the judgment of Dr. Bonar,—who has himself done more than any one else to introduce the Austrian writers to the attention of English-speaking students,— what they have given us is "rather a definition of value than an explanation of its causes."[12] Their principles have still to be applied to "the problems of distribution as they meet us in modern countries";[13] and it is not clear that in this undertaking their American disciples are being greatly helped by the new phraseology. Moreover, one cannot but observe that the early difficulty is still constantly turning up,—that economists cannot understand one another. There is a page in one of the back numbers of our own *Quarterly Journal* which makes one pause. It contains two brief letters. In one, distinguished economist A says of a criticism of his views by distinguished economist B, "I abide by my doctrines as expounded by

D

myself, and I do not accept the paraphrase of them given by Mr. B."
In the other, well-known writer C remarks of well-known writer D,
"I shall have no difficulty in showing that Mr. D, despite his denial,
did use the term 'profits' as I understood it."[14] One takes up by
chance another number of the *Quarterly*, and one's eye catches "The
misunderstanding that is the basis of President z's chief criticism [of
me] is radical and unexpected."[15] 'I see no reason to suppose,'
I should say to my inquiring friend, 'that you are likely to be
much more successful in interpreting statements of theory than
these able persons have been. Of course, if you have reason to believe that you possess a peculiar aptitude for abstract reasoning, and
are strongly attracted towards economic theory, you may find a
good deal of pleasure in turning your thoughts in that direction. I
hardly care to prophesy, with any very strong feeling of certitude,
that you will not arrive at valuable results; though I scarcely think
it probable. Further than that I am not inclined to go. But, if you
have no such strong bent, then I would suggest that you should
consider the advisability of trying your hand at economic history.
Here is an almost untrodden field: here is abundance of material;
and, even if you do not arrive at any very wide-reaching conclusions,
the facts which you may discover will themselves be positive acces-
sions to knowledge. As Lotze says,"To know facts is not everything,
but it is a great deal; and to think lightly of them because one yearns
for something further is fitting only to those who do not understand
that the half is often better than the whole." '

Before proceeding now to speak more at length of economic
history itself, there are two criticisms which it will be well to clear out
of the way. It is urged, in the first place, that 'some familiarity with
economic theory is essential to the interpretation of industrial
phenomena such as it falls within the province of the historian to
give.'[16] It will be remembered that I have advised the imaginary
enthusiast to begin by gaining even a considerable familiarity with
economic theory. But I must confess that I have done so chiefly from
a sense of justice to the man himself in the present state of opinion.
Theoretic political economy is still so strong in the support of most
teachers in England and America that it would be hardly fair to set
a man against the current,—especially if his professional prospects
as a teacher were at all involved,—unless he were in a position to
judge for himself. But, so far as the actual utility of economic theory
to the historian is concerned, I cannot help feeling that much of the
language used is unnecessarily grandiose, especially as applied to
those earlier periods which are in most need of investigation. Says
the same writer, 'All that is really given us in each case by direct

evidence is a highly complex sequence of events, in which the true bonds of causal connection may be disguised in a thousand different ways, so that, far from being patent to every observer, they can be detected only by the trained student thoroughly equipped with scientific knowledge.' But, when this same writer goes on to illustrate economic theory from history the sort of illustration he takes is a statement that 'a dry summer' in the Middle Ages 'caused much wear and tear of implements, and consequently an increased demand and a higher price, so that the bailiffs' accounts frequently mention "the dearness of iron on account of drought.' " 'We could not,' he says, 'have a better illustration of the effect of demand on price.'[17] Surely, the power of tracing so obvious a connection between phenomena demands nothing more than plain common sense: we might even use the amusing phrase of Thorold Rogers, and say that 'so much was known in the days of the Egyptian and Babylonian kings.' The author whom I have quoted would seem to have been unwittingly taking for granted that the historical economist is anxious to discuss just such problems as the modern theorist, only in a different environment. Such exaggerated estimates of the value of theory will disappear when the character of the work before the economic historian comes to be better understood. It will be seen to be almost as great a mistake to use such language in relation to the historian of economic conditions as it would be to use it in relation to the historian of constitutional or legal conditions. It is strange that this is not already apparent. No one, for instance, would deny the great value for a true understanding of social progress of two recent books touching very different periods, Mr. Seebohm's *Village Community* and Mr. Charles Booth's *Labour and Life of the People*. In neither of these books has economic theory been of any visible service.

Nevertheless, to provide against the chance that even the simplest causal connections may be overlooked, it will be a wise precaution to advise students to begin by making themselves familiar with the rudiments of modern Political Economy. Moreover, since modern Political Economy has certainly brought into prominence some of the leading characteristics of the agriculture and industry and trade of to-day, its formulæ will give the economic historian convenient standards of comparison, whereby he may the better perceive what are the distinctive features of past conditions. But more than this economic theory will not, in my opinion, do for any save those states of society to which its ablest vindicator, Bagehot, expressly restricted its applicability,—those 'states of society in which commerce has largely developed, and where it has taken the form of development, or something near the form, which it has taken in England' and America during the last hundred years.[18] And even for this very recent period a good deal of excellent work, of indispensable work, is possible without the use of 'the economic organon';[19] as is abundantly shown by the writings of Mr. Charles Booth and what may be called his school,—such investigations as Mr. Schloss, Mr. Llewellyn Smith, and Miss Collet.

The other stumbling-block to be cleared out of the way is the argument based on the imperfection of the historical record. Mr. Keynes has quoted from Richard Jones the remark that 'history has suffered to drop from her pages, perhaps has never recorded, much of the information which would now be most precious to us',[20] and, as Jones is one of the fathers of the historical church, the objection is a depressing one. But, on referring to the passage itself, it will be found that Richard Jones went on to put a more cheering view of the matter in language which, though a little rhetorical, ought always to be quoted after citing the preceding sentence: 'Yet this defect does not always exist when we think it does. The compiler and the student are sometimes more to blame than the original historian. The labors of Niebuhr, Savigny, Heeren, Müller, have proved that there is much knowledge, most important to our subject, in historical records, which has faded from the minds of men, and must be laboriously recovered from the recesses of neglected literature, like lost and sunken riches from the secret depths of the ocean. Our own scholars and antiquaries will not, we may hope, be backward in imitating them; and the historical documents, both of our own and of foreign countries, contain, we may well believe, large and unknown stores of economical instruction,—many a heap of unsunned treasures to reward their researches.'[21]

We are now in a position to look at the nature of economic history a little more closely. Let us begin by asking wherein it differs from what has hitherto been known as social history, or what the Germans call 'the history of civilization,'—*Culturgeschichte*. Social history, —so far, indeed, as it has existed at all,—has appealed to a multiplicity of interests. It has appealed, *e.g.*, to a psychological interest, curious to study forms of thought remote from our own; it has appealed still more to what may be called an aesthetic interest, the pleasure we take in mere quaintness or strangeness, like our satisfaction at seeing a mediaeval market-place on the stage. But economic history is throughout dominated by one main interest,—the economic. It asks what has been the material basis of social existence; how have the necessities and conveniences of human life been produced; by what organization has labor been provided and directed; how have the commodities thus produced been distributed; what have been the institutions resting on this direction and distribution;

what changes have taken place in the methods of agriculture, of industry, of trade; can any intelligible development be traced; and, if so, has it been from worse to better. These, and many like them, are the questions which will be asked by the student of economic history. The marking out of such a field of study is only a fresh example of the division of scientific labour: it is the provisional isolation, for the better investigation of them, of a particular group of facts and forces. And this especial study of what may at first sight seem a sordid side of human affairs is justified by its importance. For 'the two things best worth attending to in history,' as Mr. John Morley has well remarked, 'are the great movements of the economic forces of a society, on the one hand, and, on the other, the forms of religious opinion and ecclesiastical organization.'[22] Much that has been included in social history the student will now relegate to the historian of art, of literature, of technical processes, of superstition, and what not. What remains he will utilize for his special purpose, endeavoring to place in order and coherence what has hitheto been but a heap of disconnected particulars.

It may, however, be observed in this connection that the economic historian will often think it wise to postpone the consideration of many bits of information,—may even be tempted to thrust them impatiently on one side,—which are commonly supposed to be of prime importance for his purpose. This is particularly true of statistics as to prices and wages in the Middle Ages. Partly because Thorold Rogers gave his whole attention to the collection of this sort of material, partly because the economic theorists are preoccupied by the operations of the market, there has grown up an idea that what the economic historian most craves for is to learn the price of a day's labor or of a day's food in past centuries. Facts of this kind are valuable, but only when we can place them in their proper setting. Our first requirement is to understand, far more precisely than we do at present, what has been the institutional framework of society at the several periods, what has been the constitution of the various social classes, and their relation to one another. This is the explanation of what must have struck every one who has given serious attention to English agrarian history,—the infinitely greater importance of the first one hundred pages of Mr. Seebohm's work than of all Thorold Rogers's voluminous collections, and that although the former had not in all probability given to the subject one-fifth of the time and labor bestowed by the second. It is because Mr. Seebohm has given us a vivid picture of the daily life of the agricultural population, which has for the first time imparted to Mr. Rogers's facts a true significance.

'If "economic history," after all, is only a branch of history, why not leave it,' it may be asked, 'to the historian pure and simple? or, if you are not content to do that, why thrust yourself into the ranks of the economists?' Well, the time may come when those who are interested in economic history will have to turn their backs on the 'economists,' and cry, *Ecce convertimur ad gentes!* It may be granted that, as things are now, economic history belongs equally to the departments of history and economics. But this same characteristic of touching two fields which are nevertheless fenced off from one another is equally true of legal history and of ecclesiastical history. There is no reason in the nature of things why the 'pure historian,' as he is called, should not investigate both the history of religion and the history of law. But, as a matter of fact, the work of research in these two fields has usually been carried on by men who began by being theologians and lawyers in the narrow sense. So, similarly, the men who have of late done most to advance the knowledge of economic history are men like Schanz, Ochenkowski, Held, Brentano, Toynbee, Cunningham,—to mention only those writers who have given special attention to England. All these have been men who have had an 'economic' training, and have been drawn to the study of the past by their interest in the problems of the present. Professor Menger has indeed complained, in language which leaves nothing to be desired in point of vehemence, that 'the historical school has been from the very first not the result of the profound study of the problems of our own science: it has not arisen, like historical jurisprudence, from the scientific needs of economists dealing seriously with their own questions.'[23] 'Like foreign conquerors have the historians entered upon the territory of our science, to force upon us their speech and usages, their terminology and methods.'[24] Professor Menger may have had in his mind, while thus writing circumstances hidden from the world; but, certainly, his statement is very far from being precise, so far as English work is concerned. No one would, I imagine, deny the name of economist to Richard Jones, to Cliffe Leslie, to Thorold Rogers, to Arnold Toynbee. The case of Toynbee is sufficient to illustrate the motives that have been at work. Toynbee came towards the end of his life to give his attention more and more exclusively to the economic history of the last two centuries, precisely because of his inexorable desire to penetrate more deeply into 'the problems of our own science'.

But to dwell on the somewhat grudging attitude of certain writers would be to partake of their spirit. In my lectures here,—if I may speak for myself,—I shall assume such an acquaintance with the main facts of 'pure history' and also with the main ideas of 'pure economics' as may fairly be asked of educated men. My hearers may be expected, I hope, to know the centuries to which belong the Norman Conquest, the Fall of Constantinople, the Discovery of America, the French Revolution, just as they may be expected to know the general meaning of Division of Labor, and Supply and Demand. It will be cause for rejoicing if the study attracts men from the historical side as well as from the economic. But so long as students present themselves, and men are stimulated after a survey of the field to engage in new investigation, we need not greatly care to what group of studies this particular one is assigned. It is indeed one of the advantages of the elastic system of Harvard teaching that here such perplexities need hardly trouble us.

And now let us ask ourselves, before we leave the subject, why, after all, we should study economic history. First, then, we study economic history for a reason which some may think the lowest,— and others more truly will regard as of the essence of a liberal education,—in order to gratify a natural and innocent curiosity. The more we discover that history, as we have hitherto possessed it, has told us little more than the external movements of the surface waters of society, the more we shall be drawn to the search for more trustworthy and penetrating knowledge. The mere desire to know will be for many the only motive and the sufficient justification. A distinguished man of letters has indeed said that he 'does not in the least want to know what happened in the past, except as it enables him to see his way more clearly through what is happening to-day.'[25] Auguste Comte carried the principle further, and even proposed to put the continued pursuit of certain studies under the ban as unsocial, when once they had reached a point beyond which, in his judgment, they were incapable of being of service to mankind. It chanced that the very study which Comte would have proscribed, pursued, as it was, in spite of his anathema, from the mere love of truth, has since been fruitful in new and practical applications. And so it may be with economic history. Let us know all we can about it; and the application may be trusted to take care of itself. Even if the subject had no utility outside its interest for the student himself, it would widen his sympathies, enlarge his conceptions of the possible, and save him from the Philistinism of the market-place.

But with many of us it will properly be an additional motive that economic history is intimately bound up with modern discussions. This is a consequence of that peculiarly English and American trait, the love of precedent. To what is called the 'Anglo-Saxon' mind the fact that such and such conditions existed in the past is itself a strong reason why they should be made to exist in the present. It is very noticeable to any one who has come into contact with popular socialistic or revolutionary movements that an alleged historical fact has often more hold upon men's minds than any theoretic argument. Take, for instance, the belief in a primitive communism. Mr. Henry George tells his readers,—and he has doubtless a certain apparent justification in the writings of some recent authorities,—that 'the common right to land has everywhere been primarily recognized, and private ownership has nowhere grown up save as the result of usurpation'; and, again, that 'historically, as ethically, private property in land is robbery.'[26] You have only to attend a single-tax meeting to find that this argument plays a much greater part in the thoughts of Mr. George's disciples than it does even with Mr. George himself. Or, again, notice how prominent in English socialist literature has become the picture of the golden age of the English laborer in the fifteenth century,—a theory which was first borrowed from Thorold Rogers, and is now regarded almost as an accepted truth. We are even beginning to be told that the eight-hours movement is but the restoration of the laborer's long-lost happiness. We shall not, I trust, turn to history in order to find arguments for or against any such movements; but the circumstance that our study has this curious bearing on modern discussions may fairly endow it with a keener zest.

And, finally, there may be some who will be drawn to this field of inquiry by a hope akin to that which has been so stimulating in the investigation of physical nature,—the hope that they may thereby arrive at a more satisfying and intelligible conception of the evolution of human society. Just as in biological and physical science the investigator is buoyed up by the conviction that every isolated fact, could he but learn how, has its own place in a sequence, its own significance and appropriateness, so in the history of man we can never be content until we have found it a connected and consecutive whole, or until we know of a surety that it is but a chaos of meaningless fragments. We cannot cease attempting,—to use an old phrase in a more modern sense,—'to justify the ways of God to man.' How far we still are from any such unifying conception of history I need hardly say, least of all to those who have tried in vain to satisfy their hunger with the husks of 'Sociology.' May it not be that in those constant daily needs which men have ever been compelled to meet on penalty of starvation, in the never-ceasing labor to produce out of the earth the good things it contains, and in the efforts after a wiser distribution of the product, we may find the thread of continuity, the unifying generalizations, which shall at last make history something more than 'a shallow village tale'?

NOTES

1 Marshall, *Principles*, (2nd ed.). p. 92.
2 Sidgwick, *Principles*, Introduction, chap. ii. § 1.
3 J. N. Keynes, *Scope and Method of Political Economy*, p. 166.
4 E.g., Price's *Industrial Peace*, with preface by Professor Marshall; and the other publications of the Toynbee Trust.
5 Keynes, p. 167.
6 The reader who is unacquainted with the really considerable work undertaken by Professor Knapp and his friends will find some account of it in a review by Mr. Keasbey and another by the present writer in the *Political Science Quarterly* for December, 1892.
7 *Zur Litteraturgeschichte der Staats- und Sozialwissenschaften*, p. 279.
8 *Ibid.*, p. 293.
9 *Die Irrthümer des Historismus*, pp. 26, 37.
10 *Ibid.*, pp. 27, 37.
11 *Ibid.*, p. 40.
12 *Quarterly Journal of Economics*, iii. p. 26.
13 *Ibid.*, p. 31.
14 *Ibid.*, p. 109.
15 *Ibid.*, vi. p. 116.
16 Keynes, p. 271.
17 Keynes, p. 287.
18 *Economic Studies*, p. 6; *cf.* pp. 5, 17.
19 This is the happy phrase of Professor Marshall, and the text of his *Present Position of Economics* (1885). With a very great part of Professor Marshall's argument the present writer would entirely agree; though he would point out that the 'examination of facts by reason' (p. 44) and the use of the 'three familiar scientific methods' (p. 45) do not necessarily involve the use of the 'organon.' He would urge, also, that to say, as Professor Marshall does, that 'facts by themselves are silent' (p. 41) is to overshoot the mark. The lecture, however, shows the dawn of the sun of conciliation seven years ago rather than the present effulgence of its noon-tide beams.
20 Keynes, p. 308.
21 *Literary Remains*, p. 570.
22 'On Popular Culture,' in *Miscellanies* (ed. 1886), iii. p. 9.
23 *Irrthümer*, Vorwort, p. iii.
24 *Ibid.*, p. vi.
25 Mr. John Morley, *u. s.*
26 *Progress and Poverty*, Book VII. chap. iv.

2

L. L. Price

THE POSITION AND PROSPECTS OF THE STUDY OF ECONOMIC HISTORY

(Oxford, 1908)

This introductory lecture was delivered at the University of Oxford on the 13th May 1908.

THE POSITION AND PROSPECTS OF
THE STUDY OF ECONOMIC HISTORY

AN ancient custom has placed the delivery of an Introductory Lecture among the early duties of the occupants of Professorial Chairs. The wide observance of this tradition would seem to testify to its advantage; and it needs but brief reflection to discover that the opportunity then opened to the lecturer is not likely to recur in so benign a shape. For on these rare and privileged occasions, the recognized representative of some branch of learning is allowed, and expected, to display his conception of the scope and meaning of the study with which he is associated. He can examine its relations to cognate varieties of speculation and research; and he may emphasize the reasons for which, in his opinion, it should be commended to the notice and pursuit of alert and zealous students. As the first holder of a new academic office, I have thought that I might be permitted to follow the example set in more exalted circles; and that the special circumstances would perhaps extenuate the criticism which might otherwise befall the individual. For the recent institution by the Delegates of the Common University Fund of a Lectureship in Economic History is, in a sense, a fresh departure; and, while the responsibility which rests with the earliest occupant of the position is enhanced thereby, it may not be unprofitable to consider the broad conditions under which this movement is begun.

It can, I would suggest, be properly included among the signs which have recently been evident of a fuller recognition in this country of economic study. It is a fact, which calls for explanation, that, while we can indisputably claim as British some of the foremost names linked with the origin and the development of systematic thought on economic topics, a more distinctive prominence has hitherto been given to such subjects in the curricula of foreign nations. In the United States of America, especially, where an industrial and commercial atmosphere is found not dissimilar from that prevailing here, it is common to see whole Faculties of Economics, equipped with a full hierarchy of Professors and Assistant-Professors, lecturing to large classes on the various divi-divisions and sub-divisions of a comprehensive course. In the United Kingdom, by comparison, even in many of the newer

Universities which have recently arisen in our business centres, the teaching staff charged with the duty of inparting this instruction is limited. Its meagre boundaries, indeed, have sometimes been confined to the whole or part of the sevices of a single lecturer or professor. And yet, contrasted with twenty, or ten, or even five years since, the number of these posts has grown; and encouraging indications of further change are now becoming plain. The stagnant waters, it is evident, have been stirred; and in the country which gave birth to Adam Smith, and produced his classic *Wealth of Nations*, a fresh general interest is awakening in the systematic exploration of those familiar matters of the daily life of ordinary citizens which he and his successors scrutinized and expounded. It is probable, or certain, that this reviving influence will be seen in an extended recognition of economic studies in academic circles, both new and old. But those studies themselves, it should be noticed, may very possibly assume a different guise from that which they have worn in the departing days of their comparative neglect. For it is unsafe to rest content with the soporific, if consoling, creed that would-be instructors can always shift to unwilling pupils the whole responsibility for failure to enlist attention. Nor is it legitimate in this connexion to ignore the strength of feelings which have found expression lately in the urgent wide demand for what is called a 'realistic' treatment of economic problems.

In establishing a lectureship in that fertile district of the large area of economic study which is set apart for historical investigation, this University is, I believe, entitled to the credit, not indeed of initiating, but of being among the earliest in this country to pursue, a fresh direction of development. Its action, it is true, has been forestalled by the revivified University of London, where the flourishing School of Economics and Political Science commands the ability and zeal of two Readers in the subject. In the Victoria University of Manchester, the Dean of the new Faculty of Commerce, Professor Chapman, to whom the subject of Political Economy and Commerce is assigned, is assisted by a Lecturer on Economic History and Commerce. But in no other academic centre, whether old or new, of Great Britain or of Ireland, has a distinct University Lectureship or Professorship in Economic History been, so far as I know, created, although I understand that it is probable that the institution of some similar post may be soon announced in one famous seat of learning. The accident of being the first to fill this office here debars me from the grateful usage, appropriate to inaugural discourses, of commemorating the deserts of my predecessors. Yet I would claim the privilege of connecting the step which has now been taken with two names distinguished alike in the annals of this University and on the roll of writers upon Economics.

For the strenuous personality of the last Drummond Professor was shown most markedly in the unwearied zeal with which he himself pursued the study of Economic History, and in the characteristic energy with which he recommended its importance. By example and by precept Thorold Rogers gave a powerful stimulus to this particular branch of economic knowledge. He was a bold, determined pioneer in investigations which others have since developed; and in some respects at least he has suffered the hard destiny which often awaits the earliest explorers in an extensive region newly opened. Later researchers have called in question many of his favourite conclusions; but it is impossible to dispute the lasting force of his initial impulse, and the economic historian of to-day would be ungrateful if he did not pay a willing tribute to the robust intelligence, the tireless industry, and the direct incisive reasoning of Thorold Rogers. With the other name which I would mention, I can claim a closer and more personal tie; for it was to the Toynbee Trust that I owed my earliest lecturing experience. Arnold Toynbee's span of life was tragically short; but a deep impress was graven by his mind and character on his generation. He has left a memory which is still fragrant; although in the stress of fresh concern the busied world is prone to forget too soon the visage and demeanour of those who have passed away. His published writings may appear to his friends who knew him intimately to bear poor testimony to his rare genius; but economic historians cannot forget that in them Toynbee has contrived to impart an exceptional amount of human interest to a subject commonly considered dry, and often made repellent; that he himself was specially drawn to the historical side of economic study; and that by the graphic account he gave he has fixed a permanent name on that momentous epoch of social change of which he treated when he described the course of the Industrial Revolution. The author of the most recent investigation of that period, M. Mantoux, has used the same title as appropriate to his fuller narrative. An Oxford Lecturer in Economic History, then, will be fortunate if he can transmit a dim reflection of Toynbee's generous enthusiasm for the future progress of mankind, and his intense concern in the past vicissitudes of humbler folk, and can command as well a portion of the researching energy and forceful speech of Thorold Rogers. He cannot doubt at least that both these representative alumni of this University would have been interested in the departure which is marked by the institution of a special lectureship in a subject that they had made peculiarly their own.

More than forty years have now elapsed since, in 1866, Rogers published the first two volumes of his monumental *History of Agriculture and Prices in England*, and a quarter of a century has severed from the present day the death, in 1883, of Arnold Toynbee. And yet, while in the interval great progress has been made in the variety of economic study to which their energies were turned, it is still, in a sense, comparatively new. It would, no doubt, be unhistoric to regard any subject as completely new, if the employment of the epithet convey the notion that, springing into its full being in a single moment, it has no antecedents which can be traced. One fruitful consequence of the larger notice given lately to the historical side of economic inquiry has been the discovery, or re-discovery, of forgotten or neglected writings by less or more obscure economists; and among the topics which they have handled they have contributed to the more or less complete narration of periods or episodes of economic history. Some noteworthy literary 'finds' have been recently secured in this direction; and no dissimilar a result is reached by reiterated and observant scrutiny of the classical productions of the more famous masters.

The protagonist, for instance, in the onslaught made thirty years ago upon the traditional scheme of doctrine of the 'orthodox' economists of his day, used as his battle-cry the defiant declaration, 'Back to Adam Smith.' Cliffe Leslie urged indeed the claims of Adam Smith in substitution for Ricardo, because, as he contended, in the large and prominent use of facts made in the *Wealth of Nations*, the earlier economist, in contrast with the more abstract elaborate type of reasoning favoured by his successor, drew near to the characteristic methods of the historical school of modern German writers. It was the creed and practice of these writers which, their English advocate maintained, furnished the pattern for the sensible economists of his day to adopt and follow. But, whether Cliffe Leslie was right or wrong in this interpretation of the general conception of his subject formed by Adam Smith, or in his estimate of the amount of preference which that economist felt or showed for one of two contrasted modes of inference that were not in truth irreconcilably opposed, there can be no dispute that sections of the *Wealth of Nations*, not the least remarkable for their interest and importance, could take their place in a modern treatise on economic history.[1] Had he chosen, Cliffe Leslie might also have placed upon his banner of revolt the alternative inscription, 'Back to Malthus'; for not only did that economist assert a firm belief that the 'main' part of Ricardo's 'structure' of deductive 'reasoning' 'would not stand', but also, unlike his contemporary and friend, he was attracted to historical research. His praised and maligned *Essay on Population*, in the expanded shape of the second and subsequent editions, might in fact be described as being largely an amalgam of history and statistics. It was in the main a detailed review, based partly on his own notes made in personal tours, and partly on the systematic or occasional reports of other travellers and observers, of the actual facts of population. It exhibited, indeed, a distinct affinity to the 'realistic' studies of economic problems which are now in vogue. In the conspicuous writings, then, of the chief economists themselves no inconsiderable quota of historical discussion can be found; and in less-known quarters more or less detailed descriptions of past periods, or incidents, or movements, are being constantly discovered which may justly be regarded as detached anticipations of the finished and minute inquiries of the present day.

But, after all, these were the disjointed fragments of a systematic study. They were, at any rate, no more than the embryonic germs of subsequent maturer growth. A single circumstance may suffice to demonstrate this view. For a full account of the general course of the advance of English Industry and Commerce from the Early and the Middle Ages down to Modern Times, planned and executed on a similar scale to that employed long since for political or constitutional history, it is not possible to point to any earlier work than Dr. Cunningham's great book, which appeared in the full shape of two large volumes less than twenty years ago. In Oxford we may perhaps be permitted to regret that other more imperative avocations have hitherto hindered Professor Ashley from carrying beyond the mediaeval period the suggestive *Introduction to English Economic History and Theory*, of which the first instalment was published a few years before the commencing volume of the large edition of Dr. Cunningham's *History*. These facts by themselves would show the novelty of Economic History as a defined department of methodized research.

Yet, from the number of editions of Dr. Cunningham's authoritative work which have now been printed, a gratifying conclusion may be drawn upon the present state and future destiny of this branch of study. For the rank of Economic History is, we may affirm, doubly assured. It has won the recognition of the learned world as a distinct department of erudite research; and it has secured the appreciation of the general public as a subject of sustaining interest. The changes made in the successive issues of Dr. Cunningham's book have occasionally, it cannot be denied, reversed or modified an older view of primary importance; but they have more often dealt with the minor aspects of less prominent detail. They are significant; they are not discouraging. They show that economic history is not stereotyped. On the contrary, it exhibits the vitality of a progressive study. In metaphorical language, the position may thus be summarily described. So far as the economic history of this country, for example, is concerned, the broad lines of the main highways have been investigated and laid down, and it becomes less likely that they will henceforth be materially disturbed. But as yet the several by-ways have been in many instances imperfectly explored. In certain cases they remain roughly defined; and promising avenues of fresh inquiry are continually being opened out by unforseen discovery. The repeated scrutiny of dissatisfied research has not yet ceased to yield an appreciable return; and there is room for the employment to good purpose, in assiduous pursuit or opportune suggestion, of numerous recruits. But, nevertheless, such progress has been made that the commercial and industrial development of England is now an appropriate subject for correct narration; and a knowledge of its broad outlines is necessary to a comprehension of the full significance of the record of past movements and events. Without its aid no complete or final judgement can be framed on the persons and affairs of previous times.

Yet, when we look more closely at economic history from either side of its twofold relation—to history or to economics—we can hardly fail to be impressed by the difficulty with which this satisfactory result has been attained. The removal of the obstacles which barred the path has required time for its achievement. If we scrutinize, for instance, the process by which the economic historian has gained a recognized position among the students and expositors of history, we appreciate the precarious nature of his journey and are less astonished at the tardiness of his arrival. For a reference to historical treatises of high repute will show how recent is the date when any marked attention has been given by their authors to those special matters with which economic history is concerned. Until a time not yet removed by any distance from the present day, it was thought no necessary portion of the duty of a general historian to devote substantial sections of his narrative to the economic interests and affairs of the people, or the country, whose advancing or declining fortunes he was studying and describing. Political change and constitutional development, the rise and fall of dynasties and statesmen, the vicissitudes of military and naval conflict, filled the canvas and presented tempting opportunities for able draftsmanship and rich contrasted colouring. Such incidental reference as was sometimes made to economic topics, on pages occupied with more attractive or more favoured themes, was usually confined to the condition or administration of national finance.

For this last restriction, it is true, some excuse could be supplied from the practice of economists themselves. For their own systematic studies trace their origin from the exploration of the ways and means of meeting satisfactorily the need of governments and rulers for sufficient revenue. It was, in fact, because a 'poor people' implied a 'poor kingdom and king' that in France a methodized attempt was made by royal officials to discover and expound the causes of affluence and poverty. It must also be remembered that the more developed Economics, which could claim to be an orderly analysis of the growth and decay of the 'wealth of nations', and of the classes and the individuals of whom nations are composed, was elaborated in an age when trade and industry began to be conducted as a general rule on the large scale characteristic of existing business enterprise. Adam Smith wrote his treatise on the eve of the Industrial Revolution; Malthus and Ricardo witnessed its accomplishment. In previous times the more engrossing occupations of war and politics had overshadowed in actual fact the humbler dealings of plain citizens engaged on the production and exchange of goods. The 'condition of the people', for example, is in a peculiar sense a problem of the present day, when crowded populations are massed in manufacturing towns. Yet neither trade nor labour belong to the last hundred or two hundred years alone, although they have acquired in that period a prominence they did not previously possess. It would now seem antiquated to dispute the propriety and advantage of comprising in an adequate description of the doings of mankind at every stage of evolution since primitive savagery was left behind, some account of economic conduct and concerns. The origin and growth of business, and the various modes of its transaction, the development of industry from its crude beginnings to its elaborated system, the improvements successively effected in the mechanism of exchange—to select a few out of many of such topics—fall admittedly within the range of those general historians who endeavour at the present day to meet the probable legitimate demands of representative varieties of readers. But it would be no less futile to deny that until recently the space allowed for such affairs was by comparison with that assigned to other matters usually very small.[2]

In a recoil from this scant notice, or entire neglect, there is now perhaps some danger of excessive movement in an opposite direction. For the 'economic interpretation' of history exercises at the moment an obvious attraction over many educated minds. It has even taken hold of the popular imagination. The inducement to indulge in confident prediction of the future, based on bold and lavish generalization of the past, has shown its power in this particular connexion in more than one ingenious essay which has recently been published. The controversial ardour of the fiscal question is responsible for adding lately to the number of these apt 'interpretations'. But against the plausible endeavour to explain the policy and fate

of peoples, and failures and successes of prominent individuals or
conspicuous groups, by economic influences alone, the sensible
instructed student should be on his guard. For such forces should
take their proper place amid the throng of conflicting and co-operating causes to which a historical effect is generally due. Yet it is
significant that two remarkable books, which in different regions of
society have swayed the thought and conduct of large numbers in
our time, have avowedly lent their strong support to this particular
mode of representing history. The reiterated moral of Sir John
Seeley's *Expansion of England,* which endeavoured to impress mainly
upon cultered students the conception of Imperial Union, was the
dominant influence of the trading motives animating and directing
the long warfare in which our country was engaged from the defeat
of the Armada in 1588 to the Battle of Waterloo in 1815. In another
different quarter an ingenious thesis, based on the prevailing power
of economic impulse, has exercised a special fascination, with its
subtle dialectic, on the thoughts of many representative working men.
The American economist, Professor Seligman, has lately urged that
Karl Marx, whose treatise upon *Capital* has been called the 'sacred
book' of 'scientific socialism', had not received the credit due for his
prior insistence on the theory, which has since obtained great vogue,
that history can be explained by economics. And, although the more
progressive socialist thinkers now reject as obsolete the peculiar
formulae of Marxian doctrine, they do not seem wholly disinclined
to use his or a similar interpretation of past history.

The contention may not be generally accepted; but I venture to
suggest that a salutary corrective of exaggerations of the rôle of
economic forces in the drama of mankind may be found where its
existence has perhaps been least expected. It may, I think, be discovered in a just appreciation of the serviceable aid which a sufficient
knowledge of systematic economic theory, contained in modern treatises on principles, can provide for the intelligent inspection and exact
portrayal of economic history. It is true that the active prosecution
of the latter study is connected in this country chronologically with
a pronounced revolt against the alleged pretensions of the former.
It was thus that Cliffe Leslie raised his cry of 'Back to Adam Smith'.
The whole building of Ricardian economics must, he maintained,
be levelled to the ground, and a new structure gradually erected in
its place, on the firm, broad basis of a collected mass of real fact.
History was a record of past fact; and the 'historical method',
which attached supreme importance to established fact, was the
appropriate instrument to use in this new study. It was to take the
place of those imaginary hypotheses, centring round the supposed
conception of the 'economic man', from which Ricardo and his

followers had started and by long and complicated chains of abstract reasoning had reached their assured but unreal conclusions. The dogmas they had taught to a public not unwilling to avail itself of positive short rules for absolute clear guidence must, Cliffe Leslie urged, be once for all discarded.

That, in spite of the enthusiasm roused and the diligence provoked by the heat of controversy in its advocates, the advance of Economic History was for some time prejudiced with their opponents by this close connexion with the vexed debate on the appropriate method of inquiry into economic matters, is now tolerably plain. It will certainly be allowed by those more impartial witnesses who have directed their inspection of the merits of the quarrel from the detached standpoint of subsequent experience. For they can see that these angry differences on method, which, no doubt, were real to the actual combatants, were likely to conduct to inconclusive or unprofitable issues. They can discern the healing virtue of the catholic pronouncement by the chief economist of our later time, Professor Marshall, that there is no exclusive method of Economics. The economist should rather use in turn, like the students of other sciences, every means that the wit of man has found, and successfully employed, for the disclosure and the confirmation of the connexions between causes and effects. They can separate more easily than their predecessors the advantage and necessity of the full and accurate narration of the economic history of the past from the merits and defects of the analyses of present action attempted by Ricardo and his followers, and set forth systematically in treatises and textbooks on the principles of Economics. In any event we may now conclude that there are sufficient reasons for the welcome declaration that a satisfying truce has been proffered and accepted by the moderate partisans of either side; and, although in a fresh political conjuncture British economists may once again have lately found themselves divided, on somewhat different and yet somewhat similar lines, into opposing groups, the possibility of mutual service continues to be recognized.

On this occasion it is not needful to recall the lasting influence exerted by the criticisms and contentions of Cliffe Leslie and his school on the form in which the principles expounded in the textbooks are now commonly presented. In the original conception of the economic laws governing men's intentions in an engrossing portion of the daily business of their lives, in the careful delimitation of the sphere of conduct within which alone those laws can be considered to be operative, in the scrupulous enforcement of the exacting tests by which their truth or their sufficiency should be established or disproved, that influence is plainly evident. What I wish now to emphasize is found on the reverse side of the shield. It is the aid which can be rendered by a mastery of the reasonings of the textbooks in dealing with a difficulty which meets the economic historian on the threshold of his studies and bears him company throughout the course of his inquiries. It may indeed be urged with cogency that he, like the expositor of principles, should use in turn, as occasion prompts or opportunity permits, every method of discovery and inference which is capable of being effectively employed. It may also be contended with some pertinence that sometimes he may gain advantage from the actual application of the familiar notions of the textbooks to the events and persons of the story he is telling. He must beware, however, of a special danger which attaches to this process. For obviously he should not read into a former age the characteristics or ideas which belong to later times alone; and this temptation is no less subtle than it is misleading. But of the variety of help which I desire now to indicate, there can, I would suggest, be less suspicion.

It has been aptly stated by a competent expositor of the industrial history of England[3] that few conspicuous persons, and hardly any great events, are prominent in the narrative. The Black Death of 1348 occupies a solitary position as being responsible for catastrophic change; and even in this instance earlier writers may possibly have traced to a single influence what subsequent research has shown to be due to a number of different causes of which the Plague was only one. 'Economic History', the author I have quoted says, 'deals perforce with those slow but resistless movements which work below the surface of affairs.' It is the history of 'causes and tendencies and policies'; and 'what it has of dramatic interest is not gained from the rapid succession of incident or from the varying turns of fortune'. It is rather the sure but slow achievement of inevitable change which is calculated to impress observers. We may state the same judgement somewhat differently if we affirm that the economic historian must of necessity supply a philosophic rather than a picturesque conception of persons and affairs. He must seek to discover, and lay bare, the various ties which join causes to effects. But he is continually beset in this endeavour by the difficulty arising from what logicians have described as the plurality of causes and the intermixture of effects. For a historical effect is usually the consequence of more than a single cause; and a cause can rarely, if it can be ever, shown in historical narration completely isolated from the assisting or disturbing influence of other causes. We cannot, in short, experiment as we will upon mankind in the cool laboratory of scientific privacy with unfeeling instruments precisely suited to our purpose. Yet the economic historian needs in a greater measure than the political historian a trained or an instinctive faculty for noticing and disentangling the relations of causes with effects. For the forces which concern him are more gradual and less obvious in their operation than those which, lying nearer to the surface, agitate the swifter currents of political activity. The mutual interplay of motive and of consequence which he is bound to study is more profound and intricate. But it is here that a knowledge of economic theory can help. The analyses of purpose and result presented in the general reasonings of systematic treatises on economic principles would seem to meet this special need. For they would furnish an appropriate sphere for the skilled exercise of this desired aptitude. They are calculated to develop this particular capacity.

I can even conceive that in setting a keener edge upon a natural or an acquired facility for separating in a joint effect the co-operating and conflicting influence of different causes, and gauging their respective power, the nice precision and elaborate refinement of those mathematical economics, of which we have so brilliant an exponent in our midst in Oxford, may be of service to the study of Economic History. The two departments of inquiry, it must be admitted, may at first sight seem severed by a considerable distance. But it is as a preliminary mental training rather than as an instrument directly applicable to the immediate work before them that I would be bold enough to recommend to the investigators of Economic History an acquaintance with those mathematical conceptions which have been conspicuous in new developments of economic theory. The economic historian, indeed, like the analytical economist, may incur some risk in this connexion. For the sense of power gained from the apt employment of a fine variety of reasoning mechanism may possibly engender the illusion that he has solved a problem when he has contrived to give it satisfying technical expression. That appears to be the special drawback which attends the vulgar use of mathematical economics; and the danger is not unreal when in this and other countries an evident inclination in a mathematical direction characterizes popular as well as more advanced accounts of economic principles. Yet a firmer grasp of the complicated interaction of a multitude of causes in producing a variety of mixed effects should surely make the experienced inquirer modest rather than presumptuous; and on that account he will, we may assume, be less disposed to rest content with those large, easy generalizations which explain the trend of history by economic influences alone.

If this conception of the relations between Economic History and the two studies to which it is allied most intimately be correct, its future prospect should inspire confidence and not misgiving. For at the worst it would seem that it might safely count on the benevolent neutrality of economists and historians alike; and at the best their spontaneous recognition would be accompanied by their substantial help. In actual fact many indications point to the latter of these two alternatives. A large area of exploration is at any rate now freely opened; and the historian appears more likely in the immediate future to be embarrassed by the wealth than disappointed by the poverty of the material which awaits his scrutiny.

His interest is drawn in several directions. The investigations of recent years have yielded no unsatisfactory reward to that group of workers, who, addressing their attention to the problem, in some cases from the legal, and in others from the economic side, have given fresh life to the old alliance of Political Economy with Jurisprudence. They have concentrated their inspection on the origins of the Manorial System. In spite, indeed, of the pressing claims, now so vigorously maintained, of 'realistic' study, the process of reasoning 'from the known to the unknown' has not surrendered its attractions for the human mind. It is both curious and significant that in a new variety of study, which began with unreserved repudiation of the vain conceptions of the abstract imagined Economics of Ricardo and his followers, so much capacity and pains should have been applied to the skilful reconstruction of these early periods of economic life. For, without invoking the apt use of the braced and disciplined imagination, it would seem hardly possible to piece together from the scattered fragmentary evidence which is forthcoming an adequate description of the structure of society in these dim and distant ages. One of the most brilliant and successful of discoverers in this difficult but attractive region of research, has summarized the position in these words: 'A result,' Maitland remarked in his *Domesday Book and Beyond*, 'is given to us; the problem is to find cause and process.' The picture even now is necessarily incomplete; and details of importance have been drawn and coloured differently at different times by different hands. But the last few years have brought not the least happy or convincing contributions to the satisfactory solution of the fascinating riddle.

Evidence, no less gratifying and conspicuous, of the vigour and success with which the study of Economic History is being now pursued can be obtained from another quarter less remote. It can be secured by a brief comparison of our present knowledge of the industrial and commercial progress of this country, and of the various social problems which were raised and solved, in less or greater measure, in the last two centuries of eventful change, with that which was accessible, at any rate in an authoritative form and a convenient shape, ten or twenty years ago. Some notable additions to this literature have come from the industrious pens of foreign students; and it is, for example, to a Greek economist, M. Andréades, that we owe the first complete account which has been compiled of our Bank of England. Writing in French, he has traced its history from the earliest beginning of banking of the modern type, practised by those Goldsmiths who were the predecessors and the keen opponents of the Bank, to the full development of the elaborate and effective system of which it is the centre at the present day. But English research has been also busy to some purpose; and an inspection of the bibliography relating to special topics of commercial and industrial interest will reveal the skill and pains lately bestowed on the elucidation of English Economic History since 1700. The more general preparation of those *catalogues raisonnés* themselves is a sign of the zeal and competence with which such study is being now pursued. The birth and growth of Trade Unions, as narrated by Mr. and Mrs. Webb, and more recently by Mr. Unwin; the development of Factory Legislation, as described by Miss Hutchins and Miss Harrison; the extent and results of the Agrarian Inclosures, as measured and exhibited by Dr. Slater; and the course of the Commercial and Financial Relations between England and Ireland, as traced by Miss Murray, are some of the subjects which have thus received detailed attention. These books exhibit a diversified activity; and it is perhaps significant that all the writers should have been connected in one way or another with the London School of Economics.

Further examples could be readily adduced of this fresh and fruitful energy; but now I will not mention more than two which may justly be considered typical. The stimulating influence of a public controversy has been shown in the new illumination shed on the inspiring motives and the resulting facts of monetary change between the recoinage of silver in 1696 and the adoption of the gold standard in the second decade of the nineteenth century. That recoinage was described with characteristic point by Macaulay as an unique occasion when the highest speculative ability in the persons of the philosophers Locke and Newton was happily associated with the highest practical ability represented by the statesmen Montague and Somers. And yet it has been maintained persuasively by a recent writer of special erudition[4], that from a failure of the massive intellect of Newton to handle, as Master of the Mint, with sufficient speed and completeness a particular factor[5] of the situation which he recognized, momentous consequences that were not intended followed. Macaulay himself, it may be added, in spite of his evident mastery of the main problem, misunderstood the bearing of these circumstances; and later developments of monetary theory, forced into prominence by the pressure of an eager popular debate, have made the exact position plain.

In another department of research, in which the origin and growth of systematic thought on economic topics have been studied and set forth, an opportune discovery has been made which illustrates no less conclusively the new interest and great importance of the study of economic history. For a manuscript of notes taken by a student of the lectures on 'Justice, Police, Revenue, and Arms', which Adam Smith delivered as Professor at the University of Glasgow before he went to France, has been found and published. It has placed in a fresh setting the origin of the ideas which, developed later in the *Wealth of Nations*, were destined eventually to sway the opinions and the acts of statesmen. In the skilled hands of their Oxford editor, Dr. Cannan, these lecture-notes have been felicitously employed to distinguish the smaller share in those conspicuous conceptions which can be traced with reason to French sources, from the larger quota which may more justly be ascribed to Adam Smith himself, or to the instructor of his academic youth, of whom he spoke admiringly as the 'never to be forgotten' Dr. Hutcheson[6] These manuscript notes, enhancing the repute of British economic thought, have taken the rank which they have merited among the most remarkable of literary 'finds'.

It would be easy to prolong the list; but enough, perhaps, has now been said to justify the confidence I have expressed in the present state and future fortune of the study with which I am officially connected. In conclusion, I would ask permission to refer to two circumstances, deserving of some note, with which this University is more immediately concerned. The one is the assured success of the new Diploma in Economics which has lately been established. The number of students has reached respectable proportions; and there is every prospect of a further steady increase. This gratifying fact alone would seem to show that a genuine demand is arising in our midst for systematic economic training. The other circumstance, which should afford distinct encouragement to all who feel an interest in the advance of economic study here, is the recent announcement by a College[7] of a Fellowship to be awarded in that subject. That is indeed a new departure. It sets a welcome precedent which may be followed. In any case it is a plain propitious sign of the more favouring environment in which economists seem henceforth likely to be placed. For on the measure in which the interest of the younger generation is awakened and sustained, the continuing vitality of all studies must depend. From that wholesome law economic historians cannot claim, and would not wish, to be exempt.

NOTES

1 The digression on the Bank of Amsterdam and the long chapter upon Colonies in the fourth book might be cited as detached examples, while the whole third book on the 'different progress of opulence in different nations' would fall within this category.

2 Little more than a quarter of a century has passed since J. R. Green, in the Preface to his *Short History of the English People*, boasted with good reason of his conspicuous departure from the 'contant usage' of his predecessors. That change consisted in touching lightly on the 'details of foreign wars and diplomacies', and on the 'personal adventures' of sovereigns and of nobles, and dwelling, on the contrary, 'at length on that constitutional, intellectual and social advance,' in which, as he declared, 'we read the history of the nation itself.' He endeavoured to point out 'at great crises', like the Peasant Revolt, 'how much of our political history is the outcome of social changes,' and 'throughout' his book he drew more attention than he believed had been done in 'any previous history of the same extent' to the 'religious, intellectual, and industrial progress of the nation itself'.

3 Mr. G. Townsend Warner.

4 S. Dana Horton, in *The Silver Pound*.

5 This was the reduction in the rating of the gold guinea. As it was rated to silver higher in this country than abroad, the currency became preponderantly gold and the silver was withdrawn and exported to other countries.

6 Hutcheson's influence has been further investigated by Dr. W. R. Scott in his *Francis Hutcheson*.

7 All Souls College.

3

George Unwin

THE AIMS OF ECONOMIC HISTORY
(Edinburgh, 1908)

This introductory lecture was delivered at the University of Edinburgh in October 1908.

THE AIMS OF ECONOMIC HISTORY

IF there is any place in the United Kingdom where a lecturer on Economic History might feel it to be necessary to apologize for his subject, that place should certainly not be Edinburgh. A great man whose mortal remains lie in the Canongate churchyard may be claimed by the economic historian, no less than by the economic theorist, as the founder of his science. Adam Smith was the first great economic historian, and I do not scruple to add that to my mind he is still the greatest. There is scarcely a page of *The Wealth of Nations* where history and theory are sundered from each other; and, though a century, more devoted to historical research than any previous age, has intervened since his death, we must still turn to the pages of Adam Smith for that broad and lucid handling, full of constructive insight, which makes the essential outline of European economic development emerge through a bewildering mass of unintelligible detail.

To possess the tombs of the prophets is, however, not a sufficient guarantee of a due regard being paid to their precepts and their practice. It is, therefore, a still greater encouragement to know that in Edinburgh, at least, the spirit of Adam Smith still presides over the teaching of the science which he founded. During the past twenty-eight years the graduates of Edinburgh University, who have contributed in no small degree to form the educated opinion and to direct the administrative machinery of the British Empire, have learnt their political economy from a teacher who believes that the principles of a deductive science cannot be expected to bear much fruit in human practice till they have been fertilized by wide reading and acute observation, and illustrated and enforced by the experience of mankind at large in the whole recorded field of history.

But there is a third source of encouragement. The greatest body of learning which has been collected from a wide field of British economic history—a rich store from which teachers of economic history will have to draw their supplies for generations to come—is the fruit of the unremitting devotion to the subject for over a quarter of a century of a son of Edinburgh. With Dr. Cunningham's three volumes in the one hand, Professor Nicholson's three volumes in the other, and the three volumes of Adam Smith imperishably engraved, let us hope, on the tablets of his memory, the teacher of economic history, whatever fears he may very properly entertain of his own unworthiness, may at any rate approach Edinburgh in full confidence that the existence, and indeed the importance, of the science he represents will not be called in question.

It must be confessed that he might not always and everywhere have been so fortunate. At the present time, no doubt, the teachers of economic theory and of economic history are learning to work together in a friendly spirit and to recognize the value of each other's labours. But during the greater part of the last century this happy condition of things did not exist. Economic theorists and economic historians—the deductive school and the historical school—were apt to regard each other as starting from antagonistic principles and arriving at fundamentally opposite conclusions on the same subject. They were like two hostile bodies of practitioners who could not be called in for common consultation upon the diseases of the body politic. Controversial methods are, I believe, entirely destructive of the true spirit of science, and I only touch on these past differences with a view to clearing up the misunderstanding and avoiding its recurrence in the future.

Economic theory is the product of a very advanced civilization. The facts from which it sets out belong to a highly developed condition of the social mind. The economist takes it for granted that large masses of people have got the various motives on which they act carefully sorted out and separated into different compartments, so that they can act for certain definite purposes on one set of motives without being much affected by another set. A crowd of ladies struggling through a drapery sale; a stock exchange full of brokers buying and selling next year's wool and corn, or dealing in shares of non-existent mines; a great assembly of cotton operatives negotiating for an advance in wages—each of these collections of individuals are so absorbed in the act of bargaining that all their other human interests, their religious aspirations, social duties, family affections and political allegiances, are comparatively in abeyance. Not that they are by any means abolished. The shopping lady may be excellent mother, the stockbroker a devout Christian, and the workman on strike a staunch political supporter of the employer against whom he is striking. But, whilst the bargaining proceeds, all these other aspects of life are left largely out of account. Now, if the economist can safely assume that the great majority of a civilized community will habitually act in this way, he has an abundance of facts out of which to build his theories. The mind of the shopping public acts with a uniformity which is almost like a law of nature, and in the presence of which even the untrained shopkeeper acquires the habit of scientific observation. We find him embodying his successful generalizations in his alluring handbills and price-tickets. And, if the field of operation and of observation be immensely increased, if by cheapening transport, by extending the telegraph, by multiplying newspapers, by abolishing restrictive laws and customs, more and more of the civilized world be drawn within the limits of one great shopping area, a large opportunity is created, not only for the practical arts of the commercial speculator, but for the science of the economist. Just as the steam hammer of Nasmyth can be used with equal efficiency to rivet an ironclad or to crack a nut, so we find the economist, armed with the differential calculus, equally prepared to determine the price at which it will pay the Standard Oil Trust to supply their monopolized commodity for the use of less enlightened continents, and to interpret the mental operations of the poor widow as she balances the attractions of a packet of tea against the purchasing powers of a marginal sixpence.

There can be no manner of doubt that this condition of the social mind, which is taken for granted by the economist, does actually exist. It is what Carlyle used to call the Universal Cash Nexus, and, if it is not yet quite universal, it is sufficiently prevalent to supply a sound basis for the theories of the economist. When practical people protest that business is business, and bluntly ask the sentimentalist whether his scheme will pay, they imply that it would be a good thing if this state of mind were more widespread than it is. And, as a general rule, they are right, because the progress of the human race—not so much its material, as its spiritual, progress—depends on this condition. The widespread habit of keeping the economic motives in a separate compartment from the other motives does not merely furnish an excellent opportunity to the stockbroker and the economist, it also is the main condition of human freedom. In the mind of primitive man all the aspects of life, religious, political, social and economic, were indistinguishably blended in the single relationship which he bore to his tribe. The medieval craftsman divided his allegiance between the Church, the State, the city and the guild; and, though all these ties were involuntary, except the last, he found a considerable degree of freedom in playing one of these allegiances off against the other. The social life of the modern man is made up of a great number of constantly changing relationships, most of which are freely chosen by himself. He joins a church, a golf club, a political party; he adopts a learned profession, subscribes to a score of philanthropic societies, leaves one city for another or domiciles himself in a foreign State. His power to form endless permutations and combinations is only limited by his lack of material resources or of mental energy, or by the natural conserva-

F

tism of habit. And all these expanding possibilities of freedom are bound up with that painfully acquired dexterity of mankind in sorting out their motives, and keeping them in separate compartments, upon the automatic operations of which the calculations of the economist depend.

Now this liberty, when once achieved, seems the most natural thing in the world. 'Natural liberty' is the term which Adam Smith applied to it, and it is natural in one most important sense of the word. It is not, indeed, the condition in which man is born, but it is the condition for which he is born, the natural end of man, not his natural beginning. This natural liberty, this separation of the sphere of politics, religion, science and industry, so that each may be pursued on conditions proper to itself, is not only the main basis of future progress, it is the main result of long ages of progress in the past.

Progress, however, is not an easy or an inevitable operation. A considerable part of the human race has existed for thousands, perhaps tens of thousands, of years without achieving a perceptible degree of progress. The majority of the human race, represented by the present population of Asia, after reaching a degree of civilization beyond that of contemporary nations, have remained stationary or have degenerated from that level. And, what is most impressive of all, our own civilization has been slowly and painfully built up, after an interval of darkness and partial oblivion, on the ruins of an earlier civilization which had reached a level in some respects comparable to our own.

How do these facts affect the function of the economic historian? Largely interpreted, the subject of his study is the economic condition of mankind at large through the recorded past. But, over a great part of the earth, and during a still greater portion of the past, he finds he has to deal with men who have not reached that clear separation of the economic motive from the other social motives, so that, even if they are actuated unconsciously by economic motives, those motives have to act through the resisting medium of non-economic ideas. This is still the case if he confines himself to the past history of a country like Great Britain or America, where the fluidity of capital and labour and the comparative absence of restrictive laws and customs give at the present time a large scope for the calculations of the economic theorist. As soon as the economic historian takes a single step into the past, he finds the economic situation more largely influenced, if not dominated, by forces and ideas which are non-economic—the authority of the State, the power of custom and of voluntary associations, the force of nationalist sentiment or of ethical conviction. The data he can obtain from the records of the past are generally not suitable for manipulation on strictly economic methods; and if, here and there, he gets such data, they afford no sufficient clue to the development which he is trying to trace. What method is the economic historian to pursue? How is he to give that unity to his investigations which alone can invest his subject with the dignity of a science?

There is, indeed, one method open to him, the one applied with such magnificent success by the genius of Adam Smith. The central clue to the economic history of the past may be found in the emancipation of the economic forces of society from the bondage of archaic custom, delusive theory and selfish class-interest. The natural progress of opulence may be conceived as making headway against the mistaken policy of Europe. This is the subject of the third book of *The Wealth of Nations*, and no student of economic history should begin his more detailed study without the careful consideration of those fifty or sixty pages. They contain, to my mind, the best piece of economic history that has yet been written. They exhibit in a large historical field the gradual emergence of those principles which Adam Smith had expounded in the two earlier books of his great treatise—above all, the expansion of the area of human co-operation and the increasing freedom of the individual producer and consumer.

When we come to look further, and to inquire what have been the causes of this expansion of the area of human co-operation, this increase of human freedom, we find that Adam Smith very largely fails us. He was writing a treatise, not on political philosophy, but on the wealth of nations, and the truths he had to propound were sufficiently important and sufficiently overlooked to absorb his attention. He does not, indeed, entirely ignore the political conditions of economic progress. The improvement of agriculture, he points out, was largely due to the growth of towns, which served as centres of resistance to feudalism.

'The inhabitants of cities and burghs,' he adds, 'considered as single individuals, had no power to defend themselves; but by entering into a league of mutual defence with their neighbours, they were capable of making no contemptible resistance. . . . Order and good government, and along with them the liberty and security of individuals, were, in this manner, established in cities, at a time when the occupiers of land in the country were exposed to every sort of violence. . . . When men are secure of enjoying the fruits of their industry, they naturally exert it to better their condition. . . . Whatever stock, therefore, accumulated in the hands of the industrious part of the inhabitants of the country naturally took refuge in cities.'[1]

Yet, in spite of passages like this, and of that well-known eulogy of the Navigation Laws, so often cited with approval by those who are not in complete sympathy with the rest of Adam Smith's teaching, it must be admitted that, throughout *The Wealth of Nations*, the influence of organized society and of the State is generally represented as a hindrance to the natural course of economic development. If a book that contains the carefully digested thought of a life-time is to be summed up at all in a single phrase for the benefit of the man in the street, *Laissez-faire* is as good a phrase as any to designate the general trend of Adam Smith's economic teaching. But a sentence is better than a phrase, and, before passing judgment on a great thinker, we can afford to hear him to the extent of a sentence. Here is one that perhaps will serve:

'The statesman who should attempt to direct private people in what manner they ought to employ their capitals would not only load himself with a most unnecessary attention, but assume an authority which could safely be trusted, not only to no single person, but to no council or senate whatever, and which would nowhere be so dangerous as in the hands of a man who had folly and presumption enough to fancy himself fit to exercise it.'[2]

Now, in saying this, Adam Smith was not dealing in abstractions. At the time when *The Wealth of Nations* was being written, statesmen in most countries of Europe were still directing private people how to employ their capitals. In France, we read, the State exercised over manufacturing industry the most unlimited and arbitrary jurisdiction. It disposed without scruple of the resources of manufacturers; it decided who should be allowed to work, what things they should be permitted to make, what materials should be employed and what processes followed. Not the taste of the consumers, but the commands of the law, must receive attention. Legions of inspectors, commissioners, controllers, sworn searchers and wardens were charged with its execution. Machines were broken, products were burned, improvements were punished, inventors were fined. The first great blow was not struck at this system of State regulation in France till the very year in which *The Wealth of Nations* was published, when Turgot, who shared so many of Smith's ideas, published his famous edicts. In England during the sixteenth and seventeenth centuries the same policy had been pursued. The army of officials pervading every province, who served as the instruments of French absolutism, did not exist in England, and the justices of the peace, in whose hands the administration of the country mostly rested, refused to be turned into the instruments of a centralized system of regulation. The struggle between a policy of economic centralization and the free initiative of local interests was, indeed, one of the main issues of the Civil War. In the days of Adam Smith the direct regulation of industry by the State had been very largely abandoned, and the free play thus given to the forces of economic development was one of the principal causes of the rapid advance which Great Britain was at that time making over continental nations in the development of its manufactures. Internal intercourse was free. There were no customs barriers between province and province. The towns had no industrial monopoly against the country. Above all, that economic union between the northern and the southern half of the island had been effected, which has wrought such wonders on both sides of the Cheviots.

And, if the interference of the State was one of the greatest factors on the negative side in determining the rate of economic progress, so the heroic persistence of individual genius was perhaps the greatest factor on the positive side. In that same memorable year in which *The Wealth of Nations* saw the light, a countryman of Adam Smith's, born on the opposite coast of Scotland, James Watt, erected, after a struggle of some ten years, his first successful steam-engine. At the same period a young man was labouring as a stone-mason in Eskdale, who was destined to leave the mark of his genius in harbours, bridges, highways and canals over the length and breadth of Great Britain. No reader of Dr. Smiles' fascinating biographies of Watt, Telford, Nasmyth, Neilson, Brindley and the other heroes of the Industrial Revolution[3] will be inclined to belittle the part played by individual initiative and character in forwarding economic development. It may be asked, perhaps, what the policy of *laissez-faire* has to do with the appearance of these manifestations of individual genius. Granted that no amount of State interference could have produced them, could any system of State interference have hindered their successful achievements? The answer to this question will be furnished by a comparison of the projectors and patentees of the seventeenth century with the inventors of the eighteenth. There was no lack of ingenuity in the seventeenth century; but, instead of occupying itself with the task of exploiting the powers of nature for the benefit of the community, nine-tenths of it was engaged in the endeavour to manipulate the power of the State and the wealth of the community for the benefit of individuals.

But, while we insist that Adam Smith correctly diagnosed the economic evils of his time, and that, by his great vision of the gradual emergence of the economic forces of civilized nations into a freedom that would forward, not only the wealth, but the unity and happiness of mankind, he opened, as it were, the gateway to the study of economic history, we must also recognize that nothing is to be gained by lingering in the entrance thus made for us. The Moses of economic science has brought us out of Egyptian bondage, has led us through the wilderness and viewed Canaan from Mount Pisgah. It is for us to go up and possess the land. And we must make it our own by intensive culture.

I speak now on behalf of the more backward branch of the science —its historical branch. It is not at all a matter for surprise that Adam Smith's successors should have devoted themselves almost entirely to developing that side of his work that seemed to bear most on practice. The doctrine of *The Wealth of Nations* had an altogether unprecedented success, a success far beyond its author's anticipations. Within half a century of his death the principles of the economic freedom of the individual and of the non-interference of the State had come to be adopted by those who prompted the legislation and directed the administration of the kingdom. The impulse given to the development of those principles was irresistible. The interests of science, of patriotism and of philanthropy seemed to join in promoting it, and the voice of the national poet was not wanting to give the new conception of economic freedom a religious sanction. The noble lines of Tennyson written for the opening of the international exhibition mark the culmination of this great movement.

The future of the world seemed at this time to lie in the free development of its economic forces, and the inspiring duty of economic science was to push home the analysis of those forces and to secure the conscious adhesion of mankind to the natural laws of its own progress.

From this high spirit of optimism a reaction was inevitable. It was found that the past was more with us than we thought, that the economic motives of mankind were less disentangled from their social and political motives than had been supposed. In the 'sixties and 'seventies the economists of this country began to be aware of an opposing school of historical economists in Germany, and to find their own principles labelled with the opprobrious epithets of *Smithianismus* and *Manchesterthum*. Of this movement of thought on the Continent, which had produced its first fruits some twenty or thirty years before, I need not attempt to give a detailed account. The most influential figure in that movement, from a political point of view, was Frederick List, who took an active part in forming public opinion on economic matters at the time of the establishment of the German *Zollverein*. List's chief work has been translated into English under the title of *The National System of Political Economy*. It has had, perhaps, more influence than any other German economic work in forming opinion in Great Britain and America, and we are informed by Sir Donald Mackenzie Wallace that the views of

Frederick List supplied the guiding principles of the industrial policy of Russia during the régime of M. Witte.

It would certainly not be fair to put forward List as a representative of the scholarship of the historical school of economists. He was a journalist and a pamphleteer, a warm controversialist and a political exile. But his central doctrine exhibits in a salient manner the leading tendency of the historical school, and is the clearest landmark of the reaction that had set in against the teachings of Adam Smith.

Briefly summed up, the antithesis between the doctrine of *The Wealth of Nations* and the doctrine of Frederick List is this. Adam Smith regarded the economic progress of nations as a natural and spontaneous development, which had been rather hindered than helped by the policy of the State. List considered political conditions to be the determining factor in producing the wealth and the economic progress of each particular nation. Adam Smith seemed to imply that non-interference with economic conditions would have been at all periods the wisest policy for the State to pursue. List held that each of the stages of economic development through which a nation passed called for the adoption of a particular policy by the State, and that the prosperity of the various nations of Europe had been in proportion to their wisdom and foresight in adopting this policy. Adam Smith had put forth all his strength in an attack on the folly and the futility of the Mercantile System, as the main historical instance of that far-sighted statesmanship which List considered to be always the main factor in national welfare.

Here, then, we have the thesis and the antithesis of the philosophy of economic history. At bottom, you will perceive, it is the question as to the origin of progress. In all historical development we see the interaction of two great sets of forces. On the one hand, there are the forces from below, the forces of spontaneity, of germination. On the other hand, there are the forces from above, the forces of authority, of formulation. Speaking very broadly, we may express the one set of forces by the term Society, and the other set by the term the State. We may then put our question thus: Which ought to possess the dominant influence over the other—Society or the State? This is at bottom the question between Adam Smith and Frederick List. We cannot here pause to answer it. But it is worthy of remark that, whilst the main feature of British history since the seventeenth century has been the remoulding of a State by a powerful Society, the main feature of German history in the same period has been the remoulding of a Society by a powerful State.

Leaving this question for the moment unsettled, let us turn to the second set of influences out of which our subject has developed. Economic history owes even more to the science of history than it owes to the science of political economy. The science of history is the younger science of the two. Adam Smith was the last great pre-Revolution philosopher. The great thinkers whose work laid the basis for the modern science of history derived their main inspiration from the portentous events of the Revolution itself. The two poles of Adam Smith's political philosophy had been the authority of the State and the natural liberty of the individual. He looked for the peaceable and beneficient extension of individual freedom, and the limitation of the interference of the State. But in the very year of Adam Smith's death Europe saw with amazement the authority of what had been thought the strongest State in Europe successfully assailed in the name of the natural rights of the individual. The fearful struggle that followed, with its alternative phases of anarchy and despotism, aroused a deep conviction in the minds of contemporary thinkers that the authority of the State and the rights of individuals were not adequate materials for the construction of Society. They asked themselves whether liberty and order had no better safeguards than lay in these abstract conceptions. The threatened ruin of civilization gave men a new perception of its meaning and value, as well as of the age-long processes that had built it up. They looked back with a new insight upon that last great crisis of European history, when the civilization of the Romans was tried and found wanting. Out of a weltering chaos of barbarism and internecine war, the Romans had built up a nearly world-wide peace, and a strong and unified administration; out of a mass of illogical and conflicting customs they had created an admirable system of law. They had worked out a clear and logical idea of the State and an equally clear and logical conception of the individual. But this great fabric of law and government had proved inadequate to the maintenance alike of liberty and of order, because the State had lost all organic connection with the Society which it governed. The great instrument that had so long oppressed its maker was broken. The task had to be begun anew from the beginning. Liberty and order had to be built up on deeper and more elaborate foundations. Or rather, the new structure was not a building, but a growth, in which liberty and order were two sides of the same achievement. It was the slow putting on of new habits and capacities, new sympathies and new insight. It is with this great movement, in which the lapse of twenty centuries is but a stage, this broadening and deepening of the human spirit, in all its inner complexities and its many-sided expression, that the science of history has set itself to deal.

Of History in this large sense, economic history is but a specialized department. It may be said, indeed, to be still in process of separation from the closely related departments of constitutional and legal history, and it has owed no little stimulus to the discoveries of anthropologists. It is in the controversial discussion as to the constitutional origins of the Germanic nations, to which several generations of eminent scholars have devoted themselves, that the materials for a construction of economic history have been accumulated. The smoke of conflict is clearing away, and we are able, in a spirit of detachment, to appreciate the contributions of the various parties of learned combatants to our real knowledge of those early institutions—the tribe, the village community, the manor and the gild—in which the beginnings of economic development are blended with the rudimentary organization of law and government. Setting out from this broad basis of new fact, and guided by those fuller notions of social development which have been the main achievement of historic science in the nineteenth century, we are emboldened to approach the later periods of economic history—the battleground of the mercantilists and free-traders—with some hope of a better understanding of the issues involved.

When we have traversed the period of medieval history and seen the modern constitutional State gradually emerging as the organ of a slowly realized national unity, we shall be able to discuss the question of the interference or the non-interference of the State with a better sense of all that these terms imply. We shall have realized the nature of the advance which has been made by modern civilization over the civilization of antiquity. In the Roman Empire there was little or no protecting medium between the all-powerful State and the powerless individual, and the State by its very weight, even when moved by no oppressive intentions, crushed all spontaneous initiative out of the individual. At the present day there exist a great array of intermediate powers and agencies, offensive and defensive, which not only prevent the State from oppressing the individual, but actually enable initiative to gather power about itself and to bring pressure to bear on the State.

First of all, there is the element of restraint imposed upon the State by the character of the very agents whom it is bound to employ, the restraint that lies in the honourable *esprit de corps* and sense of social responsibility of the judicial and administrative functionaries who do its work. Secondly, there are the independent powers of local government (I am thinking especially of Great Britain), which are safeguarded from undue interference on the part of the State, and which have always served as the effectual basis of our parliamentary liberties. Thirdly, there is the power of, and the capacity for, voluntary association, exemplified in the fact that the direction of the State itself is always in the hands of the representatives of one of two great voluntary associations known as political parties. Students of constitutional history know that these three factors are each of very slow growth—the history of Great Britain is largely the story of their growth—and that in the absence of them mere formal stipulations and guarantees can give little assurance of political liberty. The enormous difficulties of the situation in Russia at the present moment, for example, arise from the fact that none of these essential bases of constitutional freedom can be conceived of as possessing any very effectual solidity. And it is in the direction of strengthening these natural pillars of the constitution that the instinct of the Russian reformer is rightly turned.

There are, no doubt, many historic reasons to be given for the constitutional weakness of Russia, but the most fundamental, perhaps, is to be found in the shortness of its history as a civilized people. When Russia came into the European system, the great formative process by which our western civilization has been built up was all but accomplished. In that long and glorious work of social and political construction, which lasted from the twelfth to the seventeenth centuries, Russia bore no effective part. During those six centuries western Europe built up the town, and then, on the basis of the town, built up the nation. Without the town there could not have been the nation as we know it, because it was in the earlier centuries of town history that the three great essentials to a free national constitution already spoken of—a sense of professional responsibility, the experience of self-government and a capacity for voluntary association—were painfully acquired. Russia has no towns in this historic sense of the word. She has, comparatively speaking, no middle class; and her working class, such as it is, is not, like our own, a working class inheriting largely the traditions and capacities of the middle class, but is composed of transplanted peasants of a social status resembling that of our own villeins in the days of Wat Tyler. It is for want of towns, and of those middle and working classes that only centuries of free town life can produce, that Russia finds it so hard to become a free nation.

This brings us to the point at which we were aiming. If the town may be said to have built up the nation, what built up the town? If we answer that it was the gild, we must safeguard ourselves from the possible consequences of our rashness. There are many theories of the origin of the town, mostly German, and every theorist is naturally zealous for the purity of his doctrine. Let us take shelter behind the wisdom of Aristotle. Everything, according to that eminent sociologist, has at least four causes—the material, the efficient, the formal and the final cause. If we give the town the benefit of all four, there is room for a number of theorists to live and let live. The final cause of the town—the end towards which it was unconsciously directed—

was, according to the theory we have been setting forth, the free self-governing nation. The material cause—the stuff out of which the town was made—differed, no doubt, in different cases; sometimes it was a village, sometimes a market at a ford, sometimes a military post, sometimes a deliberately planted colony. The formal cause—the legal title by virtue of which its special rights were exercised—also varied in different cases, but is probably to be sought for in the creation of a separate and semi-independent jurisdiction within a certain area. As to these causes we need not seek to dogmatize. What we are concerned with is the efficient cause or causes—the nature of the social force which, apart from mere material conditions or constitutional forms, served to bring it into existence and to make it what it became. The chief of these efficient causes was, I venture to think, the spirit of voluntary association, and that spirit found its most typical and wide-spread embodiment in the various forms of the gild.

Economic history differs, then, from economic theory, in that it deals much less with individual actions and motives, and much more with the actions and motives of groups. It is concerned, at all periods, very largely with organizations and institutions, and in the earlier periods these organizations and institutions are far from being exclusively economic in their functions and their aims. The tribe is an organ of real or nominal kinship, the feudal manor is an incipient organ of local government, the gild is partly a religious fellowship, partly a political club, and partly an organ of municipal administration. The economic historian is not concerned with the history of kinship, with the development of local government, with the growth of political associations, as such, but he finds the economic life of the periods with which he is dealing almost inseparably involved in the life and growth of these institutions. The gradual disentanglement of the economic motive from the other social motives, with the consequent increasing freedom of the individual, and increasing economic efficiency of the community, is, no doubt, the subject to which he should mainly direct his attention. But he cannot regard the other elements, the social, religious and political motives, which he finds mingled with economic motives in early institutions, in the tribe, the gild and the manor, as merely negative elements, as so much limitation and restriction placed upon the natural economic freedom of primitive or mediaeval man. The early bonds of human association—the tribal bond, the feudal bond, the fraternal bond of the gild —were undoubtedly positive economic factors of great importance. They provided, in each case, a higher degree of security than had been before possible. They supplied, in each case, a basis for wider forms of co-operation. The pastoral clan produced more wealth than the horde; the village community produced more wealth than the clan; and the town craftsman produced more wealth than the peasant who laboured in the grooves of customary tillage. But the essential pre-requisite of the economic advance was, in each case, the adoption of a higher form of association, which, whether it were kinship or lordship or fellowship, had a distinctly non-economic basis.

Now, it may be asked, is not nationality—the social unity underlying the State—simply the highest of these expanding forms of association? And, if so, does it not provide a basis for a higher form of economic co-operation, and thus justify Frederick List in his theory of the value of political influences in forwarding economic development? The answer is that national unity is one thing, and deliberate State policy another. The positive economic value of the early achieved national unity of England was, undoubtedly, very great, and this is the truth underlying List's point of view. But the mercantilism assailed by Adam Smith, and approved by List, was the deliberate policy of the State. It is possible—and, indeed, has frequently happened—for the forces making for national unity to be working in one direction, and the deliberate policy of the State, although acting professedly on behalf of the national unity, to be working in the opposite direction. It may happen, as in France, that the deliberate policy of the State has had the effect of retarding the achievement of national unity. The negative effects, therefore, of State policy, its retardation of the rate of national economic progress, as conceived by Adam Smith, are not at all irreconcilable with the economic benefits of national unity. The same is true of the gild. The deliberate policy of the gild, when in later times it came to have a deliberate policy, was of a restrictive and negative character. It was the policy of the close corporation, which was so justly denounced by Adam Smith. But, in its earlier and more elastic form, when it was continually receiving new members and lifting them out of more rigid and backward forms of association, the gild must be conceived of as a creator of economic values and a beneficent agent of human progress.

Rudolf von Gneist, who was perhaps the most learned, as well as one of the most sympathetic students of the British constitution,[4] discovers the secret of its remarkable combination of stability with flexibility and continuity in the peculiar relation between the two aspects of national existence—Society and the State. With some of Gneist's own interpretations of this relationship many of us may find ourselves compelled to disagree. But that the relationship has the fundamental importance which he assigns to it is, I believe, profoundly true, and one of its essential features certainly lies in the close intimacy in which State and Society are blended, so that it is almost impossible to tell where public functions and institutions begin. This is, I imagine, specially true of English institutions. Where should we place, for instance, the Bank of England, the Inns of Court and the Universities? They are certainly public institutions, but equally certainly not State institutions. They are private corporations, with important public functions. They are, like the political parties, part of the machinery by which Society controls the action of the State. 'It was hardly too much to say,' writes Dr. Cunningham in the latest edition of his *Growth of English Industry and Commerce*, 'that the Bank overbalanced the Crown as a power in the State.'[5]

But this peculiar interaction of social with political forces is not confined to the later stages of British history; it can, in fact, be much more clearly observed and more profitably studied in the earlier periods. It is this process that supplies a background, and gives unity and meaning, to the early stages of economic history.

We can there watch in all its successive phases that transformation of social forces into political forces which is an essential feature of what we call progress. We see class after class constituting itself a social force by the act of self-organization. Then, as the new force gains political recognition, the voluntary association passes wholly or partly into an organ of public administration. As class power generates class privilege and exclusiveness, new social forces gather to a head and find expression in new voluntary associations, which tend, in their turn, to be transformed as they are drawn into the vortex of political activity. This constantly recurring process is to be seen in the intimate relation of the gild merchant to the earliest constitution of our burghs, and in the equally close relations which the craft organizations in many cases, more often on the Continent and in Scotland than in England, bore to the more developed constitutions of cities and burghs, just as it is to be seen to-day in the formation of a Labour Party on a trade-union basis.

It is the field occupied by the operation of these dynamic forces which supplies the background out of which the economic historian has to trace the emergence of the economic man of modern civilization. He has to note the part played in forwarding or hindering that emergence by the social and political environment of different periods, by kinship and lordship and fellowship, by local custom and national law, and by the deliberate policy of the State. He has to observe the gradual disentanglement of the economic motive from other motives with which it is at first blended, its early operation in the limited area of the civic economy, and its gradual permeation of the larger areas of the national and the world economy, by which the liberty of the individual has been enlarged and the wealth of nations increased.

NOTES

1 *Wealth of Nations*, Bk. III, chap. iii.
2 *Ibid.*, Bk. IV, chap. ii.
3 S. Smiles, *Lives of the Engineers*, and *Industrial Biography*.
4 H. R. von Gneist, *The History of the English Constitution*, trans. P. A. Ashworth.
5 Cunningham, *Growth of English Industry and Commerce in Modern Times*, ed. 1921, p. 412.

4

J. H. Clapham

THE STUDY OF ECONOMIC HISTORY
(Cambridge, 1929)

This inaugural lecture was delivered at the University
of Cambridge on the 23rd January 1929.

THE STUDY OF ECONOMIC HISTORY

This chair of economic history which Cambridge has set up, and to which she has done me the honour of calling me, is—by an odd accident—at this moment the only chair of economic history in the Kingdom. There have been two others—the first, very appropriately, at Manchester, left vacant of late by the premature death of the keenest economic historian and one of the most single-minded scholars of my generation, George Unwin; and the second in London, also vacated by untimely death, the death of a Cambridge historian, Lilian Knowles, who spent her working life in building up the historical side of the London School of Economics. For the time being, but for reasons not connected with the academic valuation of economic history, these Universities—like Oxford and many others—are carrying on with readerships. There are happily besides the readers scholars of professorial quality, though I fear seldom with professorial leisure, working at the subject unlabelled or otherwise labelled—historians with economic interests, economists with historical leanings, professors of commerce, readers in currency. Lecturers in economic history are numerous; for every year, from the elementary schools up to the universities, there is a call for teachers—teachers of economic history pure; of social history which requires an economic substratum; of local history which requires one also; and of the widening study of 'human geography,' as the French say, which can no more dispense with economic history than economic history can dispense with it. If university chairs are, in wilfully mixed metaphor, the crown and fountain-head of what they call in Germany a *Disciplin*—an organized body of studies— it will, I think, be agreed that this Discipline of Economic History is lightly crowned and in some present danger of being but lightly refreshed. For the future I have no fear. The thing is growing and will grow. There are whole tracts still to be occupied. Three specialist journals in English have been started in the last three years, and new syntheses should be coming soon. My single regret, when I think of its relatively late recognition in this University, is that the man who nursed it here, and who was known in all Universities as one of the two outstanding English economic historians of his time, William Cunningham, never received from Cambridge the professorial rank which he deserved. Nor, for that matter, did his rather younger colleague, Sir William Ashley, from Oxford.

As a borderline study, lying along the frontiers of history and economics, with an ill-defined territory over which both the general historians and the economists require—so to speak—grazing rights, its late acquisition of academic independence is natural. Political economy as an established university study is itself young and history not so very old. True, Adam Smith was a professor; but, like Henry Sidgwick here, he professed moral philosophy. He was a pensioner of the Duke of Buccleuch when he wrote the *Wealth of Nations*; and his own University of Glasgow did not found an economic chair as his memorial until the end of the nineteenth century. Of his principal successors, Ricardo was a stockbroker and John Stuart Mill a clerk to the East India Company. It was only with Jevons and Marshall that leadership in economic thinking passed, it may not be finally, to the Universities and that the Universities set full value on it. Marshall, may I say, was a greater economic historian than he let the world know. He had discarded as irrelevant to his main purposes more historical knowledge than many men acquire. There are some massive fragments of these *rejecta* in the Appendices to his volume on *Industry and Trade*, of 1919. He was eager to get historical work done. Long ago—I owe the personal reference to his memory—he pointed out to me tracts of economic history which needed someone's work. Then he pointed at me and said—'Thou art the man.' I hesitated then, for Acton's power was on me, as I hope it still is. But Marshall has prevailed. To him, as well as to Cunningham, the foundation of this chair is a memorial. May it be enduring.

The term economic history is rather young; but the thing, the systematic inquiry into economic aspects of recent or remote history, is just about as old as most other systematic modern inquiry. Like important parts of economics, and so much in the physical sciences, it goes back to what Dr Whitehead has called the Century of Genius. Neglecting early anticipations and the casual economic asides of historians, Sir William Temple's *Observations upon the United Provinces* of 1672 and John Evelyn's *Navigation and Commerce, their original and progress* of 1674, though the latter is one of the slighter efforts of that distinguished Secretary of the Royal Society, might perhaps be said to mark the beginning.[1] They really have a common problem—what are the historical causes of the economic strength and the economic weaknesses of Holland? What are the forces which, as Evelyn said, have 'built and peopled goodly cities where nothing but rushes grew?' Forty years later, the same problem still occupied the mind of a very old and very distinguished French man, who has sometimes been mentioned as a father of economic history, Pierre Daniel Huet, Bishop of Avranches, at one time sub-tutor of the Dauphin under Bossuet and—I am told—an elegant scholar. He had planned and directed the publication of the Delphin Classics. At the age of 86 (1716) he has published a small octavo *History of the Commerce of the Ancients*, written many years before to oblige Colbert, a book which as an English critic said is 'chiefly a History of Sea Fights and Naval Expeditions' and, as a Scottish critic added, 'pays no sort of regard either to chronology or cos-mography.' At the age of 87 Huet followed it up with a more sub-stantial *Memoir on the Commerce of the Dutch*, written some ten years earlier, in the manner of Sir William Temple.

In the interval between these two attempts to help solve a problem in current politics by an appeal to recent economic history, the ur-gency of a very different problem had led a Cambridge man into a more fundamental and exact economico-historical inquiry. The matter can best be made clear by quoting the rather long title page of his book, which appeared anonymously in 1707.[2] *Chronicon Preciosum: or, an Account of English Gold and Silver Money; the Price of Corn and other Commodities; and of Stipends, Salaries, Wages, Jointures, Portions, Day-labour etc. in England, for Six Hundred Years—shewing from the Decrease of the value of Money, and from the Increase of the value of corn and other commodities that a Fellow, who has an Estate in Land of Inheritance or a perpetual Pension of Five Pounds per Annum, may conscientiously keep his Fellowship . . . though the Statutes of his College (founded between the years 1440 and 1460) did then vacate his Fellowship on such condition.* The College is of course my own; the author who faced this great case of conscience was William Fleetwood, subsequently Bishop of Ely, a noted preacher who had given in a sermon delivered before the University in our chapel on Lady Day, 1689, a classic account of the life of a Fellow of King's: 'We are here at perfect Ease and Liberty, free from all other cares and troubles than what we seek . . . entirely vacant to the pursuit of Wisdom, and the practice of Reli-gion.' It has been burned in on us these last ten years that nothing makes history, exalts and abases men and classes and kingdoms, like changes in the value of money. Lenin knew it. Those changes are perhaps most potent when their working is slowest and little noticed. Fleetwood first traced these slow movements over a long period. His method of studying them was unexceptionable, though he made mistakes of detail as Adam Smith pointed out. For prices he went to his College muniments because, as he wrote, 'our General Histories do mostly give us the Prices of Things, which are ex-traordinary, either for Cheapness, or for Dearness; whereas the

College Accounts deliver faithfully the ordinary and common Price of most Commodities and Provisions.' He is the father of all the historians of price, who are the most exactly scientific of all historians; for, as Professor Eddington says, 'what exact science looks for is not entities of some particular category but entities with a metrical aspect.' Thorold Rogers in the nineteenth century followed Fleetwood into the muniment rooms in search of such entities. There is still abundant material there unworked.

Though Fleetwood's more learned contemporary. Thomas Madox, is not usually classed as an economic historian, for his interests were primarily legal, yet his *History of the Exchequer* (1711) claims mention because, with his later *Firma Burgi*, it laid the foundations of the exact study of medieval public finance; because it initiated a profitable alliance between economic history, in the narrow sense, and the history of institutions; above all, I think, because it stated in a couple of sentences all that ever need be stated, by an economic or any other kind of historian, about the duty of documentation. 'For I think it is to be wished, that the Histories of a country so well furnished with Records and Manuscripts as ours is, should be grounded throughout . . . on proper vouchers.' And again—'for my part I cannot look upon the History of England to be completely written, till it shall come to be written after that manner.'

The next really important landmark, a critical landmark, was, I would suggest, Hume's Essay *Of the Populousness of Ancient Nations* (1742). He was concerned to prove that this populousness had been exaggerated. When it is remembered that he was arguing against the opinion 'that there are not now on the face of the earth, the fiftieth part of mankind, which existed at the time of Julius Caesar,' and that this opinion was Montesquieu's, it will be realized how strong was the myth of antiquity, how much sceptical discipline the best minds of Europe needed before they would consent to apply rational quantitative tests—or quantitative probabilities—to historical tradition.

The thirty years following the publication of Hume's *Essay* might be called the age of the annalists. In 1747 the Rev. John Smith, LL.B. (of Trinity Hall) published his *Chronicon Rusticum Commerciale,* or *Memoirs of Wool*, into which his notebooks vomited, but in good chronological order, extracts and analyses of every statute, proclamation, pamphlet and debate bearing even remotely on wool and the woollen industry with which years of diligence had filled them. In 1763 came the three heavy volumes of Adam Anderson's *Historical and Chronological Deduction of the Origins of Commerce.* Anderson was for forty years a clerk in the South Sea House and he had that unselective fondness for the accumulations of his leisure often found in men of affairs, and occasionally in scholars. When they would not go into his annals he pushed them into prefaces, surveys, excursuses, and appendices. He was the fore-runner of a series of Scottish accumulators and dictionary makers—Sinclair, Macpherson, McCulloch, Macgregor—who in the next seventy or eighty years heaped up material, not always well sifted but always useful, for the economist and the historian.

Meanwhile Scotland had given with Adam Smith the man who used and stimulated the accumulators, turned annals into rationalized history and unassorted observations into economic philosophy. He called his book a 'speculative work' and it was only in the avowed digressions, and particularly in the great digression in which he used and improved on Fleetwood's account of the changes in the value of gold and silver, that he adopted the pure narrative method, though there is much of it in the chapters on colonies and on the growth of towns; but his writing was informed throughout with all the his-torical knowledge of his day. What is more, there were always present to his mind the interactions and contrasts of the economic and the non-economic factors in national life. Witness the famous section on the expense of institutions for the education of youth, from which comes the known quotation about the greater part of the public professors at Oxford having 'for these many years, given up al-together even the pretence of teaching,' or the less known historical comment on musical education among the Greeks, which he thought had probably 'no great effect in mending their morals.' Smith's history was of course not like Madox's based on manuscript 'vouchers': occasionally it may have been made to serve those general propositions which he wanted to establish: in detail it has sometimes been proved wrong, as was to be expected; but never before or since in the development of economic thought have his-torical and analytical workmanship been so finely blended as in the *Wealth of Nations*. I say 'before' because one must not forget that nine years earlier yet another Scotsman, Sir James Steuart, had published a book which some German scholars have set up as a sort of rival to Smith's; a book whose very title, *An Inquiry into the Principles of Political Economy*, Smith might have taken for his own, had not he and Steuart—as Professor Cannan has pointed out—happened to have the same publisher; a book which like Smith's justifies its political title by the extent of its author's historical know-ledge; yet a book which in spite of the German scholars, and in spite of the possibility that Smith sometimes conveyed from it without adequate acknowledgement, cannot stand beside the *Wealth of Nations*.

Within a few years of Smith's death (1790), and in the early troubled years of the French wars, there appeared Sir Frederick Eden's *State of the Poor: or an History of the Labouring Classes in England from the Conquest to the Present Period* (1797) and the first edition of Malthus' *Essay on Population* (1798). Eden's book is a remarkable piece of work—he was only thirty-one when he published it—perhaps most remarkable in the way that it anticipates the social inquiries into wages, dietaries, employment and standards of life which a modern economist connects with such names as Charles Booth and Seebohm Rowntree. But it is also, unless I am much mistaken, the first attempt to write some sort of an economic history of the common man. No doubt it is far too much a survey of laws about him, and he is regarded too much as potential pauper. The research, the first hand personal inquiry, is best in the contemporary sections. That is why the book is a mine for the historian of to-day. Yet the conception is there, the conception of an historical process determining the conditions of current problems and the material happiness of humble people.

Malthus' *Essay*, in its first form, was more dogmatic than historical. But in five succeeding editions he heaped about it historical material and what statistical material was available, almost burying and at certain points deflecting the original dogmatic framework; until it became something like a history of population and of the working of his positive checks upon it. He ransacked the classics, books of travel, general histories and such books—then very few— as the *Divine Order in the Vicissitudes of the Human Race* of Pastor Süssmilch (1707–1767), the man who has been called 'the first statistician in the modern sense.' One can imagine how Malthus would have welcomed some significant scraps of exact evidence from the ancient world recently collected for us by Mr. W. W. Tarn—how 79 Greek families who received Milesian citizenship at the close of the third century B.C. contained 118 sons and 28 daughters; and how only 6 families out of 600 in second-century Delphic inscriptions reared two daughters. 'No natural causes can account for these proportions,' Mr. Tarn writes. The positive check of female infanticide is the explanation, and for those times and places we can now measure its strength.

With Malthus' historical discussion of population, following on Hume's correction of legendary views, the men of the late seventeenth and eighteenth centuries completed a first, imperfect, reconnaissance of the field of economic history. They were mostly specialists. Only Adam Smith had got glimpses of the whole territory and a clear view over much of it. The professed scholars among them had begun rather apologetically. 'The greatest (though I will not think the Best) part of readers,' Fleetwood wrote, 'will be rather apt to despise, than to commend the Pains that are taken in making Collection of so mean things, as the Price of Wheat, and Oats, of Poultry, and such like Provisions.' But he hoped 'before he had done, to show you, that the Observation of these little things may be of good Use in the Consideration of great Affairs,' and he consoled himself by thinking that 'if any ancient Greek or Latin Writer had taken the Like [Pains] and left such a Collection you would have had the Salmasius's, the Graevius's and the Gronovii almost out of their wits for very joy.' (To-day one who can rely on those ample English records of which Madox spoke, and the printed records which have succeeded them, is sorry for the Gronovii because no ancient Greek or Latin writer did.) But when the nineteenth century trampled in out of the storm the timidest pedant had no longer need to apologize. The prices of the mean things, leaping up, showed their power in great Affairs. The common man in France had lighted a candle of rich men's houses. Peasants were being emancipated in Prussia, to show that a King could do for his people as much as the Revolution. Open-fields and commons were being cleared away in England as a safeguard against hunger; for the old fear that there might not be men enough for the wars was being replaced by the new fear that there might be too many mouths to fill. A commercial empire, just ceasing to be able to feed itself, at grips with an agrarian empire—which also went hungry in years of bad harvest—was learning the truth of that old saying about the Dutch ships: 'except they go the people starve.' Modern chemistry was just beginning to show its industrial power; and in 1800 Messrs Boulton and Watt completed their 312th patent steam engine.

Watching all this, a beggared French nobleman of irregular life, who at sixteen had fought for American Independence and who died in 1825, decided that the only thing in the world that mattered was industry in the widest sense of the word. (He allowed, for example, that artists and professors were industrial persons of an inferior kind.) Politics and religion, liberty and equality, were toys. Sane history was the story of the freeing of industrial forces. The only form of parliament worth having was a parliament of economic experts, as we should say, occupied with schemes for industrial progress. He founded a school and the school a sect—the St. Simonians. The claim of economic history to dominate all history had been formulated, but vaguely and unphilosophically, by a man mainly interested in the future. To make a philosophy of it, the so-called historical materialism, was Karl Marx's work. Writing in 1894, eleven years after Marx died, Frederick Engels claimed that the Master in 1845 had made the 'discovery, that everywhere and always political conditions and events find their explanation in the corresponding economic conditions.' Marx wrote no treatise on historical method. Those who have collated and examined his various pronouncements most carefully are of opinion that he only meant that the ultimate causes of all great social changes are to be sought in the economic conditions of the age under review. Engels, as we see, claimed for him more than that; but then Engels was a pious disciple. Even Engels did not argue that each particular historical happening, of whatever kind it may appear to be, is economically determined. Fanatical Marxists—with some people who would be surprised if they were so described—seem now and then to have held this doctrine and the chase for the economic clue is conspicuous in much of the historical writing of the last thirty or forty years. There is, of course, even an economic explanation of Calvary, which those who remember the rich man and Lazarus and the tables of the money-changers must at least weigh. Fantastic though some economico-historical adventures may be, I suppose that all historians are now so far in agreement with Marx as to be unable to think of major political upheavals and important social changes into which economic causation does not enter, however great their distrust of purely economic explanations, of those who overlook so-called historical accidents, and of that kind of single-cause history which will pack the fall of Rome into an epigram.

For myself I am not convinced that the search for the economic clue has even yet gone far enough. (Should anyone say that I am professionally bound so to think, I admit that there is such a risk.) I expect, for example, that when the English economic history of the seventeenth century has been fully worked out—there is a great deal yet to do—we shall find, not an explanation of Bunyan's spiritual distress in a lag in the rise of tinkers' wages, or of Milton's harder traits in his parentage—Milton the elder was a scrivener, though a musical scrivener; and we are just learning that the seventeenth-century scriveners were often money-lenders and incipient bankers—not these, but all kinds of new things about the causes of political unrest, the successes and failures of political parties, and that profound change in the social atmosphere of England which occurred somewhere between Shakespeare and Defoe. We understand that change much better already since Mr. R. H. Tawney wrote two years ago his *Religion and the Rise of Capitalism*. But has our general history taken properly into account the fact—fairly well established long ago, though in need of more inquiry—that the food-purchasing power of wages was lower in 1600–1650 than it had been for three hundred years or has been since?

Marxism, by attraction and repulsion, has perhaps done more to make men think about economic history and inquire into it than any other teaching—especially in Germany, Italy and Russia. But not until Marx's main book, or rather that part of it which appeared in his lifetime, had circulated for over fifteen years in Germany and had been translated into French and last of all into English—that is to say not until the late 'eighties of the nineteenth century—did the stimulus of Marxism become so effective that economic history began to fall naturally into the Marxian categories. Its most remarkable product has been the *Moderne Kapitalismus* of Werner Sombart, which first appeared in two volumes in 1902 and reached the sixth volume of a remade edition in 1928. It is a gigantic attempt, full of learning, eloquence, strong feeling and strong words, to review and explain the whole history of European capitalism since the Dark Ages. Sombart is not a Marxian—far from it—but he is a passionate admirer of Marx the historian, the man who, as he says, 'discovered the new world' of capitalism, who posed all the historical problems of its origin and the speculative problems of its end. Neither precisely historian nor precisely economist (he isolates too much for the first and narrates too much for the second) Sombart is assailable from both camps. But I feel towards him much as he feels towards Marx. No none should handle any part of the industrial or commercial history of the last thousand years without weighing what Sombart has said of it. He may easily disagree. He is certain to be stirred and informed.

Strong as the Marxian influence has become—it is very conspicuous in that great book of two years ago, Rostovtzeff's *Social and Economic History of the Roman Empire*—it was by no means the first influence making for a revival of economico-historical studies in the nineteenth century. Marx himself might have argued that the economic conditions of the first half of the century imposed these studies on humanity. It may be so—in the realm of ultimate cause. But the immediate causes, working strongly in the decade before Marx made his 'discovery,' were German nationalism; English pride in England's recent economic achievement; and the ambition of a young German professor to master economic fact and thought historically as his elder contemporary, Savigny, had mastered jurisprudence. I have in mind List's *National System of Political Economy* (1841–4); Porter's *Progress of the Nation* (1836–43); and Roscher's *Political Economy according to the Historical Method* (1843).

List was not a professed historian: he was a propagandist and politician of genius. But his main contentions led the economist straight into history. They were that economic policies (in this case Free Trade) are not of universal application; and that economists must not confine themselves to studies of wealth and problems of exchange conceived of as all on one plane; but must think of living changing nations on different and shifting planes, and of the growth of their productive powers. Porter, a dry and rather limited statistician, did not look much beyond his own century but laid the foundations for the quantitative treatment of modern economic history, with the aid of material for the collection and issue of which by the Board of Trade he was himself largely responsible. Roscher, a man of more learning than discernment, contributed very little to the body of economic thought, though he put it in its historical place; but in a long life (he died in 1894) he saw the growth of a great German school of economic historians and historical economists to whom the historians of every other nation are heavily in debt. Fifty-nine years ago, for example, Brentano started the modern study of English medieval gilds. In a volume published last year the wonderful old man complains that his views have fallen into undeserved neglect latterly. His name is only one among many German names in English economic historiography, Ochenkowski, Schanz, Held, Hasbach. There is still no book in English on English railway history and policy to compare with one written by a Göttingen professor, Cohn, in the nineteenth century; and the last general survey of the medieval economic history of England written in German—it appeared by a gloomy accident in 1918—can hold its own with the last general survey written in English.

As economists, that is to say as explainers of the economic life of an existing bundle of communities with a view to its ultimate betterment—I hope the definition will be accepted—as economists, I believe that the German historical school have gone bankrupt. The aim of their left wing at least was to dissolve economics in history. Their last great leader, Gustav Schmoller, to whom Cambridge offered an honorary degree in 1913 and who died during the war, after many years of pure historical work of the first order, tried in a two-volumed *Principles* in 1900–2 to illustrate this doctrine that 'historical delineation can become economic theory.' 'He solves nothing,' I find that I noted on the flyleaf at the time, having started his book with high hopes and acquired much information of all kinds from it. My view seems to be accepted in his own country. He did not succeed 'in erecting a new scientific structure' in the place of the existing body of economic doctrine, a German historical critic wrote last year, adding—'that this situation was not satisfactory seemed clear to everyone.' Sombart, who is full of contempt for the mere historian on the one hand and for the more refined economic thinkers on the other, has accomplished more because he has used more abstraction and made all his learning bear on one problem—

though a vast and complex one—but his principal accomplishment is historical. He has not as yet taught us very much about the contemporary functioning of capitalism, though he claims to have uttered the 'modest last word about it'; and his very gratifying praise of some of our recent Cambridge economic manuals and other lighter English theoretical work suggests that he might have appreciated our severer analytical thought, given the patience to master it.

Here in Cambridge, I think I may say, economist and economic historian are at peace. We know our limitations. We can sit happily side by side under Adam Smith's great umbrella labelled *An Inquiry into the Nature and Causes of the Wealth of Nations*. The Professor of Political Economy will not cry out because I do not read a mathematical article (which, for the rest, I might not understand) dealing with taxation 'in a purely competitive system with no foreign trade,' though, for all I know, it may throw much light on the Nature of Wealth and its taxability. I shall not resent his indifference to what I take to be the final demonstration, just completed by archaeologists and air-photographers, that the now familiar strips of the medieval open-field were unknown in Roman or Celtic Britain; although the change to the strips—being connected with an improved plough—was no doubt in its time a Cause of a Nation's Wealth.

The economic historian knows that economists who wish to give precision to their study, and to fill its emptier categories with fact, are thoroughly dissatisfied even with the mass of statistical material now existing, and are always working for more. He knows, for instance, that any close causal handling of the problem of unemployment cannot go behind the first publication of the Trade Union figures in the 'eighties; and that fairly adequate material for the exact study of trade cycles is just now being assembled for the first time. So he understands the relative indifference of the more exact economists towards what little he can say about unemployment during the Napoleonic Wars or about what look like beginnings of a trade cycle under the Tudors. He knows, no one better, that any quantitative treatment of remote social phenomena to which he can aspire—even the simplest: how much of England was enclosed in 1700? how big was an average gild? how heavy was the burden of the Danegeld?—that any such treatment is likely to yield results on a plane of truth lower than that attainable, if not always attained, by the economist. If by good fortune the economic historian has one set of measured facts for a remote date—certain truths so far as they go—he will often lack that second set which leads to the illuminating conclusion. He may know the amount of wool exported in 1273 but not its price schedule, the amount of the Danegeld but not the taxable capacity of England. Very conscious of this, he is most unlikely either to rush out from under the ordained umbrella or to claim the whole shadow of it for himself. This is all on the assumption that he knows about modern economics and its opportunities. I have come across historical writers who seemed not to know these things well.

If the economic historian has his modesties in presence of the pure economist he also has his pride. He is proud because, by definition as historian, he is one to whom the tangled variety of human life is attractive in itself; one who will study alterations in the tangle for the love of it, even when his information is such that he can never hope to pick out with assurance the forces at work, or measure exactly the changes brought about by the aggregate of them between dates x and y. He cares for the beginnings of things as such. He likes to trace the growth of institutions which have been moulded by man's need to keep alive and man's desire for comfort and prosperity—village communities, trading companies, Christmas goose clubs—although he may not be able to number the community, read the balance sheet of the company, or find the slate of the goose club. It pleases him to know that in such and such an age caravans took the golden road to Samarkand, and that in such another age they went no more, even if he cannot count the camels or prove—what he always suspects—that the total amount of the rose-candy spikenard and mastic conveyed was really trifling. Some men— George Unwin was one—have turned to economic history mainly because it is so full of workings together for useful ends, of community life of all sorts, not because it is particularly rich—as of course it is—in 'entities with a metrical aspect.' Others may like best what is odd, individual, idiosyncratic in the story of how men have kept alive and as comfortable as may be. It is, in fact, a story full of attractive oddities. They weary of the general averages of statistical truth and of such human sequences as may be plotted in graphs. Others again may care most for the unmeasurable thoughts which make the measured things. But these all are within the covenant, very well within it. The historian likes his companions to be as varied as his matter; and happily there is no excluding definition which says that to be economic an 'entity' must be 'metrical.'

Yet; yet; it is the obvious business of an economic historian to be a measurer above other historians. For this the worker among English records—manuscript or printed—has immense opportunity, as Madox said and as the many Germans, Americans, and others who have worked among them, to our very great advantage, well know. While grateful to all, one is glad to think that the history of English prices begun by Fleetwood and carried on by Adam Smith was resumed, in the 'sixties of the nineteenth century, by Thorold

Rogers at Oxford without outside inspiration. I think I am right in saying also that the similar work of continental scholars—as for example, that of the Vicomte d'Avenel in France—was planned in definite imitation of Rogers. It was natural that such work should start here, because no continental country has anything approaching in continuity and completeness the records of Merton on which Rogers began, or the other College records to which he turned; just as none has a national record so old and so complete as our Domesday, from which my King's colleague, William Corbett—after half a lifetime of work—was able to give us, just before he died, a picture of William of Normandy doling out the loot of English land almost as exact as might be the secret report of some syndicate distributing the profits after a successful *coup* on the rubber market. It is only a comparatively few years since the Record Office first made available the series of Customs Accounts and Port Books, from which it is possible—given enough labour—to work out much of the English overseas trade from the later Middle Ages in astonishing detail, though strict measurement is not in this case always quite easy.

I tried just now to place the economic historian in relation to the economist. There is still a little more to be said about their joint relation to the historian without prefix. Forty years ago, and less, Seeley used to picture political economy as an invader occupying historical territory. 'When each new human science has carved out a province [from history] for itself,' he wrote in a very familiar page of his *Lectures on Political Science*, 'will not the residuum at last entirely disappear?' Historians, we recall how he went on to argue, must fall back on the province which no one can take from them— that of the State, its growth, its forms, its functions, the Kingdom of Political Science. If I thought in terms of war and the carving out of provinces, I believe I could draft operation orders for an economist's raid on that kingdom also, leaving the Professor of Political Science to draft his orders for the defensive battle; but that is not how I think.

When I picture the place of economics in history modestly, I sometimes see the economic worker as a sort of osteologist, a collector and student of historical bones, old defective fossil sets and pretty complete sets of well-articulated modern ones. I think of him saying deferentially to the pure historian, who in his fancy is sometimes himself—it is for you to call on Clio. 'Come from the four winds, O breath, and breathe upon these . . . that they may live.' I have given you to the best of my power—he falls back into specialist's jargon—the osseous structure of successive types of societies and nations, the stiff working parts, the things which condition their activity and determine its forms. Now set them to their fighting and law-making, their songs and their prayers. I am no rival. Yours is the higher work. I want to help.

It is easy, when modesty wanes, for us economic historians to glorify this bone business of ours. We can hint at the very unreal or lop-sided or dropsical historical monsters which might be reconstructed—have indeed been reconstructed—through neglect of it. Or we may choose some quite different comparison which gives more honour to the economic worker. But whether we are modest or proud, and whatever the comparison, we shall admit that there are things in history beyond and, in the scale of values, above his things. We shall not, I think, accept Seeley's easy solution that the historian can 'afford to be sketchy and summary' on 'economical questions' because a specialist has taken them from him. His practice was better than his doctrine; for in his *Life and Times of Stein* he gave a full account of peasant emancipation in Prussia.

Insisting on the full observance of his practice, even denouncing those who do not follow it, we shall still recognize economic history for what it is, a help-study—pardon the Teutonism: I know no English equivalent—a link-study between history and economics; and we shall make it our business, like the common men of our narratives, to work together with all willing historians, as with all willing economists, for useful ends.

NOTES

1   The books quoted here are of course only a selection of what seem to me the most important. For a far fuller survey, to which I am much indebted though I do not always agree with it, see Prof. Gras, 'The Rise and Development of Economic History,' *Ec. Hist. Rev.* vol. I. no. I, 1927.

2   [Sir George Clark has pointed out that Clapham later accepted the revised account of this work given in the appendix to G. N. Clark, *Science and Social Welfare in the Age of Newton*, Oxford 1937. NBH.]

5

G. N. Clark

THE STUDY OF ECONOMIC HISTORY
(Oxford, 1932)

This inaugural lecture was delivered at the University of Oxford on the 21st January 1932.

THE STUDY OF ECONOMIC HISTORY

THE holder of a newly-established chair is unable to follow our pious custom and to begin his public instruction by commemorating his predecessors in office; but a professor of economic history does not need to apologise for his subject as something novel and unfamiliar. For close on a quarter of a century the university has made special provision for its teaching and has given it a place in the examinations for honours; but Oxford has been a home of this study for a much longer period. How long the period has been I should not like to say, for like other university studies this was a component element in thought long before it was treated specifically as a 'subject.' No one who ever read those introductory chapters which are amongst the most wonderful passages of Thucydides can have failed to see that one of the keys to general history is economic. Again, no one can have been unaware of it who thought about history in the light of the scientific movement of the seventeenth century, a movement to which we may with reason attribute the translation of Thucydides by Thomas Hobbes, the greatest Oxford thinker of his time. In the, historical books of that century we do indeed find not merely anticipations but mature specimens of economic history, and it would be inexcusable, at any rate on this occasion, to make light of these early precedents. Even they were not the first. We must overcome the temptation to maintain that the first Oxford book on economic history was the translation of Orosius, with additions on the newest maritime trade-routes, made by the reputed founder of the university, King Alfred. We shall indeed do best to pass over all the stages of preparation with the mere reminder that they must not be forgotten, and to take as our starting-point a writer in whom economic history had certainly reached its full stature, Adam Smith.

Adam Smith is still by common consent the greatest of economic historians, as he is the greatest of economists, and we shall not do well if we tamely acquiesce in the belief that the six years which he spent without interruption in Oxford contributed little to the formation of his mind. It is to be hoped that one of the present fellows of Balliol will publish what he knows about the remarkable coincidence between the books referred to in the footnotes of *The Wealth of*

Nations and the books which are known to have been in the college library when its future author was in residence. The influence of Adam Smith on the writers of the next generations worked not only through the classical school of economists who, on the whole and with certain exceptions, paid far less attention to history than he did, but also through historical writers. Among the historians whom he influenced the most important strain derived from Ludwig Heeren, in Hanoverian Göttingen; but among Oxford men there was Sir Frederick Morton Eden, whose *State of the Poor, an History of the Labouring Classes in England from the Conquest to the Present Period*, though it was completed in 1797, is still often disturbed on its shelves. Eden's *State of the Poor* has been called the first of all the attempts to write a history of the common man. It is easy to forget how many Oxford authors of that age shared something of this point of view, some of them rather unexpected names like Gilbert White, who in the *Natural History of Selborne* wrote, with other things to our purpose, what may be called the *locus classicus* on the effects of the introduction of roots as winter feed for cattle. In 1830 the Rev. William Forster Lloyd, a mathematician by training, who was afterwards elected to the Drummond Chair of Political Economy, published in a slender but scholarly volume his historical *Prices of Corn in Oxford*. This is probably not much used nowadays, but it deserves mention as one of the curiosities of Oxford publishing, for the original stock has never been exhausted and copies are still on sale at the Clarendon Press.

A writer to whom we cannot fairly lay claim here is John William Burgon. His *Life and Times of Sir Thomas Gresham* of 1839, still not wholly superseded, was written before he matriculated, and we must suppose that Oriel turned his mind to the ecclesiastical interests which afterwards absorbed him. Neither the atmosphere of Oxford nor the tendencies of economic thought were favourable to economic history. That was the time when Mr. Disraeli could write, 'there is no error so vulgar as to believe that revolutions are occasioned by economical causes.' Economic historians in England felt themselves despised, a feeling which lasted to days which are still not very distant. It was said that they thought *The Pilgrim's Progress* an interesting book because it threw light on the conditions of road-transport in the seventeenth century. They pointed out very properly that at least a knowledge of the economic life of the times helps us to understand *The Pilgrim's Progress*, not to mention that other book of Bunyan's to which Thorold Rogers drew attention, *The Life and Death of Mr. Badman*. They were apt to insist, in injured and sentimental tones, that Samuel Smiles did not attain the most romantic style of which their subject permitted, and that there were even poets and artists who found their models in that world of confined horizons where

> to live men labour, only knowing
> Life's little lantern between dark and dark.

We need not prolong that argument. It has been won already, and in a wider arena than the university of Ruskin and William Morris. Economic historians no longer need to plead for toleration.

They first came into their own in Germany, and in England the outstanding figure of the new era was William Cunningham of Cambridge, who took a leading position from about 1882; but Oxford prides herself on his older contemporary Thorold Rogers. It was in the eighteen-sixties, during his first tenure of the Drummond Chair, that Thorold Rogers began the publication of his great *History of Agriculture and Prices*. His vast energy enabled him, although he had an active career as a parliamentary politician and achieved a considerable output of shorter books, to complete six of its seven volumes, and it is still in constant use as a book of reference. Subsequent historians have indeed pointed out imperfections in its workmanship, and some of the conclusions which Rogers drew in this and other books have, like so many of the over-confident opinions of the Victorian age, been revised or abandoned; but nothing can deprive the book of its place in the development of our knowledge. No other single historian in England at least has brought together so great a mass of directly economic information, and the bold conception of the book, collecting from the manuscript records of six centuries the minute facts of prices, opened the eyes of historians all over Europe to the abundance of the evidence on which they might draw. Its example was quickly imitated in more than one continental country, and it is not too much to say that it made a new beginning in economic history. Nor do writers of our time always give Thorold Rogers the credit he deserves for many incidental hints and discoveries which are now absorbed into the common stock.

Rogers founded no school in Oxford, but from his time we have had a series of writers of acknowledged eminence. Several of these have been even more notable for their influence on others than for what they themselves left behind in written form. Arnold Toynbee's posthumous volume affords in itself no measure of his vital personal influence, and we may say of Sir William Ashley, who owed his inspiration partly to Toynbee, that he too, although he left behind him a row of admirable books, effected more as a teacher than as a writer. Through him Oxford can claim a share in the ancestry of the very distinguished school of economic history which flourishes at

Harvard, as through George Unwin she is related to the younger school of Manchester. Of those who taught in Oxford, one of the first names we should all remember is that of Arthur Johnson. His Ford Lectures on *The Disappearance of the Small Landowner* are still useful after twenty-three years; and we may all envy the strength which enabled him, after a strenuous life as a college tutor, to publish the five volumes of his *History of the Draper's Company* between his seventieth year and his seventy-eighth.

With Ashley and Unwin and Johnson we have reached our own time. In Oxford, as everywhere, the study is now pursued by more people and with greater interest than ever before; but, although there is much that I would gladly say in praise of their work, it is not fitting that I should mention by name those of our living contemporaries who are or have been resident here. You would not, however, forgive me if I did not make exceptions for four *emeriti* to whom happily we still look with gratitude for guidance and example. The first is Mr. L. L. Price, who was officially in charge of this subject here from 1909 until 1921. Only the other day he published his authoritative survey of the work of English economists and economic historians in his own time. Of the other three, all are better known in other fields, but you will recognise them if I refer to them by their work in this. One is the historian of local rating and of theories of production and distribution. Another, to whom I have very special personal obligations, is the historian of the exchequer in the twelfth century. The third, the historian of Stuart England, has shown many of us the way in the economic as in the other aspects of that period.

It is indeed one of the most striking signs of the great change in the estimation of economic history, that it pervades the work of so many historians whose primary interests are elsewhere. Sir Paul Vinogradoff, though he held the chair of jurisprudence, may, to be sure, be called primarily an historian of medieval agrarian institutions; but Dicey, who was first and foremost a jurist, was also an historical thinker, and he made the framework into which economic historians have usually fitted their accounts of the English nineteenth century. Twenty years ago or more the economic history of the ancient world began to occupy the minds of our classical historians, and nowadays no teacher of history in any branch or any period would like to be accused of neglecting its claims.

The work which economic historians are doing presents a spectacle of rich variety. We may distinguish a number of directions in which the detailed work is tending to become more and more subdivided by specialisation, and although none of them is independent of the rest, each has its own problems and its own close relations with workers whom we cannot classify as both economists and historians, some of whom indeed are neither. There is, for instance, the history of technology, of tools and machines, of the chemical and other processes of production and transport. This is indisputably related to our subject; indeed it is more than that, it is a part of our subject. It is a fundamental principle of the evolution of industry that a change of tools or machines brings with it a change of business organization and of the human relationships which that dictates. Yet in finding out what the development of industrial technique has been, we must go far from the beaten path of historical studies. We must see the material evidence preserved for us in museums , and we must do archaeological field-work in the often deserted and almost forgotten mills or forges of earlier centuries. We must visit modern mines, factories, workshops, farms. We must gather information and ideas from engineers, from chemists, from geologists. For a long time the history of technology has had a life of its own. From the beginning of the nineteenth century there were German writers who attempted comprehensive and systematic surveys of it as a whole, and the existence of great technological institutes tends to keep it together. In England we have a publishing society, still young but promising, the Newcomen Society, which covers the whole field; but the complexity of modern processes of manufacture and transport is so great that this department in itself is now rather a group of special studies than a subject which single workers can master.

It has become the fashion lately to talk about 'business history' as another specialised sectional study. The expression is ambiguous, and it seems to mean sometimes the history of separate firms or businesses, sometimes the history of business in a somewhat wider sense, of business methods and organisation. Clearly the unit, to be studied to the best advantage, must be taken in its environment as one business among many, and there are more ways than one in which the story of a single business may be made to illustrate a general development. There are business histories in the heroic or epic manner, of which the theme is the rise of the good man to riches. Others, such as the history of one of our great amalgamated banks, are largely genealogical and provide useful information on the composition of the business classes in the last three hundred years. The *differentia* of 'business history' is, in fact, to be sought not in its method or point of view so much as in its materials: it is history based on the records of business itself, as distinguished from the information about business collected by governments or tabulated by economists and statisticians. In a sense material of this sort has long been in use. Account-books, for instance, provided Thorold Rogers with the bulk of his facts; but in recent years their use has changed. Rogers used them mainly as sources of information about thousands of separate transactions. He split them up and tabulated them. Attention is turned now rather to the total effects of the transactions on those who made them, to the fortunes and methods of persons and firms, the structure of economic life. A great store of materials of this kind, from the business archives of the Medici and still earlier traders down to our own time, is waiting to be explored and used. It is important that what is worth keeping shall be preserved and that the process of destruction, which has been very active among these superficially unattractive papers, shall be checked. In several countries, whether by the formation of societies or otherwise, there is a commendable movement for building up repositories in which business firms may place their records for the use of students. We in England are sometimes accused of being backward in this, but we have made a beginning and the time has come for pressing on with the work. In several universities and public libraries there are growing collections of this sort, and we may reasonably mention along with them the repositories of Lord Hanworth's national scheme for storing manorial records, of which one is the Bodleian. These manorial documents are nominally legal but in fact mainly economic, and thanks to them English agrarian history can be studied in minute detail for a long period of time. We have every reason to be proud also of the records of the East India Company, and especially of the great series of published volumes from them for the seventeenth century. The Bank of England is more secretive, even about its earliest days. Let us hope that it will allow us to thaw out the frozen records in its vaults. I cannot conceive of a good reason why any existing firm, whether semi-public or purely private, should be reluctant to throw open the whole of its records down at least to the year 1870.

Several English historians have demonstrated what really valuable results can be obtained from using business records. One of the pioneers was Professor W. R. Scott, whose *English Joint Stock Companies to 1720* is amongst the most solid and well-considered economic histories that have ever been written. He and a few others have brought to the study of these materials what it specially needs, the critical exactness of the scholar, which is the product of a liberal education and is not the mere accuracy of the clerk. They had that active sense of proportion which is necessary for work amongst records which have survived fortuitously where much else has perished, and they were skilled in the use of another kind of records of which the interpretation is a more established art, the public records. English historians are rightly proud of the immense and orderly storehouses of the records of the Crown and parliament and the courts of law. Even if they were far smaller in quantity these records would be capable of more effective use than any others in England, because lawyers, paleographers, the writers on 'diplomatic', and others have provided an excellent equipment for searching and interpreting them. It is natural that historians should have turned to them first in all their special studies, for all historians are limited by their materials, and those materials are exploited first which are most easily accessible. Among the government records in all countries are to be found considerable masses of business records, such, for instance, as account-books and correspondence impounded or put in as evidence in trials at law. These, however, like all business records, are difficult to handle: even with the assistance of the legal proceedings connected with them, it is often hard to draw conclusions from them. The same is true of the bulky records of buying and selling by governments and their departments. Far quicker results are offered by those documents which governments have collected or caused to be drawn up for the direct purpose of reaching economic conclusions. For more than a century past in England we have had so many official inquiries into population, trade, industry, finance, social conditions, and every department of economic life, so many organs of government whose business it was to watch these matters continuously, that the economic history of the period has been written mainly from blue-books and white papers and departmental files. Even for earlier periods it has been largely so, and much material of this type still awaits examination; for the period from Burghley to Walpole, for instance, the enormous collection of the Port Books is the great new source of information about English seaborne trade.

The popularity of business history is due partly to a reaction from public records, to a sense that they are for the most part only indirectly economic, that they are the results of the intervention of governments in economic life from outside. Economic activities are always conducted in a social environment, and the more complex they become, the more they tend to be regulated by law. Even in a system of *laisser-faire* individualism, legislators must concern themselves with the law of property, the law of contract, commercial law; and almost every economic act must be carried out in a prescribed legal form, being recorded, if it is at all important, in a legal document. Legal literature and legal records therefore give us something like a cast on which the lineaments of economic facts are impressed. It is, however, external to those facts, and their inner significance, their vital principle, is not easily to be inferred from it. That is why the economic essence of the history of commerce, finance and industry sometimes seems so elusive. We can easily find charters of some of the old trading companies, regulations of guilds, statutes prescribing the terms of apprenticeship, assessments of wages made by justices of the peace; but it is much harder to discover what business was done by the trading companies or by the individual members of guilds, or what wages were actually paid by farmers and master-workmen and how they were spent. Even when the state uses its great powers of inquisition to inquire into economic practice its point of view is still not that of economic science. It is necessary to allow for a subtle bias, even when the questions put by governments are answered with complete candour or so that conflicting concealments cancel one another out. These inquiries and discussions belong to the formation of the economic policy of the state, and that has various aspects. Governments are, on the one hand, participants in economic life, among other participants. On the other hand, they sometimes assume a wide responsibility for its conduct. Statesmen often sincerely believe that prosperity and adversity depend altogether on the choice of policies. That is a belief which no economist and no historian would accept without strong qualifications, perhaps also few business men. Some economic historians have been amongst the most sceptical on this point. Eight or nine years ago Unwin copied down in a private letter to me some words from his lectures on the Merchant Adventurers which now appear in the posthumously printed version:[1]

> Policy in the sense of a deliberate, consistent and far-sighted scheme . . . is more often an illusion of the scholarly mind than a fact of history. Policy, as actually found in history, is a set of devices into which a Government drifts under the pressure of practical problems and which gradually acquire the conscious uniformity of a type and begin, at last, to defend themselves as such.

Even if we do not accept this extremist view, we may appreciate the reasons which make economic historians anxious to avoid treating the state as the decisive or originating factor in economic development. We make our contribution to the history of policy, and no one now denies that it must be an important contribution. We are aware also of the reciprocal action of policy upon economic life, and consequently we must not cut ourselves off from the development of research in the political sphere, but we are also conscious of having a contribution of our own to make to the history of civilisation in the widest sense, co-ordinate with that of the political historians.

The resort to records prepared and preserved by the state has often been a step to surer ground from the more elegant but often misleading materials of literature. Pamphlets, for instance, which set out, often with finished art, what their authors believed or wished their readers to believe about economic matters, have led historians down some long byways of error, from which the clear facts of record evidence have lighted them back. Sometimes the conflict of evidence is so complicated, as in the long and mysterious history of the enclosure movements in England, that we are still far from the end of it; but even when it is proved, as it is of the earlier pamphleteers of the balance of trade, that their facts were wrong, we have not disposed of them as valueless for our purposes. They enable us to know what were the popular ideas of economics, and these ideas, developing in an intimate but far from simple organic relation with the ideas of professional economists, are also part of our subject-matter. Whatever we do we cannot reach the facts of the past except through the minds of the men who lived in that past. Even the rudest and most unsophisticated business records have their background of ideas. Book-keeping by double entry was the outcome of a long development of thought. The annual balance-sheet is the symbol of a certain historical attitude to the business concern. These things belong to the history of economic ideas in the widest sense, and that is itself a part of the general history of ideas. Much of the history of economic thought has been admirably written, but there is much still to do. In England we are somewhat behindhand in our work on the period before Adam Smith; and for the later period in all countries much needs to be done to treat economic thought not as the parthenogenetic offspring of economic facts, but as deriving also from the habits of thought which have grown to maturity in theology, in philosophy, in science, in mathematics.

It is not my object to prove that the economic historian ought to be omniscient, and I will not attempt anything so alarming as an enumeration of all the outside experts whose results he may have to take into account. That they are still growing in number will be sufficiently clear if I point out that in any work on population we have now to use the results of that science of yesterday, or rather perhaps of to-morrow, which we are learning to call 'social biology.' We cannot all engage in all these researches. We must accept much as it is given to us, and we must shut ourselves up in limited fields of specialisation. The greater part of the best work in our subject for a generation past has been done in monographs, and, although some writers of comprehensive mind like Professor Clapham compass something higher and wider, we are far from having reached that point of diminishing returns at which less of new truth results from each successive dose of specialist research. Here in Oxford I hope we shall make progress in the study of general as distinguished from merely local or national economic history. It is needless to say how important that is. This winter we have learnt, if we did not know it already, that the modern improvements in transport and in the interchange of news, operating in war and peace, have so concentrated the shocks of economic disturbances as to make the wealth and welfare of each part of the world increasingly dependent on those of other parts. Thus the economic stability of all the world depends on progress towards international co-operation and international justice. The tendency to mutual dependence may be only beginning or it may be working to a disastrous breakdown and standstill. In either case, it cannot be disputed that we need to understand it, nor should it be disputed that we are not yet in a position to understand it fully. We know too little about its history in the past. To take an obvious instance, only a beginning has been made in the difficult and urgently necessary study of the economic history of war. Not long ago Mr. J. M. Keynes wrote somewhat too severely that no one had yet begun to think how the economic history of the late European war should be written. As with the last, so it is with other wars. There is a flat contradiction between the historians who think that the warfare of the Elizabethan sea-dogs was on the whole detrimental to the prosperity of England and those who think that it began an era of national improvement and enrichment. To these instances might be added a hundred others, the sum of which is no less than this, that the foundations of general economic history are not yet well laid.

In calling it general economic history I have avoided the use of the word 'international.' There is such a thing as international economic history. The nations or, to be more exact, the political communities, have been, though not always and everywhere, the units not only of commercial law but also of currency, of tariffs and generally of economic policy. Trade between their members has therefore been in some senses trade between these communities themselves; but one of the fundamental questions which need examination is how much of the entire general economic history is comprehended in international history. Some very interesting work has been done in recent years, especially by American and continental scholars, in tracing the change from local markets to what used to be called national markets, some of which we have now learnt to call metropolitan markets. Much remains to be done in this sphere and still more in tracing the rise of world-markets. Much needs to be done in tracing the development of foreign investment and supra-national financial interests, not only in earlier centuries but throughout the nineteenth and the twentieth. The whole history of British trade must be revised in the light of the records of other countries: there are port-books waiting for us not only in Chancery Lane but in

Middelburg and Åbo. Everything that we can call the comparative study of economic developments in different countries requires further illumination: only in agrarian matters has it made much headway. The great need of economic history in England at the present time is to overstep the barriers of language.

This work on general economic history is pointed out as desirable by the needs of the current study of economic theory, and here, as a corrective to the impression of bewildering variety in economic history, I would put on record a half-humorous remark which was thrown out in conversation by the late Professor H. W. C. Davis. 'Economic history,' he said, 'is that kind of history which requires a knowledge of economics.' This may seem an austere definition. It excludes much entertaining gossip about 'the olden times' which has passed for economic history. But it provides a criterion for deciding what we ought to investigate and what we may leave aside, and to that extent it lightens and simplifies our task. It is not indeed possible, and it would not be desirable, for the theorist to tell the historian exactly what to look for, or for the historian to furnish the theorist with exactly the information which he wants. That would be possible only if a satisfactory theory could be constructed with a number of blanks into which there would afterwards obediently fit themselves illustrative or corroborative facts. As it is, the facts will dictate or contain their own interpretation, and theory will unite with history in an equal partnership. Neither will be merely ancillary and neither a mere external check on the other. In the last resort the two studies cannot, as I believe, logically be distinguished. Historians for their part ought to try to maintain a close co-operation between them. Only theory can deliver us from mere antiquarianism or aimless curiosity and make research what it ought to be, a methodical advance from the known, through the unknown, to what is worth knowing.

The definition of economic history which I have quoted was, as I said, half-humerous, for in form it was something like a definition in a circle, and in effect it evaded all the disputes about the scope and method both of history and of economics. Among the different schools of economic thought some have in fact kept a much more effective contact with historians than others. Continental writers sometimes discuss why it is that economists seem to fall into well-defined groups on one side of this line or the other. There often appears to be an affinity between the historical or positive tendency and what is called the ethical tendency, the tendency to introduce ethical criteria of value into economics, and consequently to advocate the intervention of the state in favour of various programmes of amelioration. In Germany, as is well known, there was a vigorous school of economists, running from Roscher to Schmoller, both of them authors whose work is still alive, which stood for all these tendencies and whose members were indifferently described as the historical school or as the socialists of the chair. On the other hand, the classical school was more detached from historical study. Taking not an organic and institutional view of economic life, but what I may be permitted to describe in our own Whately's word as a catallactic view, this school used a more abstract method. It disregarded all motives except self-interest and pursued an analysis of which the results, expressed in equations or identical propositions, are of a mathematical nature even when they do not involve the use of numbers. This method not only excluded ethical considerations, but its individualism also led it to stand for the principle of *laisserfaire*.

In England we do not state the relation between the two schools in this way, if for no other reason, then because a number of the leading English writers do not stand clearly on either side of a line which divides according to this deceptively simple classification. Both John Stuart Mill and Marshall, like Professor Pigou in our own time, though they were followers of the classical tradition, were much occupied with ethical considerations of what was socially desirable, and Mill was not the last economist of that school who exhibited a gradual alienation from *laisser-faire*. On the other hand, some of our historians have been individualist stalwarts. Thorold Rogers, though his work lay so much in assembling positive facts, remained in his theories as orthodox as his friend and kinsman Richard Cobden. Unwin transmitted to his school his own deep distrust of state intervention. That the historical method does not necessarily lead to a desire for changes of policy and institutions is clearly illustrated by some of our economic historians. It is shown still more clearly in the related field of jurisprudence, in which the German historical school found its example, but which was as conservative there as in England, where Sir Henry Maine was the strenuous opponent of the unhistorical individualist Benthamite radicals. We do indeed trace in the English thought of the nineteenth century certain broad currents flowing down from the *Historismus* of the romantic period and ending in collectivism of various types; but the more they are examined the more it is clear that the sequence was at many points preserved by historical accidents and diversified by irregularities and exceptions.

This is not the time to discuss the logical problems which lie behind the controversies of working historians: all that I can do is to indicate very summarily the direction in which I seek a solution. This is to regard economic history as an abstract kind of history, related to the full and concrete history somewhat as economic theory is related to the full and concrete life of the community. Economic history is to history as the economic man is to the human being. There are therefore as many different kinds of interpretation open to historians as there are to theorists: the being historians does not limit us to this opinion or to that. Nor are we to distinguish history and theory by saying that theory is more abstract than history: there are many degrees of abstraction in each. Again, each must be pursued with a single eye to the ascertainment of truth, but the truths once found will have a practical application. The more scientific our cartography becomes, the more, and not the less, certainly shall we be able to find our way by the map. Nor shall we be blamed if we select for charting those countries in which we intend to travel.

We need not hesitate then to assert that the study of economic history subserves practical ends. Not that I wish to extend any promise of immediate benefits which will ensue if we summon the seventeenth century to the rescue of the twentieth. The practical value of historical scholarship is not direct. It is no more than a part, though an indispensable part, of the combined labour of the human and social sciences. Every year now we become more clearly aware that the circle of these sciences is wider and their interdependence closer than we supposed. Economic historians find themselves engaged in an active commerce of ideas not only with the older allies of historical study, like the students of language and literature, of law and of philosophy; but with all those natural scientists whose work touches upon human needs. As in other alliances the common advance is sometimes checked by mutual suspicions and misunderstandings; but none the less there is a common advance, and the simplest way of measuring it is to see how, as they investigate the Great Society into which we have been born, all these sciences are guided by the conception of control. Three hundred years ago the control of nature by man became the conscious ambition of natural science, and in the pursuit of that ambition the scientists have made conquests which, one after another, have appeared impossible until they were completed; but these successes have served to show how distant is the more difficult control of man over man himself. Each increase of our power over nature intensifies the need for control over the forces of massed mankind, not least of them the economic forces. We recognise that the attempt to regulate such forces must be grounded in an understanding of man and of his place in the universe to which not only moral philosophy but all science must contribute. We will not grudge their pleasure to the historians who regard history as a more arduous form of story-telling, though we may well think that we have a better reason for undertaking its drudgery.

οὐ γὰρ περὶ τοῦ ἐπιτυχόντος ὁ λόγος ἀλλὰ περὶ τοῦ ὄντινα τρόπον χρὴ ζῆν. History has a share in the constructive work of justice and freedom.

NOTES

1   Among his *Studies in Economic History*, edited by R. H. Tawney, 1927.

6

R. H. Tawney

THE STUDY OF ECONOMIC HISTORY
(L.S.E., 1932)

This inaugural lecture was delivered at the London
School of Economics on the 12th October 1932. The
chair was taken by Lord Passfield (Sidney Webb).

THE STUDY OF ECONOMIC HISTORY

No one can speak in this place on the Study of Economic History without recalling the names of those who have done so before him. The first book on the subject which I read was a volume in the library of classics by one of whom we are all the pupils, our encyclopaedic chairman. The first lecture on it which I attended was by a research student of this School, later a master to whom a host of apprentices owed their instruction in the craft, George Unwin. The personality who gave it its place in our curriculum was Lilian Knowles, the most inspiring of teachers and most loveable of human beings. A student who inherits a corner of their estate must feel gratitude for their labours and humility at his own.

It is not only the memory of distinguished predecessors which fills me with diffidence. When I realised that the penalty of a Professorship was an Inaugural Lecture, I breathed a prayer to the bright goddesses of enterprise and self-help, who are ever at the elbows of teachers of this School. They frowned but did their best. 'Do not attempt,' they said, 'anything original or profound. It is not your line. Conform to the practice of the representative form, if, wretched historian, you know what that means. For once show real initiative. Study the addresses delivered on similar occasions by more illustrious persons. Aim at the median and you may hit the lower quartile.'

As always, when addressed by the voice of economic reason, I trembled and obeyed; but, as my researches proceeded, my despondency increased. If, as they inclined me to believe, one function of an Inaugural Lecture is to vindicate the claims of the department of knowledge represented by the lecturer against bold, bad men who would question its primacy, I am conscious of an incapacity for that entertaining branch of literature to be excused only, if at all, by a misspent youth. I came to the study of economic history, not as one dedicated from childhood to the service of the altar, but for reasons so commonplace that I am ashamed to admit them. When I reached years of discretion—which I take to mean the age at which a young man shows signs of getting over his education—I found the world surprising; I find it so still. I turned to history to interpret it, and have not been disappointed by my guide, though often by myself.

A student who is more interested in wild life than in museum specimens must be prepared to annoy gamekeepers by following it across country. If, in addition, he is an historian, with the historian's irreverent propensity for treating the most venerable institutions, from capitalism to university curricula, as historical categories, his need for indulgence is increased. He can only hope that he may be pardoned if he confesses to regarding what academic convention disguises as 'subjects,' not as independent entities, poised each in majestic isolation on its private peak, but as fluid and provisional divisions, with frontiers corresponding less to the articulations of the universe than to the exigencies of a world in which examinations last for three hours and a humane rubric requires that four, and not more than four, questions shall be attempted by candidates. It would be convenient if the question, Where is wisdom to be found? could be answered by referring the inquirer to the appropriate university department. But she appears to prefer the debatable land where titles are ambiguous and boundaries intersect; nor is her business much advanced by what in humbler spheres are known as demarcation disputes. So I hope that I shall not be thought less attached to the branch of knowledge which is my own, if I do not regard it as an appropriate object for proprietary defensiveness or patriotic fervour.

I

Since histories were first written, references to the work and wealth of mankind have found a place in them. But to distinguish between incidental allusions, which are forgotten as made, and the recognition of the significance of an aspect of life which leads to its systematic exploration, is the first canon of criticism; and to inflict upon you a history of Economic History is not my intention. If its springs are to be sought, they may be found, as far as England is concerned, in two movements in the century which gave both English economic life and English political institutions their decisive stamp. One of them, the attempt to offer a sociological explanation of the political breakdown, produced several *pièces de circonstance* and one masterpiece. But, when the stability of the edifice was assured, speculations as to its foundations fell out of fashion. While much of the best recent work in France has been prompted by curiosity as to the economic antecedents of the Revolution, the economic forces behind the English constitutional struggles continued to be almost ignored by historians till the theme was taken up in our own day by Russian scholars.

The highest landmark in the early history of English economic thought was the foundation of the Royal Society. The second influence found its motive in an attempt on the part of men closely in touch with the natural science of the day to apply an analogous technique to the investigation of contemporary economic phenomena of which the paradox of Dutch prosperity, a pyramid balanced on its point, was the most arresting. A generation later the realisation that the quantitative methods employed, as a conscious innovation, by Graunt, Petty, King and Davenant to the study of the present could be applied with equal effect to throw light on the past, produced the work of Fleetwood, and later of Smith, Postlethwaite and Anderson, which links the Political Arithmetic of the seventeenth century to the statistical compilations of the early nineteenth. But it was an age of annalists and antiquarians, rather than of historians, and the giants or erudition, like Madox and Hearne, eschewed generalisation. The synthesis which proved, not for the last time, that the best fish are caught when poaching came neither from an historian nor an economist, but from a Professor of Moral Philosophy.

It is a truism that the central theme of *The Wealth of Nations* is historical. It is the emancipation of economic interests from the tyranny of custom, predatory class ambitions, and the obstruction of governments pursuing sinister ends in congenial darkness. The passages devoted to that vast movement, in which Smith, a good bourgeois, sees the clue to the progress of civilisation in Europe, are among the greatest attempts at philosophical history; and no one who studies his work, not in detached snippets of doctrine, but as composed by its author, will doubt that, without several generations of historical investigation, it could not have been written. His limitations are partly those of his generation, partly the penalty of any grand construction. He brings all things to one standard; finds the similarity of man's needs in different periods and climates more significant than contrasts of environment and circumstance; and, worlds apart as he is from the *naïvéte* of his political popularisers who selected their quotations to suit their interests, is not without complacency. Writing in the age before the deluge, in which it still seemed possible that the old régime might be reformed from above by men who were his friends, he is more conscious of the solidarity which rests on a rational appreciation of common interests than of unseen foundations and subterranean fires.

In the year before his death, the deluge came. When, a quarter of a century later, the waters receded, it was evident that, with a new society, a new history had been born. As always, it took its character from contemporary interests. In the study of economic development the decisive influences were three—the Revolution, Nationalism, and the progress of Capitalist industry, for which Blanqui coined the phrase that began as an epigram, continued as a platitude, and is now criticised as a fallacy. Of these England experienced the two first only at second hand. The serious achievements were those of continental scholars, of whom one, and not the least powerful, found his materials in London.

They came both from historians and from economists. In France the pioneers were the first. It was inevitable that men who were the heirs of the Revolution should inquire into the forces which had set the cataclysm in motion, and that, as they pressed their analysis, they should find the economic to be not the least important. Writers who did not accept Saint Simon's view, that the only history which matters is the history of industry, found themselves driven behind politics and the sacred formulae of 1789 to the economic foundations. Louis Blanc's propagandist *Histoire de dix Ans* revealed the new influence, and the Revolution of 1848, with its doctrine of a fourth estate to be emancipated, underlined the lesson. De Tocqueville, whose *L'Ancien régime* appeared in 1855, has not usually been regarded as an economic historian; but his masterpiece is a watershed in the wild borderland between economic and political history, where rivers have their source. The immense body of recent work by French and foreign scholars on the economic conditions of pre-revolutionary France, and the magnificent series of volumes in the *Collection de Documents Inédits sur l'Histoire Economique de la Révolution Française,* the publication of which was undertaken by the Government on the suggestion of Jaurés, are among the streams which descend from it.

The movement which in France started from the side of the historians came in Germany from men whose interests were primarily economic. In a country economically retarded and with a strong authoritarian tradition, doctrines of relativity, of successive stages of development, of an economic apprenticeship to be passed under the tutelage of the state, found a congenial climate. List, the journalist of genius who popularised the new ideas, was a propagandist who travelled light. In his treatment of English history, his favourite arsenal of arguments, he sees design where in reality there was nothing more recondite than a commonplace struggle of interests, ascribes to far-sighted statesmanship measures prompted by the necessities of an empty Exchequer, and selects as a golden example of mercantilist statecraft an episode which subsequent research has shown to be an unmitigated disaster. The book of Roscher, whose *Lectures on Political Science according to the Historical Method* appeared in 1843, was on a different plane. His materials were inadequate, and the title of his volume, like that of Knies, *Political Economy from the Historical Standpoint*, promised more than could be performed. The work of these scholars was important less for the new light which they threw on specific topics, than because they realised that the study of economic development requires a scheme and categories of its own, which do not coincide with those either of the theorist or of the political historian. Together with Hildebrand, they have the best title to be regarded as the fathers of the science as an academic discipline, with an assured status and a continuous tradition.

Judged, however, not by its immediate effect but by its influence in widening horizons and creating a ferment which would work, by action and reaction, on future generations, the most dynamic discovery of the forties was not made in a university. It was the conclusion reached by a young German journalist, in the process of revising Hegel's *Philosophy of Law*, that 'juristic relations and political forms are neither to be understood by themselves, nor explained by the general progress of the human mind, but are rooted in the material conditions of life,' and that 'the real foundations of which legal and political institutions are the superstructure are to be found in the relations into which men enter as producers.' To examine the implications of that conception of social development is a task for philosophers, who have the wings of an eagle, rather than for a pedestrian historian, and I shall not attempt it. But the significance of a pioneer is to be judged less by the number of professed followers who march under his banner than by his influence in determining the direction taken by subsequent explorers. In setting Capitalism in its place as one phase in the moving panorama of economic civilisation, with a pedigree to be investigated and a title to permanence not more assured than its predecessors, Marx opened a new chapter in historical discussion, which, two generations after his death, is still unclosed. His hints have become books by writers unconscious of plagiarism; and, if the verdict of Croce—that his effect is that of spectacles on the short-sighted—requires be to supplemented, it is, perhaps, only with the remark that there are defects of vision which are incurable by oculists. In so far as it is concerned with the economic foundations of society, serious history to-day, whether Marxian or not, is inevitably post-Marxian.

For much of this ferment of ideas England supplied the text; from all of it she stood apart. In the period which the fashionable historian of his day described as that of 'the most enlightened generation of the most enlightened people that ever existed'—there were neither doubts as to social stability nor a grudge against history as an unfriendly stepmother, to set eyes scanning the economic past for clues to the economic future. The economic present was the province of a group of thinkers among whose virtues the capacity to see the characteristic achievements of their age as a strange, transitory episode was not the most conspicuous. Buckle in the fifties could describe *The Wealth of Nations* as 'probably the most important book that has ever been written.' But applause was not imitation; and, after Malthus, successors capable of developing the whole of Smith's estate had not been forthcoming. They were hardly to be expected.

Hence in England, while much of value was done in assembling materials, attempts at construction were few and feeble. Macaulay's famous third chapter, appropriately published in 1848, when its concluding pages on 'The Benefits derived by the Common People from the Progress of Civilization' had a topical interest, was, for all its brilliance, less argument than ornament. Rogers, who produced the first volume of his *History of Agriculture and Prices* in 1866, laid all subsequent students under his debt by his great collection of data, which only now is being superseded by Sir William Beveridge and his colleagues. But, writing at a time when the institutions which supplied them had hardly yet been explored, he was stronger as an investigator than an interpreter. With a keen eye for facts, he took his doctrines second-hand from contemporary shop windows, where they had already gathered some dust, with the result that his generalizations not infrequently throw less light on the practice of earlier generations than on the prejudices of his own. The territory nearest to economic history where progress was first made was the province of the lawyers. Maine had opened in 1861 a brilliant chapter, which was continued by Vinogradoff, Maitland, and, in our own day, Professor Holdsworth. But the best work on English economic history continued down to the 'eighties to be done by Germans—Brentano, whose introduction to Toulmin Smith's collection of gild ordinances laid the foundations for all subsequent work on gild history, and who lived to publish three volumes on English economic development half a century later; Schanz, who first explained to English scholars the significance of the commercial politics and social crises of Tudor England; and Held, whose account of the Industrial Revolution appeared three years before Toynbee's well-known lectures and may profitably be compared with them.

Partly because the legal historians had been first in the field, partly through the example of German masters, the characteristic feature of the work of the two scholars who did most to give the subject a place in English Universities was the strong institutional bias revealed when the first full-dress economic history of England appeared in 1882. Schmoller, who influenced both Cunningham and Ashley, had done much of his work on the mercantilist statecraft of the Prussian monarchy. He was somewhat heavily charged, it is perhaps fair to say, with the political assumptions natural to a German of his generation, and presented a picture of the part played by the state in economic progress, which, if a just corrective to a superficial individualism, would not always bear scrutiny. When his structure crumbled, with much else, laymen who knew economic history only through his interpretation of it, thought the blow irremediable. In reality, what had fallen was less his history than his theory. Against the latter a reaction had already been begun, not by theorists, but by historians.

It was a sign that interest had shifted from economic policy to economic evolution, that the significant problems were felt to lie in regions which elude the direct action of governments, and that a study which had crept as a *parvenu* between the elbows of economists and political historians was feeling its way towards a sociological interpretation of economic development which would find room within it for the contributions of both. The single most massive monument of the change is *Der Moderne Kapitalismus* of Werner Sombart, who took up again, on a higher plane of knowledge, the problems posed by Marx, and who emphasises his debt to him. But that impressive work is merely one peak on a continent; and, while some English reviewers of its concluding volumes sniffed nervously for heresy in the very words of its title, scholars of the most diverse opinions in half a dozen countries—Von Below, Strieder, Weber and Brentano in Germany, Sée and Hauser in France, and, a venerable name, Pirenne in Belgium, have attacked from different angles the problem of the antecedents, phases and characteristics of modern industrial civilization which is its central theme. The nearest English analogy to the discussion is the argument of the last fifteen years on the interpretation of the economic history of the eighteenth and early nineteenth centuries, the leading parts in which have been played by Professor Clapham, the *doyen* of English economic history, whose book will be the foundation of all subsequent works on the nineteenth century, and by Mr. and Mrs. Hammond, whose brilliance conceals their scholarship from those critics—a great host—who believe that, in order to be scientific, it is sufficient to be dull. The volumes of our chairman and Mrs. Webb, of Professor Scott, Mr. Lipson, Mr. Ashton, Professor Nef and Professor Hamilton, and the recent admirable work by Mr. Wadsworth and Miss Mann, supply that debate with its indispensible background.

It would be tempting to illustrate the extension in the range of economic history by referring to the specialisms—business history, technological history, the history of the economic applications of natural science—to which, itself a specialism a generation ago, it has given birth; by comparing the works on the subject when this School was founded with the monograph literature and journals available to-day; or, most significant of all, by contrasting the economic innocence of the famous historians of last century with the permeation of recent general histories—consider only those of Halévy and Pirenne in Europe, and of Beard in America—by economic interests. But the study is still in its youth, and its greatest tasks, I am glad to say, are before it. Let me state briefly my view of the spirit in which it should approach them.

II

History, as I understand it, is concerned with the study, not of a series of past events, but of the life of society, and with the records of the past as a means to that end. Time, and the order of occurrences in time, is a clue, but no more; part of the historian's business is to substitute more significant connections for those of chronology. But time is the medium in which his data are embedded, and his relation to it is analogous to that of his fellow-workers in some other social sciences to space. He finds his materials strewn about it, or uncovers them by digging, as distant regions are ransacked for data by the anthropologist and sociologist. He finds also that those drawn from one epoch or civilisation possess, like the components of geological strata, certain common features, which distinguish them from those of periods preceding or following it, and he values these uniformities as one key to their interpretation. Since the evidence as to the character of a society derived from a single century is as misleading as that offered by a single locality, these materials, which are inaccessible to the intellectual villager who takes the fashion of his generation for the nature of mankind, are indispensable to him. They are indispensable, however, not because they relate to what is called the past, but because they are specimens cut from a continuous life of which past and present—itself the past before the word 'present' can be completed—are different aspects.

If society is to be master of its fate, reason conquer chance, and conscious direction deliver human life from the tyranny of nature and the follies of man, the first condition is a realistic grasp of the materials to be handled and the forces to be tamed. The historian serves, on his own humble plane, that not ignoble end. His object is to understand the world around him, a world whose cultural constituents and dynamic movements have taken their stamp and direction from conditions which the experience of no single life is adequate to interpret. He is pursuing that object as directly when he measures the skulls of paleolithic man, studies the financial institutions of the Roman Empire, or charts prices of wheat sold on a medieval manor, as in investigating the antecedents of the latest economic crisis. If he visits the cellars, it is not for love of the dust, but to estimate the stability of the edifice, and because, to grasp the meaning of the cracks, he must know the quality of its foundations. In this sense, there is truth in the paradox that all history is the history of the present; and for this reason each generation must write its history for itself. That of its predecessors may be true, but its truth may not be relevant. Different answers are required because different questions are asked. Standing at a new point on the road, it finds that new ranges in the landscape come into view. It discovers that phenomena, which formerly appeared irrelevant, are a vital part of itself. It realises, in short, and sometimes realises too late that what it supposed to be the past is in reality the present.

If, however, the business of the historian is not merely the harmless satisfaction of an antiquarian curiosity, but the study of society, he approaches that study from an angle of his own. Human societies are not the only societies; but biologists tell us that among their qualities is one which is unique. Unlike communities of ants and bees, they are subject to change, and to change which is primarily, not a biological, but a cultural, phenomenon. Hence, of necessity, they reveal their characteristics, not simultaneously, but successively. They are not static, but dynamic; time is one of their dimensions; and, if seen only in the flat, they are not seen at all. Just as an individual human being is not known, unless known at different periods of his life and in varying social relations, so a civilisation is to be understood only by assembling the different aspects revealed in different phases of its growth. It acts in different ways at different times, and what is acting is, in spite of these differences, the same civilisation. To know it as it is, it is necessary to resist the illusion— it is not easily resisted—that it is in its essence what at one moment or another it appears to be.

When crises occur, that truism is self-evident. No one supposes that the characteristics of the peoples of England, France, and Russia are what intelligent observers supposed them to be in 1600, 1780 and 1910, or that the Europe which he knew in 1914 was the only Europe to be known. But it is equally relevant to the secular movements which alter social geology, and whose action is unseen till their effect is complete. 'This Island was blessed, sir, by Providence,' remarked Mr. Podsnap, 'to the Direct Exclusion of such Other Countries as there may happen to be. . . . There is in the Englishman a combination of qualities, a modesty, an independence, a responsibility, a repose, combined with an absence of anything calculated to call a blush into the cheek of a young person, which one would seek in vain among the other Nations of the Earth.' Temporal, as well as national, frontiers produce their Philistines; and the provincialism which erects its generalisations from observations of one aspect of one type of human being in one kind of civilisation at one point in its development, without the qualifications by which judicious thinkers limit their conclusions, is a species of Podsnappery which, though obviously superficial, is not wholly extinct even among the elect. It is the rôle of the historian, by observing social behaviour in different conditions and varying environments, to determine the characteristics of different types of civilisation, to discover the forces in which change has found its dynamic, and to criticise the doctrines accepted in each epoch as self-evident truths in the light of an experience ampler than, without his assistance, any one of them can command. The rôle of the economic historian is to do so with special reference to the interests, which at the moment I need not more precisely define, concerned with the acquisition of a livelihood in a world of limited resources, the social groupings which arise from them, and the problems which they produce. It is ultimately to widen the range of observation from the experience of a single generation or society to that of mankind.

Experience does not yield instruction to simple inspection. It requires interpretation. Methodological discussions have some resemblance to those Chinese dramas the spectator of which, after listening for five hours to a succession of curtain-raisers, discovers that the performance is over at the moment when he hoped that it was about to begin; and I shall not inflict upon you a discussion of the logical problems of historiography. I will only say that the view on which interesting, if sometimes, perhaps, needlessly portentous, works have been written—the view that the subject-matter of history precludes generalisation—is not one which I share. Whether in its cruder version, which suggests that that subject-matter is a string of events, of which each is unique and all discontinuous, or in the subtler statement that the entities with which history deals—peoples, institutions, phases of civilisation—are collective wholes which can be intuitively grasped, but not analysed by reason, it seems to me to do violence to the procedure, not only of history, but of all other social sciences, and not only of science, but of ordinary human behaviour.

To say that a phenomenon—a bone found in a barrow, a political institution, an historical event—occurs in the same setting once and no more, is not to say that it is unique, but merely that it is individual. It is a platitude that identity in difference is the foundation of thought; and, so far from the fact that a phenomenon is individual precluding generalisation as to characteristics which it possesses in common with similar phenomena whose setting is different, it is precisely that fact which alone makes generalisation either possible or instructive. The generalisations of the historian, like those of the anthropologist and sociologist, take the form, it is true, not of propositions claiming universal validity, but of statements of the relations between phenomena within the framework of a specific epoch or civilisation. But, if relative to their context, which can be as large as a thinker has the capacity to make it, they are not less instructive within it. The historian need not be deterred from attempting, what in ordinary life is habitually done, the discovery of significant connections by comparison and analysis.

That is obvious when the field is limited, and the materials to be handled homogeneous in character. Whether the historian is dealing with a period, with the generation, for example, after 1815 or the critical forty years before the English Civil War, or with a problem, such as the causes which led to the precocious development of the great industry in England and have given English agriculture and rural society their distinctive stamp, light can obviously be thrown on the subject by the establishment of relations both within the region of strictly economic phenomena—monetary changes, prices, wages, rents, the growth of trade and public revenue—and, not less important, between that region as a whole and political and intellectual movements which appear at first unconnected with it. The same method is valid, if more difficult to apply, on a larger scale. Nothing, indeed, could be less appropriately described as unique and self-contained than the stages in the economic development of European countries. Nationality is a category which is applicable only to a late phase in the history of Europe, and which to certain of its most important aspects is, except with large qualifications, not applicable at all. It has, of course, its significance, which the historian must explain; but the idea that any department of economic life, except the policy of governments, can be adequately interpreted in terms of it is an illusion to be discarded. No European nation has worked out its economic destiny in isolation. All have lent and all have borrowed. The economic civilisation of each is a cosmopolitan achievement which is the creation of its neighbours hardly less than of itself.

Whatever he thought of the generalisations in which it has been attempted to formulate the characteristics of that common evolution —whether or not we accept theories such as that which suggests that large-scale enterprise has a continuous history in Europe from the later Roman Empire, in which the landmarks are Byzantium, Venice and North Italy, South Germany, and the Low Countries; or that economic development is marked by a rhythmic movement of long alternating phases of expansion and contraction; or that economic organisation has passed through recurrent stages in which mastery over the processes of economic life oscillates between the poles of collective control from below and authority exercised from above; or that European history is the record of the rise, conflicts and decline of successive classes; or that the critical accelerations and retardations in the development of different countries are the result of tidal movements launched by alterations in the price-level; or that the main impetus to social change has come from the growth and shifting of population—there is no doubt of the part played in giving a common stamp to European economic life, not only by similarities of environment, but by migration, rivalry and direct imitation. Whether, in short, he agrees, or not, with diffusionist theories of pre-history, the economic historian, who begins where it ends, while not ignoring other factors, must pay his tribute to diffusionism. In such circumstances, comparative study reveals relations of similarity and contrast without a grasp of which neither the past evolution of economic society nor its present characteristics can be understood. It is not only, of course, within the limits of Western economic civilisation that comparison is instructive. A student is not likely to make much of the sharply contrasted Industrial Revolutions now taking place in China and Russia, if unacquainted with the conditions which produced different versions of the corresponding movement in England, Germany and the United States, and retarded it in France. Nor, perhaps, will he be unaided in understanding some of the peculiarities of industrial civilisation in Europe if he reads with discrimination such a study of a pre-industrial society as is contained in the admirable book of Dr. Raymond Firth on the economic life of the Maori.

Since the sources for economic history are vast and still largely unworked, the historian must be an investigator. But research is a means, not an end, and it is less important to discover new materials than to see the meaning of old. In handling them, he must naturally learn from both the economic theorist and the sociologist. Except as a story embalmed, with other legends, in the mausoleum of text-books, the issue between theorists and historians was never a serious affair. In Germany, where methodological discussions are popular, it struck some sparks. In England, if it arose at all, it was a skirmish of camp-followers, and is now long dead. It is obvious that the historian must be interested in theory, for more than one reason. Theories have a history, sometimes drab, sometimes exciting, sometimes merely morbid. The children of the conditions which they are formulated to explain, they reveal the traits of mortality most unmistakably when, with the *naïveté* of youth, they claim to be immune from it, and overcome the contingencies of this transitory life only by acquiring sufficient sophistication to recognise and admit them. It is the pious duty of the historian, who guards the tombs of the long line of their ancestors, without forgetting to reserve a place for those of their descendants, to explain to their exponents the peculiar combinations of circumstances which made possible their birth and occasioned their demise.

Not only, however, does he watch by the cradle of theories and follow their bier, he is interested in them also for reasons less altruistic. Correctly employed, the expression 'economic theory' should include, on the analogy of other sciences, all concepts found useful in the analysis and systematisation of economic phenomena. Part of the historian's work is done with such concepts. Not all, of course, are equally serviceable to him; nor can he restrict himself to the doctrines most prominent in the canonical books of the economic scriptures, if only for the reason that it is precisely the interaction between the economic and non-economic aspects of society which, as the example of Adam Smith should be sufficient to remind us, is a central part of his theme. But, in so far as he uses concepts formulated by economists, as for some purposes he must, he must obviously seek enlightenment from those who are their masters. No one supposes that legal history can be written without a knowledge of law, or military history without some familiarity with strategy, or ecclesiastical history without an acquaintance with the organisation and doctrines of churches; no one should suppose—though many apparently do—that the political historian can dispense with an analytical study of the phenomena which fall within the province of the political scientist. It would be equally irrational to imagine that those aspects of human affairs which are the special concern of the economic historian can be handled without some tincture of the technique devised by economic theorists.

In so far as there is a divergence between his outlook and theirs, it arises less from differences of interpretation with regard to those matters with which both are equally concerned, than from the fact that the nature of his work makes it necessary for him to take account of considerations which the theorist, with his more specialised interests, may properly treat lightly. Thus, for one thing, the historian cannot ignore the part which is played in economic development by forces other than economic. Their significance can, of course, be over-emphasised. They have been over-emphasised in my judgment by some scholars who have brought to their subject the categories of political history; and it might fairly be argued—to take a very different example—that the brilliant work of Max Weber, at any rate in the essays by which it is most widely known in England, sought in the region of ideas and psychology an interpretation of movements susceptible of simpler explanations. The fact remains, however, that the civilisation of an age forms a connected whole the different elements of which interact, and that, as a consequence, economic causation does not work in a straight line which can be traced without reference to other forces which twist and divert it. The plane on which evolution takes place is determined, in short, by factors, both positive and negative—legal systems, governmental policies, scientific and cultural attainments, class organisation, and, not least, the most neglected factor in social development, the institution of war—which, if rooted in economic conditions, can hardly be described as directly economic. An account of it which ignores them is necessarily abstract and artificial.

For another thing, the historian's scale of magnitudes is different from that of the theorist, and the difference of scale throws into relief different aspects of the landscape. The geography of the explorer is not that of the surveyor, though the latter is part of it. Working, as he does, with a large map, the historian is compelled to take account of Alps and steppes which can be provisionally neglected by those who operate more intensively in a narrower field. The difference is illustrated by the familiar contrast between the degrees of emphasis laid by economic historians and economic theorists on the institutional structure. Its importance depends partly on the length of the period which is under review. The theorist, concerned with short segments of time, over which legal and political systems may be assumed to be constant, may reasonably, for his own purposes, take them for granted, as the historian normally ignores climatic and geological changes which are of vital importance to the student of pre-history. These systems, however, are historical products; they have changed in the past, and will change in the future. In so far as it assumes the existence of any one of them, the conclusions of economic theory, some of its exponents would agree, if valid in that context, are less cogent outside it. Unless purely formal they are true *rebus sic stantibus*; with modifications in institutions and social psychology, they require to be modified. The question, it may be observed in passing, whether such modifications are possible or to be desired, the question of the permanence or merits of any particular social order, is one which the theorist who takes this view of his subject—others, of course, may be taken—properly regards, *qua* theorist, as not within his province. It is permissible to reach conclusions by assuming as a premise an existing body of institutions. It is illegitimate to argue as to the merits of the institutions by appealing to conclusions based on the assumption of their existence.

Economic historians have sometimes made too much of the institutional side of their subject; but they cannot ignore the masonry which canalises and deflects economic currents. They are concerned, not merely with the market, but with the forces behind it. They cannot investigate the rise of new forms of economic enterprise without reference to the conditions which have given enterprise its opportunity, or understand historical changes in the distribution of wealth without a study of corresponding changes in the institution of property, the class-structure of society, and the policy of states. Even were they persuaded by Professor Simkhovich that one factor in the decline of the Roman Empire was the exhaustion of the soil, it would still be necessary for them to turn to the great work of Professor Rostovtseff to study the collapse of organisation which made irreparable the effect of economic strains.

Nor, if the generalisations of historians contain a large element of contingency, are they on that account devoid of light or fruit. It is natural that the plain man who resides in all of us should regard as inevitable and immutable the economic arrangements most familiar to himself; he has always done so, and presumably always will. But, in the world as known to science, there is no such phenomenon as an 'economy' in general, any more than there is a law, religion or art which exists in independence of time and space. There are only particular economic, as there are particular legal and religious, systems. It is these particular systems which alone can be studied, because they alone exist. The individual valuations and their expression in price relationships which I understand—though I speak with diffidence—to be the special concern of the theorist, take place within a framework fixed partly by nature, partly by legal and customary arrangements, partly by the cultural and intellectual level of the society concerned. The relevance of his generalisations to any particular set of conditions can be determined only when the special features of those conditions have been investigated.

To say this is not, of course, to question their value; truths do not cease to be true because they are formal. It is merely to recall the commonplace that the tension between human wants and the limited resources available for satisfying them takes place, not in a vacuum, but in a specific cultural environment, by which the character both of the wants and of the resources is determined. If, for example, the formula that earnings correspond to marginal productivity be accepted, the question of practical importance is where the margin stands. The answer to it can be given only by a study of the objective conditions, from the law of inheritance to the organisation of industry and the system of education, which determine the accessibility of different occupations and the supply of workers competing for entrance to each. The law of diminishing utility is, doubtless, illustrated by the savage, who, having eaten one missionary, finds his appetite for a second temporarily jaded, not less than by a produce exchange in London or New York, or by the familiar procedure of exchanging nuts for apples, which is so common a transaction of every-day economic life. In so far, however, as it is true of both, it throws a somewhat less brilliant light on the special characteristics which are distinctive of each, on the conditions which cause different societies to choose different diets, and on the forces which cause a transition to take place from one plane of economic civilisation to another.

It is these distinctive conditions and forces which are the special province of the historian, as formal analysis is that of the theorist. In practice, of course, it is necessary to employ the methods of both. A student unpractised in analysis would be as impotent to unravel the morbid monetary history of the sixteenth and seventeenth centuries as that of our own day, which compared with it, is lucid; but, unless his grasp of analytical methods were supplemented by some knowledge of the special financial and political conditions of the Europe of the Renaissance, his interpretation of that history would be more hypothetical than realistic. It would obviously be presumptuous for him to consider questions relating to the distribution of wealth in different periods and societies, without having familiarised himself with the doctrines on that subject enunciated by theorists; but his account of its peculiarities in England and France would be somewhat unsubstantial, unless he knew something of the development of land tenure, industry and taxation in the countries in question, by which, among other factors, it has, in fact, been determined. To discover grounds of contention between sciences whose procedure is so different, while much of their subject-matter is the same, requires a more than ordinary degree of megalomania or muddle-headedness. Since neither is conceivable in the children of light, the most plausible explanation of such differences as may have occurred in the past is the medieval *suadente diabolo*—the intervention of the Prince of Intellectual Darkness.

Conceived in this manner, economic history obviously has close affinities with sociology. The sciences differ, it is true, in two important respects. The concern of the sociologist, as I understand his work, is primarily with the general. It is to produce a classification of societies and institutions, and to do so without more than a passing reference to the particular context in which historically they occur. The concern of the historian begins with the particular, though it does not end with it. His business is to systematise the turbulent world of concrete facts; and, while for that purpose he must make a large use, and should make a larger one, of hypotheses such as those formulated by the sociologist, he is more concerned than the latter in testing their applicability to specific situations. The sociologist brings the result of his researches to one plane; he is more interested in types than in the order in which they occur. To the historian change, or the absence of change, is a crucial aspect of life, and to establish a sequence, not merely of events, but of phases or stages of development is, therefore, vital to him. These, however, are differences of emphasis, not of substance; and, if the starting-point of the sociologist and the historian is different, their objective is the same. Both are engaged in the attempt to determine the characteristics of different types of civilisation, and to discover the causes which produce a transition from one to another; both use for that purpose analysis and comparison; and, if the sociologist must be something of an historian in assembling his materials, the historian must learn from the sociologist the critical use of the concepts by which alone they can be made to yield light. In reality, as a glance at the work of the most eminent of both is sufficient to show, the sciences meet in their higher ranges.

It would be presumptuous to suggest that sociologists have not exhausted the possible services of history to their subject. But I do not feel the same diffidence in expressing the view that the future of history, and, in particular, of economic history, depends on its ability to acquire a more consciously sociological outlook. The advance of historical technique during the last half-century has been impressive. But, especially in England, progress in methods of investigation has not, in my judgment, been accompanied by a corresponding progress in methods of treatment and interpretation.

For one thing, historians, with certain conspicuous exceptions, have continued to employ unanalysed concepts—nation, state, political power, property, progress, commercial supremacy, and a host of similar *clichés*—with an exasperating *naïvéte*. If critical in their use of sources, they have been astonishingly uncritical of the conceptions employed to interpret the data derived from them. Such scrupulousness as to facts and casualness as to categories is as though a judge should be a master of the law of evidence, and then base his decisions on the juristic notions of the tenth century. For another thing, with certain brilliant exceptions, they have preferred burrowing to climbing. They make a darkness, and call it research, while shrinking from the light of general ideas which alone can illuminate it. In the third place, the narrative form which descends from the chronicle, and which is still the commonest method of organising historical material, is not adequate to a large range of problems facing the historian to-day. It has its uses, sometimes very magnificent ones; but, as the greatest of early historians long ago discovered, it is too simple a procedure to reveal effectively the relations between different elements in a complex situation, the explanation of which is a large part of the business of economic

K

history. In these matters the practitioners of that science must learn, not only from the sociologists, but from the legal historians, whom the nature of their subject-matter compelled from the start to make a large use of comparison, hypothesis and argument.

The task before them—I do not refer to subjects needing specialised research, which are inexhaustible, but to the major problems for which research supplies the data—are of a kind to make such methods indispensable. I will give only two examples. Economic history should be, of all forms of history, the least national, for economic civilisation is an international creation. But the corollaries of that truism have still to be applied. What is needed is nothing less than a complete change of emphasis. Instead of national economic histories, containing incidental references to international economic relations, we require histories which will take as their main theme a comparative treatment of movements and problems common to several different countries—comparative studies, for example, of the rise of the great industry or of agricultural development—and treat phenomena peculiar to particular nations against that larger background. Most persons—to give a second illustration —must have felt a certain sense of unreality in reading much that is described as political history. It says so much, and explains so little. But, in so far as its defects are those of conventionality and abstraction, they are not to be corrected by placing another conventional abstraction, labelled economic history, side by side with it. Having caricatured political and religious development by isolating it from its economic and social background, we must not proceed to repeat that blunder under the guise of correcting it, or ignore the effect on the economic aspects of life of changes in the world of politics and religion. The only adequate history is *l'histoire integrale*, and the limitations of specialisms can be overcome only by a treatment which does justice at once to the economic foundations, the political superstructure and the dynamic of ideas. Such a history is, doubtless, remote. But there is no reason why savages should have all the science. It is possible to conceive economic historians and sociologists preparing the way for it by combining to treat economic and social organisation—forms of property, class structure, economic enterprise—in some modern period with the same detachment and objectivity as anthropologists bring to the investigation of similar phenomena in more primitive societies.

III

I am conscious that to many persons Economic History, as I have attempted to portray it, will appear to lack most of the qualities which give History its charm. I am not indifferent, I trust, to its literary aspects; nor am I disposed to dispute Professor Trevelyan's statement that what is significant is that men did the thing they did, not why the thing was done. At the moments when I forget that I am a teacher in a School of Economics, I confess to an unregenerate pleasure in the clang of decisive action, and in the noise which human beings make in the rare hours when they rise to it. But I do not think that a man will be less touched by the opening chapters of Michelet for having studied the economic paths which led to the precipice, or less stirred by Froude's picture of Robert Aske riding home from the cub-hunting to find his way barred by the floods and the rebels, because he knows the conditions which for a thousand years made the social problem of Europe, not the wage-earner, but the peasant. It is permissible to hope that science and art are not finally irreconcilable.

7

Eileen Power

ON MEDIEVAL HISTORY AS A SOCIAL STUDY
(L.S.E., 1933)

This inaugural lecture was delivered at the London
School of Economics on the 18th January 1933.

ON MEDIEVAL HISTORY AS A SOCIAL STUDY

THE holder of a Chair of Economic History in a school of social sciences finds himself faced at the outset by a problem of integration. In less specialised universities or university institutions, where all the arts and sciences are gathered together, he can perhaps afford to pursue his way by an inner light of his own, not very profoundly affected by what the physicist is doing on one side of him or the classicist on the other, because the roads upon which they move are widely separated from his. But a Professor of Economic History in a school devoted specifically to the social sciences cannot look upon his department as a separate entity. He is bound to regard himself as a co-worker in a common field, his subject as a companion-study both to economics and to sociology, since the object of all these social sciences is the same. They seek to elucidate the present by the discovery of how things work. Their common watchword is the watchword of the School: *Felix qui potuit rerum cognoscere causas.*

It is true that the relationship between the three studies has sometimes been distinguished by hostility as well as by cooperation. Professor F. H. Knight, writing recently in an American journal, remarked on the unsatisfactory result of polemics as to what it means to explain social phenomena, in which one group of students seem to be in possession of the problems and another in possession of the data, and the two are living in separate universes of discourse.[1] This separation among students whose ultimate aim is the same has, I fear, been due (in part at least) to a lack of mutual esteem, arising from an imperfect understanding of each other's subjects and methods. Their relations are too often those of the good and the clever in the rhyme. The historians are so hard on the sociologists, and the economists so rude to the historians, that any improvement in the world of social science seems almost beyond human hope.

What, we may ask ourselves, is the true relation between social history and sociology? It must be perfectly plain that a science concerned with the study of man in society must turn to history for one of its most prolific sources of data. Yet if we examine the best works of general sociology we shall discover that the use which they make of historical evidence is comparatively small, and that those chapters in which they deal with it are usually inferior to the chapters in which

111

they deal with anthropological evidence. They draw their best material from contemporary field-work among primitive societies or in Middletown, but the space between the Trobriand Islanders and Main Street is a howling void, and the whole process of change in time is to a great extent shirked. For this I think the blame must be placed not upon the sociologist, but upon the historian. The former cannot make use of the latter's evidence, because the historian has rarely asked himself the questions to which the sociologist wants an answer. The fact is that, in England at any rate, while historians have always regarded the moral sciences and have latterly regarded economic science as perfectly respectable, they have not yet been willing to admit the respectability of sociology. The result has been unfortunate for themselves as well as for sociology. It has led them to produce what they call social history perfunctorily and without a knowledge of the theoretical problems involved, with the result that the subject is justly held in disrepute as vague and spineless. Too often it is a mere adjunct to political history, a backcloth like the famous Chapter III of Macaulay, or a tailpiece like those paragraphs on 'the life of the people' which are sometimes tacked on to the end of each chapter in school text-books. Properly defined, social history is, of course, the very reverse of this. It is a structural analysis of society, a line of approach to historical investigation which requires as rigorous a mental discipline and as scientific a methodology as any of the longer-established branches of history. It is not that we are without examples of what social history can be when systematically treated. It is unnecessary to go as far afield as the work of Weber and Sombart for an illustration; that vast integrated study of Local Government, in which Mr. and Mrs. Webb have made all the social sciences their debtors, is an outstanding one; and in another sphere the work of Professor Tawney shows how illuminating the consciousness of a problem can be for the study of history. Nor do I despair of the rise of a school of sociological historians in this country. The English are adept at two things. They have M. Jourdain's gift for talking prose unawares; and while in learning, as in politics and morals, they are mortally afraid of names, they have a healthy capacity for swallowing facts. We must make allowances for the race which disguises the white man's dividend as the white man's burden, and while historians will no doubt continue to meet the charge of writing sociology with the indignation of a Victorian matron defending her virtue, the best of them will increasingly write it under the name of social history.

In the case of economics the boot is on the other leg, for the virtuous recoil comes from the economist, who smells a return to a bankrupt *Historismus* and rushes into the somewhat antiquated arms of Windleband and Rickert for defence. Well, we have all herded swine with the Hegelians, as Heine put it; and (I would add) if not with the Hegelians with the Kantians. It is apparently easier to detect the 'Hegelian twaddle' in Marx than the Kantian twaddle in Rickert. I shall endeavour to placate the economists by admitting that the economic historians have not fed them with pearls. The Historical School took far too much upon itself. It was mistaken in supposing that an inductive method could dispense with deduction in economics, while economic history, on its side, has suffered, just as social history has suffered, from the fact that it has not always known what questions to ask itself. The complaint of the economist that the economic historian mistakes the nature of some of his own problems through his inadequate knowledge of economic theory is often justified; and there is no doubt that the more perfected deductive method of the economist is an essential component in any methodical study of economic history. With this handsome admission I may, perhaps, be permitted to suggest that the recoil of the economist from the historical method, as an alternative line of approach, has gone too far. A purely deductive science of economics has its limitations and dangers. In so far as the laws of economics are formal and deal with formal symbols, they are inapplicable to economic reality, and before they can be applied or verified, they require the introduction of evidence drawn from the economic past, as well as from the economic present. If, on the other hand, the economist denies the social and substantial character of his science so completely as to hide his head amid a crowd of stars and consort solely with the higher mathematicians (whose speech is a tinkling symbol) then no *Methodenstreit* arises, because the spheres of economist and historian coincide at no point. Nevertheless, however much the economist may eschew a social purpose, we do have an hallucination—*nous autres*—that his voice is raised in the discussion of actuality. The pure economist is not so pure when it comes to controversy. If he will forgive me the expression, he is something of an economic *demi-vierge*. ' "History shows," commences the bore at the club and we resign ourselves to the prediction of the improbable.'[2] Very true; but 'Economics shows,' commences his twin brother, writing to *The Times*, and we resign ourselves to two rival counsels of the unattainable. Nor indeed do I blame even the purest of pure economists for these excursions into the dusty realm of reality. The essentially social character of much of his subject-matter robs it of the impersonality of physics or mathematics; and if his method be exclusively formal he tends not to rise to the position of the pure scientist, but to degenerate into that of the medieval scholastic, playing with his version of 'How many angels can stand on the tip of a needle'—or, it may be, of a gold point.

I believe that anthropologists, sociologists, economists and historians are all to-day alive to the necessity for an integration of their labours, based upon a comprehension of each other's objects, capacities and methods. If each recognizes what he properly can and cannot do, and at what point he requires the co-operation of the others, we need not be without hope that something worthy of the name of a social science *par excellence* may emerge. But if we are to find that 'dependable uniformity and regularity' in the flux of phenomena, the discovery of which is the common object of physical and social sciences alike, we can only do so by a co-operative effort. And I cannot refrain from quoting here the words of one of the wisest men who ever taught in this School, Professor Allyn Young. Citing a remark of Mill that in the study of man and society 'the besetting danger is not so much of embracing falsehood for truth as of mistaking part of the truth for the whole,' Professor Young added. 'These are words for all inquirers in the field of the social sciences to remember. Our work is retarded and our intellectual energies are dissipated in useless quarrels, because of our intolerance of methods and points of view other than our own. There are only two things of which we have a right to be intolerant, the first is positive errors of fact or of inference, the second is intolerance itself.'[3]

In speaking to you, then, about social and economic history, I am speaking about something which I conceive to stand in an integral relationship with the two studies of social and economic theory. Social history is, of course, a wide subject, and under it may be included interpretative studies whose aim is somewhat different, such (for example) as those illuminating books in which Dr. Coulton (a great scholar and a great humanist) has made medieval life live again. But the main business of the historian whose work lies in a school of social studies is to contribute his data and the assistance of his method to the general purpose of elucidating the present. We know that the object of economist and sociologist is the study of certain spheres of human behaviour, with a view to establishing the laws which govern relationships within those spheres. It seems to me that the business of the social-economic historian is to demand of his material the questions which they want answered, to the end that observation and comparison may be integrated with more deductive methods into a single scientific process. For the substance, of which they seek to descry the forms, lies spread over the field of time as well as of space, and neither can proceed to a complete mastery of his science, without taking into his calculations that vast section of the field which lies in the past. I propose, therefore, to begin by examining the method by which the social historian ought to proceed and the nature of the contribution which he may hope to make.

The first essential is to ask the right questions. This is not nearly so easy as it sounds and in order to pose the right question the social-economic historian requires a theoretical equipment. As Sombart has remarked, 'No theory, no history.' The theory, however, must be relevant to the subject, which a good deal that passes under the name of economic theory is not. Nor is it only the economic theorists who are to blame. Economic historians, on their side, have often approached their subject either with no theory at all, or with a theory that is inappropriate to it, a legal, an institutional, or a political theory. This has produced many valuable collections of facts and has deepened our knowledge of legal, institutional and political development, but it has not given us economic history in any valid sense of the term. Vinogradoff's brilliant studies of the medieval manor are written from a legal rather than an economic standpoint, and the great work of Cunningham, to which we are all indebted as a piece of magnificent pioneering, is largely not an economic history but a history of economic policy.

The second ingredient in a satisfactory method is perhaps too obvious to mention; it is the necessity for the historian to examine his own premises, before he starts trying to find an answer to the questions which he has posed. Professor Tawney has recently pointed out that while the scientific historian habitually criticises his sources, he usually fails to criticise his concepts with anything like the same rigour. Our premises rarely get examined, because we are often quite unconscious of them. If they were I cannot resist the impression that the result would be a notice: 'These commodious—these much too commodious—premises to let.'

But given that our questions have been asked and our premises examined, what is the most useful method by which the social historian can proceed towards the discovery of an answer? I am not, of course, speaking of a method of historical research. That is a matter of technique, the job of the brickmaker. We historians all have to learn how to make bricks, often with very little straw—often with the one straw which shows the way the wind is blowing. But what I am speaking of here is something quite different, a method not of historical research, but of historical analysis and synthesis— the architect's job as compared with the brickmaker's. If we turn historical research into historical narrative, we are too often content. Yet the mere accumulation of historical data, even of a statistical character, may be 'a fit occupation for an economist in his dotage,' but it is certainly no occupation for an historian in his prime. If social and economic history is to be of value in the formulation of a science of society, the historical data require to be subjected to a rigid analysis, which is different from the method most commonly applied to the study of history to-day.

There are in existence a number of methodological schemes for dealing with the facts of social history. There is the method, of which Troeltsch is the most famous exponent, by which history is regarded as the concrete representation of individual wholes. These historical individuals may be epochs or events, like the Renaissance or the Reformation; the point is that they can be apprehended only as a whole and not in terms of separate factors in interaction, and the historian's business is to arrive at their real essence by a process of intuition. This is an essentially artistic approach to history and it has certain advantages, in that it stresses the close interaction of all elements in a given social situation; but in so far as it implies that these elements are all of a piece and inseparable, cannot (that is to say) be studied by abstracting them and comparing their operation in other given social situations, it appears to be based on a misapprehension of the historical process.

It was in order to define and delimit the nature of abstraction in history that Weber propounded his method of 'ideal types,' of which Sombart has provided the best-known examples. Sombart, as is well known, claims to provide a theoretical basis for economic history by means of the concept which he calls the economic system. An economic system, to quote his own definition, is 'a mode of satisfying and making provision for material wants, which can be comprehended as a unit and is animated by a definite spirit, regulated and organized according to a definite plan, and applying a definite technical knowledge.'[4] To the different economic systems there correspond, he goes on to assert, different periods of history, in which those systems have been dominant. With the twin concepts of the economic system and the economic epoch, he proceeds to analyse the historical phenomenon of modern capitalism, as contrasted with pre-capitalism, the economic system which corresponds to the medieval epoch. In his analysis medieval pre-capitalism is a want-supplying, whereas modern capitalism is a profit-making, system. The spirit of the Middle Ages is one of tradition, whereas the spirit of modern capitalism is one of unboundedness and of what he calls 'quantitative rationality' (meaning by rationality, of course, not reasonableness but the systematic adjustment of means to the single end of pecuniary profit—which may, or may not, be rational in the conventional sense of the term). Weber, it will be remembered, endeavoured to account for the rationality of the capitalist spirit by deriving it from religious values, which came to birth at the Reformation and were directly opposed to the values prevailing in the

Middle Ages. Both Weber and Sombart lay great stress on the complete objectivisation undergone by the capitalistic system. When fully developed, it, and each separate enterprise within it, pursues its own way of life, moved by its own purpose and organic law, irrespective of the individual and his chaos of warning motives.

This method of approaching the study of social-economic history has distinct advantages. It is a real analysis and designed very successfully to bring out the distinctive features of each individual type, as compared with other actual or possible types of economic order. But the difficulty about ideal types is that those who use them are so apt to confound them with concrete historical realities. When Sombart asserts that to the economic system there corresponds an economic epoch, he is taking an enormous sideways step, without any apparent realization that he has moved out of the path. A useful piece of methodological apparatus has become an historical individual; the lexicon is imperceptibly transformed into the book, which was to be read by its aid. Hence the storm of protest with which historians have greeted his description of the Middle Ages as a period of pre-capitalism. To make it conform to his type he had to consider capital accumulation as mainly derived from urban rents and medieval trade as essentially handicraft in character. But in actual fact, as medieval historians at once pointed out, capital accumulations were largely derived not from rents but from trade, and trade itself, so far from being a mere exchange between townsman and peasant, was a large-scale international affair, animated by the most intense profit-making spirit and differing from modern international commerce only in its range. What Sombart has never grasped is that historians do not criticise him because he is a theorist, or object to his making use of the economic system as a methodological device. What they do object to is his assimilation of the economic system with the economic epoch. They claim that he has used theory not to interpret but to manipulate the facts of history. And insofar as his ideal type ceases to be ideal, his method is as unscientific as that of Troeltsch.

But it is not only because the abstraction of ideal types is always in danger of ceasing to be an abstraction that Weber's concentration on this method is inadequate. Even if the ideal type could be made and kept on the level of a perfect abstraction, it would still be neither the only nor possibly the most helpful one. There are many aspects in history which can be isolated for the purposes of scientific abstraction and comparison, and the task of a social historian is to discover and to subject to scientific treatment all the repeatable aspects of social life. His function is in the first instance one of analysis, he has to show the connections between the different elements in a phase of civilization or an economic system, and thus to reveal its true nature. If he did this alone his work would be worth while. But the next stage in his business is to detach certain elements and, by comparing their operation in different surroundings and at different periods, to discover whether certain social phenomena are habitual. If he succeeds in doing this his evidence can be collated with the field-work of the anthropologist and of the descriptive sociologist (the field-worker in modern society) and the results expanded, wherever appropriate, by the apparatus of the deductive sciences, such as economic theory. Is it too much to hope that this may result in such an accumulation and classification of experience, with regard to those general problems to which we want answers, as may lead to the establishment of laws of social behaviour? Such a question, of course, involves the often-discussed problem as to whether there *can* be anything in the nature of a social law in the scientific sense of the term, and I am aware that not only economists but also historians are sceptical as to the possibility. Naturally it depends on what is meant by a law. No one in his senses has ever pretended that the laws obtainable by the social scientist from the investigation of social reality can be as logically satisfactory as the formal laws of the deductive sciences, or even as those of the physical sciences. Both material and investigator are subject to disadvantages which do not exist in the case of the other sciences. But I conceive the whole trend of modern sociological thought to be in support of the view that it is possible to analyse social behaviour into a certain number of universal abstract relations; and if such laws are no more than rough approximations, that is already a great deal.

It should be observed that in so far as it combines sociological induction with deductive analysis the method which I am suggesting is not very different from that by which Marx approached the study of history. The Marxian treatment of history is valuable not as an interpretation of the facts, but as a method of dealing with them; it combines induction with deduction in a way that all social history must do if it is to be of any use. 'No theory, no history.' Moreover, if it be cleared of all the excrescences with which it has been covered by Marx himself, and still more by his followers, it does no more than state that all important institutions and activities can be explained in terms of other social activities (which is much what the functional method in modern anthropology assumes), and that all phenomena are social phenomena. From this it draws the conclusion that the correlations between these different social phenomena can be stated in terms of general laws, which allow the formation of reasonably valid interpretations of the past and expectations of the future. As a matter of pure methodology Marxism does not necessarily bind us to a materialist interpretation of history, nor even to a belief in the dialectical process. The difficulty is that most Marxist historians swallow whole the particular conclusions reached by Marx and refuse to allow his method to be developed and used for the discovery of new conclusions. The Marxists have not been content with asking the right questions, with realizing (in Lord Acton's famous phrase) that the great sociologist, like the great historian, now 'takes his meals in the kitchen.' They have not infrequently used their position in the kitchen for the purpose of cooking the evidence.

So far I have endeavoured to suggest, first, that the progress of the social sciences depends upon a close integration of their work towards a common end, and secondly, that historical investigation, by making a wider use than it has hitherto done of abstraction and comparison, may play an important part in discovering to what extent (if any) 'social things have habits.' It is in this framework that I want to make my claim for the study of medieval history. I would urge that the Middle Ages is far from being the subject of mere antiquarian or romantic interest, which it is too often considered by those for whom the blessed date 1760 has taken the place of the blessed word Mesopotamia. Medieval like modern history can provide the economist with empirical data for checking his deductions and the historian with material to the elucidation of which the formal deductive methods of the economist can properly be applied. It is true that the use of medieval material is hampered by the scarcity of quantitative evidence; it is, as Professor Clapham would say, weak in 'entities with a metrical aspect.' But it is not so weak in them as economists are sometimes prone to imagine. For example it is perfectly feasible to study balance of trade problems in fifteenth-century England on the basis of the customs accounts, and there is adequate material for the compilation of that statistical history of prices, upon which an International Commission is even now at work. Moreover, apart altogether from these particular economic questions, medieval history is of great importance as a field for general sociological study and by no means irrelevant to an investigation of modern social problems.

The sociological study of questions of class, family, economic motive, the degree of rationality in the approach to economic affairs, or whatever else may be the object of investigation, naturally demands the whole of history for its field and medieval history can contribute only its share. But the period has certain general advantages. If an intelligent use of the comparative method be the heart and soul of sociological investigation, medieval history provides a peculiarly suitable basis for its application. It is so far removed from the present that neither contrasts nor similarities are blurred; each problem appears small and clear; it is

> like a little book
> Full of a thousand tales,
> Like the gilt page the good monks pen
> That is all smaller than a wren,
> Yet has high towers, meteors and men
> And suns and spouting whales,

and the advantage for the study of sociology is much the same as that possessed by anthropology. Again, medieval history comprises a long period of time, in which are included ages as distinct in outlook as that of the Merovingians at one end and the Italian Renaissance at another, and for this reason it is very well adapted for an intensive study of the operation of social change.

Medieval historians, moreover, have usually been more alive than modern historians to the theoretical aspects of their work. Recent discussions all bear upon fundamental problems, which just because they *are* fundamental, are of strictly contemporary interest. The problem of stages in social evolution, the problem of culture-contacts and their results, the problem of apparent breaches of continuity in the movement of civilisation, are all matters with which medieval historians have concerned themselves. But they are all lines of approach to an examination of the processes manifested in the phenomena of persistence, modifications and change, which is also the sociologist's business. Take, for instance, the fundamental question, which has occupied historians from the time of the humanists and is in the forefront of historical discussion to-day: what was the nature of the transition from ancient to medieval and from medieval to modern times? The old picture of this change was essentially cataclysmic. The Middle Ages was born in one revolution—the fall of the Roman Empire—and passed away in another—the Renaissance. During the intervening period everything was different, political organization, economic system, the very psychology of man. But the most recent work on the subject has shown the problem of the transition in a new light, which excludes the view that anything remotely resembling a revolution took place at either end. The cataclysmic view of the passage from ancient to medieval society has been slowly breaking down for a generation, a breakdown immensely stimulated in our own time by the results of archaeological investigation. Recent treatments of the later Roman Empire, of which Rostovtzeff's is the most suggestive, have shown us a world already moving rapidly towards a complete localization of economic life; every estate striving to be self-sufficient and cultivated by *coloni* tied to the soil, every province trying to produce the wares which it wanted for itself, the great inter-provincial and foreign commerce of the early Empire petering down to a mere local exchange, supplemented by a trade in luxuries for the rich. In fact the Roman world under the later Empire was a feudal world. On the other hand, we are now learning that the Germans of the fifth century were far from primitive and that the picture of village communities of free and equal warriors is a myth. The remarkable work of Dopsch has shown us that social inequality and private land-ownership were old phenomena in their history, and that after the settlement they merely continued further along the way of social differentiation which led to the great estate and servile labour. He has, moreover, demonstrated very successfully that the actual destruction which took place in the act of conquest has been greatly exaggerated. In fine, Rome was less Roman, the barbarians at once less barbarous and less democratic than we once supposed and both were more feudal. Though the invasions gave a jolt to the social process, and doubtless heightened its tempo, they did not alter its direction. The final result would probably have been much the same if Rome had never fallen.

Similarly the change from medieval to modern times is now known to have been less relatively abrupt than it used to be represented. The economy of the central period of the Middle Ages (say, the twelfth and thirteenth centuries) did not, in fact, correspond as closely as was once supposed to the ideal type of a closed, want-supplying economy, unconcerned with the idea of profit. We begin to see that the immobility and self-sufficiency of medieval economic institutions have been greatly exaggerated. It is untrue to say of the medieval estate (to use Marx's famous phrase) that 'the walls of the lord's stomach set a limit to his exploitation of his peasantry.' The accumulation of landed property by individuals and communities went far beyond the needs of their own consumption. A manor was not a self-sufficing unit, but in most cases produced a surplus, which came from peasants' holdings as well as from the lord's demesne and which was sold. Many manors, indeed, were grouped as part of a single estate, which was considered as a whole and organized for profit. The fact that an international trade in agrarian produce (corn, wine and wool) existed from early times throws a very revealing light upon the situation. The self-sufficing manor is also a myth. Industry, too, was far from being a mere handicraft system, carried on by master craftsmen in democratic gilds. Into the picture there must also be fitted the great capitalistic industry of the Flemish and Italian cloth towns, which as far back as the twelfth century was based upon a wage system and an elaborate division of labour, and was run by big entrepreneurs for an international market. Nor was trade the handicraft exchange between town and country, which it has been represented by Bücher and Sombart. International trade and international finance, based upon an elaborate credit system, animated by the unbounded desire for gain and capitalistic to the tips of its fingers, was already in existence in thirteenth-century Italy.

Thus the capitalistic spirit was at work on all sides in the Middle Ages. Economically the Bardi and Spini of the thirteenth century belong to exactly the same species of phenomena as the Fuggers and Haugs of the sixteenth and the Barings and Rothschilds of the nineteenth century. A captain of industry like Boine Broke of Douai is of the same species as Henry Ford. The discovery of new routes, more particularly by the influx of silver and consequent price revolution which it brought with it, allowed the old spirit more scope. Puritanism, with its conception of a calling, the Renaissance, with its striving towards boundless ends, may have manured a soil in which it could flourish—or we may take the Marxian view and say that it manured a soil in which they could flourish. But the birth of capitalism does not belong to the sixteenth century.

I have insisted on this gradual view of the *modus operandi* of change, because it has important implications for the social historian. The continuity thus established opens wide possibilities for the use of the comparative method. The fundamental institutions and functions of modern times are found to be in existence far back in the Middle Ages. They have been present over a great part of history in somewhat different forms and under different disguises. Just because they are omni-present, the differences which appear in different epochs can be compared and collated, in order to yield a better understanding of the essence of these functions and institutions. A very suggestive approach to the study of capitalism along these lines was made by Pirenne in a now famous article on *The Social Stages in the History of Capitalism*. In this, by a brilliant use of the comparative method, he sketched the evolution of capitalism from the eleventh century through five historical phases, analysing the similarities and differences which appear between phase and phase. Such an analysis brings us much nearer to a true understanding of the essence of capitalism, the forces which mould it and the forms of its transformation, than would have been possible on the old individualistic and cataclysmic interpretation. Just because Bardi, Fuggers and Rothschilds belong to the same species, they can be compared; just because there are differences between them, which must be due to the presence of variables, the historian can, by analysing these variables, play his part in elucidating the present.

I have in this long excursus endeavoured to show the extremely favourable opportunity offered by medieval history for a general inquiry into the nature of the social process. In common with the rest of the social sciences, it can make its contributions slowly and piecemeal, hoping that a scientific system will eventually emerge. But in addition to this patient and long-drawn-out inquiry there are also other ways in which the student of medieval history can be of assistance to the student of society. There are certain problems of modern life and politics which are demanding an immediate solution and with which economists and sociologists are trying to deal even before their science has provided them with infallible indications. Here, too, in problems of what may be called social technology as distinct from social science, medieval history can be of at least as much service as any other branch of history, or ideed as any other study. Let me take as an illustration two problems which are of contemporary importance and towards which I hold that an approach through the Middle Ages, by way of the comparative method, might have fruitful results. These problems are first, the problem of social control of the economic system; and secondly, the problem of the industrialization of the East.

Let us consider the first of these questions. The typical characterization of the Middle Ages may be accepted to this extent, that it was the period *par excellence* in which there was least rationality (in the narrow Sombartian sense of the term) in the approach to economic affairs. A certain control was exercised upon the economic system by an outside force, which may be described as subordination to a social end. From a sociological point of view, it is immaterial that the particular τέλος of the Middle Ages was religion, for that is merely one of many possible forms which a social end may assume. In the medieval view the economic system was not a self-contained sphere, obeying its own laws; it was part of a larger whole and must be subjected to the same purpose as that which governed the other departments of human life. The modern economic system of capitalism, on the other hand, is an objectivised system, obeying its own organic laws and dominated by no purpose other than its inherent purpose of profit-making.

This reading of the contrast between two civilizations, the one dominated to a great extent by non-economic motives, the other subdued to economic ends, the one obeying the mind of man, the other its own rule of life, raises problems which are of obvious contemporary interest. Clearly it is possible to exert a teleological control over the economic system, provided that you are agreed as to what your end is to be. The Middle Ages did it; we did it ourselves to a certain extent during the late war; and Soviet Russia is endeavouring to do it to-day. But we are still largely in the dark about the power of non-economic motives over the economic system, and the extent to which social control inevitably upsets the economic machine. It is of extreme interest to consider whether in the Middle Ages the teleological control was or was not operative; and, if it was operative, then what were the social conditions at the time which enabled it to be so. I cannot answer either of these questions, but an investigation of this type would, I suggest, be of more than academic interest. It would be strictly relevant to one of the fundamental problems of our age.

Again take my second problem, the problem of the industrialization of Asia, of a society (that is to say) in which capitalism as an economic system has not arisen spontaneously. As it presents itself to Chinese thinkers this is again a problem of the relationship of the economic system to the social order. Can we, they constantly ask, industrialize China, but avoid the evil social results of industrialization in Europe? Or are the two inseparable aspects of the same thing? In my view the historical method can be used as one line of approach towards a consideration of this problem; but it will involve a much more careful study of the origins of capitalism than they have ever yet received. The weakness of past investigations has lain in the fact that they have always contented themselves with asking why *has* capitalism arisen in Europe, not why *has not* capitalism arisen in Asia. Weber alone among the historians of capitalism perceived the bearing of the second question, and his posthumous text-book *General Economic History*, roughly put together as it is from students' lecture notes, shows what line his investigations would have taken had he lived. The problem why modern industrial capitalism has not risen spontaneously in Asia bristles with significance at every point. Why did not the great medieval trading societies of the Arabs, the Indians and the Chinese produce industrial capitalism as a stage following commercial capitalism, as was the case in the West? Why did not the invention of Arabic numerals, to which Sombart assigns such an important part in the quantitative rationalization of the economic enterprise, play the same part in the business of the people by whom the invention was made? Is there a psychological explanation? What are the variables in the situation? By making use of the comparative method cannot the European Middle Ages and the modern East be made to shed a light upon each other and the problem of economic motive and social control be brought a stage nearer to its solution?

To conclude, I have endeavoured in this lecture to assert a double claim for the study of history in a school of social sciences. I have urged that to be of any solid value social history must set before itself the general problems with which sociology is concerned and must investigate them, as far as possible, by the use of a genuinely scientific method of abstraction and comparison. I have suggested, moreover, that the study of the Middle Ages has its part to play in this process; and that for certain problems it has an advantage over other periods as a fruitful field of inquiry. If these claims be justified, the amount of pure research which still remains to be done is very great. An unlimited number of monographs is required. But the subjects to be investigated must be selected with an eye to the main problems; it must be recognized that they are separate pieces of a mosaic which has in the long run, when all the pieces are assembled, to form a design. Even before such a synthesis can be made, a consciousness of the theoretical problems involved and a perfected use of the comparative method in approaching them, will strengthen the vital connection which already exists, and should exist more fully. between social history and the other social sciences.

NOTES

1   F. H. Knight. 'Historical and Theoretical Issues in the Problem of Modern Capitalism,' *Journal of Economic and Business History* (1928), i, p. 120.
2   L. Robbins, *An Essay on the Nature and Significance of Economic Science* (1932), p. 74.
3   Allyn Young, 'Economics as a Field of Research,' *Quarterly Journal of Economics* (1927), xlii, p. 6.
4   W. Sombart, 'Economic Theory and Economic History,' *Economic History Review* (1929), ii, p. 14.

8

M. M. Postan

THE HISTORICAL METHOD IN SOCIAL SCIENCE
(Cambridge, 1939)

This inaugural lecture was delivered at the University of Cambridge on the 27th February 1939.

THE HISTORICAL METHOD IN SOCIAL SCIENCE

FEW other branches of university study are more indigenous to Cambridge than the one which I have the great honour to represent. It was in Cambridge that Archdeacon Cunningham laid the foundations of economic history as a university subject, and it was out of this University that the long stream of his pioneer books issued. Cunningham was a great missionary, for economic history was to him part of his political and philosophical faith. He believed that English thought, and English politics of his time, wanted rescuing from the a-moral and a-national prejudices of liberal economics and whig history; and it was from economic history as then taught in Germany that the cure would come. This belief led him to concentrate very largely on the problems of economic policy to the exclusion of many of the topics which form the scope of economic history now. Yet it is remarkable how, in spite of his preoccupations, the work has survived the faith which prompted it and in its main outlines endures to our own day. If economic historians of the next generation were able to devote themselves to specialized study, it was because the field was occupied for them and the foundation laid by Cunningham.

But what the generation which followed owed to the man who laid the foundation, the present generation owes to the man who built on them: the first holder of the Chair, the master mason who has preceded me. On the ground on which Dr Clapham has worked and still works he found a mass of half-knowledge, overgrown with picturesque and stubborn weeds. This ground he has not only cleared, but in his own inimitable, lapidary way, has covered with a structure of facts as hard and certain as granite. On his ground and in his manner nothing else remains to be done: so in Cambridge where the first phase of economic history was begun, the second has just been concluded.

I

With these achievements to precede him, no present holder of the Chair can claim to be a pioneer. He will never know the joy of staking out the first claims and of turning the first sod, or the greatest

129

of all joys, that of inventing new names. Yet he will be a hypocrite if he pretends not to relish the advantages of his position as an inheritor; above all, the great advantage of being able not to engage in his inaugural lecture in the great controversy of history as science *versus* history as art.

In so far as science means accuracy, and art good writing, their respective claims on historians have now been settled, for we all now agree with the Regius Professor that history should be both accurate and readable. But even if both science and art are defined by their objects—science as a search for general causes, art as an exercise in imaginative creation—the issue does not present itself to economic history, though it may still concern other branches of history. For in economic history the practices of its founders, the accident of its rise and the nature of its material, deprive the historian of real choice and condemn him to dwell with the social sciences.

The facts of economic history cannot be shaped, as a personal biography or a field of battle can, into an image with a direct appeal to our artistic sensibilities. Its most effective instrument, as Dr Clapham has so well argued and proved, is the impersonal language of statistical measurements. It came into existence not as an attempt to rival the novel or the drama in the recreation of life, but as an endeavour to assist in the solution of social problems. Its founders abroad were lawyer-sociologists of the romantic period, Möser, Guizot, Lamprecht, or the economists of the mid-century, Knies, Roscher, List. Its source of inspiration in this country is Adam Smith, and its ethos derives more from Bacon than from Shakespeare. So, much as economic historians would like to rank with the richest and oldest of the arts, they are compelled to serve the poorest and the youngest of sciences.

But for one controversy they have escaped they have raised legions of others. Having gone to dwell with the social sciences they have still to decide the details of the dwelling: what it is to be—detached or semi-detached, and where—in the public halls or the servants' quarters. All these are problems of cohabitation within the social sciences, and the very fact that the sites have not yet been completely marked out makes the choice uncertain and difficult.

Regarded superficially, the mood now prevailing among history's nearest neighbours is very propitious to economic and social history. A new wave of empiricism appears to be sweeping across regions hitherto inhabited by pure theory. The most general, and the least defined of social studies, sociology, is rapidly winding up its interest in comprehensive formulae and is turning into a comparative study of institutions: family, property, legal custom, class division. When done expertly, it merges into the specialized study of social evidence;

and since all social evidence, where it is not anthropological or statistical, is bound to be historical, much of sociology has been assuming the character of generalized and universalized history. Similarly, what now passes for political science is in large part concerned with political institutions as they are revealed in recent historical experience. And finally, economics—the field in which economic historians most frequently camp—has entered into one of its empirical phases.

The economists, like the theoretical sociologists of old, only more so, tried to solve the largest possible problems from the least possible knowledge. The ingenuity which went, and still goes, into some of the syllogistic exercises of theoretical economics is only rivalled by the unreality of some of its conclusions. But if some of its conclusions are capable of illuminating real problems of economic life, and economics as a whole is something more than a soufflé of whipped postulates, it is because even the most theoretical of economists sometimes manage to mix their theorems with a little social observation. The fact that the Cambridge economists, from Marshall to Keynes, have always tried to draw upon their personal observations of reality may account for the practical importance of their theoretical constructions. Marshall's capacity for interpolating a new empirical condition at each successive stage of his argument, and of calling in new facts to redress old conclusions, is perhaps the most striking feature of his method. And no reader of Keynes's general theory will fail to observe the central position occupied in it by two acutely observed empirical scales.

But what in books of Marshall or Keynes is an occasional spark of private wisdom now promises, or shall I say threatens, to become an organized branch of economic study. The realization that their subject has been purer than it ought to be has led the economists to insist upon the need for inductive study. In this country very recently, in the United States and Germany for quite a long time, an ever-growing amount of academic effort has been turned to the collection of economic facts. Studies of individual industries, of individual firms, of price and wage movements, commercial treaties and legislative methods, have been flooding the market. Measured by bulk, most American economic study is devoted to collection of facts. Similarly measured, the syllabus of the Economics Tripos in Cambridge consists very largely of courses on this or that industry, this or that region. And to listen to fashionable economic talk, one might think that the whole race of economists has become converted to the religion of the counting machine.

So, superficially, it would appear that history, as the repository of the empirical facts which the economist and sociologist can employ, has come to its own again, and that the social sciences are once again becoming historical. And yet, if truth be known, much of the recent hankering for facts and wooing of facts and amassing of facts, appears to an economic historian as far removed from history and as irrelevant to the real business of empirical study as are the arm-chair fantasies of the sociologists or the pure abstractions of the mathematical economists. For though in a sense all facts are historical facts, and all historical facts are social evidence, the data which the economists and sociologists now accumulate are seldom employed in a way which an economic historian would recognize as historical.

History is something which is both more and less than what sociologists and economists now make of it. It is certainly something more than an assemblage of data. We all know that what now distinguishes the honourable occupation of antiquaries from the questionable occupation of historians is that whereas antiquaries collect facts historians study problems. To a true antiquary all past facts are welcome, to an historian facts are of little value unless they are causes, or parts of causes, or the causes of causes, of the phenomena which he studies. A description of an industry wherein all the facts which strike the student's eye are assembled is a piece of economic antiquarianism. Economic history ends at the point at which the facts cease to answer questions, and the nearer the questions are to social problems and the more completely the problems dominate the search for facts, the nearer is the study to the true function of history in social science.

These obvious remarks may strike economists as an admonition delivered at a wrong address, for in the past the economists were apt to justify their indifference to historical study by the alleged irrelevance of economic history to the problems of economics. With this accusation we shall presently deal: for the alleged irrelevance of the topics of economic history is not altogether the historian's fault. But even if it were, the fact remains that the amount of useful knowledge or just ordinary sense that can be derived from the flood of empirical studies is incommensurate with the effort expended on them. And if that is so, it is not because the searchers are incompetent, the evidence intractable, or other sciences uncooperative, but because the main direction of the so-called empirical economics is at fault. The economists so seldom derive from their facts the theoretical knowledge they require because they do not ask from their facts the kind of question facts can answer.

We have just said that the nearer the question is to a social problem, the more completely it dominates a fact, so much the nearer it is to history and to the true business of social science. This economists understand only too well; what they perhaps do not realize is that for the purposes of empirical study the question, the dominating problem, is not necessarily given by the theoretical conclusions of abstract economics. The prevailing tendency among economists is to believe that, having arrived at a conclusion by a long and complicated series of deductions from original propositions, they can then proceed to verify it on historical and statistical facts. I do not want to suggest that that verification is always impossible, or where possible undesirable. In fields in which the original assumptions correspond closely to an experience which is real, easily discoverable, and limited in range, conclusions are sometimes arrived at, which subsequent empirical study can check. No reader of Taussig's book on the History of American Tariffs, or Viner's on Canada's Foreign Trade, or Bresciani-Turoni's on German Inflation, can fail to notice how well some propositions of economics can be supported by historical facts. Far be it from me to deny the possibility or the value of attempts at verification such as these. But the bulk of the empirical studies do not verify any of the conclusions of economic theory, for the simple reason that most of the conclusions are so derived as to be incapable of empirical verification, and some of them are so constructed as not to require it and to be illuminating and important even though unverifiable.

Economists have lately been only too anxious to abandon the logical position which they have so proudly occupied since the days of Ricardo, Mill, Menger, and the older Keynes. The methodological assumption and justification of theoretical economics is the belief that it covers a field of problems in which knowledge could best be acquired by the exercise of deductive reasoning. In the modest opinion of an outsider like myself, this assumption has been borne out by the history of economic science. In the fields which economists have chosen as their own, they have reaped a crop of conclusions far greater in bulk and finer in substance than anything they could have obtained by the inductive study of facts. But the price of deduction is abstraction: the logical rigour and consistency of economic propositions is a direct consequence of the fact that the fundamental concepts, the original assumptions and the successive stages of economic argument are all treated in isolation from the rest of social environment. And abstraction accounts for the unhelpfulness of economics as well as for its success. Having been derived by way of continuous and accumulated abstraction, and composed of *a priori* concepts, economic propositions cannot be directly applied to facts for purposes of either policy or verification. Within their limits they are as true as, if not truer than, any other branch of scientific knowledge. Where they are unsatisfactory is not in their being wrong but in their being incomplete. And where the empirical studies can help, is not in making them truer but in making them fuller; not so much in testing their often untestable truth on facts, as in making them more relevant and tangible by supplementing them with scientific thought on those aspects of social life from which they have been abstracted.

This residium of social life fills the background of economic theories as a kind of invisible presence: mentioned frequently and always reverentially, but seldom studied, never analysed. Sometimes it makes a fleeting entry into an economic theorem in the famous disguise of 'other conditions being equal', only to pass out of discussion with its incognito intact. Even though the one thing we know for certain about the 'other conditions' is that they cannot possibly be equal, little is done to establish their true identity, to go behind their variety and flux, and to understand the intricacies of their pattern.

Sometimes these other conditions enter economic theory in the form of specific assumptions. Certain modes of social behaviour which are known intimately to affect the economic problem under discussion, but have not been selected for manipulation by economists, are then named, and left named, as special assumptions. So special are they that the whole practical value, the whole significance of the theorem when applied, indeed its very chance of being applied, depends on the knowledge of the modes of behaviour thus assumed. And yet the knowledge is not there, and little attempt is made to obtain it.

Thus in a recent restatement of the theory of international trade,[1] that trade is shown to be primarily 'caused by the uneven distribution of the factors' of production, and important conclusions are made to depend on the interregional movements of capital and labour. But what that 'uneven distribution' was and is—its causes and prospects—is unknown and taken for granted. Similarly assumed and almost equally unknown are the all-important movements of the 'factors'. For in spite of the interesting illustrations which the author draws from his Scandinavian and American experience, and a statistical sketch of the relations between prices and foreign lending, the social processes behind the migration of capital and labour still remain unexplored and unexplained.

In the same way a generally accepted formulation of the theory of wages contains a set of propositions dependent on a number of assumed social conditions, and among them population, the supply of capital, the people's ability or willingness to work, and technical inventions.[2] The theory establishes clearly that its conclusions as to wages and employment will in each concrete case be dependent on what those social conditions happen to be. But do we know enough about the conditions to be able to give reality to the author's proposition? What social causes, psychological, political, institutional, determined in the past and are likely to go on determining the changing attitudes of labour or the changing supplies of capital or the development of applied science or the outbursts of technical ingenuity?

Or let us take an example more up-to-date and nearer Cambridge. Mr Keynes's famous general theory of employment, if I understand it correctly, makes a set of conclusions about employment, the rate of interest, and in certain contingencies also prices and wages, dependent on two scales of human behaviour: the propensities of men to consume different proportions of their income, and their preferences for the different degrees of liquidity in which savings can be held. The existence of these scales is acutely observed, their importance as concepts has been universally acknowledged, their names now belong to the basic English of economics. But how much do the economists know about them? Do they know or have they explained the complex social process which throughout history has determined the employment of income and its allocation to consumption or rather to consuming classes, or have they tried to discover what social forces lurk behind liquidity preferences?

I could multiply the examples *ad infinitum*, but I hope my meaning is clear without them. Such assumptions about the social background as are made by economists, indeed the very fact that they are made, show that they are regarded as important. The fact that although they are as yet unknown they do not block the activity of the economists shows that they are regarded as capable of being known. Why then is there so little empirical economics dealing not only with the statistical verification of economic propositions, but also with the disclosure and analysis of their social conditions?

I know that by asking this question I am inviting the retort and the advice not to be in a hurry. For what the economists have not yet done they may do yet. But if that is the retort, I should like to be allowed the dismal prophecy that the same causes which prevented the economists from engaging in these problems yesterday will prevent them both to-day and to-morrow. The social topics which they themselves assume, but do not settle, belong to regions of enquiry which are outside, i.e. either beyond or beneath, the typical economist's tastes and powers. They are particles of concrete and tangible reality, their study demands constant reference to the whole combination of social forces, their logical problem is that of multiple interrelation, indeed an interrelation so multiple as to make the work

of abstraction impossible and undesirable. My impertinent suggestion therefore is that those fields which the economists are obviously
unable or unwilling to cultivate belong to other people. They are
the true regions of empirical study; and had better be left to students
who specialize in complex social situations, who search for past
causes (and all causes are past causes), and who above all do not expect their result ever to reach the precision of a mathematical formula,
and will therefore not be disappointed by the more indeterminate
results which can be derived from the study of historical reality. In
short, the regions are those of economic history, and by occupying
them and working them historians can make the one contribution
to economic science which at present nobody else seems to be
making.

III

I hope that by thus defining the character of the contribution
which empirical study in general, and economic history in particular,
can make to economic science, I have not given the impression of
extravagance. For what I have just said about the indeterminate
results of historical study recalls the statement with which I started:
namely, that history is not only more but also less than the use to
which it is sometimes turned by social scientists. If economists err
on the side of disparagement, by limiting too narrowly the range of
historical enquiry, sociologists err on the side of extravagance by
exalting unduly the function of historical facts. They expect from
them final and instantaneous solutions of all the most profound of
society's problems. And they are convinced that if history has so far
failed to yield a complete science of society and to found the engineering technique of politics, the fault is not history's but the historian's.
There is an assumption throughout the whole of their recent work
that in the hands of sociologists historical evidence can easily be
made to yield the secrets which it refuses to historians. Hence the
embarrassingly ambitious—and to an historian the embarrassingly
crude—treatises on society in general, property in general, class in
general, which are produced by sociologists on the basis of evidence
originally collected by historians. Hence, also, the attempts to wring
from historical facts theoretical lessons, lessons which send shivers
up the historian's spine for the violence they do to facts, the simplicities they impose upon life.

This aversion of historians to the maltreatment of their facts by
sociologists is a result neither of stupidity nor of ignorance, but of
experience and disillusionment. The historical method in social
science has its own history, and that history is filled with the tomb-

stones of historical schools, which claimed for their method more than it could give. The scientific employment of social, legal and constitutional history began in the attempts of people in the eighteenth and the early nineteenth centuries to derive from history useful political and philosophical lessons. Even the notions of historical relativity and anti-philosophical scepticism which mark the rise of the so-called historical schools of jurisprudence and politics in the early nineteenth century were tinged with the belief that where reason failed historical study might succeed. History, it was thought, could, when suitably employed, not only show up the imperfection of rational propositions but also support general propositions of its own. But the subsequent two or three generations, above all the mid-decades of the Victorian age, taught history yet another lesson. For while the historical school of jurisprudence, Savigny and the rest, found it only too easy to demonstrate the imperfection of the universal principles of rationalist jurisprudence and political theory, they have not been able to replace them with a single historical principle capable of direct general formulation. And similarly while Knies, Roscher and Schmoller found no difficulty in showing the relativity of Adam Smith's and Ricardo's ideas, and their dependence upon circumstances which were purely English and purely temporary, they were unable to derive from history anything in the nature of alternative principles capable of replacing the ones they had rejected.

So now at last the practitioners of the historical method have discovered, what its founders may not have realized, that even though historians and theoreticians travel on the same road, they not only use different vehicles, but also reach different destinations. For the destination of the theoretical sociologists—general universal laws, directly derived from empirical evidence and explicitly stated in generic terms—are things beyond the reach of the most flighty and peregrinatory of historians.

Why this is so all historians and many non-historians now realize. As I have already said, the degree of generalization which the theoretical economists have achieved in their field, and which some philosophers of law would like jurisprudence to achieve in theirs, has been made possible only at the price of abstraction. Now, history also can and also does abstract to some extent; but the extent makes all the difference. Abstraction of a sort is an essential condition of all processes of thought; without it we can use no language; the historian abstracts his facts and groups them into classes and types merely by using words. By calling the war of 1815 a 'war', and the war of 1914 a 'war', and the Punic War a 'war', the historian creates generic terms and abstracts up to a certain degree. But the degree, the length to which he is prepared to go on abstracting, is of vital importance. Beyond a certain point abstraction robs the fact of all historical reality. What gives facts of history, or all social facts, their worth as evidence, and their value for causal analysis, is their existence, their tangible and verifiable reality. Only tangible and concrete phenomena can be fitted into a social setting and demonstrated as a link in a chain of causation. But when abstraction has gone so far as entirely to separate the fact from its social environment, when the concept of war is so employed as to exclude all the historical circumstances of the war of 1815 and of that of 1914 and of the Punic War, the facts of history cease to be facts, lose their value as evidence, and the justification of history as a search for concrete causes goes.

The topics of history, however general in some of their aspects, have an individual existence, and it is for that reason that the historian, however generalizing he is by temperament and however sociological in interests, always writes biographies, accounts of single combinations of circumstances. The historian's work is biographical, even when the subject of the biography is such an impersonal and sociological phenomenon as my own subject of study at the moment: rural society in the Middle Ages. Where the historian shows his scientific preoccupations, and qualifies for membership of the social sciences, is in concentrating the study of his individual subject on its relevance to general and theoretical problems. He studies rural society in the Middle Ages, which is a unique and unrepeatable phenomenon, because the study is relevant to such sociological problems as the correlation of population, social structure, social class and tenure, economic technique and legal concepts. But unlike a sociologist he refuses to ask universal questions or try to formulate general laws.

Confronted with the same problems a sociologist would write a book on the connection between social structure and economic technique in all places and all centuries, as exhibited by historical evidence of every country and every age; he would write a similar book on all family, all class, all property. But to an historian these frontal attacks on theoretical problems, even when delivered with massed battalions of historical facts, are not history; and in my opinion they are not even social science. Social study in its empirical ranges deals with entire social patterns; however abstracted and however simplified, its facts are still too complex for a single and a simple prediction. And at the cost of yet another repetition, we must insist that the penalty of being sufficiently concrete to be real is the impossibility of being sufficiently abstract to be exact. And laws which are not exact, predictions which are not certain, generalizations which are not general, are truer when shown in a concrete instance or in one of their unique manifestations than they are when expressed in quasi-universal terms.

The only thing therefore which economic and social history can do for social science is to go on studying individual situations, rural society in thirteenth-century England, the rise of modern industry in the eighteenth-century midlands, labours' attitudes to wages and hours in the first half of the nineteenth century, technical education in Germany in the second half of the nineteenth century, the English wool-trade in the Middle Ages, etc., etc. But while studying social situations it must ask questions and look for answers capable of revealing the action of social causes. In studying rural society in the thirteenth century one may demonstrate the economic transformation produced by the growth of population, and in studying the labour attitude to wages one may lay bare the social forces which once converted a portion of humanity into a capitalist factor of production and still go on affecting its mobility and economic tractability. In studying technical education in Germany and the relation of factories to universities one may reveal the causes which are capable of stimulating an independent movement of technical progress. These microscopic problems of historical research can and should be made microcosmic—capable of reflecting worlds larger than themselves. It is in this reflected flicker of truth, the revelations of the general in the particular, that the contribution of the historical method to social science will be found.

IV

Is a light so meagre worth shedding? Is it worth giving implied answers, incapable of being put into words, to assumed questions which do not suffer being asked? Is not the whole enterprise of social and economic history as part of social science a mere attempt to overcome the difficulty of scientific thought by shirking it?

These doubts are not for me to answer. Had my subject to-day been 'The Value of Historical Study' I should have taken refuge in the common truth that historical knowledge has a virtue which, like that of all knowledge, is independent of its value as science. But as my subject is not the virtue of history but its scientific use, I can only plead in defence the common limitations and common hopes of all social sciences. The value of the historical contribution to the science of humanity is essentially the same as that of all the other contributions: small and uncertain. Whether it is hopeful, as well as being small and in spite of being uncertain, depends on the prospect of the social sciences as a whole, and not on that of history alone. For the uncertainty of historical results is due not to their being produced by historians, but to their being based on social facts. The real question is therefore not whether it is worth the social scientist's while to take the economic historian in as a partner, but whether it is worth his while to set up in business at all. And if I personally am hopeful about the contribution of history, it is because I am not hopeless about the task of social science.

The reason why I am not hopeless is perhaps due to the fact that I am not over-ambitious. I do not believe that the science of society will ever achieve the perfection of astronomy, but neither do I think that scientific thought is impossible or useless on lower ranges of perfection. The perfect achievement of scientific endeavour is to produce in man that certainty of expectation on which action can be based. This absolute certainty is the very opposite of the infinity of possibilities which every situation presents to a savage or a child. Between the perfect astronomical anticipation of the eclipse and the ignorance of a child as to what will follow a rapid movement of hand, a temporary disappearance of the mother, there are infinite variations and degrees in the certainty of anticipation. The path of science is that of progressive reduction in the choice of expectation, and the further the choice is reduced the nearer is thought to the ideal of science and the further it is from primitive ignorance.

Few branches of science, even astronomy, can claim to have reduced all the alternative expectations to one; on the other hand I cannot imagine social studies in combination as incapable of achieving any reduction at all. No matter how much we study wars we shall perhaps never be able to formulate a single generic law as to the cause of war; similarly, no matter how much we study rural society we shall never be able to express the interdependence of population and agricultural technique in a mathematical formula. But, as long as each concrete instance is studied with relevance to real problems, the accumulated results—that is to say, the accumulated analysis of the causes at work—does, and will still more in the future, create a knowledge of society which stands in the same relation to the savage ignorance now prevailing as life's experience or life's wisdom, with its limited range of expectations, stands to the unlimited range of an infant. That position of collective wisdom or historical experience will not be a complete and a perfect science, but for that matter so few of the sciences are. We are hopeful because we are modest; we are modest because we are historians: because the experience of a century of historiography has made us wiser than we should have been a hundred years ago as to what history can and cannot do. Our science, like charity, begins at home.

NOTES

1   B. Ohlin, *International Trade, passim*, and especially pp. 48 and 58 and ch. XVII.
2   J. R. Hicks, *A Theory of Wages*, p. 114.

9

W. K. Hancock

ECONOMIC HISTORY AT OXFORD
(Oxford, 1946)

This inaugural lecture was delivered at the University of Oxford on the 1st February 1946.

ECONOMIC HISTORY AT OXFORD

AMIDST so many animated discussions about the re-education of Germany, I have in recent years felt sometimes a sharp prick of reminder about my own thorny task, the re-education of myself. That task is now upon me, and upon many others who during the past six years have seen much paper, but few books. With too little time to fill the great gaps in our reading and thought, we find ourselves of a sudden called upon to guide the reading and thought of others, young men and women whose exile from study has been far more drastic than our own.

Our work with them, and theirs with us, will be hard; but it should be exciting. If we attack it together with imagination and zest, we shall find with each other real comradeship in the adventure of ideas. Oxford itself will be working with us, busy on its ancient task of building strong intellects, and awakening deep affections. Oxford has a life which perpetually renews itself, an ever-growing store of experience and wisdom which makes the aspirations and plans of any individual member seem by comparison a trivial thing. And yet, it is the individual contribution which enlarges the store. None of us who are in this room to-day will under-estimate the enlargement which G. N. Clark contributed, during the generation between the two wars.

If I were to recite my shortcomings as his successor in this Chair, the enumeration would be long, because there were so many things which he did supremely well. From afar I have admired his mastery of the sources of English history, his critical shrewdness in their interpretation, and the span of mind which comprehended at the same time the science of a great age and its technology, its political arithmetic and its philosophy. It is this quality of span which is in my thoughts now. I feel that if he had been giving to-day's lecture, he would have attracted many listeners from other Faculties besides those two which have a professional (or an examining) interest in economic history. He was well equipped to lead an attack which surely is long overdue, an attack against the segregation of minds, which is to-day the besetting danger of University life in Great Britain. When the attack is launched, I hope to play an infantryman's part in it. I look forward to the time when the study of economic history will spread beyond its traditional boundaries and attract to itself some at least of the chemists and physicists and engineers whose destiny it is to find their life's work in industry—not merely in its research laboratories, but in its planning and management also. The mingling of minds which is already taking place in the world of industrial production would be more creative if it were supported and prepared by a similar mingling in the world of study. Nor would the gain be by any means all on one side.

Yet to-day I must speak of the economic historian as an animal whose habitat is more circumscribed. In this University he is as yet hardly to be found outside the two Faculties of Modern History and Modern Greats. It might in consequence be thought that the classifiers of species would find his precise identification an easy matter; but this is not so; his perplexing migrations between the two tribes of economists and historians have made his nature and destiny matter for dispute.

Some of the economists have tried to cut the dispute short by imposing on the economic historian their own exclusive codes and rituals. Contrary to what one might at first expect, they have done this because they are modest people. They have not deliberately set out to make laws for their neighbours; rather have they been trying to codify their own self-imposed laws. One can trace their line of thought back at least to 1885, when Alfred Marshall explained that economic theory was not a series of propositions, but an *organon*; not universal truth, but 'machinery of universal application in the discovery of a certain class of truths'.[1] A year or two ago Professor Hicks restated the same idea, and from his original statement was carried forward by the fascination of logical elaboration to a conclusion which is rather too neat to be true. Professor Hicks began by ascribing to economic theory the modest function of preparing the questions 'which we'—we economists, that is—'want to ask of the facts'. He went on to give instruction about the proper method of approach to the facts, which sometimes are to be found in the record of contemporary life, and sometimes in the record of past ages: the element of time makes no real difference, for the method of inquiry is always the same. The inquirer asks those questions, and only those questions, which economic theory has put into his head. The result is applied economics or economic history—it doesn't matter very much which of these names one chooses; for it is 'nearly true to say' that applied economics is the economic history of the contemporary world, while economic history is 'just the applied economics of earlier ages'.[2]

By this definition, the economic historian is—no longer an historian. He forfeits his independence; he becomes merely an economist with historical leanings, or else (if he is not himself an ardent theorist) a mere hodman to the economist, a fact-collector grubbing in a field which his aloof theoretical master has defined for him. Did Professor Hicks really mean this? And did Professor Robbins mean it, when he eliminated from economic history all those impurities which he wished to cast out from economic principles—impurities of technology, law, social valuation, and such other accidentals as may befog the economist's vision of the relationship between 'ends and scarce means which have alternative uses'?[3]

I shall argue later on that economic history is bound to remain impure; that impurity is its very virtue. But first of all I wish to do justice to those elements of the Robbins-Hicks definitions which seem to be helpful to the economic historian. They do at least liberate him from an intolerable burden, the economic interpretation of history. Professor Robbins is quite explicit about this. 'There is', he says, 'nothing in economic analysis which entitles us to assert that all history is to be explained in "economic" terms, if "economic" is to be used as equivalent to the technical material.'[4] Here is a great boon—*not* to be the universal economic-interpreter, the rewriter of all history, the explorer and expounder of that alleged material basis underlying and explaining all the legal systems and constitutions, all the governments and parties, all war and peace, all religion, science, and art. I may criticize the argument which gives me my release from so dreary a servitude; but I welcome its conclusion. I turn joyfully from the economic interpretation of every kind of history to a more manageable task—the historical study of men as getters and spenders.

By the definitions which I have quoted, the subject-matter of economic history becomes specific. Unfortunately, the same definitions segregate it from the adjoining fields of historical study. Economic history ought to be specific; it ought not to be segregated. Let us not forget that the same treatment might with the same plausibility be meted out to ecclesiastical history, constitutional history, and many other branches. We should then have a series of segregated specialisms, each governed by its appropriate theory. We should have applied economics, applied theology, applied jurisprudence, and so on. What would be left to bind them together? What would be left of history?

My compaint may seem an extravagant one. After accepting with almost fulsome thanks my most welcome release from the economic interpretation of history, I have now begun to grumble about my continued subservience to the economic interpretation of economic history! It may look as if I am trying to cut loose from economics altogether—not indeed in subject-matter (for my subject is getting and spending) but in method. Let me therefore make it quite clear that the economic historian, in all his studies of getting and spending, is bound to pay the closest attention to economic theory. He will quite often find himself in fruitful collaboration with his colleagues the economists: their studies of population may help him to wring additional value from the scanty documents of Jacobean England; their theories of the trade cycle may give him new insight into the vicissitudes of commercial activity in Tudor times and the intricacies (or simplicities) of Tudor commercial policy. Whatever his investigation may be, he should always seek out the relevant body of economic doctrine.

But will he always find it? If he does, will its relevance be always close? And will its relevance be exclusive? These are questions which the economic historian is bound to ask when he is told that economic history is no more than 'the applied economics of earlier ages'. In asking them, he may with profit begin by consulting the practice of the economists themselves. Do they, when they write history, continuously ask those questions, and only those questions, which economic theory has put into their heads?

Alfred Marshall, as historian, used other instruments besides his organon. To explain the economic leadership of England he invoked geography, with a particularly keen eye to its influence upon the development of transport. He invoked war, particularly those wars from which England held aloof. He invoked technology, science, education, politics, morals, religion ('the Puritan strain'), and national temperament ('the sturdy Norse character' of Englishmen). Historians may feel that he used some of these categories a trifle indiscriminately; but they would approve his historical interpretations less, had they been the product of the organon alone.

Other economists have in our own time written history, some of it outstanding in quality. There are for example those two distinguished Swedes, Eli Heckscher and Gunnar Myrdal. Heckscher's most massive work has great depth in time, Myrdal's is 'contemporary history'; but neither work is noticeably akin to a study in applied economics. Heckscher's *Mercantilism* is an amalgam of economics and politics. Myrdal's book on the American negro has a hard core of measurable economic fact; but in explaining the existence of this fact the author ranges wide over moral, psychological, social, and political causes, no less than the strictly economic ones. He begins his book with a long chapter exploring the white man's mind. I feel in my bones that this is the right, the inevitable beginning; it is the same beginning as I myself was compelled to make when I was investigating, seven or eight years ago, the use of land and the reward of labour in the Union of South Africa. In the early mining camps at Kimberley and on the Rand the white miners had a slogan: '£1 a day for the white man, £1 a week for the black.' Since those days there have been great changes in the general economic environment, in the economic aptitude of the Bantu labourer, and in his wants; yet the gap between the wages paid to workers of the different races is still of the same order as it was more than half a century ago. This is the central fact in the economy of South Africa: if it is forgotten, no other economic facts make sense—not even the statistics of the poor white problem. Economic theory can suggest questions which illuminate the consequences of this central fact. Economic theory cannot suggest questions which will lead to its deepest causes. As for economic policy—it is in South Africa racial policy also; in consequence, the student or politician who seeks to understand it or practise it merely in economic terms is riding for a fall. Economic phenomena and economic policies are the product of a complicated reciprocal interaction of manifold forces, some of them economic, others non-economic. But do we have to visit 'mixed societies' in South Africa or the United States of America to learn so elementary a lesson? Myrdal, we may be sure, had learnt it before he left his own homogeneous Sweden.

I would not put upon these examples which I have quoted too heavy a burden of proof. They certainly do not prove that economic historians have no need of economic theory. Nor do they prove that applied economics is an unprofitable field for economists to cultivate—or for economic historians, if any of them should feel called upon at any time to try their hand at this kind of labour. What the examples do prove is that applied economics and economic history are not always identical things. The economists whom I have quoted found themselves compelled, so soon as they set themselves to the historian's task, to break free of the circle drawn by economic theory. They did not so much change the objective of their inquiry (for they were still concerned with problems of getting and spending) as its method. Economic principles still sufficed them when they were expounding the economic consequences of historical events; but when they were exploring the causes of those events they found themselves compelled to ask questions originating from many other sources besides the strict logic of their own profession.

Surely it must always be so. Consider the embarrassments which will entangle the economic historian when he tries—in all docility and with honest intention—to search out events and question them in the light of economic theory only. He will be forced at the very outset to ask himself one very pertinent question—'Whose theory?' Frequently he will have to make a choice between different schools of theory, even in his own generation and in his own country. On top of this he will have to reckon with changes of national fashion, and with the great differences which divide successive generations of economists. Must the economic historian assume always that the last generation has by right the last word? Ought he to choose his questions from the school of theory which is dominant in his own country and his own time? If he does this, his history will with a vengeance become 'contemporary'—and anybody who belongs to a rival clique or a different country or a younger generation may with good grounds protest that for him it has no validity at all.

I would not have it imagined that I am taking a sceptical and cynical view of the theoretical differences which divide economists. During the nineteen-thirties those differences were very sharply drawn; yet we now look back upon the nineteen-thirties as a creative period in the history of economic thought. The controversies of that time were a sign of life and progress. It would indeed be utterly wrong-headed to deny the immense progress in logical coherence and subtlety which economic science has made during the past two centuries and, indeed, the past generation. It would be equally wrong-headed to deny that this progress has been and still is a genuine historical force. But, if we recognize the progress, we must at the same time recognize the different stages and degrees of imperfection; we must recognize the relative aspect of economic science. The organon may be, potentially, an instrument of universal application; but, until the economists with one voice proclaim that its evolution is complete, historians are bound to conclude that its relevance is, in some respects, limited by conditions of time, place, and circumstance. They are in consequence bound to make its evolution an object of their own historical study. If it is in part a thing which evolves autonomously by the unfolding of its own logic, it is also in part a thing which bears the impress of changing economic institutions, social valuations, and political premises. For evidence of this truth we need only look around us; we need to-day look no farther than the recent controversies about Anglo-American trade policy and the American loan. How marked the contrast is with the controversies of a century ago, when *smithianismus* was dominant in Britain and the mild protests of Friedrich List were commonly ascribed to the invincible ignorance or wilful perversity of foreigners! Now, it would seem, *smithianismus* is finding a new home in the United States of America, while the national school of political economy is coming to life again in this island. Need we be surprised at the change? Has there not occurred a corresponding change in the international economic position of this island?

Some economists may perhaps chide me for paying too much attention to political controversy: a letter to *The Times*, they may say, is not to be confused with a pure statement of economic principles. Of course not: but neither are the *Proposals for Consideration by an International Conference on Trade and Employment*[5] a pure statement of economic principles; they are (among other things) proposals composed with an attentive eye to opinion in the Congress of the United States. I need not here disclose my own opinion about these proposals; but I should like to point out that their champions and their critics are in one thing alike: they both quite generously dilute their economic principles with political expediency, as they (in contrast with each other) see it. Inevitably so: for economic policy is seldom or never determined by pure economic logic; most commonly it is an amalgam of economic and non-economic considerations. Even the economic considerations sometimes contain impermanent elements of short-range validity. Such elements may be found in the text-books of economic theory themselves. Judicious economists have often shown themselves well aware of this. Even in Victorian England, which was so prone to over-rate the universality of its own ways of life and thought, prominent leaders of the prevalent economic orthodoxy recognized its contingent elements. John Stuart Mill made a distinction between those economic generalizations which depend upon 'the necessities of nature' and those which depend upon 'the existing arrangements of society'[6] Walter Bagehot, though he lived and wrote in the hey-day and at the very centre of a cosmopolitan mobility of economic resources, prophesied that it would be no more than a transitory phenomenon. 'This primary assumption of political economy', he declared, 'is not true everywhere and always, but only in a few places and at a few times.'[7] The twentieth century, as we have known it during the past fifteen years, hardly belongs to those 'few times.' We can now look back upon the Victorian assumption of universal mobility as an episode of practice and thought: on one side of it the mercantilist thinkers, on the other side of it—what? The economics of welfare, or the political economy of war? The social service state, or Moloch? Or shall we after all, with the aid of American leadership, achieve a revised and modernized version of Adam Smith's world?

If, instead of guessing at the future of man, we look back upon his distant past, we must once again confess that economic theory is by itself an insufficient guide to economic fact. Marshall's economic organon was, in aspiration, a machine of *universal* application in the discovery of economic truth: how far from actual achievement this aspiration still is must be abundantly clear to every student of the learned and fascinating books in which Dr. Firth has explained the 'primitive economics' of Polynesian societies. Modern theories of consumption and saving or of the function of the entrepreneur do not give much genuine help in explaining the economic behaviour of people who manage their getting and spending without markets or a price mechanism. Indeed, the difficulty goes far deeper than mechanism; it is the discrepancy of motive between our society and theirs which makes our standards of measurement seem so incongruous: for how are we to explain, by our system of calculating the allocation of scarce resources amongst alternative ends, the decision of an islander who stays on land to dig unproductively in his food plot when he might launch his canoe and bring home a record catch of fish? His decision is a rational one; but its rationality must be understood in terms of his own social code, where ritual observance, the obligations of kinship, and economic calculation are all mixed up with each other. Our economic theory is too sophisticated, perhaps it is also too naïve, to unravel such complications.

Would it be any more relevant if it were purged of all contingent elements? It is only by the most rigorous abstraction that the organon can be made truly universal; but by the same abstraction it becomes remote from specific historical situations. [8] Economic theory may be pure, economic life is not; for it is always intertwined with the legal institutions, the social customs, the political powers, and the religious beliefs of specific societies in specific periods of development. Economic theory, as a highly complex activity of the human intelligence needs no justification; but why should economists pretend that it is always just the thing—and indeed the only thing—which economic historians need when they go out fishing for facts? Such a pretension, which runs so contrary to the experience of economists themselves when they undertake historical research, makes me think of a craftsman who sat down to make a net so that he could catch fish. He was an accomplished craftsman, and he made a net of cunning and intricate mesh, and after a time he found himself happier working at his net on land, than catching fish with it in the sea. Indeed, he had no vulgar interest in the pot. One of the cunningest contrivances of his net was that it was just as good for letting fish go as it was for catching them. It let go all the striped and spotted fish—just as the historian who fished for economic events with the aid of economic theory only would have to throw away all the hybrids whose economic monochrome was marked and marred by religious stripes and legal spots and political stars. He would get a mighty poor haul.

He does nevertheless need the economist's net. Professor Firth himself looks forward to the time when an improved net will render indispensable service to the investigators of primitive societies; meanwhile, he thinks it a pity that anthropological field-workers have been as a rule untrained in economic science. Looking back over my own argument, I now have the feeling that I have tilted it too far on one side. In imagination I hear, and do not at all relish, the approving comment of the reactionaries who imagine that assiduity in documentary study and the gift of literary embellishment are all the historian needs. The historian also needs theory. Those historians who have no theory fill the vacuum with their prejudices, if they do not timidly shrink into antiquarianism. As an economic historian, I feel the need of enlarging simultaneously my command of economic theory and my knowledge of historical materials; it is easy enough to imagine many problems—for example, the volume of investment in relation to the growth of national income—where theory and research must go hand in hand. What I have been pleading for is a free and flexible partnership, instead of a tyranny. Do those economists whom I quoted earlier really mean what they seem to say? Do they really demand of historians that they should shut their eyes to the evidence of their documents when these testify to the profound influence of technological, or legal, or political factors? I will not believe it.

It has been Sir John Clapham's endeavour to see the economic crises of the past two centuries and a half as the Bank of England saw them—as nearly as might be. His history of *The Bank of England* would have flouted the evidence if he had explained the crises of the eighteenth century predominantly in terms of modern trade cycle theory. His account does not however in any way impugn the validity of trade cycle theory; it simply gives warning that the theory should not be 'applied' mechanically or without careful regard to the whole complex of influences—some economic, others not—operating at a particular time. It is the historian's business to explore, so far as he is able, the multiple interaction of the complex real causes which determine actual economic situations; it is the economist's business to isolate economic causes and effects and subject them to refined analysis. Surely there is room, and surely there is need, for both kinds of work. They are neighbours; but their methods are distinct. Economic history may sometimes overlap with applied economics; but between these two studies there is never identity. Economic history has its own specific subject-matter; but it cannot be segregated from the rest of history. Economic history (even when economists write it) is historians' history. I would submit that it is for this very reason an essential part of the education of economists in the School of Philosophy, Politics, and Economics. Indeed, it may be nourishing fare for the politicians also; for they too have (quite properly) their own abstracting tendency which needs correction. As for the philosophers—I, personally, have far more to ask

N

from them than to offer them. I would in particular ask them to give what help they can towards the solution of those problems of method in the investigation of social evidence, which I have been so inexpertly discussing during the past half-hour.

What range of economic history should the economist study in his undergraduate days? Alfred Marshall argued that he ought to be confined pretty strictly within the limits of very recent history, and this for two reasons: first, because the materials of study are abundant and lend themselves to a precise training in scientific method; secondly, because the content of very recent economic history has a direct bearing on the economic problems of the present and the near future.

I do not think this advice sound; nor do I accept the reasons—at any rate the second reason—which Marshall advanced in its support. I must however take pains not to let myself be misunderstood on one important matter. Provided the history of our own times is not isolated from the history of what has gone before, I am no less convinced than Marshall was, that we can study it, and must study it. I know that some people argue that the true historian should have nothing to do with it, for fear of being overwhelmed by the brute mass of evidence or of falling a victim to his own bias. I suspect that this scruple about bias is rooted in a sense of sin—the sin of the historical writer, who for the sake of a lively story and in the know-ledge that the dead cannot answer back, has allowed his Whig interpretations or Tory interpretations to run riot; or the sin of the reader of histories, who confesses or even boasts (as a dilettante Prime Minister of this country did) that he finds historical bias so much more interesting than historical truth.[9] Bias is never easy to conquer, truth is never easy to discover; but the conquest and the discovery come no easier to the historian of the Elizabethan wars than to the historian of our own wars. Did they, we wonder, come without great labour and stern self-discipline to the historian of the Peloponnesian War? A eunuch 'detachment' (as distinct from the zeal for justice which overrules our partialities) is only possible to us when we find our subject boring.

The test of an historian's integrity is always most searching when he is handling the great issues of politics and morals which are contemporary to him, either in the purely temporal or in the Crocean sense. The historian of high politics is more severely tested than is the economic historian, for the latter is more concerned with the continuing processes of society than with the great moments of moral and political decision. Yet the economic historian must not delude himself into believing that the processes which he is studying can be detached from the value-measurements of society, in which ethics and economics are mingled. These value-measurements exert a powerful influence upon economic fact (for example, upon the actual material make-up of what the nation calls its wealth). The economic historian who fails to criticize his own standards of value, be they mercantilist or individualist-cosmopolitan or national-socialist, will slip insensibly into biased conclusions about such seemingly instrumental matters as tariffs and wages and the location of industry.

Bias, then, is always a danger, even when—or specially when—the historian is unconscious of temptation. But it is not a danger which need frighten the economic historian away from the study of contemporary evidence. Far more frightening is the vast bulk of evidence. But are we to wait until the neglect of man and his violence have reduced the bulk to manageable proportions? The I.R.A. destroyed a large pile of documents in Dublin Customs House, and no doubt the Americans with their atom bomb (and ours) have destroyed a vaster pile still at Hiroshima. But shall we historians wait upon the expectation of our problems being eased this kind of way? And shall we in the meantime leave it to the gossipers and the guessers to expound the historical problems of our own time? If, through laziness or timidity we take this easy line, we shall earn the maledictions of future historians, who depend upon us to do at least the rough work of exploration and explanation. If w ecannot see any end to the mass of evidence, they will be unable to find even the beginning, unless we blaze the way for them. Their judgement will in some things be truer than ours. because their prospective will be longer; but our judgement will in many things be truer than theirs, because we can, often in the literal sense of the words, cross-examine the evidence. They may expound more truly than we can the deeper causes of our wars; but we can expound far more truly than they can ever do the way we have fought our wars. I speak now of what I know; for the accidents of this troubled time have compelled me to spend many years in the study of very recent history (far too many years, as I shall find when I endeavour to guide others along remoter, half-forgotten paths). It is a formidable task, as any historian will soon discover when he finds himself set down in a government department among two million files, and these only a part of his evidence. It is nevertheless a task which can be mastered, and has been mastered. In mastering it, the historian achieves a new and illuminating understanding of the meaning of historical evidence; he toughens his mind and sharpens his technique; he will in consequence write better history when he returns at last to his customary and chosen field of study—whether it be the legal institutions of Tudor England, or politics and administration in the age of Charles II, or the economic development of Italy, or the public finance of Great Britain and France.

These statements, dogmatic though they may sound, cannot now be further supported, for that would start too long a story and lead too far from to-day's theme. To return: Marshall was surely right when he argued that the study and teaching of very recent economic history should be given a place in the Cambridge Faculty of Economics; but he was surely wrong when he suggested that very recent history was by itself a sufficient historical diet for young economists. By itself, it would be a most unbalanced diet, if not a positively poisonous one. Sir William Ashley gave a better prescription; he believed that economic history for under-graduate economists ought to be 'not too mediaeval, but not exclusively modern'.[10] Exclusively modern history (to say nothing of exclusively contemporary history) would, he thought, mould young minds in the worst kind of provincialism in time. This danger can be demonstrated by one of the illustrations which Marshall used. Marshall wanted his pupils to understand the world market and its rules of operation—and where else, he asked, would they discover the intricate operation of these rules if not in recent economic history? That question would still have seemed fairly plausible in 1929; it would have been quite unplausible in 1939. If all our history is crowded onto the small-scale map of our own times, how shall we find our bearings when all of a sudden our times move right off the map? We need maps of larger scale; we need them even when the present time itself constitutes our absorbing interest. Marshall himself was in his heart aware of this, for he suggested that the study of contemporary India would enlarge our understanding of Europe's economic past, from which we should in turn derive a truer insight into the economic problems of contemporary India. Here is a most illuminating clue to the method of the economic historian, and its value. Who else but an economic historian with Tawney's span of imaginative insight and critical understanding could have written *Life and Labour in China*—the best short book, I believe, which any scholar of this generation has written about another country, and one of the greatest services—so a Chinese friend has told me—which any Englishman of our time has rendered to the Chinese people?

It is never easy in historical teaching to strike a balance between knowledge which is too thinly spread and myopic knowledge; between a period or subject compact enough for exact study and broad enough to suggest the larger contrasts and changes. The teacher should not overstrain his curriculum. It may well be that Sir William Ashley's prescription would demand too much from economists reading Modern Greats. The recognized period of study which purports to open in 1760 may represent a workable compromise, provided its chronological boundaries are not too rigidly drawn. Teachers and their pupils must be free to trace some of their problems back to earlier times and to follow others right up to the present day. They must also be free to treat their problems comparatively. The purely nationalist definition of economic history, if it were seriously intended and observed, would be a real blot on the curriculum of Modern Greats. Provincialism in space is almost as bad as provincialism in time. Economic historians ought not to swallow without criticism the national system of political economy. The economic aspects of sovereignty are, no doubt, an important object of study, and there is in a sense an English or British economic system, just as there is an English or British science, or religion, or art. But none of these things make real sense apart from their European context. (And during the past century or two the context has become 'Western', or something still wider.) I therefore assume that the teaching of economic history in this University does not too slavishly follow the printed syllabus; that it does not stay within this moated isle, even when it starts there; that its method is consciously and persistently comparative. It should indeed be rather more than that; for the need is not merely to observe the similarities and dissimilarities of economic institutions on different sides of a frontier, but also to examine the reciprocal interaction of forces and causes operating across frontiers and in despite of them.

I wonder whether my colleagues in the History Faculty have been thinking that this lecture has been too little addressed to them? Yet it has been a defence of historians' history. I have told the modernists that historical thought must have depth in time; I have told the economists that it must have breadth of content. I have not invited either of them to undertake work which is not their strict academic business; but I have suggested to both that the healthy progress of their own studies depends in large measure on the healthy development of the entire body of historical studies. When I was an undergraduate I did not read Greats; but I read History more intelligently than I would have done had not so many of my friends been reading Greats. In recent years there has been a very great expansion of modern studies; this expansion and its further continuance are desirable; but the life of the University will suffer, and modern studies will themselves suffer, unless classical and medieval studies continue vigorously alive and growing. We must nourish our roots.

If I now suggest that economic historians can render valuable service in making a healthy tilt, I hope it will not be imputed to my excessive partisan zeal. I have sometimes thought that the products of our Schools of History in this country are rather too delicate; for I have known men who took a First merely on the strength of the information they had stored in their heads and their capacity to fiddle cleverly with other people's ideas. Some of them wilted when they were asked to tackle, under their own power, difficult intellectual problems. We should take pains to teach our pupils to think. Economic history will serve us well in our attempt; stiffened by its close contact with economic theory and statistical measurement, it will be a toughening influence in the History School. Nor need anybody fear that this toughening will also be a coarsening. Ability to write the King's English—so an English historian ironically suggested a few years ago—is an unfair advantage which some historians enjoy over the rest. Economic historians will seldom be found amongst 'the rest'. If one were to choose from among the historians of the past generation the six most distinguished masters of English prose, three at least of the six, by my private estimate, would be economic historians. And where amongst British (or American) historical periodicals shall we find so impressive a combination of exact research, significant thought upon important problems, and good clear prose, as in the *Economic History Review*?

Should some foreign scholar attempt to classify by academic origin the historical and economic writings of the past ten or fifteen years, he would in all probability conclude that economic history was more alive in Cambridge, London, and Manchester than in Oxford. Perhaps his conclusion would be wrong? I have entitled my lecture *Economic History at Oxford*, but the title should have a question-mark at the end of it. My task of rediscovering Oxford, after a twenty years' absence—or almost that—is not such an easy one as I had anticipated. I am beginning to learn that some of my notions, some of my plans, may need considerable revision.

I am however convinced that economic history is to-day a main growing point of historical study, just as constitutional history was in the half-century after Stubbs. The greatness of the opportunity excites me; but I am correspondingly cast down when I remember my own limitations. That personal problem of re-education to which I referred at the beginning of my lecture demands a five-year plan— and another five-year plan after that. Such special skill as I can achieve will always be primarily exercised in the brief span of time from Adam Smith to the present day; but gradually I shall work back into earlier centuries also. It will not happen quickly. Meanwhile, I am well aware that no single individual, not even my predecessor in this Chair, could hope to be expert over the whole range of medieval and modern time in all the manifold problems of agriculture and industry, commerce and finance, and the relations of all these to law, politics, and science. Nor can so wide a field be cultivated systematically by a Professor and Reader, even when one of them is able to correct the modern (or medieval) bias of the other. I therefore hope that more labourers will come into this vineyard. Should they be hired to come in? Financial provision and formal appointment are only part of the story of any growing study, above all at Oxford, where so many vigorous minds choose freely the fields of research and teaching which attract them most. I hope that an increasing number will choose economic history. The way of the economic historian may be hard, but it is not a narrow way, with a single entrance at one wicket gate. It is good that some of the wayfarers should come in (like those two bad men in the *Pilgrim's Progress*) by jumping over the wall. Nor need the pilgrims reckon it a backsliding if once in a while one or other of their company turn aside into another way.

NOTES

1 Alfred Marshall, *The Present Position of Economics* (Inaugural Lecture, 1885), *passim*.
2 J. R. Hicks, *The Social Framework* (Oxford, 1942), pp. 8–9.
3 L. Robbins, *The Nature and Significance of Economic Science* (London, 1932), pp. 37, 38.
4 *Ibid.*, p. 41.
5 Cmd. 6709 of 1945.
6 J. S. Mill, *Autobiography* (London, 1873), p. 247.
7 W. Bagehot, *Economic Studies* (London, 1880), p. 23.
8 On the different methods of abstraction employed by historians and economists see M. Postan, *The Historical Method in Social Science* (Cambridge, 1939), especially p. 30, [and above pp. 137–8.].
9 I realize that my 'sinners' are not at all apologetic or abashed, and they that are able to quote eminent authorities (Bury, for example) with whom on this issue I disagree.
10 *Economic History Review*, vol. i, p. 8.

10

T. S. Ashton

THE RELATION OF ECONOMIC HISTORY TO ECONOMIC THEORY
(L.S.E., 1946)

This inaugural lecture was delivered at the London School of Economics on the 7th February 1946. The chair was taken by Professor R. H. Tawney.

THE RELATION OF ECONOMIC HISTORY TO ECONOMIC THEORY

THE obligation to deliver an inaugural lecture must rank high among the impediments to vertical mobility in academic life. After some weeks of meditation on the matter I am constrained to suggest to the august personages who determine these things that the cause of learning and academic mobility might be advanced by the abolition of the requirement. If some ceremony were thought to be essential the newly elected professor might simply be sworn in and enrolled on the acceptance by him of the sum of one shilling in legal tender money. Or, if it were considered that this would impose an unwarranted strain on the University chest, the initiation might follow the tradition, long established in other fields of human endeavour, by which the apprentice, elevated to the rank of master-craftsman, 'stands his footing' in a form which, unlike a lecture, can hardly with accuracy be described as dry.

In my own case there are special reasons for wishing that the obligation did not exist. By training I am more of an economist than a historian. In the first decade of this century I was one of a small group of students at Manchester who took draughts of Marshallian theory at the hands of Sydney Chapman, a teacher whose virile beauty of form and clarity of mind can never be forgotten by any of us who had that stimulating experience. Chapman, like Marshall himself, always insisted that high theory must be supplemented by realistic and historical investigation; it was under his direction that I made a few halting enquiries into the growth of businesses in the textile industries. Some years later, as lecturer in Economics at Manchester, I had the supreme fortune to be the colleague of one of whom Eileen Power spoke as the most original of English economic historians—a man in whom faith and scepticism, tenderness and irony, daring speculation and austere scholarship were combined in a way that only a biographer of exceptional insight and skill could possibly convey to those who had not been in daily contact with him. (Happily, I may add, such a biographer was found.) The personality of George Unwin was magnetic. One by one, the young theorists ceased to twitter in their nests of indifference curves and fluttered down to earth. If only the first World War had not deflected

163

Chapman's abilities from academic life to government service, if only it had not broken Unwin's constitution, Manchester might have effected that synthesis of theory and history about which, at a later stage, I propose to offer a few remarks.

These autobiographical details have been mentioned, not out of egotism, but simply in order to explain how it has come about that one who until recently made a living by teaching Currency and Public Finance now appears in the robe of the historian. When I think of the superb equipment of my predecessor in this Chair, of the learning that she bore so lightly, of her gifts of speech, of her literary grace and wit, of her personal charm, I can only say that the early death of Eileen Power was a catastrophe to historical studies comparable to that occasioned by the death of Unwin. If I say no more than that, it is because my knowledge of her (as distinct from her writings) was little more than could be gained in brief conversations before, after and (I must admit) during, examiners' meetings. To an audience of those who knew her as a colleague and loved her as a friend, it would be a clumsy intrusion for an outsider to offer mere words of praise.

One thing at least, however, I have in common with Eileen Power —there is her own word for it—a constitutional inaptitude for philosophic speculation. That is why I shall not attempt this afternoon to discuss at any length the ultimate purposes of the study of economic history. I will say only this. Interest in history, so it seems to me, arises out of the simple delight we all take in watching things grow— whether it be babies, or puppies, or delphiniums or social institutions. That in itself would make the study worth while. But the adult mind asks for something more than narrative: unlike that of the young heroine of *Northanger Abbey*, it is not satisfied with the book that is 'all story and no reflection'. It seeks not only to see things grow, but also to know how things grow, and what circumstances are favourable, and what hostile, to growth. Now historians, political, constitutional and economic alike, are doing their best to satisfy that demand. They are increasingly preoccupied less with the configuration and more with the geological structure of their territories. Or, to change the metaphor, they are looking less to the physiognomy, and more to the bony framework and organic processes, of the societies with which they are concerned. And, however it may be with other kinds of historians, economic historians, by their very nature, can hardly look at the past, as H. A. L. Fisher looked at it, seeing 'only one emergency following upon another as wave follows upon wave, only one great fact with respect to which, since it is unique, there can be no generalisations', seeing only 'in the development of human destinies the play of the contingent and the unforeseen'. It is, of course, true that every historical fact is unique, just as it is true that every individual body and soul is unique. But the uniqueness of the individual does not preclude the possibility of statistical generalisation where large groups are concerned. Economic history—whatever may or may not be true of political history—is concerned with large groups: with the general, rather than with the particular; with processes, rather than with events; with the typical, representative or statistical fact, rather than with the unique, individual fact. And it is about such groups, such processes, such facts, that the modern mind seeks to satisfy its curiosity.

But it is not curiosity alone that draws men and women to the study of history. Interest in the past arises as often as not out of the urgencies of the present, and it is because of a belief that history has some meaning and message that so many people, especially of our own unhappy day, turn to it for both guidance and solace. Even if some who seek fail to find in it direct answers to the questions they ask this does not mean that the search has been in vain. For the fruits of history, like those of all humane studies, are things not only of the mind but also of the spirit. Let me recall the words of one of the greatest sons of this University and of this School, a man whose energies were given to pursuits not closely related on the surface to historical studies. 'I set great store by objective actuality.' wrote Lord Stamp, 'not merely because it creates a sense of history, the base of sane judgment of things relative, and of economic sense in arranging them, but because that same historic sense is the best nursery of resolve, selflessness and public spirit'. What more need be said?

II

Economic history is but one country in a great hemisphere of scholarship. Its position between History on the one hand and Economics on the other reminds me of that in which the diminutive Boswell found himself when acting as interpreter between Dr. Johnson and the Corsican General. 'I compared myself,' he said, 'to an isthmus which joins two great continents.' Now an isthmus may either connect or separate. Those who inhabit it may build up an independent life and character of their own or, as more often happens, they may fall under the tutelage of one or other of the neighbouring powers. For long, economic history remained under the domination of the politically minded historians. Like the British in Egypt, or the Americans in Panama, these brought with them a developed technique; they raised the subject to academic status; and, on the whole, they exercised a civilising influence. But their work is now done, and labour is required to clear away some of the traces of their occupation. The very periods into which economic historians divide, one from another, their varied specialisms, are still described in terms drawn from the vocabulary of politics or political history. 'The Feudal System,' 'Mercantilism,' 'Laissez-faire,' 'Collectivism': the ideas behind words such as these are associated with the policies of government rather than with the postulates of economic science. Not many years ago in one university the special period of English economic history, prescribed for students in the Honours School of Economics and Modern History alike—the period 1830–48—was described, not as the age of the railways, or of joint-stock, or of Free Trade, or of the Chartists, not even as the Age of Cobden or Peel, but as the Age of Louis Philippe. One widely read text-book announces that Napoleon I restarted the Industrial Revolution in France—as though that series of inter-related technical, economic and social changes were a mechanism to be stopped or started at the bidding of a dictator. There are still writers who believe that some Colbert or Frederick or Bismarck, some Marx or Lenin, was really 'the obstetrician of a new age'. And there are even some who so confuse Economics with Technology as to think that, because wars sometimes lead to inventions, those who make wars are to be given a place among the pioneers of social development.

In face of such crude interpretations it is the duty of economic historians to point to those spontaneous forces of growth in society that arise from ordinary men and women and find expression in voluntary association, as well as in the state. 'Society,' Unwin once said, in one of those *obiter dicta* which every good teacher uses to arouse his students from their habitual torpor—'Society cannot direct its destiny by policy'. As it stands, that is perhaps an overstatement. But it sprang not from any spirit of negation, but from exasperation with those so obtuse that they fail to see in History any territory in which the writ of the sovereign state does not run.

It is not, however, only the political historians and political theorists that have occupied the isthmus. At a later stage there appeared a swarm of sociologists and economists of the so-called Historical School, bringing with them an avidity for classification that might well have done credit to a contemporary academy of botany or zoology. With great ingenuity they traced out stages of economic development through which all societies were supposed to travel: from barter, through money, to credit; from a subsistence economy, through a village, town and national to an international economy; from an eotechnic, through a paleotechnic, to a neotechnic phase; from household production, through a gild and a domestic, to a factory system; from pre-capitalism, through mercantile capitalism, industrial capitalism, finance capitalism, monopoly capitalism, and several other forms of capitalism to wherever you will. Those who constructed them hoped that in time their schematic presentations might come to be regarded as a body of doctrine, parallel to, and perhaps in the end destined to supersede, what used to be called the laws of Political Economy. That hope was a fond one. Take only the first of the series: Hildebrand's master-generalisation about the development from barter, through money, to credit. Professor Postan has pointed out that when documented history began money was already in use; that though there have been many periods of advance towards, there have also been others of retreat from, a greater money economy; and that in times of which it was assumed that men exchanged their goods and services only through the medium of the precious metals there was, in fact, a highly developed system of credit. There is no need to proceed with the other pedigrees of economic institutions. 'Everything we know about economic history warns us against belief in steady advances and unbroken lines of progress.' The quotation is from Eileen Power's posthumously published work and expresses her mature judgement on this matter.

It is not to be denied that the effort to discover stages of development has yielded some useful results. It has at least presented us with a set of labels which we can attach, if we are so minded, to the files in which we assemble our facts. But facts are stubborn, wilful things. You can arrange then in either logical or chronological order, but very seldom at the same time in both. Therein lie at once the difficulty and the fascination of historical composition.

It is not only the systematisers who have, as I think, on balance done harm to the subject. The whole practice of coining phrases and attaching them to particular periods of time has tended to cloud, rather than illumine, our vision of the past. The attribution to the years 1760–1830 of the epithet 'The Industrial Revolution' is the outstanding case in point. We now know that the essential changes began long before the year of the accession of George III. Has not Professor Nef called attention to a remarkable speeding-up of industrial development in the hundred years from 1540 to 1640, and has not Miss Carus-Wilson discovered an industrial revolution as early as the thirteenth century? Every first-year student is now aware, moreover, that 1830 was in no sense a terminal date, and that many of the processes which the phrase Industrial Revolution connotes were made manifest far more fully in the forties, fifties and sixties than in the earlier decades of the nineteenth century.

It is now too late to alter this particular superscription, for the words have entered the currency of common speech from which there is no recall. But for other periods something may yet be done. Take, for example, the years 1873–96, to the whole series of which the term 'The Great Depression' has come to be attached. Thanks to the work of Lord Keynes, Mr. Beales and Mr. Rostow, we now have a clearer view of what was really going on than was open to the members of the *Royal Commission on the Depression of Trade and Industry* which issued its final report in the middle of the period. We know that in the technical sense of a fall in the marginal efficiency of capital there *was* depression. But we also know that, alongside the dwindling of profits, there took place a great expansion of the national income, an increase in the proportion of that income that went into the pockets of the workers, and a substantial rise of average real wages. These are not movements of the kind that the plain man normally associates with depression. To him (quite wrongly no doubt) the word means unemployment, falling wages and distress. That unemployment was particularly marked during the period is disproved by the figures of the trade unions. Yet the belief persists and finds expression annually in the scripts of many candidates for degrees of this University. It has been encouraged by a curious incident of literary scholarship. In a footnote on a page of their great work on English Local Government the Webbs point out that the first recorded instance of the use of the word 'unemployment' known to the compilers of the Oxford English Dictionary was in 1888, and the first use of 'unemployed' as a noun in 1882. The statement is elevated to the text in Mr. Ensor's *England 1870–1914*; and it appears again (with some reference in the text) in a footnote to the third volume of Sir John Clapham's masterpiece. Now a few years ago it fell to me, as external examiner, to read two theses submitted for the degree of Ph.D. of the University of London. In the first of these, written by Mr. H. J. Carr (now Dr. Carr) my eye caught, in a quotation from John Frances Bray's *Voyage from Utopia*, the words 'unemployment results in begging or street-singing'. These words were written in 1840 or 1841. In the second thesis written by Mr. W. McLaine (now Dr. McLaine) again my eye caught, among a statement of proposed alterations in the rules of the Journeymen Steam Engine and Machine Maker's Friendly Society, under the date May 31st, 1841, 'That no allowance be made for office bearers for the benefit of the unemployed'.[1]

If there is any significance in the fact that these words did not become current in literary circles until forty or more years later, it does not lie in any increasing incidence of unemployment. Nor do any of the distinguished historians whose names I have mentioned draw any such inference. In the early decades of the nineteenth century middle-class observers of working-class life failed to distinguish between the new wage-earners who were pouring in and out of the factories and that amorphous mass of the 'poor' from which most of them came. But the trade-unionists and Bray saw more clearly. By the eighties—and not least because of developments during the so-called 'Great Depression'—it had become plain to all that an independent working class had emerged. To those who belonged to it temporary loss of work did not necessarily mean destitution. Observers were at last learning to disentangle the problem of unemployment from that of poverty. It was the beginning of wisdom in social investigation.

Perhaps it should be added that there is no reflection on the watchfulness of the compilers of the Oxford English Dictionary: it could hardly be expected that they should be familiar with the sources I have mentioned, or, indeed, with the vocabulary of early Socialism and Trade Unionism in general. But it is not without profit to observe some of the results that might come of relying on lexicography as a means of reaching to the origins of economic institutions. We should find ourselves attributing, for example, the beginnings of industrialism to the year 1831, of trade unions to the same year, of capitalism to 1854, of inflation (in the monetary sense) to 1864, and of deflation to 1919.

But to return to my theme: the phrase 'The Great Depression' is one of the few of these established captions which bear an economic rather than a political import. Attempts have recently been made to introduce others. One by a writer who heads his chapter on the years 1858–73 with the words 'The Great Boom' must encounter mental resistance from anyone bred in Lancashire where, until quite recently, it was possible to meet people who preserved lively recollections of the Cotton Famine. There is, it is true, something to be said for these attempts to set the milestones at the periods at which cyclical depression turns to recovery, or, more widely, at those at which major downswings of general prices give way to upswings. But it is a misfortune that those who would divide up the past in this way are not content to say what they have to say in plain English. There is a model set by an early historian which ran as follows: 'And the seven years of plentiousness that was in the land of Egypt were ended. And the seven years of dearth began to come.' But such words are too direct for these sociological surveyors. After reading Professor Schumpeter's otherwise admirable work on *Business Cycles*, I am dismayed at the thought that the pages of economic history may come to be littered with Juglars, Kondratieffs and the like.

What is the drift of all this? Simply to say that economic history is concerned primarily with processes that persist over long stretches of time. It is preoccupation with these that binds economic historians

o

together and differentiates them from other kinds of historians. Some specialisation by periods there must be, since to elicit information from a Charter or Pipe Roll requires skill of a different order from that needed to draw out the meaning hidden behind the magisterial pronouncements of a Royal Commission, or submerged in the detail of a nineteenth-century business ledger. But the centuries and years of the calendar should supply all the palings we need : it is unnecessary to plaster these over with signs. 'Stick no bills', and 'Leave no litter', are maxims of conduct for the historians as for the citizen.

III

Understanding of the processes which it is the business of economic historians to trace through the centuries does not come by the light of nature. The data do not wear their hearts on their sleeves: it is only by selecting and grouping them that they can be made to yield a meaning. But (as others have said) as soon as the historian begins to select his facts from the myriads available to him he becomes a theorist of sorts. The poorer type of historian is one who allows the stray reflections that pass through the mind to serve as a substitute for the thought that the processes of selection and grouping demand. And even the historian of disciplined intellect requires some more or less systematic body of principles to which he can relate his facts; for, as Ben Jonson remarked, 'Very few men are wise in their own counsel or learned by their own teaching'. To repeat: the economic historian, like the fisherman, needs a net, to help to separate those fish that may be marketable from those that may as well be left in the sea. But it must be a net made by skilled hands and not just a reticulation of odd ideas. The men who make the special nets for the craft are the economists.

This somewhat blunt statement will appear as a platitude to some, but as a rock of offence to others. Is it not, these latter will ask, an attempt to justify yet one more of the long series of efforts to interpret the human story in the light of a docrtine? Even if that were so it would not dispose of the matter. For the question might be answered by asking for the alternative. 'Don't forget,' wrote James Wilson in an early page of that great journal of which he was founder and first editor, 'the people who attack Political Economy have a Political Economy of their own; and what is it?' But the real answer to those who shrink from the suggestion that modern economic theory should be applied to the study of earlier forms of society is that they misunderstand the nature of Economics. For, whatever may have been its origin, the subject has ceased (or almost ceased) to be a set of conclusions and has become an apparatus of thought; no longer a doctrine, it has become a method. The only question is whether this method is appropriate to the study of history.

Until recent years the answer might have been in the negative. For though Adam Smith had provided a nursery in which it was possible for theory and history to play happily side by side, as theory grew up it became cold and abstracted; and a later preoccupation with margins completed the rift. The static analysis on which most of us were reared had its uses, but it had little or no bearing on the problems of change over periods of time. Professor Robbins put the correct relation between the two disciplines neatly when he said that Economics is concerned with the form, Economic History with the substance. Most of what I have to say this afternoon is a variation on that theme. But it can hardly be said that at the time when he coined the aphorism the form was really appropriate to the medium: economic historians were offered a set of implements devised for other jobs than theirs—tools that would cut only *across* the grain, and not, as they required, *along* the grain. It is true that about the same time, in one brief article, Allyn Young pointed the way to that theory of economic development which is what is needed: had historians taken more heed of this we should have been spared some barren disputation as to whether expansion of trade precedes or follows expansion of industry, and so on. But economists as a whole were beset with so many problems of current concern that they had little time for sustained thought on these wider questions. If, in the event, they have shaped an instrument that may be of use to historians it is by accident rather than design.

It was during and immediately after the first world war that there took place the first of those developments in thought that have made possible a closer intimacy between economists and historians. Under the pressure of events, economists became increasingly less theoretical and more statistical in their approach. It would be too much to attribute to contagion the tendency of economic historians to concern themselves with the statistical aggregate or average, rather than with the outstanding or picturesque incident. For that tendency had long been at work. The senior British economic historian, Sir John Clapham, certainly did not wait for the impetus to a quantitative treatment to come from the professional statisticians, though he would, one imagines, be among the first to recognise the great service that Professor Bowley has rendered to our subject. The work of Bowley and those he has trained and stimulated is certain to have a profound effect on the future of historical studies. It has made us all less tolerant of the loose, unsupported generalisation: it is to be hoped, one may add in passing, that the infiltration of statistics will not make our text-books any less readable.

The violent movement of prices during and after the war turned attention to the causes and social consequences of changes in the value of money. Here was a field which required the skills of economists, statisticians and historians alike. Where so much valuable work has been done by so many students it is invidious to mention individuals, but I cannot refrain from reference to the light thrown on the social history of the sixteenth and seventeenth centuries by Professor Hamilton's study of the effects of Spanish Treasure; to the clearer understanding of the economic background to the French Revolution that has come from the brilliant and scholarly work of M. Labrousse; and to the enormous debt that every student of the last quarter of the eighteenth, and the first half of the nineteenth, centuries owes to the statistical labours of Professor Silberling. More recently, the assembly of material on prices by Sir William Beveridge and his colleagues for England, and of Posthumus for Holland, opens possibilities of new interpretations of large tracts of the past. The part played by the banking system in the upward and downward swings of prices from 1914 to 1925 led to investigations by Hawtrey, Cannan, Feavearyear, Angell, Viner and Morgan into the similar movements of the years 1793–1821; and it has not been without effect on scholars, like Mr. Judges, who have worked on the same set of problems in earlier centuries.

Out of the exigencies connected with the growth of the national debt between 1914 and 1920 came a revival of concern with the theory of interest; and this, in turn, led to a study of the effects of changes of both long- and short-term rates on investment and activity. I wish it could be said that here too there had been enquiries by historians parallel to those of the theorists. But the field has remained almost entirely without cultivation. We have, it is true, detailed information about the course of Bank Rate and the yield on Consols over the last two centuries. But until relatively recent years these official rates were but loosely tied to those that prevailed in transactions between merchants and manufacturers. What we need is tables of rates in force in long-term business contracts and in day-to-day operations of credit.

Chronological tables of rates of interest, similar to those of the price series, would be valuable in a variety of ways. Changes in short-term rates, as Wicksell pointed out, have important effects in determining the nature of the medium of circulation. The high rates of interest between 1797 and 1815 stimulated the substitution of small bills of exchange for notes and even for coin; and the fall in the rates that followed the Napoleonic war was accompanied by a reversal of the process. It may be that if we knew more of these things we should find that those earlier oscillations from money to credit or from credit to money, to which I have referred, were susceptible of similar explanation. Changes in the long-term rates of interest, it may be supposed, had even more potent effects. Long ago Philip Wicksteed made the interesting observation that the substantial quality of the houses in many Dutch cities might be attributed to the fact that, at the close of the eighteenth century, interest on good security in Holland was as low as two per cent. I have often wondered whether the first country textile factories of the north of England (so different, at least in outward appearance, from the satanic mills of text-book imagination) do not owe their permanence and their beauty to the accident, if accident it was, that they were constructed during the period of low rates of interest between 1783 and 1797. And these low rates may also have had an effect on such things as the depth to which mines were sunk, the size and type of the dwellings of the workers, the state of the highroads and the development of canals.

It would not be an easy task to trace the changes in the rate of interest in earlier centuries. Something might indeed come of a re-examination of the transactions of those usurers with whom Professor Tawney has so close an acquaintance. ('Acquaintance' rather than 'friendship' would seem to be the appropriate word.) And it should be possible to follow the major changes in long-term rates by careful study of mortgages and the terms of purchase of farms or fixed annual payments. The results might well justify the labour. Mr. Habakkuk has shown how enclosures declined as the rate of interest rose between 1690 and 1715; and a chronology of interest rates during the two preceding centuries might throw light not only on the breaking-in of the waste and the development of more capitalistic methods of cultivation, but also on changes in the technique and structure of early manufacturing industry.

The reconsideration by the economists of the nature and effects of national debt had results in other spheres. There is need for historians to rewrite their essays on the financial policies of, for example, Peel and Gladstone in the light of new ideas. If it were possible to extend to earlier periods those methods of estimating national income and capital that have been devised by economists and statisticians of this generation, we should be able to speak with more assurance about the wider social effects of these policies. We might also be able to answer with less hesitation the question as to how far what seem to us the miserably low standards of comfort of the labouring classes in earlier times were the inevitable consequences of low productivity and how far they resulted from avarice or want of social sympathy on the part of employers and landowners.

Again, in the nineteen-twenties, the problems of external debts and reparations led to re-examination of theories of international trade and the foreign exchanges. The principles laid bare by Taussig, Angell, Ohlin, Viner, Whale and others are now beginning to inform the work of historians. The concept of the terms of trade, essentially a historical concept, might be used to enlighten discussion on the economic relations between nations in earlier centuries, and, applied internally, on those of the relative rates of growth of agriculture and manufactures.

Yet again, the development in the 'twenties of monopolistic forms of organisation led other economists to refine that theory of value which had hitherto seemed to serve their purposes. Studies in imperfect or monopolistic competition provide tools better shaped for work on the past, no less than on the present, than those in perfect competition or pure monopoly on which most of us were brought up. How effective these tools may be has been demonstrated by several historians, notably by Mr. Burn in his scholarly study on the history of steel-making.

Unemployment and labour disputes in the same period drew the attention of other economists to the unsatisfactory state of the theory of wages, and new formulations resulted. Mr. Rostow has applied Professor Hicks' analysis to one period, at least, of the nineteenth century. But it can hardly be said that the second thoughts of economists in this field have yet been reflected in the works of economic historians in general. Thanks to Professor Bowley, we know something about the course of real wages in the nineteenth century, and others, like Knoop and Jones, and Mrs. Gilboy have provided valuable material for earlier times. There are excellent histories of trade unionism, detailed studies of labour movements such as Chartism, monographs on factory reformers, and chronological accounts of industrial and social legislation. But we know very little about the gradual changes in the status of the workers, and in their personal relations with the employers. Let me give one example of the kind of relation I have in mind. No one who glances through the records of industrial concerns of the period we call the Industrial Revolution can fail to be struck by the almost universal tendency of the workers to borrow from their employers on the security of future earnings. The effects on the mobility and bargaining strength of labour are obvious. To-day, as John Hilton has reminded us, debt is the key to all working-class life; but the debt is no longer owed to the employer, but to agencies outside the factory—moneylenders, pawnbrokers, above all instalment-selling concerns. Where and how was the change effected? I know of no economic historian who has investigated this or similar matters. Or, to mention a wider problem: we are almost entirely ignorant of the changes in the relative scarcities of different kinds of skill and of the elasticities of substitution between labour and capital at particular periods of time. Yet these are matters which may in the end prove to have been of at least as much account as the self-sacrifice of Lord Shaftesbury or the devoted energy of Ben Tillett. Labour, in the sense in which the word is used by the economist, still awaits its historian.

It was in the decade before the recent war, however, that there occurred the most spectacular of those developments in thought which make possible a closer co-operation of economists and historians. In this many played a part, but the work of Lord Keynes is outstanding. The introduction of an income-and-expenditure approach to the problem of money and prices and the analysis in terms of aggregates, rather than of marginal differences, were of some consequence. But what is even more important than these is that, at last, the theorists have provided an organon that can be applied to explain those alternations of activity and depression that have characterised the last two centuries or more of economic society. If we accept Lord Keynes' teaching that (except in conditions of full employment) the growth of capital is retarded, rather than advanced, by a low propensity to consume, we must seek the causes of that growth, no longer in the parsimony of the early factory employers, but in the relatively high expenditure of others (including the government) during the formative years of the Industrial Revolution. Already the economic outlines of the nineteenth century are seen in a new light. It should be an exciting experience for some young specialists in, say, the fourteenth century to discover how far the modern analysis can be used to explain the trends of a period in which land and money were virtually the only alternative ways of holding wealth, and in which credit institutions were still rudimentary.

The effect on the study of the development of particular institutions is likely to be profound. For to write of these, as some have done, without reference to the periodic variations of activity is like writing the life-history of a tree without reference to the climate or the seasons. The fluctuations of interest, investment, incomes, employment and prices are not just incidents to be mentioned in passing: they are an essential part of the environment in which social and political institutions flourish and decay.

(Among other conditions of appointment to the Professorship of Economic History, Mr. Chairman, is one which lays it down that the holder 'shall direct research'. A nineteenth-century novelist put the matter in other words when she wrote of 'that form of authorship which is called suggestion, and consists in telling another man that he might do a great deal with a given subject, by bringing sufficient amount of knowledge, reasoning and wit to bear upon it.' Interpreted so, there is one duty of this office for which I hope I have indicated if not an aptitude, at least a relish.)

What has been said so far may be read by some as an invitation to theorists to occupy the isthmus. That is not the intention. The interest of the economist in the past arises, as often as not, out of a wish to test his conclusions in a series of different environments: the interest of the historian is wider than that. The theorist has taught us that economic phenomena are bound together in ways that the uninstructed would not suspect. He has created an apparatus which explains any given economic situation in terms of profit expectations, the propensity to consume and so on. But beyond that he cannot go. It rests with the historian to trace the causes, or as he would prefer to say, the antecedents and predisposing circumstances of these expectations and propensities: to say how it came about that at one time men were inclined to spend freely, and at another to hoard their resources, how it was that men were enterprising and optimistic in this year or this decade, cautious and penurious in that. Sir William Beveridge tells us that in his pursuit of prices and wages through the centuries he was like one driving a car by night through unfamiliar country, with the glare of headlamps lighting up a narrow strip of road, and giving only occasional glimpses of the surrounding country-side. The historian can be no mere tourist: he must be a native who knows the fields and hedges and hidden valleys, as well as the highroads. All that is urged is that, when moving along some more or less defined route he should trust less to unaided vision or native wit and more to the processes of systematic thought: that he should make some use of imported headlamps. Not all the gadgets that the economist carries in his toolbag will be of direct use to the historian; some are whetstones for the sharpening of other implements; others, one suspects, are little more than ingenious toys. But that some of those I have mentioned can be used to make a cleaner job of our work on the past seems to me already to have been set beyond doubt.

I have said something about what the historian may learn from the economist, but little or nothing of what the economist may gain from a closer contact with historians. It is often urged that some acquaintance with history may save him from the hasty conclusion, the easy generalization, the belief that because an idea is new it is true, the tendency to dogmatism. I would not lay stress on this, for, in my experience, economists are no more prone to these weaknesses than other specialists. The poor fellows, indeed, have so often been reproved for being unrealistic and dogmatic that some of the best of them have developed an inferiority-complex and are apt to hold their golden peace when matters are in debate on which, it might be supposed, words from them might be of service. Nor is the gain merely that of being able to try out theoretic models at different altitudes, though there is something in that. It lies in the reminder that the institutions or factors about which economists generalize are concrete realities, with a past without knowledge of which they cannot be apprehended: in that widening of experience in time which history offers to us all.

Given patience, I am not without hope that we may break down that suspicion of all empirical generalizations that lurks in some of the more remote caves of the economists. For there are still theorists who are wounded in their pride at the suggestion that an historical fact or argument might sometimes be injected, with advantage to their dialectics. When, greatly daring, the historian ventures to put in a word the impression created is like that which might follow the entry to a drawing-room of a ploughboy with the mud of the fields fresh on his boots. If, however, the historian is called upon to apologize for his 'brute facts' he may reasonably ask for similar courtesy when the economist pays a return visit and brings, as his contribution to historical discourse, the hypothetical reactions of a hypothetical Robinson Crusoe to his hypothetical surroundings. But the whole discussion as to whether deduction or induction is the proper method to use in the social sciences is, of course, juvenile: it is as though we were to debate whether it were better to hop on the right foot or on the left. Sensible men endowed with two feet know that they are likely to make better progress if they walk on both.

To sum up: the historian is increasingly feeling for the structure that underlies the surface of events, for explanation and interpretation. The economist is increasingly concerned not with static equilibrium, but with the transition from one equilibrium to another, with problems in which *time* is one of the dimensions. If they will take counsel together they may move towards that ideal in which no longer will the one look at his facts in the hope of inducing from them a theory, and the other deduce from first principles a theory in the hope that it may be found to fit the facts, but in which the two cooperate so that, in the words of Croce, the facts and the theory demonstrate each other.

A word of warning: in order that there should be discourse between the two disciplines it is not necessary that historians should incorporate into their speech the phrases in which economists reveal, or conceal, their thoughts. For the language of economists is full of strange sounds and is apt to change with all the disconcerting inconsequence of American slang. The economic historian must know about, for example, the Multiplier: but the Multiplier is an ugly brute (especially when seen in reverse!) and there is no need, I suggest, to give him prominence our in pages. All that is wanted is some form of Basic English in which theorists and historians can converse: there might well be a conference called to consider the matter.

IV

Economic history, though an isthmus, is a wide territory. In this lecture I have said nothing of many of its outlying provinces: nothing of that area in which the demographers are sinking their shafts to strata deeper than the economic; nothing of that terrain, explored by Mr. Beales, where industrial and social streams of development mingle their waters; nothing of that region of battles between old privilege and new aspiration which the Hammonds have observed with their clear eyes and described in their sensitive speech; nothing of that coast, known to few as to Professor Tawney, where the waves of economic impulse beat on the eternal verities. That is not because I count these provinces as of small importance. It is, in fact, precisely in them that the moving frontier of the subject is likely to be pushed forward with most benefit. But, even in these, no economic historian is likely to add much to the work of the pioneers unless he brings with him some at least of the appliances of modern thought.

There is a group of historians who are disposed to argue that the course of events of each age expresses, in some way not very clearly defined, the spirit of that age. In the writings of some that spirit or *Zeitgeist* ceases to be merely an habitual character and becomes a demon, sometimes almost a malicious personal devil. There are others, less apocalyptic in outlook, who write of some abstract idea, such as Capitalism, as though it had the attributes of a living human being. It would be foolish to deny the existence of the phenomenon of Capitalism: the whole set of influences of which I have been speaking this afternoon may, indeed, be usefully described as manifestations of it. But what is to be resisted is the tendency of some who make much use of the word to a teleological interpretation of events: Capitalism required this, demanded that, necessitated everything. Now these interpretations of history in terms of brooding spirits or personified forces press heavily on the mind, especially of the young, who are apt to take them seriously. They lead not to faith and effort, but to pessimism and inertia. It may even be that the larger infiltration of the ideas of the economists for which I have pleaded, will in less degree, have something of the same effect. If, by the grace of God, we managed to cast out the devil of Teutonic mysticism from the house, of what profit would it be if we let in seven more demons under the name of Economic Determinants?

The best antidote I can think of to all this is detailed work on the records of some one merchant, manufacturing concern, banking house, trade union or other organization. The sense of the individual or group overcoming obstacles and building some fragment into the social fabric is heartening. And since, until within the last hundred years, life had not become departmentalized, the ledgers and letters and pay books tell us much, not only about prices and terms of credit and wages, but also about the people of whose work they are the record. The student will learn from them, it may be, little about the Spirit of the Age, but he will come to know more about the spirit of men. And in the light of that knowledge some of what pass as works of history will come to appear as shabby caricatures, often little better than crude libels on the dead.

The study of what by yet another misfortune of terminology has come to be called business history should be pursued alongside the interpretation of the past with the aid of the apparatus of economic thought. For it is in the business unit that economic forces can be seen in operation, as it were in the front line. Business history may serve as a reminder that demand and supply, the various elasticities and multipliers, the determinants and stabilisers, are all generalizations, useful indeed, but causal factors at one remove; and that it is the wills and choices and acts of men and women that are the ultimate data for economists and historians alike.

NOTES

1 Even in the eighteenth century the use of 'unemployed' as a substantive was not unknown. 'A perpetual influx of the unemployed from the north pours into Edinburgh and its vicinity . . .' George Robertson, *General View of the Agriculture of the County of Midlothian* (1793), p. 26.

11

F. J. Fisher

THE SIXTEENTH AND SEVENTEENTH CENTURIES:
THE DARK AGES IN ENGLISH ECONOMIC HISTORY?

(L.S.E., 1956)

This inaugural lecture was given at the London School of Economics on the 6th March 1956. The chair was taken by Professor R. H. Tawney.

THE SIXTEENTH AND SEVENTEENTH CENTURIES: THE DARK AGES IN ENGLISH ECONOMIC HISTORY?

TRADITIONALLY, an inaugural lecture should be used by the new occupant of a University Chair to expatiate upon the nature, methods and significance of the subject which he professes. But those are matters which my predecessors at the London School of Economics have so illuminated, both by precept and by example, that I am forced to choose a more modest theme. My purpose is merely to offer some comments upon the present state of the study of modern economic history in this country and, in particular, to draw attention to a tendency which has recently developed for modern economic history to be split, somewhere in the eighteenth century, not merely into two periods but almost into two separate subjects.

Despite the convention that modern economic history begins with the sixteenth century, it has, of course, long been realized that some sort of dividing line was to be found somewhere or other in the eighteenth. But, until recently, historians working on either side of that line tended to plough similar furrows. Not only did they ask similar questions; to a surprising and even suspicious extent they arrived at similar answers. On either side of the line one could find the small land-owner always disappearing and the middle classes always rising; capitalism always growing; trade always expanding; the standards of living of the working classes always falling. And but two decades ago, almost perfect equilibrium was obtained; for it was discovered that the sixteenth and early seventeenth centuries had produced an industrial revolution to balance the more notorious revolution of the eighteenth and nineteenth. So great was the emphasis on the continuity of English economic life and on the basic similarities between the various centuries that at times one was led to doubt whether anything happened in the eighteenth century at all.

In recent years, as I see it, the trend has been in the opposite direction. The emphasis on continuity has been seriously weakened. But it has been weakened, less by changes in historical interpretation, than by changes in historical method. A generation ago, the main requirement of an economic historian was that he should be able to read, since most of his sources were literary. The archetype of the learned

183

monograph consisted of a thin rivulet of text meandering through wide and lush meadows of footnotes. Though much derided, there was much to be said for that type of work. The brevity of his text made it difficult for an author to obscure his argument; the copious quotations in his footnotes were often more entertaining than anything the author himself could contrive. Today, that type of monograph has gone. To some extent it has been the victim of economic progress, for it is one of the eternal verities of history that as societies become wealthy they are no longer able to afford pleasures that were well within their reach when they were poor. But, very largely, it has been the victim of a change in fashion. Today the first requirement of an economic historian is that he should be able to count, for his materials are largely statistical. The archetype of our modern fashion is one in which a stream, often a less than limpid stream, of text tumbles from table to table and swirls round graph after graph. In his inaugural lecture my predecessor asked that a greater use should be made of statistics in the writing of economic history. The Almighty has answered his prayer, not with a shower, but with a deluge.

So far as an amateur in these matters can tell, the application of statistical methods to the study of the English economy in the eighteenth and nineteenth centuries has yielded highly valuable results. It has enormously increased the precision of our ideas about that period; it has in some measure increased the accuracy of those ideas. But, like most improvements, it has not been made without cost. The economic history of the eighteenth and nineteenth century is in some danger of becoming a specialized subject in the sense that only those with a peculiar mental equipment will be able to understand it. It is already becoming a specialized subject in the sense that, since quantitative methods can be applied only to such phenomena as are by their nature measurable, the economic historian is tending to contract his field of interest. In this respect it is perhaps relevant to notice the number of proposals that have recently been made for the development of social history; a discipline which seems to be designed, at least in part, to take over the field from which the economic historian is retreating. But the most serious cost of these new developments has, perhaps, been the break in the continuity of historical study between the sixteenth and seventeenth centuries on the one hand and the eighteenth and nineteenth centuries on the other. So long as literary sources are being used, historians in either of those periods can deal with very similar questions—and tend to get very similar answers. For literary sources often have their origin in the complaints of the disgruntled or of social reformers, and the literature of economic and social protest shows an almost monotonous uniformity throughout the ages. To take but one example, the lament that 'artificers and labourers . . . waste most part of the day and do not deserve their wages, sometimes in late coming to their work and early departing therefrom, long sitting at their breakfast and their dinner . . . and long time at sleeping in the afternoon' might, so far as its substance is concerned, have been made in any of the last five centuries. Only the cadence of its phrasing suggests that it comes, as indeed it does, from the early sixteenth.

But once statistical sources have to be used the historian of the early modern period rapidly gets out of step. Not, to be sure, because of any objection to quantitative methods as such. In fact, the application of statistical techniques to the study of the early period has sometimes been taken almost to extremes. Thus, if I am correctly informed, the history of the Papacy has recently been re-written on the basis of two statistical indices—one of managerial efficiency and the other of religious zeal. It would appear that the index of managerial efficiency stood at a respectable 60 in both the sixteenth and seventeenth centuries, but that the index of religious zeal fell from a low 35 in the sixteenth to an even lower 25 in the seventeenth. It would, however, be dishonest for the historian to claim the credit for that particular application. Like so much that is bold and imaginative in the interpretation of the past, it is the work of an economist. Professed historians have worked at a lower level; but they have worked assiduously and by now have accumulated a not inconsiderable volume of statistical data. Unfortunately, those data are more impressive in their volume than in either their quality or their range. They are largely confined to the fields of prices, government revenue and foreign trade; and even in those fields they are highly suspect. Having collected his figures, the historian is too often in the position of not knowing whether it is better to use them or to explain them away. Nor, in that quandary, does he often get much help from his literary sources; for contemporaries wrote in an even greater statistical void than does the modern historian. Admittedly, the seventeenth century saw the birth of Political Arithmetic—'the art of reasoning by figures upon things relating to government'. But the figures even of Petty, the father of that art, were seldom more than guesses. And although it may have been mere coincidence that Petty's guesses were usually 'very grateful to those who governed', it was certainly no accident that the guesses of other people were normally highly favourable to themselves. One example of the wildness of contemporary guesses may perhaps suffice. In 1694 a committee in the House of Lords was debating a bill to allow, for the duration of the war, the importation of Italian raw and thrown silk via the Netherlands. Counsel for the London Silkthrowers, arguing for the importation of thrown silk, asserted that the throwers numbered nearly 200,000. Counsel for the

P

London Weavers, arguing for the importation of raw silk, challenged that figure and the committee adjourned for a more exact total to be produced. When it reassembled it was presented, not with one total, but with two. The Beadle of the Silkthrowers claimed that there were 80,000 workers in the industry; one of the Company's Assistants thought there were only 30,000. It is, perhaps, not surprising that the Lords were among the advocates of improved statistics at the end of the seventeenth century.

To the teacher and student, at least, this tendency for modern economic history to split virtually into two subjects, by asking different questions and using different methods, is a matter of some moment. Those undergraduates who, selecting economic history as their special subject, direct their attention mainly to the eighteenth and nineteenth centuries complain—and complain bitterly—that there is no precision in what they read or what they are told about the sixteenth and seventeenth. Those whose interests lie mainly in the earlier modern period complain that the history of the nineteenth century is full of every sort of figure except the human. Since quantitative data are also lacking for the Middle Ages, it might seem that all my argument amounts to is that, in this respect as in many others, the Middle Ages really lasted until the Glorious Revolution and that the problem might be solved simply by altering the periods into which history is conveniently divided. But this as a solution—if solution it be—is one which historians as a whole will not accept. If the student of the sixteenth and seventeenth centuries is deficient in the statistical techniques now being applied to the nineteenth, he is almost equally deficient in those more esoteric methods by which the truth about the Middle Ages is discovered. The position has been recently put, quite bluntly, by Professor Heaton in a passage which, too long to be quoted in full, may be summarised as follows: the great growth of population, production, trade, migration and capital investment of the eleventh to the thirteenth centuries is well established. The stagnation and recession in population and enterprise from about 1350 to at least 1450 is supported by much gloomy evidence. After at latest 1750 the emphasis is on the abnormal growth of population. The central problem becomes how to feed and clothe generations of children outnumbering by far those of any earlier times. Some countries failed to solve it, with consequent starvation, disease, falling living standards, revolution and emigration. The British solved it because sufficient landlords, farmers, manufacturers, merchants and others had the wit and resource to devise new instruments of production, evolve new methods of organising and administering production, and dig out unprecedented quantities of capital for fixed plant and operating expenses. But what of the period between 1450 and 1750? 'In many respects this early modern period is the Dark Ages of economic history'.

Although this problem presents itself in its most acute form to those historians who are mainly concerned with such measurable things as the population, output, and the national income, it is not peculiar to them. If one may judge by the very interesting discussions which have arisen out of Maurice Dobb's *Studies in the Development of Capitalism*, the sixteenth and early seventeenth centuries are a period of some difficulty for the Marxists also. It is part of the Marxist creed that feudalism was overthrown by capitalism. But it is also generally accepted by Marxist historians that whereas feudalism was in an advanced state of disintegration by the end of the fourteenth century, the capitalist period cannot be said to open until considerably later. Indeed, at a conference of British Marxist historians held in 1947, it was agreed that 'the Tudor and Stuart state was essentially an executive instrument of the feudal class more highly organised than ever before. . . . Only after the Revolution of 1640–1649 does the state in England begin to be subordinated to the capitalists. . . . The revolution of 1640 replaced the rule of one class by another.' Thus the Marxist is faced by the problem of finding for the sixteenth and seventeenth centuries an interpretation which, while permitting feudalism to disintegrate in the later Middle Ages as the evidence requires, will nevertheless preserve it to be slain in the seventeenth century as theory demands. One suggestion, that of Mr. Sweezy, is to call the system which prevailed in the fifteenth and sixteenth centuries 'pre-capitalist commodity production' to indicate that it was the growth of commodity production which first undermined feudalism and then, somewhat later, after that work of undermining had been substantially completed, prepared the ground for capitalism. But it seems that any such suggestion, however reasonable it may superficially appear, leads only into the 'Pokrovsky-bog of merchant capitalism' and will not serve for a revolutionary view of historical development. The alternative method—that of keeping feudalism alive by subtly changing its definition—has the demerit of keeping it alive too long. The problem, it would seem, is still unresolved.

Hence the historians of Tudor and Stuart England at present stand indicted by their fellows. Their labours, it would seem, have been outside the main field of historical enquiry. Whoever seeks to trace the development of the English economy through the ages, whether he is primarily interested in such matters as population, output and national income, or whether his main concern is with class structure, finds that he loses the thread of his story at some time in the fifteenth century and picks it up again only some two hundred years later.

Between, to repeat the accusation of Professor Heaton, come the dark ages of economic history. That is an indictment which demands an answer.

One thing is clear enough. There can be no reasonable doubt that the sixteenth and seventeenth centuries saw an increase in the output of English agriculture and industry. The England of the early Tudors was rich in unused physical resources—idle land, unexploited woodlands, unworked minerals. By the end of the seventeenth century these resources were being used to a far greater degree; more land was being cultivated; woodlands were being either carefully managed to provide fuel or grubbed up to make room for corn and pasture; the growth of mineral output had been spectacular in the case of coal and substantial in the case of iron, lead, and salt. Nor was expansion confined to primary production. There was a marked widening of the range of England's secondary industries with the introduction of new forms of woollen textiles and the development of the cotton and silk manufactures, glassmaking, papermaking, brassmaking, sugar refining and of other trades hitherto practised, if at all, only on an insignificant scale. And in the country's economic relationships with the outer world, although change was gradual, its cumulative effects were profound. At the beginning of the sixteenth century England was still mainly an exporter of wool and unfinished cloth to north-western Europe. By the end of the seventeenth she was not only exporting a wide range of woollen fabrics to all of Europe, the Near and Far East, Africa and America; in addition she was sending both men and capital across the Atlantic and, with the aid of a vastly expanded mercantile marine, carrying on a substantial re-export trade in Asiatic and American produce. The problem is to relate that undoubted expansion to the demographic changes which accompanied it. From the taxation records which have survived it seems reasonably certain that the population of England approximately doubled between the late fourteenth and late seventeenth centuries; and although the evidence for the intervening years is inconclusive, it seems likely that most of that growth occurred after 1500. A growth of population in a country with abundant unused resources is likely to be accompanied by an expansion of output. The problem of the historian of Tudor and Stuart England is to decide whether the expansion so induced was also accompanied by progress; i.e. by an increase in income per head.

In the absence of statistical data, no direct approach to that problem is possible. Moreover, for a number of reasons, the most obvious of the indirect methods of approach do not yield conclusive answers. It might seem an elementary matter to compare the conditions which obtained at the beginning of a period with those obtaining at its end; but such a comparison is made difficult by the changes which occurred in the nature of historical records during the sixteenth and seventeenth centuries. In the early years of the sixteenth century whole categories of records which the medievalists find invaluable begin to peter out or disappear completely, partly as a result of the Reformation, partly as a result of the new administrative methods introduced by the Tudors. After the middle of that century there emerges another body of materials extraordinarily rich but significantly different from that which preceded it. Then, after the Restoration, those materials peter out in turn with the decline in the powers of the Privy Council and their place is taken by a new pamphlet literature and by the tax records which eventually develop into the statistical sources used by my more up-to-date colleagues. At first sight, it is true, the economy in 1700 looks very different from what it had been in 1500. But it does so partly because the most easily available records illumine different facets of it.

Something, one might suppose, could be deduced from changing habits of consumption. And it is clear that by the end of the seventeenth century the upper classes, and the more prosperous farmers and tradesmen, enjoyed a wider range of goods and services than had their ancestors of two hundred years before. But changing patterns of consumption do not necessarily mean that the incomes of consumers have increased. It was a constant complaint of the times that the new habits meant a decline in 'hospitality' and at least one pamphleteer attributed the sluggishness of agricultural prices in the late seventeenth century to the fact that gentlemen paid for their new-fangled pleasures by going without their suppers and demanded that, in the public interest, all gentlemen should have suppers prepared for them whether they partook of them or not. Moreover, there is abundant evidence that some of the gentry paid for their new standard of living by dissipating their capital. Finally, there is the problem of the poor. Even at the beginning of the sixteenth century the lot of the poor had been hard. 'Poor labourers, carters, ironsmiths, carpenters and ploughmen', wrote Sir Thomas More, 'by so great and continual toil as drawing and bearing beasts be scant able to sustain . . . get so hard and poor a living and live so wretched and miserable a life that the state and condition of the labouring beasts may seem much better and wealthier. . . . These silly poor wretches be presently tormented with barren and unfruitful labour, and the remembrance of their poor, indigent and beggarly old age killeth them up. For their daily wages is so little that it will not suffice for the same day, much less it yieldeth any overplus that may daily be laid up for the relief of old age.' The little we know of the movement of real wage rates suggests that the lot of the poor was to deteriorate still further; and both the history of the Poor Law and the calculations of such men as King and Davenant suggest that by the end of the seventeenth century the poor may have constituted a larger proportion of the population than at the beginning of the sixteenth. The inequality with which the national income was distributed makes it dangerous to deduce changes in that income from changes in the consumption habits of the wealthier classes.

Nor is the detailed history of agricultural and industrial production as helpful as might be hoped. By the end of the seventeenth century, it is true, writers extolled the virtues of machinery as saving labour and increasing output per head. But labour-saving devices played an insignificant part in the economic changes with which we are concerned; and when they appeared they were bitterly opposed. From Starkey to Davenant all were agreed that the country's major economic problem lay in the under-employment of its labour force. Partly that underemployment was due to the seasonal fluctuations in agriculture, mining and transport; partly to the fact that many men were producing for local markets too small to keep them continuously occupied; partly to the high leisure preference which the inhabitants of poor countries so often possess. When the rewards for toil were meagre, the temptation to toil no more than was necessary for a bare subsistence was great. Whatever the relative importance of those different causes, the path of wisdom seemed to contemporaries to lie less in the provision of equipment to save labour than in the provision of more working capital to set that labour on work, in the creation of new markets to absorb its output, and in the provision of a legislative and economic environment in which the costs of voluntary leisure should be painfully high. The purpose of the inventions of the sixteenth and seventeenth centuries was less to save labour than to bring the forces of nature under greater control. In so far as national income per head changed during that period, it is more likely to have changed because of changes in the level of employment than for any other reason. And of all economic phenomena, the level of employment is one of the most difficult for the historian to assess.

Consequently, as is so often the case, the historian is driven back on to the coherency theory of truth. When the direct evidence relating to his problem is so scanty, can he construct a consistent and plausible argument from such material as he has? It is in the light of that question that recent work on the economic history of the sixteenth and seventeenth centuries must be surveyed. Most of the recent studies in that field deal either with overseas trade, or with local history, or with the relationship between religion and economic life, or with the fortunes of the landed gentry. To what extent can materials collected on topics so diverse be used to illuminate the problem of economic growth?

The relevance of foreign trade to that problem is obvious enough. It is the one field in which statistics are reasonably abundant, and despite their many imperfections there can be little doubt that foreign trade and shipping grew rather more rapidly than population; and with them grew employment in the exporting industries, the mercantile marine, and in the increasing number of trades dependent upon imported raw materials. But foreign trade accounted for only a small fraction of the national output; most production was for home consumption and it is in this field that the crux of our problem lies. Fortunately, it is above all on this field that the local historians for the most part cast their light. One of the difficulties which beset the student of the sixteenth and seventeenth centuries is the fact that most of his material is narrowly local. Not only is that obviously true of records which relate to a particular manor, or parish, or town, or county, or business; it has constantly to be remembered that most of the general statements about the economy as a whole were made by men whose knowledge was essentially local. It is not until the very end of the seventeenth century that much effort was made by the government, or by economic interests, or by writers to bring together similar information for different parts of the country so as to afford a conspectus of the whole. It was not until the eighteenth that those efforts were crowned with spectacular success in the work of Defoe. For the period with which we are concerned the historian is constantly puzzled to know whether the progress or decay which he finds in any specific place is purely local, and to decide whether a process which appears to be continuous is in fact so or merely appears so because it occurs in different parts of the country at different times. In such matters only detailed work in local history can resolve his difficulties and in that sphere much detailed work remains to be done. But even from the work that has been done so far, two developments of major importance emerge. One is the growth of London from a city with a population of some fifty or sixty thousands to one with a population of half a million; a growth based partly on foreign trade, partly on manufacturing, partly on the provision of financial and professional services, partly on its role as the country's political and social centre. The other is the economic development of the hitherto backward west and north. That development was reflected in the growth of the textile industries of Devon, Lancashire and the West Riding, of the metallurgical and leather industries of the Severn Valley and the Black Country, of the potteries of Staffordshire and of coal, glass, and salt production on Tyneside; it was reflected also in the rise to commercial importance of Bristol and Liverpool with their easy access to Ireland, Africa and, above all, America. Nor, it seems, was that growth restricted to industry and overseas trade for, at least in the West, there was much land over which cultivation could be extended once the industrial areas provided a market for foodstuffs and once the introduction of artificial grasses facilitated the reclamation of hitherto barren land. By the end of the seventeenth century, if contemporaries are to be believed, those regions were characterised by cheap food because of agricultural improvements, by low wages because of cheap food, and by low poor rates because of the industrial demand for labour.

Those developments, taking place on opposite sides of the country, had one effect in common. They greatly stimulated internal trade. London did so primarily by virtue of the large market which its population offered to provincial producers. It was fashionable to bewail the growth of the capital as draining the life-blood of the country, and it may be that in some measure that growth did, in fact, depress industrial and mercantile activity elsewhere in southern and eastern England. In overseas trade the Southern and Eastern ports found it difficult to compete with London; and there may be some substance in the argument that the metropolitan demand for food raised prices and wages in nearby industrial areas. At least, it is noticeable that by the later seventeenth century the major industries in the Home Counties were those such as spinning, knitting, lace-making and strawplaiting that depended on female rather than on male labour. But the benefits which flowed from the city's expansion were too obvious to be missed by more perceptive commentators. 'It may be well worth the enquiry of thinking men', wrote Davenant, 'what truth there is in this common and received notion that the growth of London is pernicious to England; that the kingdom is like a rickety body with a head too big for the other members. For some people who have thought much on this subject are inclined to believe that the growth of the city is advantageous to the nation'. Among those who thought thus was Houghton. 'Let us,' he wrote, 'consider what the consequences will be of making London as big again. . . . In likelihood we should spend twice as many coals, which would double the shipping to Newcastle and that double the trade and people at Newcastle. . . . Whatsoever is said here for Newcastle will likewise serve for Norfolk for stuffs, stockings or fish; for Suffolk and Cambridgeshire for butter; for the counties about London for most sorts of food; for the West for serges, tin, etc.; for Cheshire for cheese; for Derby and Yorkshire for lead, alum and several other; and in short, for all counties and places in them; for I believe there is no county or place in England but directly supplies London, or at one hand or other supplies them that do supply it.' In its turn the development of the North and West stimulated internal trade, not only because of the demand which the growing industrial population created for foodstuffs, but also because the industries upon which it was based were all producing for more than a local market.

This development of inland trade, it may be argued, was one of the most significant features of economic life under the Tudors and Stuarts. But it is difficult to speak of it with precision for, since most of it passed overland, it has left no statistical record. Fortunately, it is the habit of men to bewail their blessings and in some measure its story can be reconstructed from the complaints to which it gave rise. Under the Tudors the villain most frequently consigned to eternal damnation was 'that caterpillar which cometh between the bark and the tree'—the middleman in primary produce. By the early seventeenth century he had come to be accepted as a necessary evil and criticism was being directed at shopkeepers who sold goods which they had not produced; but by the end of that century even they had acquired the respectability of a vested interest demanding protection from intruders. 'The inland or home trade of England', it was asserted in a slightly later broadside on that theme, 'is an ancient establishment of business, form'd from the beginning in the mere nature and consequence of things, from the situation of places, the growth of materials, and other conveniences of the manufactures. This method of trade consists not in the bare producing or manufacturing the first principles of our trade, such as the wool, leather, metals and minerals, in which our country abounds, but in the buying and selling, carrying and re-carrying the goods from place to place for sale. This is very significantly called the circulation of trade, by which every part of the island is fully supply'd with what they respectively want. Trade going on in this happy progress, has for many ages increased to a mighty degree, so that manufactures of one kind or another are carried on in every county, shops are open'd in every corner, and in the most remote parts well furnished with goods of all needful kinds, as well of our own produce as of foreign importations. The shops, with the wholesale dealers and manufacturers who supply them are infinitely numerous, and being generally kept by the most substantial people, are the support of the whole trade of the kingdom; these may be said to pay the landed men their rent, the government their taxes, the parishes their assessments, and the poor their allowances; they bear all the burthens and chargeable offices in the towns and parishes where they dwell.' Such men, it was argued, clearly deserved and needed to be nourished and defended. 'For now, to the infinite and unexpressible loss and discouragement of all these fair traders, they find this beautiful constitution of trade broken in upon and invaded by the frauds and arts of the hawkers and pedlars, and private clandestine traders, who, upon pretence of selling cheaper than the shops, insinuate themselves into the opinion of the buyers, which pretence also is a delusion in fact (except where smuggling, or dealing in prohibited goods, and other unlawful practices, may enable them to do so). On this occasion the fair trader, as well by wholesale as retale, as also the woollen and silk manufacturers of this kingdom, humbly represent; first that these people travelling or rather wandering from place to place, and having no legal abode, thereby avoid all the several payments and assessments which the fair tradesmen, who are house-keepers and settled inhabitants, are subjected to. Secondly, that by carrying their packs from house to house they invert the order of trade, supplant the fair dealer, and forestall the markets: and thus the scheme of our inland trade is broken, and the manufactures know no regular motion. The carriers are intercepted, and must in time cease to travel, for want of double carriage; or the foreign goods (which the shop-keepers must have) will come heavily charged with the said double carriage: the inns and houses of entertainment on the road (which are now, beyond comparison, the best in the world) will sink, and the whole commerce feel a sensible and terrible decay.' And by the end of the seventeenth century the growth of inland trade was inspiring more important demands than that for the taxation or suppression of hawkers and pedlars, for it was the major cause of a spate of projects for improving harbours, roads and rivers.

The significance of this needs no elaboration. The growth of internal and foreign trade meant that an increasing amount of production was for more than local markets, and Adam Smith's explanation of how larger markets lead to the division of labour and the efficiency which specialisation engenders has long been an integral part of economic doctrine. Moreover, it would seem that production for a large market permitted more regular employment than production for a small, so that the changes which increased efficiency may well have served also to raise the general level of employment.

The changes which, during the same period, took place in the relationships between religion and economic life have inspired a literature to which justice cannot be done in any brief summary; but the nature of these changes can at least be crudely indicated by the contrast between two well-known prayers. The first is the Prayer for Landlords officially published in 1553 and then abandoned by the Anglican Church for ever:

'The earth O Lord is thine, and all that is contained therein; we heartily pray thee to send thy Holy Spirit into the hearts of them that possess the grounds, pastures, and dwelling places of the earth that they, remembering themselves to be Thy tenants, may not rack and stretch out the rents of their houses and lands, nor yet take unreasonable fines and incomes after the manner of covetous worldlings, but so let them out to others that the inhabitants thereof may both be able to pay the rents, and also honestly to live, to nourish their families, and to relieve the poor.

Give them grace also to consider that they are but strangers and pilgrims in this world, having here no dwelling place but seeking one to come. That they, remembering the short continuance of their life, may be content with that that is sufficient, and not join house to house, nor couple land to land to the impoverishment of others, but so behave themselves in letting out their tenements, lands and pastures that after this life they may be received into everlasting dwelling places.'

The other is to be found among the papers of a financier who was considered shady even by the unexacting standards of the early eighteenth century in which he lived.

'O Lord, thou knowest I have mine estates in the City of London and likewise that I have lately purchased an estate in fee simple in the County of Essex. I beseech Thee to preserve the two counties of Middlesex and Essex from fire and earth-quake. And as I have a mortgage in Hertfordshire, I beg Thee likewise to have an eye of compassion on that county. For the rest of the counties; Thou mayest deal with them as Thou art pleased.'

Whatever the reasons for it, that transformation of Divine Grace from an instrument for perpetuating the uneconomic allocation of resources into a protection for economic enterprise and business foresight was among the intellectual achievements of the age. The influence of public opinion upon individual action is, admittedly, one of the imponderables in history. But it is surely not fanciful to suggest that, for men whose skins are not abnormally thick, the incentive to acquire wealth is strengthened by the belief that its possessor will deserve well of the Almighty and obtain social acceptance by all right-minded people.

Nor were such factors the only ones operating to create a social climate favourable to the entrepreneur. 'To what purpose', wrote Weston, 'do soldiers, scholars, lawyers, merchants and men of all occupations and trades toil and labour with great affection but to get money, and with that money when they have gotten it to buy land,? It is by now a commonplace of the textbooks that, between the middle of the sixteenth century and the closing years of the seventeenth, sales by impecunious gentry and an even more impecunious Crown made land more easily available to moneyed men than ever before. And if land by itself was not a sufficient passport to social bliss, gentility was not out of reach. At first sight it is true, the status-system of the sixteenth and seventeenth centuries does not seem highly favourable to the rising man. As I understand it that system, at least in its cruder manifestations, was essentially biological. It was based upon a colour bar; though the relevant colour was that of the blood rather than of the skin. A man's status depended less on his own distinction than on the possession of an ancestor who had been distinguished before him. And the more remote that ancestor, and hence presumably the less of his blood which flowed through an Elizabethan's veins, the higher the status of that Elizabethan was. One of the most pathetic stories of the sixteenth century is that, I think, of the efforts of Lord Burleigh—a man of distinction by any rational criteria—to prove his descent from a Welsh princeling who probably never existed and who, if he did exist, was probably hardly distinguishable from the sheep of his native hills.

The advantages of a colour bar to those on the sunny side of it are too obvious to need exposition. But, as modern experience shows, the operation of such a bar raises certain philosophical problems. For the proposition that socially valuable qualities are the monopoly of a biological group is not one that is easily reconciled with experience. It was this dilemma which inspired, no doubt, the remark to be found in that curious work *The Blazon of Gentry*: 'Jesus Christ was a gentleman, as to His flesh, by the part of His mother . . . and if He had esteemed the vain glory of this world (whereof He often said His Kingdom was not) might have borne coat-armour. The Apostles also were gentlemen of blood . . . but through the tract of time and persecution of wars, poverty oppressed the kindred and they were constrained to servile works.' It was that dilemma which, solved in some countries only by revolution, was so magnificently dealt with in England by the College of Heralds. That College was set up to prevent men of low birth from passing as gentlemen. If contemporaries are to be believed, its labours produced exactly the opposite effect. To quote the well-known words of Sir Thomas Smith, Elizabethan ambassador and secretary of state, 'as for gentlemen, they be made good cheape in England. For whosoever studieth the lawes of the realme, who studieth in the universities, who professeth liberall sciences, and to be shorte, who can live idly and without manuall labour, and will beare the port, charge and countenaunce of a gentleman, he . . . shall be taken for a gentleman: . . . (and if need be) a king of Heraulds shal also give him for mony, armes newly made and invented, the title whereof shall pretende to have beene found by the sayd Herauld in perusing and viewing of olde registers, where his auncestors in times past had bin recorded to beare the same: Or if he will do it more truely and of better faith, he will write that for the merittes of that man, and certaine qualities which he doth see in him, and for sundrie noble actes which he hath perfourmed, he by the authoritie which he hath as king of Heraldes and armes, giveth to him and his heries these and these armes, which being done I thinke he may be called a squire, for he beareth ever after those armes.' Nor was that written in terms of disapproval. Posing the question whether that manner of making gentlemen is to be allowed or no, Smith came to the conclusion that 'it is not amisse'.

Thus it is arguable that economic development in Tudor and Stuart England was more than the simple result of population growth. Quite apart from such external factors as the rise of Antwerp and the influx of American silver, the social climate was becoming more favourable to business men and, braced by that climate, business men seized their opportunities to build up a volume of internal and overseas trade that brought with it at least some of the benefits of specialisation and possibly raised the general level of employment. For that reason it is possible to think of this period in terms of economic progress as distinct from mere economic expansion. Yet a caveat must at once be entered. Even when all allowances have been made for the changes in the nature of the records, it is difficult to resist the conclusion that such progress as occurred was a feature of the seventeenth century rather than of the sixteenth—and of the later seventeenth century rather than of the earlier. The growth of London, of the extra-European and entrepot trades, and of western and northern industry were Stuart rather than Tudor phenomena. Although the new attitude to business enterprise was being reflected in the House of Commons at the end of Elizabeth's reign, for another generation it was to be denied full expression by the policies pursued by the privy council. Admittedly, the land market was brisk from the middle of the sixteenth century, but the most prominent purchasers in it seem to have been professional rather than business men. Partly, no doubt, that was because government service and the law did not permit the ploughing back of profits. But partly it seems to have been the result of a relatively under-developed economy in which the professions offered higher rewards than more mundane business. If, in the early seventeenth century, one wishes to find competition at its most fierce it is to be found, I suggest, not in trade or industry but in the conflict of jurisdictions between the Courts. That conflict is part of the constitutional history of England, and I would not insult my legal colleagues by implying that the lawyers who fought it were inspired by any motives other than the desire to protect the liberties of Englishmen. But the economic historian cannot but notice that, in their case, the financial rewards of civic virtue were considerable. Today, it may be, the stories of the large earnings to be made in the law are purely figments of envious imagination. In the seventeenth century they seem to have been better founded.

This distinction between the earlier and later parts of the period can obtain some support from other evidence. It is, for example, suggested by what we know of the movement of prices and wages. Admittedly, our data are but fragmentary and were influenced by changes in the supply of money. But a feature of the later sixteenth and early seventeenth centuries seems to have been a rapid rise in rents and agricultural prices combined with a much slower rise in wages and industrial prices. Such a combination suggests an economy in which agriculture was not expanding sufficiently to provide men with all the food, the farms and the employment that they needed and in which industrial development was too slow to make up for the deficiencies of agriculture. Nor is that suggestion implausible. Commercial statistics suggest that under Elizabeth foreign trade grew but little and that the later years of James's reign saw a series of major depressions. Coal-mining apart, there is little evidence of rapid industrial expansion before the second quarter of the seventeenth century. The main form of agricultural improvement was the enclosure of open fields and commons—it was estimated that two acres of enclosed land were worth three in the open fields or seven on the commons—but that was not always easy. In the more densely populated areas common rights were highly prized and were defended by their owners with great bitterness and, perhaps, with less obscurantism than the improvers alleged. The less densely populated areas, in which the institutional obstacles to enclosure may have been less, were often remote from the main centres of consumption and cursed with large areas of marshy or relatively infertile soil. It needed the greater urban and industrial markets of the seventeenth century, cheaper capital, and better methods of drainage and land reclamation to spread agricultural improvement throughout the country. Nor were the Fates always kind; there is some evidence that bad harvests were particularly frequent in the late sixteenth and early seventeenth centuries and that the efforts of men were in some measure frustrated by the vagaries of the weather. Today it is unfashionable to think of Elizabethan England as a country in which population pressure was gradually reducing many to poverty and possibly diminishing the national income per head; but that was a view which some contemporaries held. The argument of over-population was repeatedly used by the advocates of America colonisation; there is no reason to doubt their sincerity; it is even possible that they were right. One reason why the middle and later years of the seventeenth century present a rather brighter picture may be that population growth was temporarily checked by emigration and bubonic plague, to be resumed only when agricultural, industrial and commercial expansion were more fully in their stride.

Thus it is possible for the historian of Tudor and Stuart England to give at least a tentative reply to the indictment of Professor Heaton; although he cannot measure the changes which occurred during that period he can at least suggest the directions in which affairs were moving. To the Marxist he has scarcely any reply at all. The most striking thing about the social analyses made by Wilson at the end of the sixteenth century and King at the end of the seventeenth was that their categories, unlike those used by Colquhoun at the end of the eighteenth, were essentially medieval—landowner and merchant; clergyman and lawyer; petty trader and handicraftsman; seaman and labourer. Despite the contemporary murmurings about 'monied men' neither of those authors—and neither of them was a fool—saw any need for any separate category of industrial or financial capitalists. Nor, perhaps, is that surprising. Most of the entrepreneurs who brought about the economic changes were small men readily included in the category of properous artisans or tradesmen. Those who provided the considerable fixed equipment in the mining, metallurgical or shipping industries were easily thought of as landowners or merchants, for that in fact is what they were. The effect of the economic changes of the sixteenth and seventeenth centuries was less to create new categories of men than to offer the existing categories new opportunities and to inspire them with a new spirit.

It is important, however, that an economic historian should not even seem to accept the suggestion that he is concerned solely with the story of change. If his interests were so confined the sixteenth and seventeenth centuries would indeed be an unrewarding field, for the economic changes which they saw were not great. A historian's function is, surely, to discover how men have behaved in the various environments within which they have lived. In that respect the historian of the Tudor and Stuart economies may perhaps claim some modest success. Whether his discoveries and conclusions are of interest and value to workers in other branches of social study is, of course, for them to say. But perhaps a historian may be permitted two comments. One is inspired by a remark recently made at dinner by one of my most distinguished colleagues in this University. It was, if my memory serves me, 'Despite what Professor Fisher thinks, I say that history should be based on facts. If it is not based on facts it is sociology'. And, in my experience, the economic historian working in the sixteenth and seventeenth centuries finds it particularly easy to hold sympathetic converse with sociologists. Whether or not it is because they have a similar attitude to facts, they share an interest in similar problems. I suspect that, if a social history of the eighteenth and nineteenth centuries ever develops, it will cover many of the topics with which the economic history of the earlier period now deals.

My final comment is inspired, like so many of my views on this subject, by the work of Professor Tawney. Just consider some of the more obvious features of the Tudor and Stuart economy. It was one in which the methods of production were simple and the units of production were small; in which middlemen and usurers were both hated and indispensable; in which agricultural progress was seriously impeded by the perpetuation of communal rights over land. The chronic underemployment of labour was one of its basic problems and, despite moral exhortations, among the mass of the people the propensity to save was low. Consider the comments made by the rector of Bodsworth on two of his parishioners in 1551. 'These men earn twenty shillings a year each. Their masters with whom they dwell find them all manner of tools, so they spend nothing in getting their wages save find themselves in clothes. Either of them might save at the year end clearly five shillings and eightpence.' And what was their reply? It was that they could not save a penny. Moreover, if contemporaries are to be believed, both the incentive to work and the propensity to save were being undermined by that crude form of social services known as the Elizabethan Poor Law. It was an economy heavily dependent on foreign sources for improved industrial and agricultural methods, and to some extent for capital, but in which foreign labour and business men were met with bitter hostility. In it ambitious young men often preferred careers in the professions and government service to those in business, and fortunes made in business were too readily converted into land. It was an economy in which monetary stability was periodically threatened and sometimes upset by unwise policies on the part of the government, and in which an embryo money market had its efficiency impaired by a glut of government paper that it could not digest. Men increasingly pinned their hopes on industrialization and economic nationalism to absorb its growing population; but industrialization was slow to come and the blessings of economic nationalism proved to be mixed. Such an economy may have little in common with our own; but at least some of its characteristics are still to be found in countries so different from ours that we call them underdeveloped. I would suggest—and in this I am fortified by the example of Professor Tawney's classic study of *Land and Labour in China*—that an understanding of the economy of Tudor and Stuart England is not the worst equipment for a study of the economically less developed parts of the modern world. In the last resort, perhaps the darkness of the sixteenth and seventeenth centuries depends upon the angle from which they are approached and upon the questions that are asked about them.

12

W. Ashworth

THE STUDY OF MODERN ECONOMIC HISTORY
(Bristol, 1958)

This inaugural lecture was delivered at the University of Bristol on the 13th November 1958. Some brief introductory remarks, appropriate to the occasion but not essential to the themes of the lecture, have been omitted.

THE STUDY OF MODERN ECONOMIC HISTORY

THE purpose of the remarks in this lecture can be explained very easily. I believe that there are sound reasons for encouraging an increased attention to the study of modern economic history in universities, especially among undergraduates—it may be that the subject already has its fair share of research workers, though not of research funds—and I wish to suggest what are some of those reasons. I also wish to consider what is involved, educationally, in teaching people to understand modern economic history more fully, since fuller understanding among those who can hardly avoid all contact with the subject is more important than the attraction of greater numbers who will make economic history their special study.

An expansion of the teaching of economic history is, of course, not something that still awaits a beginning, and the present discussion is best introduced by a brief consideration of some of the changes that have recently taken place. One of the odd things about the development of economic history as an academic subject is that it has happened in spite of there being no agreement about what it is and where it belongs. Some universities have introduced it as a minor element in the economics department, some in a similarly minor position in the history department. A few have found an odd corner where it could be tucked away by itself without bothering anyone. There have been plenty of economists and plenty of historians who were equally ready to disown it and quite willing to concede the claim of those economic historians who maintained that their subject was neither economics nor history, but something between the two.

Yet, despite the suspicion of the bar sinister, it has come to be less and less excluded from polite society. In the last three years five British universities have established new chairs of economic history, almost doubling the number previously in existence, and this gratifying result has been achieved without the employment of a single public relations officer or, so far as I know, any of that useful field research into economic incentives which jealous non-beneficiaries are apt to describe as corrupt practices. The most plausible explanation is that accumulating experience must have made students of many other subjects aware that the advancement of their own work is helped by some study of economic history.

It is easy enough to see how the economists and the historians were affected. Economics is not just inner light made manifest in refulgent chains of pure and eternal logic. Even some of its most abstract propositions claim an ultimate derivation from some sort of general observation. The appetite for conceivable but non-experienced worlds can be sated; the conflicts and setbacks of the recent past have presented urgent challenges; and, let it be whispered, the market for economic advisers who can tell governments and business firms, reasonably accurately, how the affairs of this world are working out and how they can be altered has grown appreciably. More and more are economists drawn from the contemplation of general hypotheses to the explanation of the actual course of events; and they cannot do this for very long without finding themselves writing economic history, whatever they meant to do. Historians may begin with single-minded devotion to the activities which they count as supreme in the affairs of men: the business of state, the creation of the edifice of law and justice, the maintenance of religion. But then they find politics distorted by threats of governmental bank-ruptcy, the balance of power disturbed by the rise of new industrial techniques, the content of parts of the law moulded by new com-mercial practices, the spread of the gospel hampered because dearth (or sometimes its opposite) reduces the numbers of the faithful and the revenues of the Church; and either they leave their subjects in-complete, or else they find themselves writing economic history, however much it goes against the grain.

But this sort of development does not stop with economists and historians. Once the geographers leave behind their exclusive concern with the physical terrain and start on its human inhabitants they forgo all hope of a pure intellectual life. They find themselves drawn irresistibly from settlement to production, from production to commerce, and immediately the explanation of their problems compels them to look before and after. Who can go very far in human geography or economic geography or historical geography without finding something that looks very like economic history? Indeed, the only definition of historical geography known to a non-geographer like myself is that it is economic history with the hard bits left out and maps put in instead. I understand that this definition does not command universal assent among those professionally concerned, but the fact that economic historians scan works written across the border, just in case a geographer has (by sheer inadver-tence, of course) put in a hard bit that they had not thought of for themselves, suggests that at any rate it may be half true.

Or consider for a moment the sublime heights of classical studies. When all else fails for novelty, what nowadays is more ready to hand as a pick-me-up (or a death-blow) than the economic argument? When the ignorant but interested observer hears of the opening of a new field of knowledge through the decipherment of Linear B he confidently awaits the turning of the field into a battlefield, in the customary academic manner, and wonders only what grounds the experts will choose for opening hostilities. And he has only to look at recent issues of the *Economic History Review* to be rewarded by a fine sequence of controversy and warm denunciation, all about the kind of economic organization that may properly be inferred from the newly deciphered inscriptions. One may even go well beyond the boundaries of the arts subjects and still be unable to escape from economic history. I myself once found, in pursuing the industrial history of a particular town, that the only place in which one large segment of it was conveniently gathered together was in a thesis which had gained for its writer a master's degree in chemistry.

If one adds to economics the still wider terrain of social history, the places in which it can be found become still more numerous. How much more difficult it would be to keep up the output of literary theses if it were not possible to discuss the social development of one little period after another as an influence on the novels of X, the poems of Y or the plays of Z, perhaps even the anthologies of Q. Recently, too, there have been more examples of the inter-penetration of social history and psychology. It is true that the writers probably regarded themselves as social historians with a new line in explanations, but the impression conveyed is rather that of a selective search into the historical record for empirical confirmation of theories of both social and individual psychology. Whichever way the connexion is meant to be used, there is no doubt that it has been made.

This discussion suggests two significant points. One is that economic and social history serves as a useful background to a surprisingly large number of other branches of study, helping to deepen and clarify them. The other is that the training and equipment of the economic historian is likely to be inadequate unless it has a wider range than the name of the subject might seem to indicate. The first point suggests some reflexions on the use of economic history as a subsidiary element in courses of study centred on other subjects, but these are so plain as to need little comment. Instead, I shall try to develop the second point a little further.

Economic historians have always shown a certain eclecticism in their methods of work, which has given rise to the suspicion that they have no methods of their own and rely on a miscellaneous assortment of borrowings. This has never been wholly true and is less true than it used to be, but the element of truth in it has probably retarded the acceptance of the subject as academically respectable. Yet it can be argued that it has been hampered by borrowing too little rather than too much. The widespread belief of history students that economic history was too much crossed with (to them) unfamiliar and difficult economic theory, inadequately tested against the facts, had very little foundation before the last quarter of a century. The main reason for this is that for about a hundred years, during which economic history emerged as a subject of study, the leading economic theorists gave only a minor part of their attention to the kind of problems which attract historians: problems of growth and decay, of the things that cause the wealth of nations to be greater or less. From the eighteen-fourties to the nineteen-twenties experience in the western world suggested that economic progress could be taken so much for granted that it would be superfluous to spend much time and effort enquiring into it. Consequently, originality in the development of theory was diverted to the refinement of static analysis. This change in the central preoccupations of economic theory was a partial abandonment of one of the liveliest traditions within the subject, which had attained great intellectual peaks in Adam Smith and Malthus. It deprived economic historians of what could have been valuable guidance and encouraged them to neglect some of the most important influences on economic change, such as the relation between incomes and investment, and the effect of changes in the supply and mobility of the factors of production on variations in economic growth. It is only thirty years ago that Sombart could argue (and make out a strong case) that the existing body of economic theory was of no service to the economic historian.[1] It was not that all the able economists lacked an interest in history. M'Culloch was not only a leading expositor of classical economic theory but the possessor of a vast knowledge of the history of economic doctrine and of the course of trade, manufacture and policy. But he used his knowledge of history mainly for a different set of works from those in which he concentrated on the presentation of theory. Alfred Marshall, the dominant figure in a later generation of economists, had likewise a keen awareness and wide knowledge of the concrete world of affairs. He had much to say that is still of direct value to economic historians, but they will find only a little of it in his *Principles of Economics* (chiefly in appendices) and will turn instead to his *Industry and Trade* and *Official Papers*. In fact, for many years, the influence of economists on the study of economic history was exerted very little through the application of economic theory. It came chiefly through the extension backwards of an interest in contemporary descriptive economics and the working of economic institutions. It was an indispensable and, as far as it went, wholly beneficial influence, which established one of the main streams of writing in economic history, within which some of the greatest work in the subject was produced, notably Clapham's *Economic History of Modern Britain.*

But it did not provide complete guidance to what was needed in economic history, nor was it the only influence at work. The other important contributions came from historians trained in non-economic aspects of their subject and from a group of scholars, mainly German, who are much harder to classify; they included some who regarded themselves as part of a historical school of economists, but they are perhaps most accurately described as early sociologists concerned with the evolution of types of society, though the ablest of them, such as Marx, transcended the limitations of this description.

Of the non-economic historians some developed an interest in economic subjects and others revealed much of economic interest in the course of investigations with a different object. Together they served economic history not only by first uncovering many of the facts but also by their insight in interpreting them. But these non-economic historians rendered a still greater service. They enabled economic historians to master the techniques of the critical use of documentary sources as soon as these were perfected, and, by so doing, greatly reduced the scope for future error. Not all was gain, however. The techniques of historical research were developed and, to some extent, stabilized at a time when medieval and Renaissance studies flourished more than those of more recent periods, and some modern economic historians were trained in ways not altogether adapted to their needs. In addition, political historians who turned to economic subjects tended to retain their predominant interest in the doings of governments and to draw their information mainly from the public documents with which they were familiar. Not surprisingly, they revealed what public authorities had tried to do, claimed to do, and sometimes even accomplished, but not what they had neglected to do or never thought of doing and not what had been done by countless other institutions and individuals. The result, for many years, was the acceptance of general versions of economic history in which policy occupied an unrealistically large place. Economic historians had to learn how to retain the technical skills of other historians while adapting them for different purposes and they had to discover new kinds of sources to which they could apply them.

Much the same mixture of gain and loss was derived from those I have called the sociologists. The concentration of attention on the indissoluble links between economic and other social aspects of organization and activity gave valuable new insights into the nature of social processes. The effort to study how and why, over long periods, complete transformations of society have been accomplished helped to impart a more dynamic conception of society than was provided by other scholars and to give that broadening of vision which is so necessary a complement to the intensive study of more strictly limited topics. Moreover, no other approach gave the economic historian such an assurance of the importance that the subject of his study has in human affairs. But there were many disadvantages. The systematization, which facilitated many fruitful comparisons and opened the way to many useful generalizations, was carried much too far. The more historical knowledge grew, the more evident it became that the postulated social types rarely, if ever, existed in pure form, and that they did not invariably follow one another in an orderly, irreversible sequence. The student trained on the ideas of any of this school needed a corrective injection of the pure historian's virtue, which will abandon the theory for the sake of the awkward fact and help him to be tolerant of the untidiness of history.

It was a subject whose methods and equipment were moulded by these three sets of influences that the economic historian a generation ago was expected to master. If he were to become capable of turning at will to the use of any of the types of material or any of the concepts of social change which they suggested he needed to be a man of considerable trained intellectual versatility and wide general knowledge. If he were to make an original contribution to his subject he had also to be capable of elucidating economic relations that were buried in his materials and with which ancillary subjects gave him little help. Just so in the early twentieth century some economic historians, particularly those concerned with the very recent past, were groping rather imprecisely towards an explanation of some of the main aspects of economic growth while economic theorists were neglecting them. In short, economic history was a subject in which breadth, adaptability and a capacity to notice unfamiliar combinations of events and to reflect on their significance were specially important. But it was not a subject whose practice depended very much on the application of refined and recondite techniques.

More recently it has seemed that this was changing. The most obvious characteristics which distinguish much of the economic history written in the last twenty years from earlier work are that it makes more use of the concepts and the jargon of economic theory and contains many more statistics. The chief reason for this is that events have induced economists to renew their interest in dynamic problems, which has led them to develop concepts which economic historians can appreciate and use. The shattering experience of world economic depression in the early 'thirties made it obvious that economic progress is not automatic and unquestionable, and created a demand for practical remedies. It also made the safety of governments more dependent on the maintenance of prosperity and thus brought economists face to face with governments' questions, which are apt to take the form of 'how much is needed for how big a return how soon?'. In the 'forties the effects of war and the more general diffusion of information created a vivid awareness in many Asian and African countries that the economic growth of the western world had passed them by and a demand to be let into the secret of how it was achieved. The development of under-developed areas became the most fashionable branch of economics. With this changed focus of attention and the brilliant advances in dynamic theory, made by Keynes and his successors, and in the measurement and analysis of national income and its constituents, there was an immensely larger area of common interest for economists and economic historians than existed even at the time, not yet so remote as to be forgotten, when I began my own undergraduate studies and was diverted from my intention to become a specialist in economics by what seemed to me the excessive attention given to the less realistic aspects of the subject.

But there have been other reasons for new methods in economic history. Economic historians themselves, as they turned their attention to the emergence and development of highly industrialized communities were presented with novel phenomena to study and with source materials that were novel in both character and abundance. They were bound to find that some topics previously little regarded had acquired fundamental importance and they were forced to seek new methods of treating their subject. The things which most clearly mark off western society in the 19th and 20th centuries from all previous human history are the speed of change and the ever-increasing specialization and complexity of organization. To describe, and still more to explain, the history of such a society is impossible without a more elaborate analysis of the relations between its different activities and institutions than was necessary or possible before. In that analysis quantitative methods must have a large part. Many of the changes are so vast and so rapid, yet so irregular, that without some kind of measurement any discussion of them risks being blurred into meaninglessness. At the same time the day-to-day running of such a society requires the recording of an unprecedented amount of quantitative information and leaves an immense deposit of other material, much of which can, with a little ingenuity, be fitted into the categories used by economic theorists. Thus the nature of the sources and subject-matter of economic historians of more recent times, as well as the new interests of economic theorists, has helped to strengthen the connexion between economic history and theory.

How has all this affected the writing of economic history and the training of those who study it? As far as concerns history before the late 18th century in this country, and somewhat later in most others, only a little. Economic historians have benefited from occasional eavesdropping on theorists and have consequently sought and found new material and deepened their notions on such things as the relation between recorded price movements and the supply of different factors of production and on the underlying causes of long periods of apparent depression or revival. But on the whole these earlier periods lack the abundance and variety of statistical records which would make it practicable to use many of the techniques of contemporary economists. In any case, it would be inappropriate to do so, since much modern theory of employment and economic development assumes the existence of a network of institutions (capable of spreading their influence rapidly throughout the economy) which is incomparably more complete and sophisticated than anything found before the 19th century.

On the study of the economic history of the last two hundred years the effect has been more profound. Much work has been produced which appears different in kind from that written earlier. Its main substance is often embodied in a set of graphs and tables, and the figures found therein will very likely not have come direct from any surviving records but be the result of various arithmetical operations which turn them into index numbers, moving averages in a time series, measures of growth rates, and so on, with missing evidence made good by interpolation and extrapolation. The commentary is in terms of which all are familiar to economists but many are unfamiliar or even incomprehensible to the rest of the educated public, and the really polished performer will add a little algebra in the footnotes and appendix. It might well appear that, for this period, economic history has been turned into or (as some economists prefer to think) replaced by a new and specialized branch of economics, some of whose practitioners do, in fact, choose to call themselves economist-historians, rather than use the old name.

I do not think the revolution has been as complete as that. It has demanded that the modern economic historian should become more versatile than ever but has not made him obsolete. Quantitative analysis has greatly enlarged and clarified our understanding of economic change and represents a gain that should never be thrown away. But those whose training is confined to it have very serious limitations. Economists using historical statistics have made some sorry blunders for lack of the historian's habit of criticising his sources. They have taken figures at their face value without considering by whom, in what circumstances, by what methods and for what purpose they were compiled. Consequently, they have sometimes used incomplete figures as though they were totals, have submitted very rough figures to statistical methods that can safely be applied only to data with little margin of error, and have used available figures as though they were reliable indicators of other activities on which, at best, they could throw only a distorted light. Moreover, this approach is too impersonal to be, by itself, realistic and it yields incomplete answers to fundamental questions about historical change, partly because it is too impersonal. While it is most useful to be able to sort out and measure the relations among a complicated set of mutually dependent economic variables, it is an incurious mind that does not go on to probe what makes the variables vary and what makes it necessary to keep changing the equations which express their inter-relations. At once such a quest brings in again all the studies which economic historians have formerly been accustomed to pursue and which, if they work in the pre-1750 period, are still regarded as their normal work.

It brings in even more. Not only does the large number of other subjects in which the economic historian can find something of professional interest suggest that his predecessors might with advantage have spread their net even wider, but there are at least three specific features of the last 200, and especially the last 100, years which make further demands on the attention of historians of that period. One is the tremendous role of technological innovation as the most powerful driving force in economic and social change. Though there are some grounds for thinking that the history of science and technology and economic history might make a good pair of complementary studies, it would be impracticable as well as unnecessary to demand that economic historians should have a training in technology and natural science. But they are likely to get a peculiar idea of their own subject if they make no effort to understand what conditions foster or retard technological progress and how technology affects the practicable range of products and their cost. Teachers are familiar enough with the fantastic misconceptions of students who, because their elementary text-books terminate their catalogue of industrial inventors with Crompton, Cartwright and Watt, believe that technological change slowed down in the first half of the nineteenth century, with all sorts of odd consequential conclusions. But they will not provide an effective correction unless they attempt to appreciate the way in which economic expansion was influenced by the state of scientific knowledge and to understand the technical limitations on the type and quantity of equipment which could be produced at different times. To be able to do this requires at least an outline text-book knowledge of the history of science and some insight into the way in which scientists think.

A second relevant feature is the swifter growth in the area of commercial influence exerted by industrialized countries. Since the early nineteenth century the elements of local and national self-sufficiency (very incomplete even then) have greatly diminished and in many countries the supply of daily necessities and the maintenance of prosperity have become overwhelmingly dependent on international conditions which they themselves can influence only very partially. Such a state of affairs makes necessary a change of historical approach. A British student who concentrates historical study down to the eighteenth century on his own country, and pays attention to the outside world as it is shown through British foreign and colonial policy and trade, has a manageable and informative field of study. But for any more recent period he must find much of it incomprehensible unless it is supplemented by a fuller study of what was happening simultaneously in a number of other parts of the world. Only in that way can he discover the continuously changing characteristics of the international community into which his own country has had to fit itself, and at the same time there are opened to him invaluable opportunities for comparisons in historical development which make it easier to detect what is most influential in the activities of any community to which he is paying special attention.

The third feature of recent development which I must emphasise is the extreme complexity of society in all its aspects, not only the economic: an ever-increasing specialization of structure; a greater fluidity (directed by new influences) such as is shown by more rapid changes in occupation, class, income, outlook and habits within one family or from one generation to the next; and a greater variety of objectives to which the fruits of economic growth may be directed. In these circumstances it is impossible to go on looking at the social setting of economic change in the rather rigid terms of nineteenth century sociology, which were once much used for the purpose. Not that sociology has become impossible. It has become more subtle and more detailed, and the modern historian would be well advised to take note of its investigations and results, at any rate those that are recorded in words to which an intelligible meaning can be attached. But there is also an almost infinite variety of social questions and relationships that must be unravelled in a historical way before they can be understood.

There is no time in this lecture to discuss the nature and scope of social history, and in any case the damage that more eminent historians than I have done to their reputations, when they have tried to do just that, is an inducement to caution. In practice, social history has tended to take in all that has not been already annexed by the well-established branches of historical study, as well as trespassing frequently over their boundaries. Thus for anyone who has to spend a good deal of time in bondage to the rigorous requirements of economic history it has the attraction and value of a safety-valve. I should be grateful to the University of Bristol for its unusual step in including a reference to social history in the title of my chair, since this permits me to read, write and say almost anything (including, I dare say, blasphemy and sedition) without deviating in the slightest from my academic duties. The important point in relation to my present argument, however, is not so much that social history may be a relief from economic history as that it may be an essential illumination of it. It is in social history that the economic historian must find the explanation of most of his questions about the quantity and quality of the labour supply—about incentives, training, physical fitness, mobility and turnover—and there, too, he will find guidance about the causes of some of the most striking shifts in market demand and of the type of control exerted by public policy over economic activity.

Moreover, a close link with social history helps the economic historian to give proper weight to personality and human nature in his explanations. Impersonality is one characteristic that many people have attributed to economic history and which has repelled them. Against some of the statistical compilations of economist-historians it is a just charge and various remedies have been attempted, such as the recent American development of entrepreneurial history. But, in general, economic history neither is nor should be impersonal. More exclusively than other branches of history, it deals with the activities of large groups and not with individuals, but it cannot explain the achievements and relations of those groups without reference to motives, aptitudes and values. To estimate reliably which among these are so strong and so widely spread as to exert decisive influence on the doings of not one but a whole category of people is not possible without sympathy and insight into personality. The economic historian must draw on his own human experience and imagination. He will also be helped by studying activities which are obviously not wholly conditioned by economic aims and interests and which show up the influence of individual quirks and irrationalities on undertakings that have an economic effect.

All these various considerations influence one's judgment about the best way to pursue the study of modern economic history. And here I should insert two points of explanation. First, about my use of the word 'modern'. I do not wish to go over the arguments that have been used for and against a revision of the established nomenclature and dating of historical periods, in which modern history begins in the middle or at the end of the fifteenth century. Much of what I have had to say in this lecture is relevant to the study of economic history over many centuries, but in many of my remarks I have had to distinguish sharply between periods before and after the eighteenth century. It is clear that the coming of industrialism brought greater changes in the problems to be studied and the material available for studying them than anything in previous history. Because of this I have chosen to use the word 'modern' only for the period since rapid industrialization became noticeable, which did not happen anywhere earlier than the late eighteenth century. Second, in thinking of methods of study I have in mind mainly the education of undergraduates. But similar considerations, with some additions, would apply to research students and professional historians.

No one whose studies are centred on modern economic history can be just an economic historian or even just a historian. His economic history must be firmly set in social history and he must have at least an outline knowledge of political history in the same period; and, however localized his most detailed work, he must be able to see it in relation to those major historical developments that have had something like world-wide influence. He must also have some knowledge of the social sciences, at least of economics, and be able to deal with numbers without making foolish mistakes. In the past, some most distinguished work in economic history has been done by people who knew hardly any economic theory. For the most modern period that is no longer possible. The historian has to get hold of many of the economist's concepts, which he can do clearly only by seeing how the economist uses them and relates them to each other. He has no need of all the refinements of the advanced economist, but he must have a thorough grasp of the elements of those parts of the subject which are concerned with large aggregates and of such other pieces of elementary analysis as are needed to make those parts comprehensible. This is not a small requirement. In statistical theory his needs at present are much less. The great majority of historical statistics before the Second World War are too approximate to be suitable material for the application of mathematical methods of any but the most elementary kind, and attempts to treat them in that way can usually be ignored not only with safety but with advantage. But the economic historian does need to know something about the simpler methods—to know something about the compilation and use of index numbers, to understand the different types of averages and their use, to be able to use logarithms and do simple arithmetic. Very likely, as more of the twentieth century becomes part of history, he will need to know more. The greater quantity and reliability of economic statistics and the development of new econometric methods to throw light on the nature and effectiveness of business decisions and on the efficiency of production will inevitably bequeath new materials and methods to historians, some of whom will have to equip themselves to deal on equal terms with the ablest econometrician. Fortunately, there is in my contract a clause about retirement which gives some hope that that particular deluge may come after me.

What I have suggested as the minimum range of knowledge for the modern economic historian is very wide and if it is applied to undergraduate study there is an obvious danger of encouraging superficiality. The remedy is in specialization, for which no apology is called. Much glib nonsense is talked about the educational errors of specialization, as if its advantages and perils were much the same in all fields. For the student of modern history the most useful approach to specialization is by limitation of the period to be studied. Lord Acton's famous advice to historians to study problems, not periods, is based on an antithesis that is no longer valid. In the modern world, change is so rapid that most problems are inextricably bound up with particular, often quite short, periods. The most advanced undergraduate work in economic history ought to be the study of either the whole economic history or a group of related economic activities in a defined area over a short span of years—two generations at most. If it is properly done the student will find himself drawing an on ever-widening stock of material—economic, social, technical, political—to explain the phenomena which he observes and discovering an ever-increasing variety of links among them. Nothing can do more to impart an awareness of the complexity and variety of modern society and yet to help understanding of the way it works and of the objectives which men seek to attain through it. And it is partly because it is specialized that it can be simultaneously both a broadening and a deepening educational experience.

But even with specialization there are limits to what can be attempted. It is impossible, for instance, to find time for undergraduate reading of original documents on all aspects of a subject of special study. The intensive effort to squeeze the last drop of blood from a single document and let it flow in minutely detailed comment, which has doubtless done much to advance knowledge in other sectors of history, is seldom much of an aid to the discovery of the truth in modern economic history. In this field the questions that matter are mostly questions of relationships, and to illustrate or to answer even the simplest of them requires selection from and comparison of a large number of diverse source materials. Do not mistake me. I am not suggesting anything so absurd as that history students should stop studying primary documents. Modern economic history uses more, not less, of them. The undergraduate student must know the main categories of sources from which knowledge of his subject is derived, how they came into existence, for what purposes they can be used; and he cannot get to know what they are like without sampling some of them at first hand. But because of the increased complexity of the subject his sampling is bound to be very partial, and more documentary work must be postponed to the postgraduate stage than used to be the case. We must remember that our first purpose in undergraduate teaching is to train citizens, not professional historians. If, even at the cost of a reduced appreciation of the methods of historical research and a lessened ability to pass straight on to it, a deeper understanding of society can be encouraged, then the price is worth paying, though one would prefer to avoid the loss if possible.

Some such compromises, in deference to the boundlessness of knowledge and the shortness of life, are inevitable. Even when they have been made they do not dispose of all the main difficulties in the use of modern economic history as an educational medium. Though they set limits to what is attempted they do not get rid of the necessity for unusual width of knowledge and reading as a foundation. Unusually wide reading depends on unusually large libraries, which cost money; not as much as laboratories, but more than is spent on them in most places. Nor do these compromises make much concession to those with a limited intellectual range. It is not just the familiar academic wish to have the leaven while somebody else looks after the lump that makes me suggest that modern economic history, as a special study, is not suited to weaker students. The nature of the subject is responsible. It is not among those (not less valuable) which can be readily taken apart and assimilated in small stages, and in which quite a limited progress may be a most useful training. It is not unique in being a subject where it is necessary to bring into focus a bewildering variety of facts and relations before one understands much of anything at all, and where, once that difficult threshold is crossed, interest and insight may grow quickly. I believe there is a real need for more people to be trained in the social studies, towards which modern history (and particularly economic history) increasingly leans, without pulling up its firm roots in the humanities. For some of them to concentrate on modern economic history, with a back-ground of other social studies, might be the most helpful and illuminating training they could have. But there would be something wrong if they were more than a small minority of the total.

That is not to say, however, that some knowledge of economic history cannot and should not be given to many other people. Any specialized work in the social studies suffers if it has no economic history in the background, and I have already tried to indicate how few are the fields of study to which some knowledge of it is entirely irrelevant. Such a background it ought to be well within the competence of the trained economic historian to provide. He can select the events and forces that appear to have dominated the life of society and promoted the greatest change within it, and he can try to describe their mutual inter-actions. In an exposition of this kind much has to be taken on trust by the reader or listener without specialized knowledge, though the key tests of consistency and plausibility can be applied by anyone. Nor does such a treatment provide an opportunity for that discovery and pursuit of fundamentals for oneself which is the real heart of an advanced education. But it can provide additional knowledge which makes it easier to gain that experience through other media; and it is probably one of the most direct roads to the sort of knowledge on which depends the ability to make a realistic commonsense appraisal of the way the human world rubs along.

All this may seem to raise unduly large claims for the study of modern economic history. It is all very well, one may say, to cata-logue its advantages and make the list as long as possible; but it has to be weighed against many competing claims. Is it worth more than a minor place? The fact that it is often immensely fascinating in its content may not nowadays be valued as highly as I think it should and a more severely practical answer may be demanded. It is not hard to find one. Without exaggeration it can be said that economic history is at the core of some of the most bitter and troublesome problems of the day. How much more than ever before are inter-national politics moulded by demands for a share in the benefits of an industrial revolution and by an attribution of their absence, or of the hardships on the road to their achievement, to wickedness, exploitation, robbery. And how can truth in these matters be demonstrated without close examination of what has, in fact, been involved in changes of a comparable kind? If this is not enough, I would remind you of the tremendous ideological conflicts that rend the world. The ideology underlying the spread of communism that has so transformed the world in our time is intricate, various, constantly evolving, and liable to sudden, contradictory twists. But

R

later accretions and convenient doctrinal adjustments to new situations have not concealed its derivation from Marx and Lenin, whose teachings, wide-ranging as they were, were centred in argument about economic history. There are many grounds for thinking that the implications which that presentation of history has for the possibility of future economic development are still, in practice, in a large part of the world, the most powerful element in the appeal which communism may have. A subject that may provide one of the hottest sparks to ignite revolution and affect for millions the choice between destruction and happiness can hardly be deemed remote and unpractical. And though its quiet and dispassionate study may appear like a silence destined to be drowned in the world's roar of raging propaganda, there is all the long experience of liberal studies in universities to counter so pessimistic a view. It is not a vain thing, nor unproductive of practical changes, to pursue the truth about matters which have a great part in men's lives; and here, in modern economic history, is one among them that it would be foolish to neglect.

NOTES

1   W. Sombart, 'Economic Theory and Economic History', *Econ. Hist. Rev.*, II, (1929), 1–19.

13

A. J. Youngson

PROGRESS AND THE INDIVIDUAL IN ECONOMIC HISTORY

(Edinburgh, 1959)

This inaugural lecture was delivered at the University of Edinburgh on the 16th January 1959.

PROGRESS AND THE INDIVIDUAL IN ECONOMIC HISTORY

MR. DEAN, Ladies and Gentlemen, when I first learned some thirteen or fourteen months ago that I was to be the first Professor of Economic History in the University of Edinburgh I experienced sensations at once of pleasure and alarm: pleasure—I hope not altogether vain—at the honour done me, at the prospect of working again in Scotland, in this ancient and famous University, and in the hope of being able to further the study of Scotland's own remarkable economic history; alarm at the thought that one day I should have to give an inaugural lecture. But, I reminded myself, I am one of those who believe that ancient customs should be preserved (unless good reason can be shown to the contrary); I recalled the words of a nineteenth century economist to the effect that the way to preserve old customs is to enjoy them; and so I have come here this afternoon hoping to demonstrate to myself and perhaps to you that this is a custom which should be preserved and can be enjoyed.

Economic history is not a new subject. Economic history of a kind was written by Karl Marx a hundred years ago; of another kind by Adam Smith two hundred years ago. Nor is the subject, I am glad to say, without long and strong connections in this University. It was a graduate of Edinburgh, Dean William Cunningham, who wrote, towards the end of the last century, *The Growth of English Industry and Commerce*, one of the most scholarly and profound surveys of British economic history ever written and a book still, in many respects, in my opinion, unsurpassed. And it was George Unwin, later Professor of Economic History in the University of Manchester, very distinguished, very learned, erratic, restless, penetrating, often profound, who was appointed to be the first lecturer in the subject in this University in 1908, just fifty academic years ago.

But the very title, economic history, does not suggest, I am aware, a separate, autonomous academic discipline, however old or however new; and it is right that it should not do so. Economic history has its own contribution to make to our knowledge of man and his affairs and I believe that that contribution is a very important one, never more important than to-day; but the study of economic history is linked with, and in many ways it depends upon, those great branches

221

of learning, history and economics. Economic history is a kind of history, that is true; but it is also a kind of economics. The special interest of economic history is in the economic problems set and solved, or set and shelved, in the past. And so the economic historian is obliged to develop a kind of schizophrenia—I use the word in its popular sense, begging pardon of the Dean, who uses it more often than I and I suspect in a slightly different sense—a kind of schizophrenia in his work; he is interested in two different sorts of things at once; on the one hand he is interested in books and the past, on the other hand in theories and the present. And this is not to be deplored. On the contrary, this tension, this conflict, this contradiction is the life in him. This has never been better demonstrated than in the work of Adam Smith himself, and Adam Smith's work has never been better appreciated in this respect than by the great Cambridge economist, Alfred Marshall:

'I began to look for Adam Smith's originality', says Marshall 'more in the general conspectus he presented than in particular doctrines. And as regards this, the more I knew of him the more I worshipped him. It was his balance, his sense of proportion, his power of seeing the many in the one and the one in the many, his skill in using analysis to interpret history and history to correct analysis (especially as regards the causes that govern human nature, but also in other matters), that seemed to mark him out as unique'.

The economic historian who tries to escape from this inner conflict by writing history with a minimum admixture of economics, or economics with a thin veneer of history, is simply running away from his subject.

Of course, the need to combine economics and history raises many problems. The economic historian requires not merely a working knowledge of history, but also that more vague and equally valuable possession, a sense of the past, a feeling of how men's minds worked in other times. Along with that he must possess a sure, though it may be a limited, grasp of economic theory. This necessity sometimes presents him with the difficulty of choice. There are so many theories. George the Third, it is reported, once said to his great minister, 'Mr. Pitt, you must take a wife'. And Mr. Pitt replied, 'Yes, Sire. Whose wife shall I take?' Our situation in economic history is a little like that. Are we to believe, for example, that an increased volume of investment will generate the additional savings necessary to finance it, *or* that there must be new savings before the additional investment is undertaken? Are we to believe that no practicable changes in the rate of interest can offset fluctuations in the market estimation of different types of capital *or* that the rate of interest is the natural equilibrator in the economic system and is the price of time? Are we to believe that a general reduction of wages is likely to increase the volume of employment *or* that wage reduction will not have that effect? Economics does not return a very clear answer to these questions. I do not think, however, that such doubts need be pressed very far. They concern, as a rule, not principles but generalizations, i.e. non-particular statements based on a more or less inadequate supply of evidence. Concerning these, there are of course many differences of emphasis. But on all or almost all the important and fundamental points of analysis the extent of disagreement in modern economics has been on the whole, I think, exaggerated.

Differences of emphasis, however, are not confined to economics. When he gave a general lecture shortly after coming to Edinburgh in 1908, Unwin spoke about the conflict, in economic affairs, between individual freedom and the power of the State; and his eyes were turned, it is interesting to note, towards the Russia of his day, towards the rapid economic development going on there, accompanied by an insurrectionary movement for political reform. Sixteen years later, in another general paper on economic history, he spoke on the degree to which a sensible man can and should believe in the economic interpretation of history. Neither of these topics is dead today—far from it. The economic development of Russia has changed the face of the modern world; the force of her example may change it still further. And in the struggle between communism and the free nations of the world the economic interpretation of history is an important weapon. But there is another topic, or perhaps not so much another topic as another way of looking at economic history, which catches our attention in the 1950's, and which, I am quite sure, will live as long as these others; that is, the idea of economic history as the study of economic progress itself. And this will live in economic history because it is the fundamental problem. It was the heart of the matter for Adam Smith, just as it was for Cunningham. Economic history is a record of economic progress. Of course, it is not a record of continuous unceasing progress. Not only are there ups and downs in economic progress, cyclical advances and retreats, but there may even be in the history of our own country, if we go back six or seven hundred years, some phases of rather prolonged economic retrogression. And yet, if we look at the whole span of the economic history of western Europe for a thousand years, what we see is a long record of gradual, possibly of accelerating, advance. We stand now on a level of achievment which, in some respects, previous generations could never hope to reach. My father, if I may strike a personal note for a moment, who worked as a doctor in Aberdeen and knew well many of the poorest districts in that town between 1890 and 1940, said to me half a dozen years ago 'There are no poor people now'. And that is more or less true. Material poverty has been more or less eliminated in this country. At last there exists an economy—and ours is not the only one, although it is one of the very few—which is not degraded and depressed, materially and spiritually, by the existence of what used to be called a submerged tenth—of what was, we know in the seventeenth century and probably in earlier centuries as well, more nearly a submerged fifth or a submerged quarter of the whole population. It has taken all of recorded history to make possible the appearance of the poverty-less economy. It is a marvellous fact. And it helps to give to economic history a grand pattern which history lacks, this pattern of progress. But the pattern does not make the economic historian's task any easier; instead, it poses a question. The fact of substantial material progress, the fact of its achievement here and there and the possibility, perhaps, of its advent everywhere, is the central challenge to economic history. Along what lines are we to explain the recorded economic progress of nations?

One of the best general books on economic history is C. R. Fay's *Great Britain from Adam Smith to the Present Day*, first published in 1928. This book, as I understand it, tells the story of the growth of economic freedom and the working of 'the invisible hand' from the time when Adam Smith first proclaimed the necessity of the one and the inevitability of the other down to about 1920. It explains rising income in these terms. It thus fulfils the vision of Adam Smith, brings Adam Smith up to date, in a manner of speaking. It is a brilliant book; but it no longer satisfies us. Why? Not because more recent research has made it out of date, but, I suggest, for two reasons:

first, because Soviet Russia has proved that economic progress is compatible with unfreedom;

second, because statistics and econometrics form an influential departure in modern economics, and have made their impact since 1928.

The economic rise of Soviet Russia is not a matter for me to discuss today; I have already referred to its importance. But I should like to say something about the role of quantatitive economics. No modern economic historian can afford to ignore this development. It has been suggested, even, that that close marriage of economics with economic history, so long proposed but never accomplished, is to be realized at last in the form of econometrics. What are the possibilities here? Is the work of Fay, Mantoux, Cunningham to be superseded by volumes of statistical time-series—some of which, incidentally, have already reached us?

I must confess, that, as far as the explanation of the past is concerned, I myself do not think that this approach is going to yeild any great quantity of useful results. There are a number of reasons. One is that good work in this field requires a lot of statistical information, and there is seldom enough for almost any decade before 1920. There is no doubt that if the modern economist's standard of living is measured by his consumption of statistics, then his standard of living has risen a lot in the past twenty years. But nothing much can be done about the economic historian's standard of living measured in this way. We can dig up more statistics relating to the past and it is important that we should. Those which throw light on rates of investment and on relative price movements are, in my view, especially valuable. But we cannot now obtain the quarterly series which for many purposes we need; often, and for periods earlier than 1870 usually, we cannot get even annual series of any value. For example, what evidence is there for the general belief that unemployment in Great Britain in the nineteenth century was generally at a low level? I will not say none, because there is a little; but of that scarcely any is direct evidence and very little is statistical, and none of it can be used without very careful historical interpretation. That then is a severely practical limitation on the use of purely or even largely quantitative methods in economic history. But it is not the main ground for my scepticism about the value of historical investigation carried out mostly in statistical terms. The main ground is, that many time-series—including those which it is fashionable nowadays to regard as the most important ones—show merely the movements in aggregates. They deal, not with persons and intentions, but with quantities and averages. They are therefore, in an important sense, results. But what produces the results? Decisions—that is the answer—decisions made by people working within a changing framework of institutions. And so we come back to history, to human nature. What we want is an explanation of economic change; time-series are not an explanation. Let me quote from the high priest of historical time-series himself, Professor Kuznets:

'The social aggregates dealt with by statistical methods are only results *en gros* and cannot reveal the underlying motivations and aspirations of the human agents and of the institutional factors at play. What is worse, they necessarily drown the strategic, the revolutionary, the dynamic, in the mass actions of groups and thus tend to obscure the elements that may most deserve emphasis'.

Indeed, the mere collecting of figures is in my view often no more than a reversion to that old and slightly child-like, and, dare I say it, first-year form of history as just a narrative. The point is not a new one. It was made almost a hundred years ago in that book of constant reference which stands, I imagine, on every modern professor's bookshelf:

> 'I could tell you my adventures—beginning from this morning,' said Alice a little timidly; 'but it's no use going back to yesterday, because I was a different person then.'
> 'Explain all that,' said the Mock Turtle.
> 'No, no! The adventures first,' said the Gryphon in an impatient tone: 'explanations take such a dreadful time.'

And that hits the nail right on the head. Explanations in economic history must, to be at all satisfactory, involve economic and social and institutional minutiae. They must be detailed, they must be lengthy, they must be personal. It is no use to write economic history and to begin by squeezing the juice of humanity out of the subject. The past in which the economic historian is interested is not just a repository of economic problems. It is also an ever-changing society composed of individuals. Therefore the economic historian must try to understand the play of social forces in different periods. And the evidence for this is almost solely literary in character. There came to my notice recently a scrap of this kind of evidence from the underworld of Scots literature a hundred and fifty years ago:

> 'In the county of Fife, on the sea-coast, there stands a little town, inhabited by few but fishers, called Bucky-harbour, because of sea-buckies and shells to be found so plenty on the rocks about that place. There is little mention made of this town by Historians. . . . these people are said to have descended from one Tom and his two sons, who were fishers on the coast of Norway, who in a violent storm, were blown over, and got ashore at Buck-harbour, where they settled; and the whole of his children were called Thompsons, and soon became a little town by themselves as few of any other name dwelt among them. This is a traditional story, handed down from one generation to another.—They kept but little communication with country people about them, for a farmer, in those days, thought his daughter cast away, if she married one of the fishers in Bucky-harbour; on the other hand, Witty Eppie, the ale-wife, wada sworn, Be-go, laddie, I wad rather see my boat an a' my three sons dadet against the Bass, or I saw ony ane o' them married to a muck-a-byre's daughter; a whin useless tappies, it can do naething but rive at a tow rock,

and cut a corn; they can neither bait a hook, nor rade a line, houk sand-eels, nor gather perriwinkles.'

That is not economic history; it is partly folk history, suggestive in itself; but partly it is evidence, of a very interesting kind, relating to several matters which an economic historian concerned with Scotland's economic history should have somewhere at the back of his mind.

Now, I am not trying to belittle the importance of statistics or of econometrics. Figures are very valuable, as far as we can trust them. They help us to ask the right questions; sometimes they prevent us from asking unnecessary or wrong questions; often they enable us to correct mistaken ideas about the scale of things—exaggerations concerning the extent of evictions due to enclosure, for example, or the number of children employed in the early factories. And there is an exception or a partial exception to what I have said. It may be that when changes in certain aggregates take place—such as the rate of growth of population, or the capital/output ratio—then the situation facing the individual taker of decisions changes, in a way over which he has no control, which he does not completely understand, and for reasons which he does not understand at all. But it is difficult and I think that as a rule it is going to be impossible for the economic historian to judge the importance of these half-hidden changes because his evidence is not in the right form. He deals with particular cases. The aggregate studies of the econometricians may provide hypotheses which the economic historian may find it useful to work with, but which by the nature of his studies he will be able to do little to confirm or refute. True econometric work is for econometricians. It is valuable. Economic historians should try to understand it. But they should not nurse the secret ambition of taking the bread out of the econometrician's mouth by doing his work for him instead of their own. There is room for both kinds of study. The course of history is like a rush of cars to the seaside. The historian watches the driving from the pavement; sometimes, circumstances permitting, he even gets underneath the cars: the econometrician observes the scene at large from a helicopter (the implication that his feet are not on the ground need not hold). Both the man on the pavement and the man in the helicopter contribute to our understanding of the causes of accidents and the flow of traffic.

My contention that the economic historian is properly concerned with persons rather than with generalised trends or relationships is reinforced by looking at the matter from the other end, so to speak. I have been speaking about the individual as the ultimate cause of change. What about the nature of the result, of change itself? When we are told that the national income, in real terms, increased four fold between 1870 and 1950, for example, what does that mean? The answer to that question, in economics, involves some of the most difficult reasoning in the entire range of the subject. But the economic historian does not have to try to produce a formal answer. His answer is to point to the conditions of say, 1950 and to compare them, roughly or more elaborately, with those of, let us suppose, 1870. Then the changes which took place between the two dates are seen to be more confused and complex than could be inferred from any merely quantitative record, and they present themselves in the first instance in what can only be called particular rather than general forms. To make clear what I mean, may I put this under four headings, not necessarily in their order of importance.

First, the economic historian may point to institutional changes. These may promote or they may hinder or they may alter the character of economic progress; they can hardly leave it unaffected. The greatest institutional change of our time in this country—namely, the assumption by the State of indirect but ultimate responsibility for the rate of capital formation—has a very definite bearing on the rate of economic progress.

Second, the economic historian will want to examine the details of technical change, the great immediate mainspring of progress. This is a far from inhuman topic; it is a record of scientific inquiry, of investment and enterprise, of ingenuity, determination, risk and success—and let us not forget, of disappointment. The world's first all-jet airliner was not the first innovation to come, temporarily, to grief. There were, in earlier centuries, trans-Atlantic cables which parted, systems of colliery ventilation which failed to ventilate, improved methods of cultivating the soil which produced smaller crops. But the enquiring scientific spirit which has played so large a part in our lives for three hundred years, love of gain, curiosity about new things and sheer resolution have overcome difficulties and triumphed over disappointments.

Third and *fourth*, the economic historian will want to work out the consequences of successful technical change along two especial lines:

I how do some goods—like porter, or television sets—come into existence and on to the market? How do others—let us take the twentieth century—like tons of coal become scarcer and dearer while others like tons of aluminium become more plentiful and relatively cheaper?

II how do people in large numbers come to change their jobs?

Let me close by enlarging for a moment on that last question. If I look at the Census returns for Scotland for 1851 I find that the second commonest occupation was that of domestic servant. There were 115,000 domestic servants, about one for every 25 of the population. Only agricultural workers were more numerous. By 1911 the number of domestic servants had increased a little—to 133,000—but the population had increased much faster, so that the situation—from the viewpoint of the recipients of service—had deteriorated; each domestic servant had now not 25 but 35 non-servants to look after. Pass on to 1951. How many domestic servants remain? A mere 4,000, a remnant of the great army of the nineteenth century; and most of these, I suspect, unlike their predecessors, worked in boarding houses and colleges and lunatic asylums and other institutions. But look at the Census returns again. In 1881 there appears for the first time a new category—electricians, and those engaged in the manufacture of electrical apparatus: 78 of them. At the beginning of this century there were only 4,000 employees of this sort in Scotland; in 1951 there were 33,000. These two changes are obviously connected. Just think of it—just think of all the electric cookers, the electric washing machines, the electric mixers, the electric floor polishers, the electric vacuum cleaners, the electric hair dryers, not to mention those devices we take completely for granted like electric lights and electric fires—think of these and of how impossible the lives of our mothers, our wives, our sisters—and therefore our own lives too—would be without them. The appearance of these things and the disappearance of domestic servants are obviously connected. It is not, of course, a matter of cause and effect. But there is clearly a connection. But what exactly is the nature of that connection? How on the one hand were the new devices developed, whe developed them, who paid for their development, who persuaded people to buy them? And on the other hand how did the domestic servants get out of domestic service? What and who induced them to leave, what obstacles did they encounter, and where did they go?

There is a problem in economic history. I don't say that it is the most important particular problem that I can think of: but it is an example of a very fundamental kind of problem. It is a problem, like all other problems in economic history, of general principles in action. It is a problem of technical innovation on the one hand, of social movement, and therefore of human nature, on the other. And, since even technical innovation must be regarded as having an economic motive as well as a purely technical aspect, we should regard the whole problem of innovation, of new tastes, and of changed occupations—of progress, in short—as a problem of economic motive acting, to borrow a phrase used by Unwin in this University fifty years ago, 'through the resisting medium of non-economic ideas' in the past.

14

J. D. Chambers

THE PLACE OF ECONOMIC HISTORY IN HISTORICAL STUDIES
(Nottingham, 1960)

This inaugural lecture was delivered at the University of Nottingham on the 19th February 1960. The chair was taken by Professor J. S. Roskell, Dean of the Faculty of Arts.

THE PLACE OF ECONOMIC HISTORY
IN HISTORICAL STUDIES

THE chair which I have the honour to inaugurate tonight is a new one, and my first duty is to pay a tribute to those pioneers whose labours made its establishment possible. In particular, my tribute must go to Professor Robert Peers who himself taught economic history as a labour of love for many years to students of the University College preparing for the Economics and Commerce Degrees of the University of London, and who, in his capacity of Deputy Vice-Chancellor, suggested that Economic History should be given the status of an independent degree in the Arts Faculty of this University when it received its charter in 1948. He, therefore, is the true begetter of the Chair to which I have had the honour of being elected; it is one among many innovations by which he has left his mark upon the scholastic history of this University and the region that it serves, and it will be my hope and endeavour to discharge the responsibilities which it imposes in such a way that it will always remain an achievement in which he can take pride.

For historical reasons of which I am ignorant, the teaching of Economic History was at first associated with the Department of Economics, but in 1952 it was restored to the History Department where is was believed (and I think rightly) it more properly belonged.

I have chosen tonight to try to define the place which the economic kind of history holds within the field of historical studies for three reasons: first, there have been some misapprehensions expressed, from time to time, as to the nature of the subject, and I felt that this was the right time and place to try to clear them up. The question—a very natural one—has been asked whether it was a species of history at all; was it not a branch of applied economics? And if it was a branch of history, why separate it from the majestic flow of events over which Clio is reputed to preside? Could it not be tacked on, much as Macaulay tacks on his third chapter, as a brilliant after-thought to the stream of political events which really constitutes the glittering panorama of historical change? In any case, the business of earning a living is already too much with us; getting and spending we lay waste our powers; why not forget about it and concentrate on the real content of history, the rise and fall of parties and dynasties, the record of sedition, privy conspiracy and rebellion, of battle, murder and sudden death from which we ask, from time to time, to be delivered—that is, all of us but political historians who have a professional interest in such matters.

Secondly, since Economic History is closely associated with economics, the recognition of a separate subject under that name might be regarded as a part of the conspiracy that seems to be afoot to dismember Clio's empire and hand over the less political parts of it to those branches of the social sciences which need, as it were, a top dressing of highly selected historical facts to give suitable nourishment to their speculative systems. And of course we have all heard about the empty boxes of the economists into which economic historians have been able from time to time to drop a little something from their store.

It will be remembered that, on the occasion of his own inaugural lecture, Professor Wood sounded a note of alarm at the extent and frequency of the depredations which were being committed at the expense of the rather indeterminate boundaries of historical studies; he spoke of acts of petty larceny at Clio's expense on such a scale that he feared he would wake up some morning to find that history, like the kingdom of Poland, had been partitioned by hungry neighbouring disciplines and had disappeared from the academic landscape without a trace. I would like to take this opportunity of saying that we who are concerned with Economic History in this University are in no way a party to these misdeeds; on the contrary we place ourselves squarely by his side, and ask only to be allowed to spy out new lands, and to occupy them and bring them, unromantic and even repellent as they may be (such as, for instance, population statistics and urban sanitation) to be incorporated in the Empire—or rather the Common-wealth—over which he presides so benignly. It is, alas, a Common-wealth which lies under the shadow of his own impending retirement, and it is sad to think that he will no longer be here to require the teachers of Economic History, at most unexpected times and places, to stand and justify the profession of a branch of learning of whose very existence he is himself in doubt; and I sincerely hope he will return again and again and confront those shadowy wraiths—in the academic not the corporeal sense of the word—who have the hardi-hood to profess it, with the problem of their insubstantiality, and put them to the amiable but sometimes acid test of his wit and learning.

There is another reason for raising the question of Economic History in relation to other branches of history. The problem of the under-developed areas of the world which wish to enjoy the benefits of industrialisation has come to trouble the minds and consciences of economic historians as well as of economists. They are beginning to examine the circumstances of economic growth in its classical setting of Europe and above all, England, with a new urgency. They are pointing out that the possession of natural resources alone is not enough; in fact it is nothing if it is not accompanied by the possession of the propensities to develop them, the propensities to save, to invest, to take calculated business risks, to invent and pursue scientific knowledge for its own sake, and perhaps especially to prefer the material fruits of honest work to the pleasures of idleness in a state of squalor. Economic History, therefore, is not simply the history of economic facts and figures; it is also the history of economic attitudes which have developed under favourable historical conditions, and without which the economic facts and figures as we know them would never have come into existence. If the history of economic attitudes and propensities as well as economic facts is to be taken into account—as indeed it must—the relation between Economic History and other branches of history which have contributed to their growth becomes one of great importance. It is also one in which wide differences of opinion may be expected to be held, and therefore all the more suitable subject for an occasion of this kind when there is nothing to lose but a whole hour to spend in the invigorating pastime of baiting the cognoscenti while not—or trying not—to bore the laity too much.

A suitable starting point for the discussion is provided by the blunt declaration of Sir John Clapham:

'Of all varieties of history,' he writes, 'the economic is the most fundamental. Not the most important; foundations exist to carry better things. How a man lives with his family, his tribe or his fellow citizen; the songs he sings, what he feels and thinks when he looks at the sunset; the prayers he raises—all these are more important than the nature of his tools, his trick of swopping things with his neighbour, the way he holds and tills his fields, his inventions and their consequences, his money—when he has learnt to use it—his savings and what he does with them. Economic advance is not the same thing as human progress. The man with a motor car may have less imagination, and perhaps a baser religion, than the man who frequented Stonehenge. But economic activity, with its tools, fields, trade, invention and investment, is the basement of man's house.'[1]

This passage, so typical of the four square, fact finding approach of a great modern economic historian is not so John Bull-ishly simple as it looks. Let us accept the metaphor for what it is worth and admit that the economic historian is busy exploring the basement of the house of history; it soon becomes apparent, however, that the basement of the house of history is very different in some parts of the world from what it is in others; in the older civilisations of the world such as India or China, it has remained virtually unchanged for thousands of years; in the west, although it has existed for a much shorter time, it has continuously grown until in the last two hundred years it has transformed the house of history into something unimaginably different from anything that has gone before.

Economic historians are not usually consciously concerned with the problem of this fundamental difference between East and West; they are content to explore their own selected corner and make their contribution to the understanding of those aspects of the past which have an economic content, that is to say, that relate to the way men have satisfied their material wants through the administration of the means at their disposal. It will be obvious, of course, that most of the data of these studies will be of the kind with which economists are concerned: the relations of buyers and sellers, of producers and consumers, of borrowers and lenders, of masters and men, but it will be equally obvious that the economic historian is concerned with problems that lie outside this restricted framework, with problems that arise, for instance, when the economic ends of the individual come into conflict with those which the state in its wisdom may have designed for him. William Cecil, in 1559, made it clear that the maximisation of production and profits was *not* the objective of Tudor industrial policy, whatever enterprising cloth merchants might assume to the contrary; and as for working men who in spite of the law ran from one master to another in search of higher wages, they should be reduced to obedience for, 'by the looseness of the time, no other remedy is left but by awe of the law to acquaint men with virtue again.'[2] Virtue, as understood by the Tudor State, was the objective of industrial policy, not the maximisation of economic opportunities. There are also striking economic contrasts to be considered between great States at the same period of history, as may be seen, for instance, in the meteoric rise of the diminutive Dutch Republic and the contemporaneous collapse, on the economic side, of the massive Empire of Spain; or the long adherence by French industry to highly ornate quality production and the early transition in England to quantity production.

All these questions involve something more than short term economic analysis; they raise questions of motive, of religious and intellectual influences, of the nature of political and legal institutions, of differences in social structure and national outlook, and involve the consideration of data which lie outside the field of specifically economic enquiry.

As an example of the composite nature of Economic History, even in the hands of one who rarely transcends the categories of the economist, I would like to refer to the treatment of the Industrial Revolution by Professor T. S. Ashton. Here is a specifically economic treatment of a great national economic event; but though the author is almost wholly concerned with the process of maximising the use of resources, e.g., in the substitution of fixed capital in the form of machinery for labour, and the economising of circulating capital by improvements in transport and so on, he is also concerned with institutional and psychological factors which explain why these things were done in England at that time. He notes, for instance, the importance of social mobility both up and down and between landed and commercial classes, as well as geographical mobility from place to place; he comments on the background of political stability that induced the confidence to invest and made possible a steady fall in the rate of interest; he notes especially the high level of education of most of the leaders of enterprise and the lively interest they had in scientific investigation; he emphasises the part which thrift and hard work played in the accumulation of capital for industrial enterprise, and the willingness of entrepreneurs to forego immediate satisfactions in order to plough back profits for future enterprise. He is, in other words, concerning himself with institutional factors of long historical growth and with economic attitudes and propensities which possessed Englishmen at that time beyond all their neighbours and caused them to take, for the first time in history, the kinds of action which led them to the transition to the technological age.

The question of the propensities which induced the economic growth of the West, first of Britain, then of other advanced countries, is given a new significance in the light of the contemporary problem of the underdeveloped areas with which economic historians are coming more and more to concern themselves. The question was raised as a matter of scholarly curiosity by Adam Smith, who discoursed at some length on 'the different progress of opulence in the different countries' and referred specifically to China which, he says, 'was a much richer country than any part of Europe' but had long been stationary while Europe had been advancing. Since his time, the gap has continued to widen until, in 1947, it was said on the authority of the Oxford Bureau of Statistics that 'the national income yard stick will not begin to measure it'; and the disparity in income between the rich strong nations of the world and the poor nations of Asia is greater today than it was ten years ago. A question that was raised as a matter of scholarly curiosity in the last quarter of the eighteenth century is now one of international significance, and invites the economic historian to the highly dangerous but not unexciting quest for historical explanation. Why, to return to Sir John

Clapham's metaphor, was the physical basis of the history of the West expanded until it transformed the whole superstructure while in the East it remained essentially unaltered and apparently unalterable except under Western influences?

This is, probably, one of the unanswerable questions of history, but an enquiry into the propensities and institutions which have made economic growth possible in the West may have its value; to take for instance that which distinguishes western society from all others most sharply: the propensity to pursue truth for its own sake by the scientific method. Controversial as this question is, there are certain historical landmarks which will help to guide enquiry. It will be generally agreed, for instance, that though the development of scientific thought in medieval Europe was slow, it was never proscribed. This was due to the relatively materialistic metaphysic of Christianity as taught by the Church which recognised the material world as a necessary counterpart of the spiritual world and set an appropriate value upon it. Matter was good so long as it was not misused, i.e., so long as it did not endanger the mortal soul; and the pursuit of material ends, e.g., for maintaining oneself and one's family at an appropriate station in life, was a moral obligation. We hear an echo of the dual nature of the Christian metaphysic when we are summoned every Sunday, not only to confess our manifold sins and wickedness, but to ask for those things which are requisite and necessary as well for the body as for the soul.

The Church also taught that human intelligence finds its natural field of activity in the sphere of the sensible and the particular as well as in the contemplation of the abstract and the eternal. Thus, when Greek science was brought to Europe by the Arabs in the twelfth and thirteenth centuries, it was incorporated into the intellectual tradition of the West, and, by the contributions made by medieval mathematicians, it prepared the way for the Copernican revolution in astronomy in the 16th century. The Arabs, on the other hand, under the influence of their religious leaders, turned their back on the science they had preserved and relapsed into an intellectual dark age.

The question, therefore, is not whether the Middle Ages made a contribution to the scientific revolution which ushered in the modern age, but why that contribution was so small. The answer seems to be partly, that in an age of faith when theoretical speculation was essentially theocentric, scientific enquiry was felt to be unnecessary, or at best, peripheral, and also because technical improvements that might have thrown light on natural processes were few, and such as they were, were regarded as secret and not to be divulged to strangers beyond the limits of the community that practised them.[2] Where these limitations were absent, technological advance was striking:

in the art of war, for instance, which was under the control of princes, not of the gilds; in the fabulous building industry which was carried on by migrating masons immune from the interference of town governments; and in the English cloth industry which owed its technical progress to the flight of workers from the towns to the freedom of the countryside. The commercial and political revolutions of the 16th century carried forward on a flood of American bullion broke down local exclusiveness still further and stimulated a fruitful alliance between the abstract speculation of the philosophers with the practical experience of the craftsmen and engineers. The scientific revolution of the 17th century thus had its roots in the relatively materialistic metaphysic of the Medieval Church and the technical experience and requirements of an expanding commercial society.

A second propensity, that of regarding work as the normal means of satisfying wants in preference for instance to theft, pillage or sheer asceticism, also received encouragement from the same theological source. The Medieval Church accepted and carried on the Biblical Doctrine of Creation and the Biblical Doctrine of Work— that is, a recognition that the performance of ordinary tasks of life had an ascetic or purifying value[3] and that among the snares which men should try to avoid was excessive indulgence in leisure. The West was taught to believe that work was a good thing in itself, and from the time of St. Benedict who ruled that his monks at Monte Cassino should go to bed broken with toil, to Thomas Carlyle who said that 'properly speaking, all true work is religion,' there is a continuous thread of social theory which regarded work as a form of moral discipline.

Alongside the medieval conception of work we must also consider the medieval conception of the worker. Although he might in law be merely an instrument, a human tool owned by another, he was also an agent of his own redemption, working out his own destiny, a person in his own right, with indestructible attributes no different from those of his master. To what extent this purely theological conception of the ordinary man affected the course of change towards the growth of a free labour force, with all the economic consequences which that implied, is a difficult question, but its significance to the economic historian is made clear in the following comment which was made by Marc Bloch,[4] perhaps the most eminent of French economic historians until he met his death at the hands of the Nazis:

'The Church,' he writes, 'refused resolutely to sanction the enslavement of Christians, true Christians, that is Catholics. If a Christian captured another Christian he was obliged to respect his free status. Perhaps one of the finest triumphs of Christian ethics was the enforcement of respect for this maxim, slowly to be sure, for it is still being recalled in England early in the 11th century, but in the long run most effectively. So it came about that the perpetual wars among Catholics left numberless dead; prisoners who sometimes sighed their lives out in dungeons, but, after the age of the great invasions, hardly any slaves. Yet you could hunt for slaves in the countries round about: Celtic Christians of the far West, generally treated as heretics; Islam; Slavonic, Baltic or Finnish 'paganries'; and even, from the 11th century, Greek Christians who by that time were all but cut off from the Catholic world. But these were all distant lands, or difficult of approach. They could supply warriors or traders with a few slaves; they could not maintain a great servile economy.'

The door back to slavery was closed: if there was a movement at all, it must be towards freedom.

We should also remember that all these ideological influences making for the freedom of the individual in his mind, his person and his property were operating within a loose political framework in which the conception of the State as an all-dominating sovereignty, though not unknown, was an impractical ideal. There was, therefore, no overmastering and unchallenged authority to impose its fiat upon the process of change, either legal, intellectual or economic, and within the interstices of this pluralistic structure of political and theocratic power, the seeds of liberty of thought and also liberty of person under the law had an opportunity which might have been denied if Church and State had combined to impose a unitary conception of orthodoxy or of social relations.

If the fruits of intellectual liberty began to be gathered first in Italy, the benefits of liberty under the law made themselves felt most effectively in England. In his *History of English Law,* Professor Holdsworth observes that both legal and ecclesiastical authorities accepted the same set of assumptions about rights and duties, namely that legal definitions regarding them were derived from Christian revelation and human reason, that is Natural Law, which was common to all men in that they were rational creatures, or as Professor d'Entreves, the Italian legal authority says, 'Human equality is the direct consequence of natural law, its first and essential tenet'; and to quote Professor Holdsworth again, '(this) common body of assumptions and methods made for that theoretical supremacy of right, legal and moral, which all through medieval history we see both in public and private law.'[5]

In England, the struggle for legal equality took place within a context dominated by two interconnected influences: a succession of kings—admittedly not unbroken—with a passion for order and a genius for administration and the emergence of that unique achievement of the English legal mind, the English Common Law. As a result, a shield of legal protection was thrown over the small freeholder as well as the large feudatory; and there was a period in the 13th century when the villein also appeared to be on the verge of receiving a similar degree of protection. By the beginning of the 14th century, however, the Court of Common Pleas—perhaps because it had built up as much business as it could comfortably handle—decided (in the words of Professor Plucknett) that 'it could not be bothered' with the affairs of the villein and he remained subject to the custom of the manor as administered in his lord's court. It was often possible, however, to argue as to who was and who was not a villein, or whether a man held land of ancient demesne; and such cases came before the King's courts. The lead was taken by villeins of substance, men of 100 acres or more who were protesting not against oppression and fear of starvation, but against feudal restrictions which hindered their further economic advancement.[6] Owing to the absence of recognition by the Common Law of claims of younger sons, the English peasantry, like their feudal masters, were generally under the rule of primogeniture, a further factor making for economic differentiation among them. Both before and after the Black Death, the Common Law was thus permitting the process of differentiation between larger and smaller cultivators which later led to the growth of a class of substantial yeoman farmers over against a class of semi-landless labourers by the process of economic evolution among the peasantry themselves apart from the action of landlords through enclosure and eviction. Moreover, the demographic effects of primogeniture among the peasantry should not be overlooked. Younger sons faced obstacles to marriage which were reflected in the relatively low birth rate[7]; and since the Christian tradition, unlike that of the Orient, made no demand for sons as a ritual necessity but rather honoured celibacy as an alternative to marriage and the production of children, the religious outlook contributed to the maintenance of a per capita level of income that, by the end of the Middle Ages, made the term 'the sturdy peasantry' something more than a cant phrase. Thus, some of the most important features of a commercial agriculture and a proletarian labour force were implied in the legal and demographic evolution of the medieval village.

A similar process of economic differentiation within a context of legal equality was taking place in the towns, and here the influence of underlying conceptions of equality derived from religious sources appears to have been unmistakeable, and indeed, decisive. In his essay on 'The Roots of the City,' Professor George Unwin observes that a distinguishing feature of medieval cities was the high degree of race fusion which they permitted compared to the cities of the East in which the different nationalities were separated by the rigidities of caste.

> 'The germ of western progress,' he writes, 'lay in a mighty sympathetic power of a new moral relation which drew together Celt and Saxon, Saxon and Dane, Frank and Gaul, Goth and Lombard and Italian and enabled them to co-operate in building up a new and wider civilisation. In the London of the 13th century the Saxon worships at the shrine of the martyred East Anglian St. Edmund; the Dane honours St. Olaf, and the Normans St. Botolph and St. Mildred, whilst a sense of a still wider Christian community is felt in the Churches of St. Martin of Tours, St. Giles the Provencal, St. Laurence the Italian and St. Nicholas the Syrian.'

The doctrinal fellowship thus created was not merely a solvent of antagonisms; 'it was,' he said 'a positive force, a creator of new social unities' which prevented racial division from hardening into a sterile hierarchy of castes which condemned the cities of the East to economic stagnation.[8]

The existence on the one side of a free agrarian society engaged in market operations and the rise of a thriving urban bourgeosie organising trade and industry through channels of credit dependent on mutual trust and the fulfilment of contracts, provided the twin pillars on which the exchange economy slowly raised itself from the inchoate economic life of early feudalism. In England, this upward progress was relatively steady owing to the greater freedom which she enjoyed from the ravages of war. For this—and for other reasons —economic life proceeded in relative peace and quietness, and the propensities making for economic growth through the rational use of resources were permitted an unusually large measure of freedom. The bourgeois life of the urban centres was assimilated into the life of the nation and the reciprocal influences between town and country were allowed to operate with maximum effect. Successful city merchants became absorbed into the landed classes; the landed classes reflected the rational approach to the administration of resources which in less economically developed societies would have been regarded as a vulgar attribute of a despised merchant class. In Spain, we have recently been told, the landlords in the 18th century were too proud even to keep accounts; and younger sons found the bread of poverty sweet so long as it was eaten in the shade of the genealogical tree.[9] These esoteric forms of satisfaction were not usually appreciated by the English landlords; though there were exceptions. The outstanding one is that of the Duke of Chandos in the 19th century who, with an income of £72,000 a year, raised the already crushing debt on the estate to £1½ million and after the sale of his effects in 1848, spent his remaining years cultivating the genealogical tree as a lodger in the Great Western Railway Hotel at Paddington.[10] He is the exception that proves the rule of the English landlords: they had come to regard estate management as part of the ordinary duty of their class and they generally aimed at handing over the family estate to their heirs in a better condition than that in which they received it from their fathers. They had learned that it paid them to attract good tenants and they had gradually developed a quasi co-operative system of land tenure by which the landlord provided and maintained the fixed capital and shared with the tenant the profits and to some extent even the losses of their joint enterprise. On this basis was built an advanced agriculture and a prosperous internal market which provided an indispensable condition for the acceleration of economic activity.

It is platitudinous to say that by the beginning of the 17th century the currents of change were running strongly in favour of the propertied classes, but they felt themselves thwarted in the rational pursuit of their interests by the fatuous irresponsibility of Stuart governments, particularly in regard to public expenditure and taxation. How far this factor entered into the causes of the English revolution of the 17th century is a question which I would not dare to raise; the dust of controversy which now obscures it, is, however a measure of the inextricable intimacy with which economic factors are combined with other historical circumstances to bring about great events. Whatever the economic causes, the economic results contributed to the overthrow of the irresponsible Stuart regime and the establishment of the more rational mercantile State in which political ends were adjusted to economic means and in which State policy was determined by the unspoken assumption that the national life must be related to the sources of the national livelihood.

One important characteristic of the new regime may be mentioned as a factor in the release of economic forces which is sometimes overlooked. Among the complaints which the propertied classes brought against the Stuart government was the burden of taxation; but if the Renaissance State of the Stuarts chastised the propertied class with whips, under the auspices of the mercantile state, which they themselves ruled, they chastised themselves not with whips but with scorpions. In his book on the *English Land Tax* Mr. Ward writes that by the end of the 17th century, 'The principle that all types of income should bear their share of the national burden had now been written into British fiscal policy,'[11] and the proportion of taxation falling on the propertied classes at this time is roughly represented by the following figures: on Excises £900,000 per annum; on poll taxes on the general public £120,000 per annum; on land tax paid as a rent charge on landlords £1,300,000 per annum. Compared to the sporadic spoilation of the Stuarts this was a tidal wave of revenue, but it was acceptable because it satisfied the contemporary theory that taxes should be 'equal' and 'general'.

Such voluntary immolation on the altar of fiscal rectitude by an all-powerful ruling class is so unusual as to be almost improper; it is I believe unique; it is perhaps the sovereign difference between the economy of Britain and that of her neighbours and certainly an important reason why Britain experienced an industrial revolution while France endured the French revolution. It also helps to explain the confusion which clouded the mind of the British governing class as to where their interests ended and those of the nation began; and they were encouraged in this amiable illusion of identity by the chief political philosopher of the day who demonstrated to them that the sanctity of property was a natural right which it was the duty of the State to defend, on pain of forfeiting their loyalty; and they could find further encouragement if they wished in the work of the leading poet of the day who expended the iridescent brilliance of his verse in celebrating the doctrine of deistic hedonism embodied in the famous tag:

> So two consistent motions act the Soul;
> And one regards Itself, and one the Whole.
> Thus God and Nature linked the general frame
> And bade Self-love and Social be the same.

It is hardly surprising, that with such distinguished authorities at their elbow as John Locke and Alexander Pope—ignoring the warnings which the latter offered in other of his writings—[12] landlords tended to assume that the self-acting mechanism for identifying private interests with public good had been providentially designed for their express benefit, and those of them who were given to speculation in land values felt no compunction in giving this beneficient contrivance a surreptitious shove in the right direction when circumstances demanded, as Dr. Mingay (a former student of the University) has shown.[13]

The emancipation of the propensities for economic growth could hardly go further; and the subsequent period of headlong advance into a new world of industrial technology presents the economic historian with a problem of peculiar difficulty. Is Economic History henceforth no more than a record of unleashed acquisitiveness, directed, at the best, by intelligent self interest? Is the task of the economic historian concluded by expressing economic achievement in terms of indices of growth, of income flows and movements of the trade cycle, in manipulating the technical apparatus of applied economics? It has recently been said, on another inaugural occasion, that 19th century Economic History is full of every kind of figure except the human,[14] and if economic historians are to avoid the aim of this shrewd shaft they will have to look round for a less inhuman approach.

It seems to me they will find it by emphasising those classes of economic facts which are not susceptible to purely economic kinds of historical analysis and that require something more than the exigencies of the market economy to explain. I have already mentioned the ideological and institutional factors which made for the rise of a flexible tenurial system of agriculture, of an urban bourgeoisie, of mobility between the social classes, of political stability which provided the security for investment and enterprise. Another well-known aspect of the problem is the disproportionate part played by members of Dissenting organisations in the transition to machine industry. Many reasons have been advanced for this, but the most convincing explanation appears to be that Dissenters combined a respect for work as a form of moral discipline with a passion for education which gave them a command of useful knowledge and of habits of intellectual application. They were also for the most part men of conscience and humanity who could secure the loyalty of their labour force and the trust of their customers; and some of them went on to create factory communities such as those of the Strutts at Belper and the Gregs at Styal with something more in mind than the maximisation of their economic interests.

Another field of enquiry which economic analysis alone will not elucidate is the factor of interdependence of industrial innovation and scientific investigation; nothing illustrates this more clearly than the story of the central innovation of the age, the steam engine of James Watt. If Professor Black and his colleague Dr. Anderson had not been demonstrating the principle of latent heat to their students at Glasgow University, they would not have had occasion to call in James Watt to repair the model of the Newcomen engine on which their demonstration depended. The steam engine, therefore, marks the point of intersection between two lines of historical advance: that of empirical adaptation of means to ends on the part of skilled craftsmen, and that of pure science in the tradition of Boyle and Newton and Galileo and the medieval mathematicians who paved the way for Copernicus.

A third set of facts which enter into the total economic situation but which are not susceptible to economic explanation is the ambivalent attitude of the economists themselves to forms of economic behaviour which they did so much to promote. Adam Smith, who was Professor of Moral Philosophy at Glasgow, and wrote the *Theory of Moral Sentiments* before he wrote the *Wealth of Nations,* did more than anyone else to give the principle of self interest the sanction of scientific authority. His object, however, was not the apotheosis of acquisitiveness but the promotion of freedom. 'The note of liberty rumbles through the book,' it has been said. 'He advocated capitalism not because it *was* freedom but because it made freedom possible.'[15] Again no one did more to demonstrate the economic importance of division of labour but no one was more alive to its ill-effects and to the necessity of preparing against them.

'The man whose whole life is spent in performing a few simple operations has no occasion to exert his understanding: he becomes as stupid and ignorant as it is possible for a human creature to become. The torpor of his mind renders him, not only incapable of relishing or bearing any part in any rational conversation but of conceiving any generous, noble or tender sentiments and consequently of forming any just judgement concerning many even of the ordinary duties of life.'

And so, to avoid a society populated with 'mutilated and deformed' spirits, he advocated a programme of national education. Similarly, the advocacy of competitive individualism by the classical economists was not simply to maximise output; on the contrary they thought

'the struggle of men for larger incomes was good because in the process they learned independence, self-reliance, self-discipline—because in short they became better men.'[16]

Even to the much misunderstood Samuel Smiles the object of self-help was not the acquisition of wealth but, in the last resort, of the qualities of the true gentleman—and

'a true gentleman,' he said 'was not the creature of inherited privilege, but the person who was polite, civil, tolerant and forebearing.'[17]

In practice, the gospel of self-help imposed a sterner test upon its votaries than modern economic theory would have found necessary or than their contemporaries were prepared to endure. It was associated with Malthusian doctrines of population and Ricardian doctrines of the self-regulating economy based on the supposition that consumption was co-extensive with production and that the answer to unemployment was to be found in the accelerated accumulation of capital and the increased mobility of labour. The stigma of pauperism as well as the discipline of the workhouse was felt to be the appropriate treatment for able-bodied labourers who sought support from public funds, and the surplus labour of country districts was to be forced to seek a productive union with surplus capital in the towns. But in the slump of 1837–42 there was surplus labour in the towns too, and the fires of Chartism were stoked to revolutionary fervour by this application of the New Economics so that many observers feared a break-down of the new capitalist society. If this was the best that the new science of wealth had to offer, it is not surprising that men looked round for an evangel of a different order, and English thinkers began to develop an alternative structure of thought that laid the foundation of modern socialism and anticipated some of the ideas embodied in the Communist Manifesto and Das Kapital.

The British working class movement was on the march; but it represented something more than a crude clash between capital and labour, and it drew its strength from historical roots that go far beyond the immediate circumstances that called it into being. Lord Attlee has given it as his opinion that

'The first place in the influences that built up the socialist movement must be given to religion.' 'It is significant,' he writes, 'that the gap between the end of Owenism and the birth of the Social Democratic Federation is filled by the Christian Socialist Movement of Kingsley and Maurice. Here one sees a feature which distinguishes the British movement from most of those abroad. . . in no other socialist movement has Christian thought had such a powerful leavening effect.'

As a general statement about the British working class movement this is no doubt true, but the Christian Socialist Movement of Kingsley and Maurice was, in the circumstances of the time, a step backwards, since it opposed the extension of the franchise to working men and put its faith in a change of heart on the part of the aristocracy. Marx and Engels pounced on this with savage delight: 'Christian Socialism,' they said, 'is the holy water with which the Priest consecrates the heart burnings of the aristocrats.'[18]

But events proved that the Marxist prophecy of proletarian revolution was as much a mirage as the Christian Socialist hope of a conversion of the aristocracy. Where then did the solution of the immediate problem lie? It lay in the economic process itself and in the minds and characters of the leaders of thought and action which it had thrown up. The new capitalist society had discovered the revolutionary principle of economic growth and was learning how to adjust its policies for the advancement of welfare as well as the production of wealth: railways and steamships solved the economic problem; free trade was pursued as part of laissez-faire planning for employment, and the new capitalist economics, in accordance with its moral origins, was in its objectives not only utilitarian but ultimately equalitarian. Certainly, it was a negative approach to equality. As Professor Tawney has drily observed, it meant,

'not the absence of violent contrasts of income and condition, but equal opportunities of becoming unequal';[19]

but by promoting the extension of political and civil liberties it opened the door to new political influences which have brought the equalitarian ideal nearer to realisation than the 19th century formulators of it might have approved. The Philosophical Radicals who whipped up the fury of the Chartists through the New Poor Law were also champions of free trade, of manhood suffrage, compulsory education, public health and factory reform, and the formation of an efficient, honest and devoted civil service as an approach to what has been called 'Social Socialism.'[20] Even the much abused classical economists supported these reforms, including factory reform, and as the danger of over-population gradually receded before the advance of mechanical production, their emphasis switched to the problem of distribution and the social evils of unregulated competition, and no less a pillar of orthodoxy than James McCulloch was asking in 1843 'whether "artificial means" ought to be used to check the disproportionate growth of manufacturing'[21] while J. S. Mill was confessing his leaning towards socialism. Industry itself produced radical leaders such as Cobden and Bright who challenged the Chartists for the support of the working class and Chartist leaders noted with a tinge of envy that working men contributed generously to a memorial to Sir Robert Peel. It was especially significant that Trade Union leaders found that there was some virtue in a cotton lord though he passionately opposed, in the name of economic freedom, any form of State interference such as factory reform, health reform, even the licensing laws and the laws to check the smoke nuisance. John Bright, who embodied these characteristics of the text-book capitalist, was the recognised leader of the radical forces which won the vote for the working men in 1867, and the political split which had threatened to divide the social classes was solidly and permanently bridged.

How different things might have been if the Industrial Revolution had been merely a phenomenon of market forces, or if prevailing economic ideas had been nothing more than a rationalisation of the interests of a capitalist class exploiting a proletariat sinking into deeper and deeper misery. In the famous incident of the reform meeting of 1866 when the railings of Hyde Park gave way under the pressure of unemployed workmen demanding the vote, Marx wrote that if only the railings had been used against the police and twenty of them had been knocked dead, the military would have had to be called out and 'then there would have been some fun.' He was disappointed of his fun. Instead, the trade union leader Robert Applegarth and the cotton lord John Bright combined to carry the law for manhood suffrage,[22] and the working class were admitted as equal partners into the political community.

In his series of lectures on *Economic Theory and the Undeveloped Countries*, the distinguished Swedish economist, Gunnar Myrdal, tells us that 'the Great Awakening in the very poor countries reflects the equality ideal of Western civilisation,' and he goes on to raise a question which I hope does something to justify the kind of approach to the study of Economic History that I have been indicating:

'It is still,' he writes, 'a largely unsolved sociological problem why and how it happened that this shining idealistic vision of the dignity of the individual human being, and of his basic right to equality of opportunity, originated, and how it maintained its strength through untold centuries of blatant inequality and oppression.'

He relates it to the influence of Natural Law through which he says, the equality doctrine 'had fastened itself at the rock bottom of Western economic speculation.'

It can be seen therefore that the free market economy was something more than a convenient instrument for maximising the economic satisfactions of a class of wealthy capitalists, or even a group of wealthy capitalist states; in its historical development and in its contemporary manifestation it has been associated with an ideal conception of man first as a person then as a legal entity, and now as a citizen of a free society in a community of free societies. If Professor Myrdal is correct, the problem of the undeveloped nations raises more than a question of a re-deployment of resources within the framework of the contemporary market economy; it presents a challenge to the moral assumptions from which the free market itself arose. These, I have suggested, have their roots in a historical past that is coeval with Western civilisation and which call for their proper understanding upon a range of reference that includes other branches of history—in particular those of religion, science, law, and

T

politics—as well as the strictly economic. Economic History is thus a unifying force within the field of historical disciplines, and, while being an autonomous discipline in its own right, it has an important part to play in the study of historical inter-relations; it is an agent, as others have observed, for

'reducing rather than increasing the numbers of compartments into which scholarship is now divided,'[23]

a role which provides additional justification for its inclusion in the recognised schools of study of a modern university.

NOTES

Corrected notes to J. D. Chambers' Lecture.

1 J. H. Clapham, *Concise Economic History of Britain to 1750*, 1949, p. xvii.
2 See M. M. Postan, 'Why was Science backward in the Middle Ages?' in *History of Science Symposium*, 1953.
3 See Alan Richardson, *The Biblical Doctrine of Work*, 1952.
4 Marc Bloch, *Cambridge Medieval History*, II, p. 27.
5 W. Holdsworth, *History of English Law*, II, p. 131; A. P. d'Entrèves, *Natural Law*, 1951, p. 22.
6 T. F. T. Plucknett, *Concise History of Common Law*, 1956, p. 310; R. H. Hilton, 'Peasant Movements in England before 1381', *Econ. Hist. Rev.*, 2nd ser., II, 2, 1949, pp. 130–1.
7 See G. C. Homans, *English Villagers of the Thirteenth Century*, 1942, p. 137; H. E. Hallam, 'Some Thirteenth Century Censuses', *Econ. Hist. Rev.*, 2nd ser., X, 3, 1958; J. T. Krause, 'Some Neglected Factors in the English Industrial Revolution', *Journ. Econ. Hist.*, XIX, 1959 and discussion by M. D. Morris, *ibid*, p. 568.
8 George Unwin, *Studies in Economic History* (ed. R. H. Tawney), 1927, p. 49.
9 A. Goodwin (ed.), *The European Nobility in the Eighteenth Century*, 1953, p. 55.
10 F. M. L. Thompson, 'The End of a Great Estate', *Econ. Hist. Rev.*, 2nd ser., VIII, 1, 1955, p. 50.
11 W. R. Ward, *The English Land Tax in the Eighteenth Century*, 1953, p. 20.
12 Epistle III: *Of the Use of Riches.*
13 See for example G. E. Mingay, *Land Ownership and Agrarian Trends*, (Ph.D. thesis, University of Nottingham, 1958), p. 112:
'O Lord thou knowest mine estates are in the city of London and likewise I have lately purchased an estate in fee simple in the County of Essex. I beseech Thee preserve those two counties of Middlesex and Essex from fire and earthquake. And as I have mortgages in Herefordshire, I beg Thee likewise to have an eye of Compassion on that county. As for the rest of the counties Thou mayest deal with them as Thou art pleased'.
14 F. J. Fisher, 'The Sixteenth and Seventeenth Centuries: The Dark Ages of English Economic History?', *Economica*, NS., XXIV, 93, 1957, pp. 2–18, [and above pp. 181–200.]
15 C. R. Fay, *Great Britain from Adam Smith to the Present Day*, 1928, p. 28; J. Cropsey, *Politics and Economy*, 1957, p. x.

16 G. J. Stigler, *Five Lectures on Economic Problems*, 1948, p. 14. For his support of high wages and general well-being of the poor see A. W. Coats, 'Changing Attitudes to Labour in the Mid-Eighteenth Century', *Econ. Hist. Rev.*, 2nd ser., XI, 1, 1958.
17 Asa Briggs, *Victorian People*, 1954, p. 145.
18 C. R. Attlee, *The Labour Party in Perspective*, 1937; Marx and Engels, *Communist Manifesto*, 1848; J. Saville, 'The Christian Socialists' in Dona Torr (ed.), *Democracy and the Labour Movement*, 1954, p. 153.
19 R. H. Tawney, *Equality*, 1931, p. 138.
20 D. H. Magregor, *Economic Thought and Policy*, 1949, chapters 3 and 5.
21 M. Blaug, *Ricardian Economics*, 1958, p. 241.
22 Asa Briggs, *op. cit.*, and *The Age of Improvement*, 1959, pp. 514–523 for a valuable analysis of the cross-currents of opinion that made possible 'the leap in the dark'.
23 See J. U. Nef, 'What is Economic History?', *Journ. Econ. Hist*, Supplement 1944.

15

M. W. Beresford

TIME AND PLACE
(Leeds, 1960)

This inaugural lecture was delivered at the University of Leeds on the 28th November 1960.

TIME AND PLACE

A FEW moments ago there was a procession into this room—

> clothéd all in a livery
> Of a solemn and a great fraternity—

language which you will recognise as Chaucer's and not mine. In Chaucer's day a livery signified membership of a fraternity. Students of economic history are familiar with one fraternity-type especially, the guilds, whose main purpose was economic and whose members had in common some handicraft or trade. But a university was also a fraternity, with masters and apprentices to a craft, the craft of knowledge. The apprentices had their own badges and dress and the masters of arts had theirs, that which I wear this afternoon. When apprentices to a craft came out of their time there were initiation ceremonies. In Leeds breweries the apprentice coopers who learn to make barrels still mark the end of their time by being rolled out in a barrel. In *higher* education we have more dignity. Taking its tune perhaps from *The Mastersingers of Nuremberg*, the University demands of a new professor something like a mastersong. It commands him to make an exhibition of himself.

I suppose these public exhibitions are most useful when a new professor is a newcomer to Leeds. How economical for a stranger to be introduced to a roomful of people at once! But no amount of ceremonial dress can disguise me. I am not a stranger. I am the 3.0 o'clock on Tuesdays and the 4.0 o'clock on Thursdays man. For more than twelve years I have lectured in Economic History, more than half of those years in this very lecture room.

But what is new, and what I am honoured to initiate this afternoon, is the Chair itself. The actual study of Economic History in this University is half a century old, for when Leeds appointed John Harold Clapham as its first Professor of Economics in 1902 it gave him so few students that he had leisure to work in the field both of Economics and Economic History. Indeed, one might say that Leeds converted him: for after he left Leeds for Cambridge in 1908 his principal work *was* in Economic History, and in 1928 he became the first Professor of Economic History there. If it is the creation of professors that makes a subject respectable, the frock-coat period of

255

Economic History has been since the end of the Second World War. One for Birmingham, one for Bristol, one for Nottingham, one for Glasgow, one for Edinburgh . . . and Leeds came tumbling after.

It might look as if we historians were getting near that specialisation and division of labour that Adam Smith noted in the pin factory. But the scope of the subject I am called to profess is rather larger than a pin head. It is concerned with all past economic behaviour. *English* Economic History alone now has a literature too bulky for any one person to know thoroughly. We even have our subspecialists: agrarian historians, business historians, transport historians, to name only the subspecies who now publish their journals.

It is not part of my task this afternoon to apologise for my subject or to take further time defining it. Definitions of subjects can have a brief notoriety as examination questions but that is about all they are good for. I would rather find historians too busy writing to have time to define their subject. I have great sympathy with the film director whom John Grierson once described: 'He demonstrated the limits of his art in the most effective way—by persistently going beyond them.' Nor do I want to demonstrate how the model Economic Historian should behave, nor to claim that all Economic Historians should be interested in what interests me. I am still enough of a newcomer from a non-professorial world to remember that professing a subject is not quite the same thing as possessing it. In so far as a year in a new environment has corrupted me, I will dare to be mildly possessive in one direction only. When the History of Technology comes to be a respectable subject in universities—and where else if not here?—I hope it will not go the way of the History of Science, i.e. to the place where the philosophers are kings. Technological change and economic change are so connected that I would regard them as already married, married as it were by repute and no marriage service necessary.

I have said earlier that this inaugural lecture invites me to make an exhibition of myself. And now I can proceed, so long as it is clear what I am exhibiting: one of many ways of looking at the subject; one of many ways of working in it; and one of many ways of teaching it. Self-analysis, public self-analysis is a risky business, but if I have to define a Beresfordian approach to Economic History it is an emphasis on visual things. By 'visual things' I mean not only the traditional sources of historical inquiry, books and documents—they are visual enough; nor do I add merely maps, a visual summary of the real world. I add the visible real world itself, or rather those visible remains in it by which past economic activity can be detected. In this sense my profession is Time and Place.

These visible remains in the real world enter into two parts of my professional life and indeed help to weld these parts together. They help me as an inquirer, a researcher, for they suggest questions and sometimes answers. They help me also as a teacher. You may have wondered why for seven years I have lectured in this particular theatre. It is because it has the best lantern for showing slides; and this has been easier since we who teach in Leeds are aided by Mr Blackledge's department and have a photographic service which is the envy of my colleagues in Oxbridge and Redbrick alike.

I would call my approach a 'field-approach' or 'archaeological approach', were it not that 'field' sounds like the countryside and 'archaeological' sounds antique. The visibles of which I spoke come from town as well as country and from any century. The Baines wing of this University is as much a piece of Economic History of its day as the Man-made Fibres Building. I shall not flinch if this gets me called a 'local' economic historian, so long as 'local' is not a term of abuse. Visible evidences cannot help but be local. One looks at *particular* streets, *particular* fields, one cannot look at England in one glance.

One of my colleagues, knowing that I am a time-and-place man, said to me recently 'What do you do when you get to the commercial crises and booms and slumps of the nineteenth century? Surely you cannot illustrate them with reference to places and buildings!' Booms and slumps . . . commercial crises. . . . A short bus-ride could take us all to Tadcaster Bridge. I invite you next time you cross it to look north upstream. You will see the River Wharfe and a railway bridge crossing it. It looks an ordinary railway bridge. If you walk up to it, it appears very extraordinary: for it has no railway line; on one side there is no sign that there ever was one, and on the other there are cuttings which end in mid-field. This is in fact the debris of a Victorian commercial failure, the uncompleted railway line of 1848 which George Hudson planned to go direct from York to Leeds and not round the two sides of a triangle—York to Church Fenton and Church Fenton to Leeds—which a rival company's line then followed and (alas) still follows. The documents, the plans of the route that Hudson's line hoped to follow, can be seen in the British Transport Commission's Record Office in York.[1] But the real bridge in its isolation is more eloquent than the plans, for they might suggest that the line was built. In Tadcaster they know better, for they still have to come into Leeds by bus.

I should like to come into Leeds myself for my next illustrations. Ten minutes' walk from the University there is another occasion for an observer to interpret time and place, and again the theme is nineteenth-century boom and slump. Plate I*a* shows Prosperity

Street. The name of this street is itself a Victorian period piece. It matches *Hard Times*, the other side of the coin, for which the visible evidence is the Leeds Workhouse. Hard Times and Prosperity Street succeeded each other pretty regularly in the nineteenth century, and if one had to guess when Prosperity Street was built and christened one could write off half the years of the century to begin with. In which of the prosperous and optimistic Victorian years was our Prosperity Street christened? It does not appear in a Leeds directory of 1873 but it does appear in White's[2] of 1875. So it was christened in 1874 or 1875. Professor Cairncross's figures show that in 1875 there was virtually no unemployment among building workers, and residential building all over the country had been on the increase for the previous five years.[3] Artisans—like the saddlers, cabinet-makers and upholsterers who were the first occupants of Prosperity Street— were then experiencing nearly full employment. Beveridge's index[4] shows only $1\frac{1}{2}$ per cent out of work in 1874: clearly, the never-had-it-so-good situation, just the time for Prosperity Street.

But only just in time. Between 1874 and 1876 unemployment doubled and by 1879 it was nearly 11 per cent among the skilled, and obviously higher among the unskilled. One in twelve building workers was now unemployed. It was the worst unemployment figure between the Great Exhibition of 1851 and the post-war slump of 1921. The name of Prosperity Street was not changed, but what happened was that building stopped. Three houses on one side and seven on the other was the sum total of Prosperity Street until, near the peak of the next boom in 1882, ten more houses were built— filling up as far as the half-way mark, the crossing with Hawkins Place. Then the slump of 1886, the boom of 1890 and the slump of 1894 were to pass before the street was completed in 1898–1901.

I must add one bizarre footnote which will be meaningful to economists present, especially students of the trade cycle. In the directory giving the first occupants of Prosperity Street in 1876, who lives at no. 12? His surname is Macro, William Macro, brickmaker. And in the slump? In 1881 his house was empty. Macro had gone.[5]

I have not yet wrung the last drop of Economic History out of this unfortunate street. Let us now look at it and its neighbours from the air (Plate I*b*). There seems to be some pattern in the grouping of the rows of back-to-back houses. What dictated where these streets were placed?

They were laid out by speculative builders, and to build they needed land. Blocks of houses like these were determined, as Mr David Ward has recently shown, by the existing units of agricultural ownership.[6] In a city like Nottingham the late survival of open fields and common rights made it almost impossible for builders to buy up

PLATE I

(*a*) Prosperity Street, Leeds, 1960.

(*b*) The pattern of fields imposed on back-to-back houses.

PLATE II

(*a*) Incomplete back-to-back housing at former field edge.

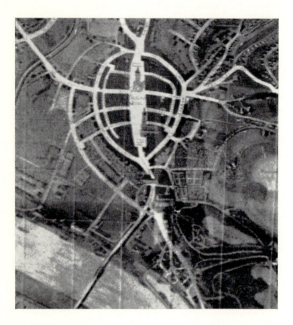

(*b*) Plan of Deggendorf on Danube, Bavaria.

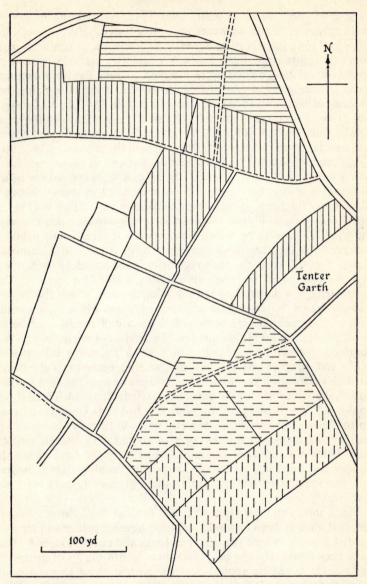

Fig. 1. Fields to south-west of Meanwood Road, Leeds, 1847. Four different owners are shown by shading; a fifth owned the fields shown unshaded.

farm land near the town until after 1845, so that the houses of Nottingham remained compact and compressed.[7] But in Leeds the fields had long since been enclosed and there were no obstacles from common rights over them. Builders could buy up fields piecemeal whenever existing owners were tempted to sell. People sometimes speak dramatically of green fields drowned in a sea of building, but in terms of land ownership the part of Leeds in 1847 shown in Fig. I was not one continuous sea but a chain of pools, many small owners side by side. The units of purchase by builders were fields, and houses and streets had to be fitted into them. Five of the owners are indicated by different shadings.[8] You will notice that one of these grass fields was a tenter garth, a field where the frames were erected on which the cloth was stretched in the open air by local weavers. This next plan shows the back-to-back terraces as they were fitted in (Fig. 2). Mr Mortimore, who drew this plan for me, spotted an acute case of the shoe-lift process by which houses were squeezed into fields. It concerns the Oxbridge area between Camp Road and Meanwood Road. You will see a curious irregularity in the length of the terraces and the placing of the open-air lavatory yards (top centre). This irregularity was dictated by the limits of the field which the builder had purchased, but to explain *why* the hedge was where it was would take me far back into the agricultural history of Leeds . . . where I don't propose to go at this moment. Instead I commend to you two common examples hereabouts which show the same influence of field- and property-boundaries on housing patterns. Behind Mr Austick's bookshop you will find a good example of the ship's-prow-house, shaped to fit into the corner of a triangular field. Then, if you go down Elland Road (as if on your way to Leeds United) and look up to the steepnesses of Beeston Hill you will there see how rows of ordinary back-to-back houses come to an end with a single terrace, there being no room for a complete house on the land which the builder had bought. In view of the sporting locality dare I christen this phenomena (Plate II*a*, right) the full back-to-back and the half-back?

Fig. 3 shows another block of Leeds fields in 1847. Some, you will see, had already been captured—not for housing artisans in terraces but for gentlemen with gardens, paddocks and coach-houses.[9] These have been fitted into the fields but there is still plenty of green. To these fields might be applied Keynes' words: these ghosts rule us from their grave. Whose lives do these ghosts rule? The Vice-Chancellor's, the Faculty of Arts', the Department of Economics and Commerce's and so mine. One of the gentlemen's houses is now the home of the Department of Education, and the Union and University House have been fitted between the groves on the left.

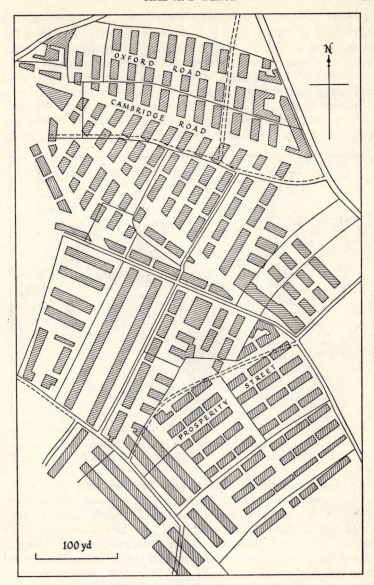

Fig. 2. The area of Fig. 1 as finally filled by back-to-back houses;
the former field-boundaries emphasised.

In 1847 the fields in the centre of the plan, which I have shaded, all belonged to John Hillary Hebblethwaite. In 1852 he proposed to sell them off in building lots, making up a new road to be called Cavendish Road. The road was cut but there were no takers for the plots.[10] In 1859 he put them on the market again[11] and a purchaser was found for the first plot to be built upon, the present Department of Student Health (no. 3), originally the home of Joseph Horsfall, machine-maker and partner in the Victoria Foundary.[12] The two houses which now (1960) shelter most of the members of the Faculty

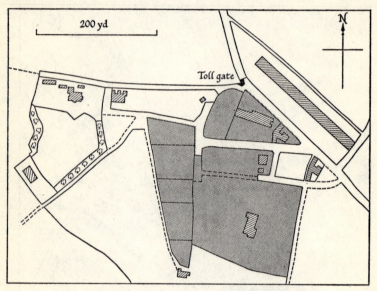

Fig. 3. Fields to the south-west of Blenheim Terrace, 1847.
The property of J. H. Hebblethwaite is shaded.

of Economic and Social Studies were built in 1864. No. 6, the northernmost, was built by Jonathon Pulleyn, stationer and engraver.[13] This is the house where Professor Grebenik—appropriately enough for a demographer—occupies the best bedroom; while Professor Brown and I occupy the front rooms downstairs, one to dine and one to draw. No. 8 (the other half of Economics House) and no. 10 (Geology) were both built in 1864 by Miss Matterson. Here her *Seminary for Young Ladies Day and Boarding* brought the first light of education into the precinct. She died in 1898 and in 1899 no. 10 was bought by Sydney Rumboll, the surgeon.

The houses on the south side of the Presbyterian Church, a number of which now shelter university departments, were built between 1886 and 1888 but for a different sort of customer. They have shorter back gardens with no room for coach-houses; their front gardens are narrower; and they have the family conformity of a terrace. No. 32 has no room for any back garden. If we ask why the building plots were so cabined and confined and why Tonbridge Street treads on the very heels of no. 32 we are back again among the fields which Hebblethwaite had inherited from his great-uncle in 1840. It was the Far Pasture, the Lane Close and the Low Close whose hedges determined where builders should build.

Most regnant of all the ghosts are the hedges a little to the north of Cavendish Road, those which determined the bounds of Beech Grove Terrace. It was a ghost which Messrs Lanchester and Lodge were powerless to exorcise when they designed the new Arts Block. What our architects had to do was to squeeze the building in between the two public roads which had been laid out between 1847 and 1852 on either side of what the plan of 1847 shows as 'no. 174: Lyddon's Trustees'. In this long-determined length and breadth my Arts colleagues had to be squeezed, 'a fair field full of folk'.

The theme to which I now move can also be stated in terms of Time and Place. It, too, begins in Leeds but it is far from parochial and takes us to the Danube and to the feet of the Pyrenees. I begin with two innocent questions: Why is Leeds parish church so far out of the town? Why is Briggate straight?

Strangers will need to know that Leeds parish church is neither the one in Boar Lane nor the one in upper Briggate, for these are daughter-churches, latecomers in the seventeenth and eighteenth centuries. The mother-church, the only true parish church, is St Peter's at the far (east) end of Kirkgate, tucked away behind the railway embankment which overlies part of its graveyard, its spire just visible from the city bus station. Why so remote? and why so remote from the market-place of old Leeds, which was the wide street of Briggate? Town market-places were usually *next* to their parish church. The oldest market-place in York was alongside St Sampson's; the largest market space in London was alongside St Bartholomew's church: but Briggate is not alongside St Peter's, Leeds. Why was this?

The answer was suggested in 1945 by Mr Geoffrey Woledge in a paper to the Thoresby Society. Simply, it was that the houses and yards on both sides of Briggate made up the little borough which Maurice Paynel, lord of Leeds, created in 1207. Mr Woledge argued that Paynel had not promoted the old village of Leeds into a borough but tacked a new borough alongside the old village, planting the borough in the fields (Fig. 4).[14] The village church continued to serve the borough, which had no church of its own until St John's was founded more than 400 years later at the north end of Briggate. In this view, Briggate is straight because it was laid out as a single venture in town planting, possessing the two essentials of a medieval town: sixty building plots for the houses of craftsmen and traders; and a market-place to serve the surrounding countryside each Monday.

In economic and social life a straight line is always suggestive. If you have to lay out a street in the fields and put building plots alongside it, the easiest way is to have straight streets and right-angled plots. The straight line in any period is usually a symptom of something sudden, something planned, something added, something altered. In contrast, village streets and roads-through-fields (which have grown, as it were, inch by inch, slowly and without design) tend to wriggle and to wind. Compare Kirkgate or Woodhouse Lane with its double wriggle and Briggate with its set-square sides.

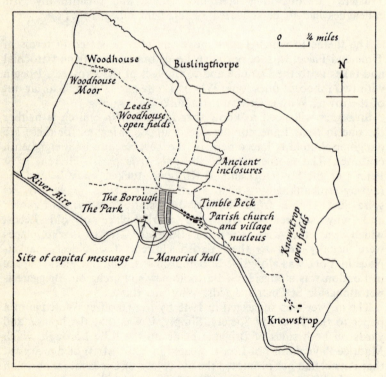

Fig. 4. Conjectural plan of Leeds borough village and fields in 1341.
(Based on *extent*, P.R.O. E. 36/176, ff. 79–87.)

Straightness as the mark of the town-planner appears in many centuries in many countries. It is the pattern of the streets of New York; it is the pattern of the boulevards which Hausmann drove through Paris between 1852 and 1870; and of the streets of Louis XIV's town of Versailles; it is the pattern, you will remember, of Prosperity Street and its neighbours.

But Versailles, Paris boulevards, New York and Prosperity Street are not of the same century as Maurice Paynel's creation of Leeds in 1207. Where can we match this? Where in medieval towns shall we find straight streets and right-angled building plots? In Hampshire is a little borough, Stockbridge, planted in the fields of King's Somborne about seven years earlier than the borough of Leeds. It has not grown in later years and its skeleton is less covered with flesh than Leeds. But there are the burgage plots (sixty-four of them by 1256) on either side of the broad market-place. The economic advantage of this site must have been thought excellent, for it was a remarkably damp place to choose. The meanders of the River Test swirl along the edge of the burgage plots, making it the most Venetian of all English boroughs. This little borough, contemporary in its foundation[15] with Leeds, is not far from Briggate even in name. In *Briggate* we have our northern form of 'bridge': and further, the original name of Stockbridge was simply *Le Strete*, and what else is the '-gate' in Briggate but the northern word for 'street'? Our borough of Leeds was simply one street also, and at the end of it was Aire bridge just as Stockbridge had its bridge.

There are medieval plantations which are not so very far (in some respects) from New York. One late thirteenth-century foundation with street-names akin to New York's was Edward I's plantation of New Winchelsea. In an early rental[16] of 1292 its streets were simply *Prima Strata, Secunda Strata*, and so on, and the very building blocks were numbered off. We may match the straightness of the streets of many North American plantations with the straightness of Gascon streets such as those of Grenade sur Garonne; or, in England, of Portsmouth, Stratford on Avon, Salisbury, Ludlow, Windsor, Bury St Edmunds and Liverpool: to name but a few of the 120 towns which were planted in England between the Norman Conquest and 1300.

In Wales about forty towns fall into the same class; in that part of France which remained English in the thirteenth century the total of English plantations is also about 120. Many of these Gascon towns were simply small market centres where the local wines were collected for shipping down river to the sea-ports of Bordeaux or Bayonne. Once a week since their foundation there have been markets in such planted towns as Sauveterre de Guyenne and Beaumont du Périgord.

U

I hope you will now recognise in the straightness of Briggate the evidence of its plantation and also its function as a market-place. Can the remoteness of Leeds parish church from the borough be matched in other planted towns? Is the absence of a parish church convincing evidence that a town came late on the economic scene? Visual, topographical, non-documentary evidence of this sort is necessary since so many towns have few or no documents from the period of their origin. It is exceptional to find rentals like that of Winchelsea in 1292 or of Newtown (Francheville), Isle of Wight, in the first year of its life (1257).[17]

Stratford on Avon, whose grid-pattern of streets has been mentioned, is one such town. You have to walk out of the town to find the parish church if you are in search of Shakespeare's monument. At Hull, another planted town, the walk was even longer. There is a true story of an archbishop of York in the early fourteenth century

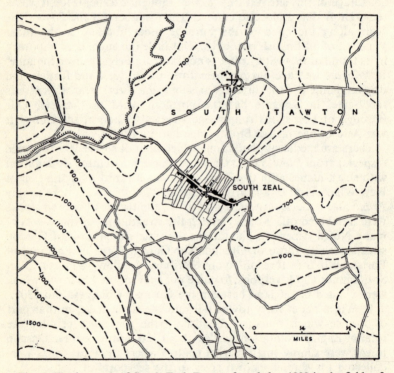

Fig. 5. The borough of South Zeal, Devon, founded c. 1299 in the fields of South Tawton parish. The borough has burbage plots on either side of the single broad street, like Leeds; it later acquired a chapel subordinate to South Tawton church, as St John's Briggate was subordinate to St Peter's, Leeds.

being astonished to meet a funeral procession wending its way on a stormy night along the dangerous shore of the Humber. It was on its way to the parish church of the townspeople of Hull, that of Hessle.[18] Hull had been planted in the fields of Hessle. Young Liverpool, founded in the same year as Leeds, had no parish church; nor had Boroughbridge; nor had South Zeal, Devon (Fig. 5). And all for the same reason: they were like seatless latecomers at a crowded lecture; they arrived too late.

I spent September 1960 in another part of Europe where the expanding economy of the thirteenth century induced landowners to speculate by planting new towns. A plan of one such town is painted inside the town gate, and it makes a dark photograph (Plate II*b*). But this plan of Deggendorf shows the regularity and artificiality of its shape: an oval. To the south can be seen the Danube. Deggendorf resembles Hull in having no parish church inside its walls. To find the church and town graveyard you must go outside the gate to the church of the village in whose fields Deggendorf was planted. The tall building in the market-place is not a church but the *rathaus*, the town-hall and market-hall. Until nineteenth-century improvements the Moot Hall of Leeds stood in just that position, right in the middle of Briggate, though in a less attractive style.

Fig. 6 shows the planted towns of Bavaria to match the plantations in England, Wales, Scotland, Ireland and Gascony. And these Bavarian towns are but a few of the hundreds of planted towns of the twelfth and thirteenth centuries along the whole moving eastern frontier of the Germanic peoples. These towns are the visible signs that new land was being colonized and new market centres called into existence. In plan, as in function, the Germanic foundations were akin to the Gascon and English *bastides, villes neuves* and Newtowns (Fig. 7).

Our English plantations were also part and parcel of expanding cultivation and expanding markets. It was not, of course, an expansion on the German scale, for England and France were not starting from scratch, even in those parts of Gascony where there had been great depopulation during the Albigensian wars. In England there were plenty of old-established towns eager for promotion. It seems to me that this makes our record of town plantation the more impressive. Our economic expansion found work not only for our existing stock of old towns; but also for many promotions of villages to towns; and also for all these additional ventures, the New Towns, so many of which turned out to be successes. There was room at the bottom, room in the middle and room at the top.

In Cornwall, Devon, Wales (and perhaps even Yorkshire) one might accept plantations as being on a frontier of colonization. But

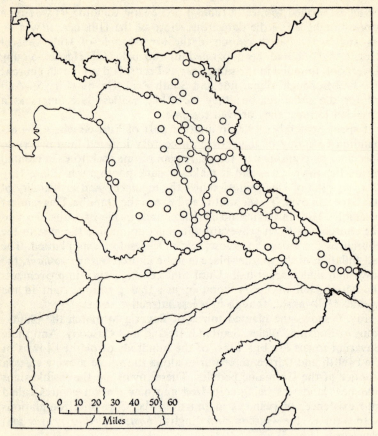

Fig. 6. *Bastide* towns in Bavaria, 1150–1350. (Plantations over the border of Czechoslovakia and East Germany are not shown.)

what can be said in the face of the fact that within a forty-mile radius of Winchester, the old capital of southern England, seventeen new towns were planted alongside a good crop of old-established boroughs and promoted villages?

I must not leave you with the impression that every venture prospered. That would have made the plantations a certainty and I have rightly called them 'speculations'. Fig. 8 shows the plan of Beauregard in Gascony, its grid of streets but a shadow of its former self. In England, Ravenserod has gone beneath the Humber and the site of Warenmouth in Northumberland was so little remembered that a chancery clerk once sent its charter to Wearmouth. One or two

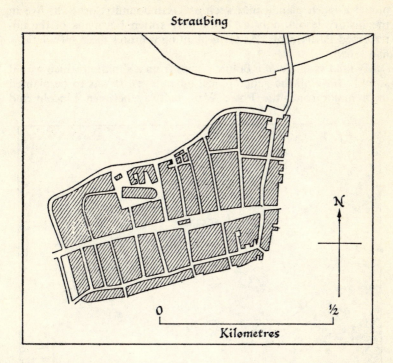

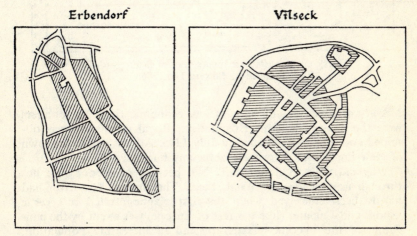

Fig. 7. Three Bavarian plantations. Straubing on the Danube is a walled town with a long central market-place; Erbendorf is of similar plan; Vilseck is walled and moated with a castle in the north-east corner.

of the English plantations, such as Grampound (Cornwall) live in
the history books only as half-empty rotten boroughs of the un-
reformed Parliaments. As town-planting ventures these speculations
had failed.

My final example of a failure comes from a situation which would
seem to have all the geographical advantages. It was to be planted
on a major road, the Fosse Way, halfway between Lincoln and

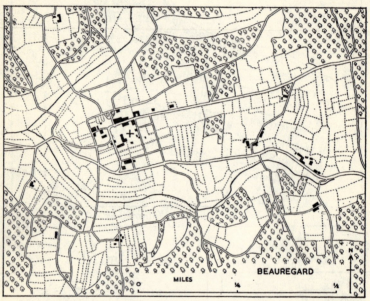

Fig. 8 The shrunken *bastide* (*sc.* plantation) of Beauregard, Dordogne,
founded by Edward I in 1286.

Newark and well out of sight of any economic rival. Its founders
were the wealthy Knights Hospitallers. Royal permission was obtained and a charter[19] issued in July 1345. All was set for the town
of New Eagle. But there were never any burgesses.

Why did the speculation fail? Not because of a poor site; not
through any legal snag. What, then? The timing. The town had
hardly been conceived when the first plague-infected rats came
ashore and England (like the rest of Europe) was swept by the pan-
demic of the bubonic plague. Instead of increasing population,
colonization, more villages and towns there was contraction. There
was not even enough to keep all the old towns going and there was
certainly no room for new ones. Perhaps the best simple commentary

on the drastic change in the economic climate after 1349 is this empty field; and the knowledge that, whereas the previous 250 years in England had added at least 120 towns, there are only two foundations in the whole of the next four centuries.[20] New towns did not begin again until the spa-towns and the cotton mill-towns of the late eighteenth century.

I have almost done, and I hope that the bricks, the small pieces of local and visual evidence, have begun to make something of a building and that I have brought an aspect of urbanization into its proper proportions.

I prefaced my lecture with no text: may I be allowed an epigraph? In 1897 the Cambridge historian Maitland delivered in Oxford those Ford lectures which were later published as *Township and Borough*. He was conscious that his Oxford audience, used to thinking of history as the decline and fall of empires, might think the walls and fields of Cambridge a petty, parochial subject. 'Will you think me ill-bred', he said, 'if I talk of the town in which I live?'[21] This afternoon I have been even more parochial. If he was ill-bred to talk of his own town in a public lecture to an academic audience, I, who have talked of my own street, must be simply disgusting.

POSTSCRIPT

The ideas about medieval towns that were germinating in my mind in 1960 were subsequently embodied in Maurice Beresford, *New Towns of the Middle Ages: Town Plantation in England, Wales and Gascony* (Lutterworth Press, 1967; pp xx + 670). The Prosperity Street theme was developed further in 'Prosperity Street and others: an essay in visible urban history', in M. W. Beresford and G. R. J. Jones, eds., *Leeds and its Region* (British Association, Leeds, 1967) pp 186–199; and a full-scale book on the building history of inner Leeds is envisaged in the 1970s.

M.W.B.   1970

Thanks are due to Mr M. J. Mortimore who drew Figs. 1, 2, 3, 5, 7 and 8; to Mr David Ward for Fig. 4 and Plate II*a*, taken from his unpublished thesis; to Mr P. M. Gulland for Fig. 6.

Plate I*b* is by Aerofilms Ltd and is reproduced by permission. Plates I*a* and II*b* are from photographs by Mr K. J. Woolmer.

Acknowledgment is also made for help received from Mr Harold Nichols, Reference Librarian, Leeds Public Libraries; from the Acting City Archivist; and from the Bursar's staff.

NOTES

1   B.T.C. Record Office, York: Deposited Plans, vol. vii, p. 18.
2   1873: Johnson's *Directory*; 1875: White's *Directory* (in a supplement of 'smaller streets').
3   A. K. Cairncross, *Home and Foreign Investment, 1870–1913* (1953), p. 149.
4   W. H. Beveridge, *Full Employment in a Free Society* (1944), p. 312.
5   Occupations and dates of completion of the street from: McCorquodale's *Directory*, 1876, 1878, 1882; White's *Directory*, 1881; Robinson's *Directory*, 1898 and 1901.
6   David Ward, unpublished M.A. thesis, Department of Geography, Leeds University, 1960.
7   J. D. Chambers, *Nottingham in the Making* (1945), pp. 5–6, with plan of 1831.
8   Drawn from the Tithe Award plan of 1847: Leeds Public Libraries, Archives Dept. RD/RT/142/1.
9   *Ibid.*
10 S. D. Martin, 'Plan of an estate . . . the property of J. Hebblethwaite, etc.' (1852): Thoresby Society Manuscript Plans (Bonser and Nichols, catalogue no. 126).
11 S. D. Martin, 'Plan of an estate . . . the property of J. B. Hebblethwaite Esq. etc.' (1859): Thoresby Society Manuscript Plans (Bonser and Nichols, no. 144).
12 University of Leeds, Deeds of Property in the Bursary: *re* nos. 3, 6, 8, 10 Cavendish Road; these take the ownership of the property back to 1788; also Charlton and Anderson's *Directory*, 1864.
13 Charlton and Anderson's *Directory*, 1864; White's *Directory*, 1866, 1870 and 1875; Kelly's *Directory*, 1867; Porter's *Directory*, 1872.
14 G. Woledge, 'The Medieval Borough of Leeds', *Proc. Thoresby Soc.* XXXVII (1945), p. 298.
15 P(ublic) R(ecord) O(ffice): C. 53/2, m. 21; C. 54/24, m. 8; C. 132/21/12; Just. Itin. 1/778, mm. 57 and 63.
16 P.R.O., SC. 11/673–4; trans. in W. D. Cooper, *History of Winchelsea* (1850), pp. 44–53.
17 Rental reproduced from original now in County Record Office, Winchester, in M. W. Beresford, 'Six New Towns of the Bishops of Winchester', *Medieval Archaeology*, III (1959), fig. 76.
18 W. Brown, ed., *Register of [Archbishop] Corbridge* (Surtees Soc. CXXXVIII (1925)), p. 161; J. Bilson, 'Wyke-Upon-Hull in 1293', *Trans. East Riding Arch. Soc.* XXVI (1928), p. 72.
19 *Calendar of Charter Rolls*, v (1916), p. 40; T. Hugo, *The History of Eagle* (1876), pp. 14–21.
20 Queenborough, Kent (1368); Falmouth, Cornwall (1613).
21 F. W. Maitland, *Township and Borough* (1898), p. 3.

16

S. G. E. Lythe

THE HISTORIAN'S PROFESSION
(Strathclyde, 1963)

This inaugural lecture was delivered at the University of Strathclyde on the 18th October 1963.

THE HISTORIAN'S PROFESSION

THERE exists a venerable tradition that a newly appointed professor should begin his inaugural lecture by heaping laurels upon his predecessor. As the first occupant of this Chair of Economic History I am exempt from this often hypocritical exercise, but it would be churlish of me not to refer with sincerity to the long and productive line of economic historians in this City, a line stretching back through Scott to Adam Smith and vigorously sustained in recent years by Professor Checkland and his Department of Economic History within the University of Glasgow. Similarly the occupant of my Chair cannot avoid a keen consciousness of the historical background of the Royal College, an institution which had arrived at full manhood when the University of Manchester was but a conception in the brain of John Owens, and when the University of Durham was no more than a gleam in a bishop's eye.

Unfortunately the guidance one derives from the pronouncements of our founder, John Anderson, is more of moral than of academic value. 'The Professors in this University', he wrote in his Will, 'shall not be permitted, as in some other Colleges, to be Drones, or Triflers, Drunkards, or negligent of their Duty in any manner or way'. In this hive of academic industry we are unlikely to become Drones, and a casual glance at the prevailing scale of university salaries indicates the improbability of our becoming drunkards.

I have chosen to speak of the Historian's Profession, and I use the word profession to imply specialisation in an academic discipline rather than to mean a body organised—as Shaw said—to defraud the lay public. We do not, of course, dispute the title of oldest profession, but we are clearly more ancient than most. We have our patron goddess: Clio—daughter of Zeus, who is traditionally represented as holding a book and a stylus as evidence of her readiness to record what happened to mortal men—and indeed to the immortal gods with whom she consorted on Mount Olympus. We recall, and not without pride, that the founders of our profession—Herodotus, Xenophon and Thucydides—are honoured not simply as recorders of the events of ancient Greece, but were themselves participants: Xenophon indeed was a national champion in an age of heroes.

From remote periods in all parts of the world come evidences that once a people becomes literate it begins to record its history: in this sense the historian becomes the custodian of the social memory and the interpreter of the nation's heritage—indeed I put the question (without attempting to answer it)—'If man had not been possessed of a sense of history and of a desire to record and remember it, could there have been any feeling of nationality?'

But for this very reason—because our material is part of the fabric of human heritage—we contend, more I think than any profession except perhaps medicine, with a tangle of legend, of half-truth half-fiction, of caricature rather than character, and of rank fallacy. In popular thinking the rulers of the past are either saintly (Edward the Confessor), chivalrous (King Arthur), perpetually engaged in felonious or murderous enterprise (King John), or else living a life of open profligacy with a succession of mistresses who either came from the fruit business of finished up on coins of the realm, (King Charles II). Much of this caricature arose from the capitalising of historical figures by dramatists and novelists who, by the nature of their money-making craft, select and exaggerate to titillate the public fancy. How can we expect a full-blooded 17 year old schoolboy today to distinguish between Cleopatra and Elizabeth Taylor? Or direct your minds to King Henry V of England. There we see him, before the battlements at Harfleur, naked sword flashing above his noble head: 'Once more unto the breach, dear friends, once more, or close the wall up with our English dead'. But that isn't the Henry V of history. That is a mixture of Will Shakespeare and Larry Olivier. The corridors of non-professional history are thick with these hoary cobwebs of half-truth, and I doubt if any country's history is one-half so spider-ridden as that of Scotland.

At a very early stage in the evolution of our profession, certainly by the time of the Roman Empire, historiographers could be classified within two general groups. First there was the writer of the *commentarius*, who claimed simply to set down the happenings which came within his own experience, with no pretence at theorising or interpreting, and with no axe to grind. The classic example, Caesar's *Commentaries* on the Gallic and Civil Wars, reveals at once the duplicity of ostensibly objective reporting, and the dangers of what nowadays is popularly called contemporary history (later I shall have occasion to use this phrase in another meaning). We are told, indeed I paraphrase my colleague Professor Potter, that historians never write about anything until those concerned are safely dead. Now admittedly Caesar had removed some who might have been potential critics, but nevertheless his history was essentially contemporary, written with such economy of vocabulary and with such a wealth of ablative absolutes that he might have known he was providing a text for the 3rd Forms of all future generations. In fact he created a wholly fallacious air of ingenuous honesty: the simple soldier telling plainly about the events he had seen. I will return again to the problem of objectivity in historical writing: here let me simply say (with Adcock) that Caesar's *Commentaries* reflect the personality, the mind and the prejudices of the writer, and let me add that there can be as much guile in the laconic sentences of a professional soldier as in the flowing periods of a professional politician. The world is full of monosyllabic rogues.

Theoretically, however, the *commentarius* was a straight record, source material if you like, from which others might subsequently write the *historia*. In the *historia* the writer might have, indeed generally had, a purpose in view beyond the simple process of informing his public. So Livy set out to show how the foundations of Roman greatness were based in primitive morality; or so Tacitus exalted conquest and military glory. There was claim neither to originality of material nor to objectivity in selection. Equally the *historia* was a conscious exercise in literary art, indeed according to Quintillian 'proxima poetis'. From this there stemmed the thesis, wholly laudable in my view, that history should be presented in the common language of the urbane world, and that—within the rules of grammatical exactitude—the historian is entitled to use any literary device appropriate to his theme and his requirements. In this we differ from some of our fellow practitioners within the broad field of Social Studies who have either created their own terminology or have arrogated to themselves the questionable right to attach special meanings to common words. We suffer, as the philosophers hasten to point out, from absence of precise definition in this employment of common words: we do not, for example, adequately examine the meaning of 'cause' when we say that one event was the cause of another; we fling around the words 'revolution' and 'revolutionary' with reckless abandon. These are real weaknesses in most historical writing, but they do not, in my submission, modify the right of the historian to express himself in standard Queen's English, the resources of which are adequate to transmit any thought of which the normal mind is capable.

Let me therefore say plainly that my colleagues and I in this new Department will look for quality of presentation in the written work that comes before us. Above all we shall look for clarity—for though I speak with the tongues of men and of angels and have not clarity it profiteth me nothing. The language of historical writing must be clear in meaning and appropriate to the theme. If a man feel strongly; if he sincerely believe that his feeling is well justified by fact, then by all means let the vigour of his language reflect the depth of his feeling. Let me read you two sentences to illustrate my point:

'It is not eighteen months since I got the first glimpse of light, three months since the dawn, very few days since the unveiled sun burst upon me. Nothing holds me: I will indulge my sacred fury: I will triumph over mankind by the honest confession that I have stolen the golden vases of the Egyptians to build up a tabernacle for my God. If you forgive me, I rejoice; if you are angry I can bear it; the die is cast, the book is written: it may well wait a century for a reader, as God has waited six thousand years for an observer.'

That is not a hot gospeller about to expound a new plan for human salvation, nor is it an 'Eng. Lit' letting off steam. It is no less a scientist than Kepler, about to pronounce his laws on the movement of the planets.

I want us to maintain the tradition of historical writing as literature. I am not thinking of the massive rounded periods proceeding from the mouth of Gibbon. I do not want verbosity to obscure meaning. Nor am I thinking of the sabre-rattling of a Churchill. If I am pressed for a model it would be R. H. Tawney whose prose, handsome in itself, was always appropriate to its theme.

We have arrived thus far: the *commentarius* and the *historia* of the ancient world are the founts of the twin streams of tradition in historiography right down to the nineteenth century. The wealth of diaries—the salaciousness of Pepys makes his the most famous— and the contemporary history of men like Burnet and Balfour, represent the equivalents in English of the Latin commentaries. The *historia* provided the model for a huge library of multi-volume works, written in the main by men of great literary stature, of great insight into human character, of experience in affairs, and of evident (though maybe misplaced) sincerity—the Gibbons and the Macaulays. Though they left unexplored vast territories of human experience, notably in social and economic affairs and though they ignored sources and selected evidences to suit their purposes, their works occupy a permanent place in historical literature as much as case-studies in *ex parte* interpretation, as for the hypotheses which they advanced.

Whatever their individual political beliefs, the historians of the past were by nature conservative in their technical approach, and it was not until the nineteenth century that any radical change overtook historiography. Revolutionary changes in industry and transport at a rate hitherto unknown in human experience produced—at the humble level—the specialist study of economic history (the phrase

'Industrial Revolution' came into general use in the 1880's), and—on the grand level—the economic interpretation of historical change which lies at the heart of Marxist philosophy. Similarly historiography could not escape the influence of the revolution in scientific thought—hence the argument that if history were to rank among the social sciences it should be susceptible to the same disciplines as the natural sciences: should be handled in the same de-humanised manner and should evolve generalised conclusions possessing the same degree of universal applicability as the 'laws' of chemistry and physics. To put the outcome plainly: there grew up a school of so-called Scientific History whose first exponents—Hegel and Comte—gradually made their impression on British minds. Its earliest dogmatic expression in English is in T. H. Buckle's *History of Civilisation in England* (1857) in which he presents an uncompromising insistence on the need to interpret history so as to exhibit the operation of universal laws, 'a great principle', says J. S. Mill, 'eminently promoted by the great work of Mr. Buckle'. Resistance in Britain was powerful: listen for a moment to J. A. Froude speaking before the Royal Institution a hundred years ago on 'The Science of History'—'One lesson, and only one, history may be said to repeat with distinctness; that the world is built somehow on moral foundations; that, in the long run, it is well with the good; in the long run, it is ill with the wicked'. And he adds, somewhat superfluously one might think, 'this is no science; it is no more than the old doctrine taught long ago by the Hebrew prophets'. And with this comforting riposte most Victorians were content and the average historian went ahead with his writing without, as Cobban has said of us recently, any undue consciousness of what he was up to.

And then, in his inaugural lecture in 1903, J. B. Bury, an historian of unquestioned ability, made the dramatic pronouncement that 'History is a science, no less, and no more'. In the succeeding 60 years this assertion has come up repeatedly in the debates on historical method: it occurs there with the same unfailing regularity as—'A man's a man for a' that' on the night of Jan. 25, or 'unity is strength' at any political conference any time.

In one respect Bury had a good point, and one highly relevant to the theme of my lecture. In the two generations before 1900 historical study had become increasingly academic—more professionalised if you will—in its character. The trend can be detected most tangibly in the establishment of University Chairs and Lectureships, and in the editing and publication of massive series of state papers, charters, guild records and similar primary materials. 'As regards modern history,' wrote J. C. Morrison in 1881, 'we are almost overwhelmed with the mass of new materials and new discoveries which have been launched upon us'. In consequence the stock of historical material—of 'facts' if I may use the word loosely—was enormously enhanced, and the validity of the material was—as a result of checking and comparison—as secure as any reasonable being might demand. In short, history, in the later nineteenth century, underwent the same kind of technical revolution as archaeology has undergone in the mid twentieth. In Britain in particular the cult of historical facts fitted amiably with the empiricist tradition in philosophy from Locke onwards: facts impinge on the observer from outside, they are independent of his subjective judgment, and around this comfortable proposition there has grown up a forest of seemingly common-sense dicta, an anthology of homespun philosophy: facts alone are wanted in life, says Dickens; they are sacred, says C. P. Scott; they are chiels that winna ding, says the national bard. So, to paraphrase E. H. Carr in his Trevelyan Lecture in Cambridge two years ago, the facts are available to the historian like fish on a fishmongers slab. He buys which he likes, takes them home and cooks them in whatever style suits his palate.

If any discipline is to claim the title of science, its first requirement is that its raw materials, its facts, be methodically determined and subjected to all available tests of accuracy. In this basic requirement we have become increasingly competent. But it is no matter for praise. Accuracy in fact is not a virtue, it is a duty. The accumulation of materials by a diversity of techniques has carried us far: we know, for example, far more about what used to be labelled 'The Dark Ages' than did the Norman chroniclers who were 800 years nearer in time than we—indeed if we go on much further we shall have to find a new label for the Dark Ages. But equally it is certain that we shall always labour under the disadvantage of gaps in our basic knowledge, and one takes comfort from the words of a great nineteenth century jurist (J. F. Stephen) 'The one talent which is worth all the other talents put together in human affairs is that of judging right upon imperfect materials'.

If I were to stop at this point—your reaction—apart of course from the welcome feeling of relief—would be that history is nothing more than a gracefully presented assemblage of facts and that, in consequence, the historian operates at a low intellectual level. You would, indeed, be in agreement with Dr. Johnson:

'Great abilities are not requisite for an historian; for in historical composition all the greatest powers of the human mind are quiescent. He has the facts ready to his hand; so there is no exercise of invention. Imagination is not required in any high degree; only about as much as is used in the lower kinds of poetry.

Some penetration, accuracy, and colouring, will fit a man for the task, if he can give the application which is necessary.'
The Life of Samuel Johnson (Boswell quoting Johnson).

The mere recital of superficially related facts in chronological order—in essence the method of the *commentarius*—is acceptable only in the absence of other possibilities. It is a barren exercise, and it leads to a whole houseful of fallacies of the post *hoc ergo propter hoc* category. Whether he realises it or not the historian daily encounters the kindred problems of selection and interpretation, and even the most elementary process of selection involves some way of determining relevance, and, because I suppose historians are naive souls, much of the discussion in this field has been conducted for us by philosophers. It is as if a gardener grows the tallest hollyhock in captivity, but it takes an organic chemist to tell him what he has been up to.

The philosophical discussion on historical method focuses greatly on sophisticated variations on a theme by Bacon: the theme of scientific method. I pause to remark that scientific method in this Baconian sense is by no means universally employed in the natural sciences: thus Sir Charles Ellis writes of Rutherford 'I do not believe that he searched for an explanation in the classical manner of a theory using certain basic laws; as long as he knew what was happening he was content'. Few natural scientists to-day would speak of universal laws with the same assurance as their predecessors in the nineteenth century: to-day I think the natural scientist would claim little more than observed regularities which, however soundly based on his existing stock of knowledge, never have the same quality as the conclusions of logical proof based on unassailable premises. I say this, not to denigrate natural science, but to praise it, for these manifestations of modesty lie at the heart of true intellectual greatness. In this sense, I think, the old sharp antithesis between the apparent order of natural science and the shapelessness of the arts has lost some of its edge.

If we import into our work a conviction that history displays the operation of a consistent force (as Froude was doing in the sentences I quoted from him), or if we believe that history is simply the unfurling of a grand design, our problem of selection and interpretation is simple. Throughout the Middle Ages (and after) men attributed events to 'the inscrutable working of Providence' or to 'the Hidden Hand'. The mere fact that these forces were inscrutable and hidden rendered them immune from rational examination, and consequently so long as these views prevailed historiography could not proceed much beyond straight narrative. Then, with the nineteenth century,

x

there was a real risk that historians would succumb to a crude Darwinism, and allow their selection and emphasis to be dominated by concepts of progress and natural selection, hence, I think, the 'Master Race' theme and the eulogies of empire. When these devices were outmoded, some sought for a working hypothesis in the nature of man himself: his lust to acquire or to dominate, hence *homo economicus, homo politicus* and so forth. Taken singly these concepts have their value; taken singly they lead to what Marc Bloch called 'the fetish of the single cause', and commit the historian to the monomania of the party politician.

The problem of selection and interpretation arises at two levels. If we operate on the level of a Marx, a Spengler, or a Toynbee, our product is shapeless and valueless unless we construct it around some universal principle, theory, model, call it what you will. This is the end product of Baconian scientific method. But my concern is rather with the thousands of historians whose field of thinking is— deliberately—restricted by theme, character, locality or a combination of such boundaries. And here again I think we march with the typical natural scientist. What proportion of current scientific intellectual effort is directed to the universal themes with which Newton, Kepler or Einstein dealt?

But however restricted our theme we still face the problem of selection and interpretation. Partly because our craft is ancient, we inherit a variety of concepts—let us call them hypotheses—tools of thought, bases for analysis. The Manorial System; Protestantism and the Rise of Capitalism; the Industrial Revolution—you recognise the chapter-headings of our standard textbooks in Economic History. These are comforting formulae and, as Sombart said, if we abandon them we feel like drowning in a sea of facts until we find a fresh foothold. The production of fresh formulae—as in Rostow's book on the British economy of the nineteenth century—represents real progress in historical interpretation. We constantly produce additions to our stock of facts, and periodically we advance from one fragmentary hypothesis to another. In this again we are, I think, closer to the natural scientists than the exponents of the Two Cultures would have us believe.

But, you say, there is a radical difference, for once the natural scientist had selected his materials and set up his experiment his personality is abstracted from his work. Once he has put the elements in the crucible the outcome of the experiment will be the same even if he is converted from Wesleyanism to Zen Buddhism during the coffee break. History—in the sense of historical writing—is made in the brain of the individual, and can never possess the depersonalised nature of a science. It has been argued, with great force and cogency, that the real function of the historian is not simply to explain historical phenomena by showing causal relationships, but to understand them by uncovering the motives of the human agents who added their contribution and who thus diverted the course of events this way or that. 'A great man,' said Buchan in the first sentence of his *Oliver Cromwell*, 'lays upon posterity the duty of understanding him'. And Professor Butterfield concluded his David Murray Lecture in this City some years ago with the obvious inference from this: 'In the last resort insight is the greatest asset of all'. This approach lies at the core of the idealist theory of historical method, expounded in Britain by Collingwood, and it amounts to saying that the historian works from his knowledge of events and actions to the purposes they embody, and from the purposes he penetrates ultimately into the minds of the actors and participants. The word 'imagination' has acquired a sinister connotation in academic circles because of the writing of historical fiction in which imagination runs riot, yet Collingwood and his followers would not hesitate to claim that imagination—trained, critical and cautious—is the historian's supreme tool. This is the final stage in the historian's process: the stage he reaches when he is completely familiar with all available facts and when he has explored all the relevant hypotheses. Then, say the idealists, he will be far enough inside Caesar's mind to know why he crossed the Rubicon, and he will know the mental turmoil which thrust Newman on the road to Rome to kiss the Fisherman's Ring.

We arrive, then, on the frontiers of the almost untrodden territory which lies between the field of the historian and the field of the psychologist. The historian can rarely hope to penetrate beyond the conscious rational thinking of the character under examination. He is, normally at least, either unequipped or ill-equipped to penetrate and analyse the unconscious, either on the level of individual psychology or on the probably more difficult level of mass psychology. He cannot put Garibaldi on the couch, let alone the whole Italian people. And when the professional psychologists have tried their hands at the interpretation of history the results have been, to put it mildly, curious.

But even if these psychological barriers could be surmounted, the Collingwood approach seems dangerous and lopsided. Pressed to its conclusion it implies that the only historical phenomena of significance are those which reveal human purposes and human thoughts. Thus the Price Revolution of the sixteenth century would appear only as the outcome of the colonial ambitions of the Spanish, or as the force which turned the minds of landowners towards sheep-farming and of Charles I towards ship-money. It is certain also to involve us in a highly personalized view of history. We shall conclude that history is simply the essence of inumerable biographies, or, with Emerson, that there is properly no history, only biography, or, with Pascal, that if Cleopatra's nose had been shorter the whole history of the world would have been different.

And worst of all, in my view, it involves an interpretation technique which is esoteric in the extreme. He, and he alone, who—in the mind—sat with Ceasar in the tent, can know with certainty what motives led Caesar to cross the Rubicon. The rest of us cannot enter the mental process: we cannot criticise because we cannot know; and, being human and sceptical, we raise the charge of subjectivism.

Let me say at once that when I speak of subjectivity in history I am ignoring—with contempt—all those who deliberately select for consciously propagandist purposes: to 'prove', for example, that 'We' have done more for the working-class than 'They'. Nor, I think, is anyone seriously disturbed by those whose minds are so obviously predisposed that their bias is plain to all save the most innocent. We all know about Wells' dislike of military commanders and Belloc's views on the Reformation, and make due allowance. It is, indeed, arguable that the non-specialist forms the best impression of an incident or a period by comparing the interpretations offered by various specialists of known conflicting views. Certainly current studies of the social consequences of the Industrial Revolution conform to this pattern.

Our real problem is to enquire whether 'objectivity' is possible, or must we for ever endure the play of the present prejudices on past passions. Everybody is, wittingly or not, involved in the emotional and intellectual currents of his own age, either floating in the fashionable streams or creating his own private whirlpools. In the nineteenth century most political historians accepted the contemporary liberal sentiments about human relations and institutions— hence the 'Whig View' of history from Macaulay to Trevelyan. The unfashionable writers equally reflected current reactions. In a challenging phrase 'All true history is contemporary history' Croce meant that all history has to be seen through the eyes of the present, and that historical phenomena are of significance only in so far as they satisfy present interests.

'Saint Augustine looked at history from the point of view of the early Christian; Gibbon from that of an eighteenth century Englishman; Mommsen from that of a nineteenth century German. There is no point in asking which was the right point of view. Each was the only one possible for the man who adopted it'. I quote Collingwood. This can be taken as a sweeping expression of historical scepticism, and if we press it to its conclusion we shall conclude that there is no single meaning in history: there are as many meanings as there are historians, and none with any greater title to truth than the next. *Quot homines*: *tot historiae*. In fact, of course, there is no scientific evidence that the statements or the standards of judgment of the individual historian are determined by his cultural setting or by his personal attitudes towards other matters. There is no scientific proof that a rabid teetotaller is incapable of writing a balanced history of the social repercussion of the invention of whisky, yet common experience and common sense would lead us to suspect his interpretation. What I am saying, in this roundabout way, is that we cannot invoke a theory of knowledge which sharply distinguishes between object and observer. It may be that the same problem arises in natural science: it may be that some chemists regard sodium sulphate with the same detestation as Belloc regarded Henry VIII, and therefore attempt to denigrate its no doubt valuable qualities, but I assume that such are rare. In strictly philosophical language, history cannot, by any techniques at present available to us, become objective.

Because of this our profession is essentially argumentative. In Hegelian fashion we progress in historiography by thesis, antithesis, synthesis, and the synthesis then becomes the thesis for a fresh cycle. You must not ask of a piece of historical writing 'Is this true?', for the truth is not in us. What you may ask is 'Is this intellectually respectable?'. And I would say that a work is intellectually respectable if its inferences are warrantable, if, in other words they conform to the known facts and to the known hypothesis of the writer. History, the greatest living Dutch historian has said, is 'argument without end'. That, I would add, is the measure of its academic stature.

I take this proposition as the lead to a few final remarks about the usefulness of our profession.

In the final analysis the distinction between professions and trades is neither legal nor economic. It rests rather on the mutual relationship between a profession and society, whereby society accords a measure of semi-respectful recognition, and the profession for its part accepts an obligation to perform a social function without exclusive regard to material rewards. It goes without saying that our prime obligation is to present as balanced and accurate a picture of the past as we are able and so straighten the distortions in the public's impression of history. Whether we should pass moral judgment on the characters in history or whether we should suggest 'lessons' from history raise issues too large for present discussion.

Indeed I find myself entirely in accord with the distinguished and much lamented Richard Pares who told an Edinburgh audience that 'the professional historian is of most use to the general public if the general public goes to the University'. Most obviously we have, in this setting, the duty of submitting ourselves and our students to a specialised form of intellectual exercise. If the student has the capacity, if he derives intellectual satisfaction from the discipline, he may in turn become a professional historian, and in this production of honours and post-graduate historians there is, normally, immense mutual pleasure. But especially in a broad-based School of Social Studies like ours in this institution, the production of a fresh generation of specialists—however attractive the prospect—is not our prime duty. When a student joins our first-year class it matters not whether he is destined to become another Gibbon or another Gladstone: a Hume with a 'U' or a Hume with an 'O'. Our job is first to enable him to benefit from exercises in the basic techniques of historical method. What we teach the mass of our students will not be directly useful—in the sense that instruction within a Faculty of Medicine is useful to future doctors, and instruction within a Divinity College is presumably useful to future ministers of religion. We are not in any narrow sense, seeking to provide vocational education, and in these terms (though not in others) it is irrelevant whether we study Britain in the reign of Victoria or Rome in the reign of Vespasian. By this process we can hope to cultivate a sense of judgment; an ability to make rational decisions; an anxiety to look for justification and to present a reasoned case in competent terms. This I would argue is an educational project in the best sense of the expression. Thus, I think, we discharge our obligations to our employers, and, through them, to society at large.

Nevertheless this is essentially a teaching responsibility. I said at the beginning that written history is a part of the nation's literature, and we must consider the kind of image we present to the literate public at large. In his *Agrarian Problem of the 16th Century* Tawney said that because we focus attention on those forces which have triumphed, we give an appearance of inevitableness to the existing social order. In this sense history reads like a success story, or, as Sir Isaiah Berlin put it, the criterion of history seems to be 'that which works best'.

To say this, to say that history demonstrates the inevitability of the present social and economic order and thereby casts some sort of justification over it, is to ignore vast territories of historical thinking and writing. Nobody, for example, could deny that historians ignore movements such as Chartism. Fifty years ago they used to invite students to write essays on the theme 'Why did

Chartism fail?'. To-day, I suspect, we should not set so loaded a question. At the most we might ask 'Did Chartism fail?'. What I am saying is that history deals as much with delayed achievement as with immediate success. Who can say how long a seed of thought will lie dormant? No historian will say with conviction that any seed is dead.

Rather, therefore, than teaching the inevitability of the existing order, history puts its emphasis on the inevitability of change. I am disposed to think that the citizen with a feeling for history will be the more likely to adopt a rational and a calmer attitude towards change in whatever field of public life it comes. You may infer from history that society is progressing: you may infer the opposite and speak of decadence: you cannot, by any warrantable mental process, infer that society is static. The readiness to cope with change is the beginning of wisdom, and as Bacon said 350 years ago, the purpose of history is to make men wise.

POSTSCRIPT

I think it desirable to point out that the foregoing symbolized the institution of the first chair in any historical discipline in this University and for that reason I thought it wise to speak of history in general rather than of economic history in particular. I would also ask readers to bear in mind that it was delivered before a University which consisted, in 1963, overwhelmingly of natural scientists.

S. G. E. L.   1970

17

Sidney Pollard

ECONOMIC HISTORY—A SCIENCE OF SOCIETY?
(Sheffield, 1964)

This inaugural lecture was delivered at the University of Sheffield on the 28th October 1964.

ECONOMIC HISTORY—A SCIENCE OF SOCIETY?

THE academic discipline of Economic History is, as its name implies, of mixed parentage. In this, as one of the most distinguished living economic historians has remarked recently,[1] it resembles the mule. But while he went on to muse that it was not for him to decide which of the two parent-subjects was equine, and which asinine, I would rather draw attention to another characteristic of this most appropriate animal: its inability to reproduce its own kind.

It is worth noting how recent is the position of Economic History as a discipline in its own right in British Universities. When I was first introduced to its teachings, there were only two chairs in the subject outside London and the two older provincial Universities; these were in Manchester and Birmingham. It is true that there were several other economic historians to be found disguised as Professors of this or that subject, including the Professor of Economics at this University, but this rather serves to underline the point that it was not the lack of distinction among its practitioners, but the lack of regard for the subject, which kept down the number of chairs. Today, Sheffield University is among the majority in having established the Chair which I have been greatly honoured to have been asked to occupy. Chairs in Economic History have become status symbols not only among the older institutions, but even among others so new that they may not even have time to advertise them before filling them.

More important, perhaps, than the status of the teacher, is the place within the curriculum. Here there was virtual uniformity in my student days. Economic History was taught in subsidiary or dependent courses, but never as the core of the teaching, to economists, to historians, or to both. The teaching staff, the specialists, necessarily also bore the marks of this dual carriageway of approach: for they, themselves, had come to Economic History either as historians in search of a soul, or as economists in search of a body. Things have changed very little in most British Universities. In Sheffield, also, we intend to continue to provide auxiliary courses to departments close to ours, partly because we feel that our studies will be of value to them, and partly because the stimulus we receive from students of different academic backgrounds seems to lend support to the widely held doctrine that there is fertility in the border areas between two or more major disciplines. We have, however, not been satisfied with the traditional limits to our role. We have gone further, and have raised Economic History to a substantive subject standing on its own: in doing so, we have joined a very small, not to say fringe, minority. You may take the rest of this lecture as part of our justification for this action.

It should be said at the outset that Economic History has not always occupied its present subordinate position within the economic sciences. Adam Smith, who may be regarded as their founder, made no such distinction in his great work, first published in 1776, between the theorems and their accompanying historical illustrations, from which, indeed, they had often been derived. 'There is scarcely a page of "The Wealth of Nations" ' as Unwin put it, 'where history and theory are sundered from each other'.[2] In the next generation, Ricardo's terse language, and his quest for water-tight laws, were in the greatest imaginable contrast to the leisured, classical prose and the pragmatic conclusions of the eighteenth-century Scotsman; yet Ricardo also, like his contemporary Malthus, thought in terms of the long-term evolution of societies. In other words, they also possessed a historical perspective.

It was men of the following generation, making their mark about the middle of the nineteenth century, who were, for the first time, faced with the prospect of finding the social system they had set out to describe and to foster, to be in some way at its maturity, so that a look into the future might reveal signs of a decline which they were unwilling to contemplate; it is at times like this that ideologies turn conservative and begin to look for 'eternal' laws. By about 1870 the transition was made. In several quarters at once—a sure sign that the need for this re-interpretation was widely felt—the first halting steps were taken towards that 'marginal analysis' or neo-classicism which, by concentrating on problems which could be expressed, and solved, in mathematical terms, ultimately transformed 'political economy' into economics and relegated Economic History, as indeed every other social science, to auxiliary status.

In Britain, the empirical tradition was strong enough to delay the total victory of the new school for the best part of two generations. The dominant Cambridge economists, Marshall, Pigou, Robertson and Keynes, continued to treat economics as a social science while mastering its mathematics, and their brilliant fruitfulness served to mask the immanent divergence. In Germany, however, where economics was taught in faculties of law or of philosophy, economists were more self-conscious regarding their philosophical foundations, and quickly brought the dualism into the open.

The powerful school of relativist economists or, as their critics dubbed them, historicists, which developed there in the second half of the nineteenth century, opposed the optimistic view of Say that the 'absurd opinions'[3] and 'errors' of the past were best forgotten, and held with Karl Knies

'that political economy . . . is a result of historical development; . . . that its fund of arguments arises out of economic life, and its results must bear the description of historical solutions; that even the "general laws" of political economy are nothing but an historical explanation and progressive manifestation of the truth. It is only the study of historical development, and the advancement to a recognition of an order and regularity within it, which can allow us to reach a full understanding of the economic position of the present and of the direction in which we are moving.'[4]

These views found some significant, though curiously neglected echoes in this country. Thus Thorold Rogers discovered as a result of his historical researches 'that much which popular economists believe to be natural is highly artificial; that what they call laws are often hasty, inconsiderate and inaccurate inductions; and that much which they consider to be demonstrably irrefutable is demonstrably false'.[5]

The opposition came largely from the marginalists, and was expressed in its most extreme form by the Austrian, Carl Menger. He thought that it was part of the duty of the economists,

'in analogy, though not in identical manner with the natural sciences, to reduce the real appearances of political economy to their simplest and purely typical elements, in order, by isolation, to set out its laws'.

Both the natural and the social (or as he called them, ethical) sciences were searching for 'real types' and 'empirical laws',

'and in the above point of view, at any rate, no *essential* difference between the ethical and the natural sciences exist, but at most only one of *degree*'.[6]

The dialectic of this so-called 'Methodenstreit' was resolved into an uneasy synthesis by about the outbreak of the first world war, though echoes of the battle could still be heard in the nineteen-fifties.[7] Meanwhile, however, in Britain, the gentleman's agreement to treat economics as a social study, while exploring the exciting new mathematical possibilities, proved increasingly difficult to sustain. It was shattered in 1932 by a young London economist who, stepping forward boldly where his elders had kept respectfully aloof—his present eminence as Lord Robbins inhibits me from using the phrase which readily springs to mind—proclaimed a new definition of the subject-matter of economics. It was to be no longer in terms of 'a study of mankind in the ordinary business of life', which was Marshall's definition, or 'the general causes on which the material welfare of human beings depends', which was Cannan's, or more intriguingly, 'the relation between unwelcome exertion and the remuneration which induces that exertion', a definition used by Taussig, but was to be in terms of the *manner* of approach: economics, he declared, was concerned with

> 'human behaviour as a relationship between ends and scarce means which have alternative uses'.[8]

At one stroke, economics was to be taken out of the muddy waters of political overtones, personal value judgments, social pressure and class interests in which real economic life takes place, to be studied in the serene clear waters of universally valid mathematical relationships, like the natural and neutral sciences. Economists could draw up sequences of causes and effects, and it was only at the point of actual decision-making, to be left to others, that political and other practical considerations need be re-introduced. The idea caught the spirit of the time. Extreme though it was, it became absorbed quickly into the text-books—it was adopted even by some economic historians[9],—and certainly dominated all the formal definitions to which I was introduced as an undergraduate fifteen years later. Nevertheless, it was a hollow victory. There was no danger at that time that anyone would take it seriously, least of all Professor Robbins himself, whose social conscience is second to none. For one thing, men brought up on the broadly-based pre-Robbins curriculum, were conscious of the residue of political bias. As Gunnar Myrdal had written in 1929,

> 'on the one hand, it is emphasised that economic science only observes social life and analyses what can be expected to happen in different circumstances, and that it never pretends to infer what the facts ought to be. On the other hand, practically every economist draws such inferences. And the various specific theories are most of the time arranged for the very purpose of drawing them'.[10]

But secondly, the purpose itself was mistaken. For despite all protestations, one looks in vain in economic textbooks for non-economic instances of relative scarcity, as for example that of a conductor who has to share out a limited time among hosts of desirable orchestra pieces; by contrast, the economic literature of the time was filled with problems of unemployment, or resources which far from being scarce, were only too plentiful.

There was a reason for the almost unanimous acceptance of what was a patently false emphasis and inadequate definition; it allowed economists to ignore completely the broader social and historical framework, and to concentrate on the more congenial and less dangerous mechanics of manipulating units within it. 'A major task of economic analysis', the textbook on which I was brought up stated baldly, 'is to explain *why* the price of butter is eighty cents per pound'.[11] Far be it from me to question the importance of that task, particularly for people who want to make a profit out of selling butter; but you will find that in the solution, all relationships except those expressed as a price/quantity are omitted. The buyers and sellers could be combines, individuals, slaves, Greeks, Turks or Kalmucks; the time could be war, peace, this century, the last, or the next: the answer, and its significance, is the same in each case.

The value of this approach of isolating one problem is evident, and on it is based the reputation of Economics as perhaps the most exact, or at any rate the least inexact, of the social sciences. But it depended on a self-denying ordinance, embedded as a standard warning found in all courses and in all textbooks, against the danger of giving economic *advice* on the basis of pure analysis without taking other factors of the concrete social situation into account. As long as economists were compulsorily educated in social and political theory, in history and in related subjects, they were unlikely to suppose that they could ignore these warnings. In the past ten or fifteen years, however, the analytical side of the subject, making its burdensome demand on the normal economist's limited mathematics, has become so large, so difficult and so elegant, that he has neither the time nor the inclination to go farther afield in his quest for knowledge. He is happy to rummage among Clapham's empty economic boxes;[12] what is worse, he may even imagine that they are filled. The more unaware he is of the complexities of the social setting, the more confident he becomes that his solutions are alone relevant. Thus we find solemn discussions on the future of the National Health Service oblivious of such unquantifiable values as the gains in security, equality and human dignity created by it; or advice is proffered by economists on steel nationalization in terms solely of profit and loss, forgetful of the fact that the issue is a battle-ground of ideologies, concerned with the ultimate control over the economy and the location of the responsibility for British industry.

I regret this refining process in the development of economic studies. I think that Economics has been impoverished by it. I also believe with Professor Parker, that 'economic theory and statistics may suggest explanations of economic change consistent with a hypothesis of economically rational behaviour. But a complete economic history must bring to bear a wide variety of non-quantitative variables and a generous amount of speculation about motivations',[13]

Otherwise we run the danger of measuring the waves, and forgetting the tide. Pope may have been right in his belief that the only proper study of mankind is man: I am old-fashioned enough to hold that the only proper study of the social scientist is society.

In this odyssey of academic economic teaching, which I have sketched for you as one-sidedly as I dared, you will have noticed one continuous theme: the steady decline of the reference to the social, concrete historical setting in which economic discussion takes place, ending, at present, in the complete disappearance of the historical dimension. It was thus that Economic History came to occupy the peripheral place in Schools of Economics which I have sketched at the beginning.

Of course, this is not the whole story. In parallel with the study of micro-economics, where the tendency to disregard society has gone farthest, there has developed, in a painfully uneasy common harness, the sub-science of macro-economics, based on the categories of Keynes, who himself was blessed with an uncanny historical sense. While some of his successors may be less well endowed, others, particularly in America, have recently turned to the problems of the under-developed countries of the world. Here they operate within vastly enlarged parameters, as they are witnessing not the substitution of some units of resources for others at the margin, but the total transformation of societies from their basic economic and property relations upwards to the top of their cultural and spiritual superstructures. As they find themselves turning into amateur historians, sociologists and anthropologists, these economists are eager to collaborate with the disciples of other social studies. With them, the economic historian makes his most fruitful and happy contacts; but he must not forget the others at home, blinded by the exuberance of their own science.

If he sees it as part of his task to persuade economics that it is an art as much as a science, is he equally justified in trying to persuade his other parent, history, that it is a science as much as an art? Here is the expression of one extreme view:

'Men wiser and more learned than I have discerned in history a plot, a rhythm, a pre-determined pattern. These harmonies are concealed from me. I can see only one emergency following upon another as wave follows upon wave, only one great fact, . . . one safe rule for the historian: that he should recognize in the development of human destinies the play of the contingent and the unforseen'.[14]

These are words we shall have to take seriously, if only because their author was, for a time, Vice-Chancellor of this University. It is easy to call this view trivial, or to find amusement by counting the number of occasions on which Fisher refers to the 'inevitability' or 'necessity' of historic developments in the very work prefaced by this quotation.[15] Here I wish to make only two observations. The first is that there is inherent in this view a danger of which Camus was so terrifyingly conscious:

'those who rush blindly to history in the name of the irrational', he warned, 'proclaiming that it is meaningless, encounter servitude and terror and finally emerge into the universe of concentration camps'.[16]

I, also, fear that those who have given up trying to make sense of the past, must have given up hope for the future. The second is that in practice no-one acts upon it. Even Ludwig von Mises, one of the most articulate of the enemies of historical determinism, has to admit that in an undetermined universe,

'no action could be designed, still less put into execution. Man is what he is because he lives in a world of regularity and has the mental power to conceive the relation of cause and effect. . . . If you want to attain a definite end, you must resort to the appropriate means; there is no other way to success'.[17]

Professor Popper, if anything a more severe critic still, agrees, in his inimitable prose, that causality is a

'typical metaphysical hypostatization of a well-justified methodological rule'.[18]

I shall return to historical nihilism later, in its guise of the worship of the individual and the accidental, but meanwhile we must assume, with W. H. Walsh, that most historians are desirous of 'making sense of' or 'understanding' their material.[19] There are many possible approaches. Seligman, writing about the turn of the century,[20] felt he had to deal with the claims of idealistic, of ethical, even of religious conceptions of history, but I think today we need waste little time on these exotic creations of nineteenth-century philosophy. Geopolitical and psychological explanations, though vital for an understanding of the mechanism of concrete historical events, suffer from

Y

the fact that a constant cause is called upon to explain a process of change; and an age which has seen men of English and Dutch race, who were, with the Swiss, the first to bring human freedom to Europe, became the last (together with the Portuguese) to deny it in Africa, will have little faith in explanations in terms of national character. Sir John Clapham might have been somewhat optimistic when he supposed, in his inaugural lecture in 1929,

> 'that all historians are now so far in agreement with Marx as to be unable to think of major upheavals and important social changes into which economic causation does not enter',[21]

but I think we can at least say that the only types of explanations which command any substantial measure of support in the mid-twentieth century are those which ultimately derive the motive force of historical change from underlying economic developments. To those of you who suspect that I am eager to pursue this course of argument because it appears to enhance the importance of my own subject, I can only say that you are probably quite right.

May I say at once that an economic, or better, a materialist conception of history does not presuppose that men obey mercenary motives only. It is pleasing in view of what one hears nowadays about the high ideals of business, to come across this beginning of what is probably the first (manuscript) set of systematic instructions to a British mill manager, dated January 1818:

> 'The first and great object', the owner writes, 'to be aimed at by the Manager of the East Mill is PROFIT'.[22]

But if all historical human action were so clearly directed towards making money, it would not have needed a Marx to discover it, nor could even a Popper deny it. It is rather that every man's material needs and interests predispose him to certain attitudes which appear subjectively to be of general validity, but can be shown to be objectively selfish. Who would deny today that the emancipation of women in this century derives directly from their opportunities of economic independence? Yet this is not how it appeared to the generation involved in it. Then, the women were the champions of human liberty, while the Victorian father, thwarted in his habitual petty domineering, was either defending the sanctity of the family, or acting in the girl's best interest—a true selfless and Christian gentleman. And conversely, the reason why few of us would today have any sympathy for that father's point of view, and why we would grant women the right to full individual development, or at least to a fuller personality than the nineteenth century was prepared to concede, derives, not from any growth in our belief in liberty as a concept of some high level of theoretical abstraction, but from our unspoken assumption, based on observation, of the ability of woman to maintain her economic independence.

On a broader canvas, we may take as another example the upsurge of the French democrats in 1848, representing the interests of the petty bourgeoisie. Yet even in the heat of battle, in that remarkable piece of polemical journalism, the '18th Brumaire', Marx stressed that

'one must not form the narrow-minded notion that the petty-bourgeoisie, on principle, wishes to enforce an egotistic class interest. Rather it believes that the *special* conditions of its emancipation are the *general* conditions under which modern society can alone be saved'.[23]

This disposes, I hope, of crude selfish or 'economic' motivation; but we must begin at the beginning.

Man, from birth, has certain material needs. Their importance is not an invention by historians who are looking for a convenient theory of history, as Rickert used to allege:[24] their primacy is a physiological fact.[25] In a primitive society, always on the edge of starvation and unable to allow its members the satisfaction of any but the most basic wants, this primacy would scarcely be disputed. It is, however, equally significant in more highly developed societies, such as in ours, although here it operates through the social division of labour and our position within the social structure, or, in other words, the way in which we gain our living.

The critical fact, from our point of view, is the truism that we simply cannot live as isolated individuals. Man on his own would die quickly of starvation and exposure: he *must* become a member of society. 'All human labour is social labour, and the problem of human labour is therefore always sociological'—these are Sombart's words.[26] And, as soon as we are born, in Mr. Carr's phrase, 'the world gets to work on us and transforms us from merely biological into social units'.[27]

'In the social production which men carry on they enter into definite relations that are indispensable and independent of their will. . . . The sum total of these relations of production constitutes the economic structure of society—the real foundation, on which the legal and political superstructure arises and to which definite forms of social consciousness correspond. . . . In broad outline, we can designate the Asiatic, the ancient, the feudal and the modern bourgeois methods of production as so many epochs in the progress of the economic formation of society'.[28]

Put still more tersely,

> 'the hand mill gives you the feudal lord; the steam mill the industrial capitalist'.[29]

Here is the link between physiological need and the driving force of history.

History takes in all of man's social activities, including his beliefs and superstitions, his science and knowledge, his political organization, personal eccentricities and artistic achievements. All these act and react on the material and class-oriented bases of life. But perhaps it will now be evident in what sense the economic aspect of history is primary. We may express it in the generalised form of saying that physical survival is the first essential. More specifically, we may express it by saying that the social productive base provides not only the character or ideal type of each age in the sense of Max Weber or of Spiethoff, but its momentum and direction of change.

Of course, there are no pure and simple one-way causes in history. As every historian knows, historical explanation has to proceed along at least two lines: the immediately preceding events, as well as the general social setting. Any particular history, religious history, perhaps, or theatrical history, must take both into account: the Reformation can be understood only by studying both the church as it was found by Luther or Calvin with its own laws of development, and the contemporary rise of capitalism; or the English Restoration Theatre only by studying both the theatre under the Puritans and the classes that came to patronise it under Charles II. These other spheres of human endeavour, like churches, theatres or military affairs, or the spheres enumerated by the aged Engels in his famous letter to Conrad Schmidt,[30] including politics, law, religion and philosophy, have a logic and possibly a science of their own, and are not entirely without influence on the economic base; but that influence is minor only, and becomes negligible in a survey of its general direction of advance.

The men engaged in the process necessarily forge their new appropriate ideologies, to combat the ideas of those who resist the change. It will surely be generally agreed today that the reverse order of influence would be contrary to all experience. We just 'cannot assume', S. G. Checkland remarked recently in a study of the decay of Highland Society,

> 'as Maitland did with English open-field strip agriculture, that the community in some sense chose to accept a wasteful system of exploitation in the interests of maintaining a set of notions about human relationships'.[31]

Those of you who have followed the recent dialogue between Sir Isaiah Berlin and Mr. E. H. Carr[32] will know that there are two main, and linked, objections raised against the view of history which I have been trying to put before you. The first is that history is made by individuals who are unpredictable; and the second, that for practical as well as epistemological reasons,[33] history cannot be turned into a 'science'.

The voluminous discussion about the role of the individual in history has always seemed to me slightly off the point. May I use an analogy?

I believe that if I took a bar of polished steel round to my colleagues in this University, the members of the Department of Mechanical Engineering might describe it as solid, with a smooth surface, the members of the Department of Metallurgy might describe it as solid with a very rough surface, and the members of the Department of Physics might describe it as a collection of numerous particles in motion in a largely empty space. Now we do not find them quarrelling about this, and accusing each other of being unscientific: they know quite well that they are each using 'microscopes' of different powers of magnification.

Historians are too often at cross purposes because they use different microscopes. On the scale of the individual, the scale appropriate to the biographer, perhaps, the interest lies in the diversity, the caprice, the accidental or contingent and the emphasis is on the power to make decisions, though even here it would be more useful, and more valid, to study all great individuals as the products of their age, and to derive the extent of their influence from the success with which they fit into the historic process of which they are a part, and with which they were able, in Burckhardt's phrase, to 'rescue the ideals of their time'.[34] On the scale of the political unit, regularity and historical causation are much more in evidence than on the individual scale, yet here also I am willing to admit that the accident of personality will produce real and significant variations: it would be too ungallant to deny any power to Cleopatra's nose[35] or, better, Helen's face, though few historians would follow Sidney Hook in ascribing such major events as the Bolshevik Revolution, and with it the rise of Nazi Germany and the Second World War, to the survival of Lenin in the critical October days of 1917.[36]

The dimension in which I am interested, however, is the dimension of the laws of change of society as a whole. Perhaps I may quote to you from a recent, and unjustly neglected, book by Witt-Hansen:

'In contradiction to social sciences such as jurisprudence, political economy, historiography', he writes, '. . . historical materialism deals with the human society and history as a whole. The subject matter of historical materialism is in fact *social formations* or *economic formations of society*, as exemplified in the capitalist economic formation of society or "capitalist society" '.[37]

On that scale of magnification, the individual is too small to be caught in my microscope. Even a Peter the Great was as unable to speed up the development of capitalism in Russia as Joseph II was in Austria, and Catherine II was as powerless to affect the basis of serfdom in her dominions as Frederick the Great was in his: yet who was ever more powerful than they? Notice, too, that they were all, clearly, children of their time, and not eccentric Utopians. The fortress of holistic determination has been for so long under siege by Professor Popper's heavy guns,[38] charged with the prejudice against its likely predictions, and firing their shells labelled 'piecemeal social engineering', that few have the temerity to entrust themselves to its walls. I believe, on the contrary, that it is precisely at the level of whole societies that we can use the laws of the social and the natural sciences to make sense of history, just as it is precisely at the points at which the material needs of society enforce a violent political change, that the political historian is most inclined to accept the validity of historic determinism. At such times, Sidney Hook admits, 'the forces unloosed will sweep away anybody who seeks to stop them'.[39]

The triviality of the discussion on free will and fatalism in this context will now, I trust, be apparent. I need not dwell on the fear of Sir Isaiah Berlin—wayward as he is brilliant—that deterministic views breed fatalism.[40] This is just bad observation. They *may* do so on occasion, but equally no historian can fail to note how many of the most determined actors of history, the Calvins and Cromwells, the conquering early followers of Mahomet and the Bolsheviks under Lenin, were sustained in their remorseless drive precisely by the unquenchable belief that they expressed the will of God, or were on the side of the forces of history.[41] After all, as Fichte observed, everyone chooses the philosophy that suits him best.

As far as free will is concerned, the responsibilities of the individual are not impaired by the fact that societies as a whole obey social laws. As in the tribal ritual in which many of us took part some thirteen days ago, our choice may be limited, but we do have a choice. We may choose, for example, to uphold the social order, or to join forces with those who wish to subvert it. On the other hand, we may *not* choose to become slave owners, and this is so, not only because the institution of slavery does not exist and cannot now be created, but also because we are not conditioned to aspire to it. Further, since our freedom of action depends on our power of understanding and controlling our destiny, those who wish to increase that freedom must seek to enhance that understanding. Conversely, those who say that there cannot be any understanding, do not only diminish our hope, but take away our freedom.

Of course, men are less predictable than chemical elements, and the laws of social science are not as accurate as the laws of chemical science, but social scientists have long since learnt to make allowances even for the eccentric, the wayward, and the brilliant.

Yet does this then make a wide breach in the walls of our fortress? If a few can oppose the march of history, why not the many? What if a majority decided to defy and thereby to change the course apparently laid down for them? To answer this, we must turn to the other objection, that history by its very nature can never be a 'true' science.

In order to defend a scientific approach to history it is not, of course, necessary to prove that history is exactly like the natural sciences, in methology, in aim or in exactitude;[42] after all, even the natural sciences differ greatly among themselves in these respects. At the same time, modern science has itself shown a remarkable shift towards the approach of the historian. As Professor Frisch has told us.

'we are no longer faced with a smooth, unbroken chain of events; we are faced with distinct, separate observations. In atomic physics . . . there are gaps in what we can know: and there is no longer any strict causality to bridge those gaps'.[43]

Historians, like scientists, are willing to be persuaded by disproof, even if not necessarily by proof. Further, both history and the natural sciences, according to Hempel,

'can give an account of their subject matter only in terms of general concepts, and history can "grasp the unique individuality" of its objects of study no more and no less than can physics and chemistry'.[44]

In both cases, also, the degree of reliability depends in part, on numbers.[45] I should like to commend the adoption by W. W. Rostow—as an American presidential adviser, surely an impeccable source—of the scientific notion of 'problems of disorganized complexity', in which,

'in spite of (the) helter-skelter or unknown behaviour of all the individual variables, the system as a whole possesses certain orderly and analyzeable average properties'.[46]

We need not venture into nuclear physics; the school-physics I remember will do as an illustration. Water contained in a vessel placed over a gas burner will boil in due course. Before the process begins, it is quite impossible to predict which molecule will enter the stream phase first, and which will turn into steam last, say, ten minutes later. Any molecule can be in either position. How then can we predict an orderly process of vaporization? What if no molecule, as it were, takes the initial plunge, and all evaporate together a little later? The answer would be, I suppose, first, that unless there are special conditions, with their own laws, present, water does not behave in such a way, and second, that there are other laws of physics which help to explain why it does not. These other laws can be 'explained' by others still, and so on backwards, but although the series is constantly being extended, there is no final certainty.[47] These are exactly the answers I should give to the question as to what would happen if the majority of a society behaved erratically with respect to a law of the social sciences.

Of course, if the gas supply were interrupted, or if the vessel leaked, the water might not boil at all; but we would not thereby declare our laws invalid. The historian's laboratory is constantly beset by failing gas supplies and leaking vessels, and it has to be visualised, moreover, situated somewhere in the main hall of Paddington Station where a rush of passengers to the trains periodically knocks over vessel, burner and lab. assistant. Accidents, in other words, are part of the material with which the historian works.

Their importance, however, should not be exaggerated. First, they are, of course, themselves within the orbit of science: Lenin's survival in 1917 and his death in 1924, did not violate any canons of medicine. Secondly, what may appear as an accident to one generation, may fall into a recognised pattern or law for the next: our lab. assistant may get to know the Paddington timetable, and protect his burner accordingly. The task of the social sciences as a whole, indeed, is to reduce our area of ignorance in exactly this way in order to take appropriate action. But thirdly, as Mr. Carr has reminded us,

> 'the historian distils from the experience of the past . . . that part which he recognises as amenable to rational explanation and interpretation, and from it draws conclusions which may serve as a guide to action',

and for this, the 'accidents' are irrelevant: they are 'dead and barren'.[48] With this reminder of the purpose of history, we may return to the mainstream of our argument.

It is a curious fact that many historians who see their own society as chaotic and unpredictable, are willing to allow a coherent materialist explanation of history for societies which are distant in time or space. Owen Lattimore's explanation of Asiatic migration, or Gordon Childe's of European Pre-history,[49] may be widely accepted, while those of Marx or Sombart, relating to our own society, are not. Yet to me it has always seemed that the opposite position would be much more defensible. I for one, in my ignorance, would be quite willing to be told of a distant culture so fanatical in its religion or its quest for power as to ignore the demands of its material life,—though I should also expect to hear of its speedy demise. But it is quite different with Western bourgeois society, particularly the later stage of industrial capitalism.

Starting out from some of the more neglected corners of these islands two hundred years ago, it has spread over the absolutism of the European Continent and over the liberty of the North American, it has pervaded and defeated the dark and brooding serfdom of Russia, the many-coloured landlord's rule of India, the oriental splendour of China and the chivalry of ancient Japan. Today there is no corner of the world, from the Fiji Islands to the northern Eskimo, from Africa across to Asia and to South America, where societies are not adapting, changing and rebelling, in order to embrace this new mode of production in the Western image. Can there be anyone who bears the appellation of historian, who does not stand in awe before the power and the grandeur of this design?

This march, unlike the spread of Christianity, which proceeded in a similar, though far less successful course, has had no conscious organization behind it. There have been no missionaries, no text societies, no spiritual soup-kitchens. The motive force was the action of millions of men seeking their own private purposes and achieving an unintended social result.

'The bourgeoisie . . . has accomplished wonders far surpassing Egyptian pyramids, Roman aqueducts, and Gothic cathedrals, it has conducted expeditions that put in the shade all former Exoduses of nations and crusades. . . . It has created more massive and more colossal productive forces than have all preceding generations together. . . . The need of a constantly expanding market for its products drives the bourgeoisie over the whole surface of the globe . . . by the rapid improvement of all instruments of production, by the vastly easier means of communication (it) draws all, even the most barbarian, nations into civilization. . . . It compels all nations . . . to adopt the bourgeois method of production; it compels them to introduce what it calls civilisation into their midst, i.e., to become bourgeois themselves. In one word, it creates a world after its own image'.[50]

These last few paragraphs were not written by me, though I might wish that they had. They were written 116 years ago by the youthful

Marx and Engels, in the most seminal of all their works, the 'Communist Manifesto'.

There is here no contrast between the generalizing method of science and the uniqueness of the events dealt with by the historian. Our history contains both.[51] In one sense, it is unique, for no one will again invent the steam engine, or spread its use around the earth: there is a single Western bourgeois society with a single chronology. In another, the general process has been repeated again and again, in every country, in every region, in every town.

It is, in turn, from this repetition that the other social sciences draw the observations for their inductive laws: 'history', Mill admitted,

> 'does when judiciously examined, afford Empirical Laws of Society'.[52]

Conversely, behind all historical generalizations are the laws and the regularities discovered by the other sciences. Thus we draw from biology the notion that man must have food and shelter to survive; from social psychology the notion that in any human group, some individuals will emerge as leaders, and others will be content to follow; and from economics the notion that, given free competition, the low-cost producer will drive out the high-cost producer. We can then re-assemble these generalizations, and apply them to a given historical situation, as for example the modern Western world. To this extent, the historian is, as Popper would have him,

> 'not a producer of general laws, but a consumer of them'.[53]

These laws furnish the implicit framework within which we attempt to derive the laws of motion of the whole of our society. It is a field in which Economics, Sociology, particularly as conceived by Comte, Mill and Spencer,[54] as well as other social sciences necessarily meet; but its cultivation is peculiarly the task placed upon the Economic Historian.

It may be considered relatively easy to survey the development and predict the extension of modern industrial capitalism now, in the second half of this century. It required nothing short of genius to have attempted it in the middle of the nineteenth. All of us owe an incalculable debt to the genius of Marx, and it has been a tragic loss for our study of history that his teaching has been so often banished or traduced because his latter-day followers have become closely associated, not merely with one political movement, but with a particular region of the globe; or, to put it differently, because, as he himself could have predicted, historians have been unable to separate his methods from his conclusions which their own position in society made certain they would abhor. Yet to date, no more fertile method has been discovered. The method itself is only a guiding line and not a certain key to success. It did not preserve Marx himself from error, particularly where arithmetical, or rather differential calculations were involved, as in the doctrine of the *relative* increasing misery of the advanced working classes,[55] yet it allowed him to make some remarkably enduring and widely valid discoveries also. I should like to end by drawing your attention to two in particular: the first is the description of capitalism as essentially an expansive system, and the second is its inevitable need for growing social control.

Both ideas have entered so firmly into our thinking habits that their very familiarity may reduce their potential fruitfulness. For the causes of this expansionist drive, which extends even, as Dr. Eric Williams has recently reminded us, to slavery under capitalism,[56] have been among the most potent in shaping our modern society, and its consequences have included not only the series of economic crises with which its history has been marked, but the gradual conquest of the world. Twentieth-century man, like his ancestor in less enlightened centuries, is still essentially parochial, and he does not often realize how exceptional measured against historical times, are the restlessness, the instability and the fundamental propensity to change of our society. Compare it with the social stagnation of a feudal society, of an Eastern Empire, even of a slave-owning civilization. There may be changes due to outside influences, such as contacts with other peoples, or to contingent events, such as a population increase leading to assarting of forest land to an extent which upsets the balance between arable and forest. But there is no inner drive to change in fundamentals, and the world familiar to the father is still the world familiar to the son. The changes that occur are too slow to be perceptible.

Not so our universe, which has discovered the secret of perpetual motion or, more accurately, of 'self-sustained growth'. In Rostow's words, 'The innovational process has ceased to be sporadic and is a more or less regular institutionalized part of the society's life'.[57] Many of us may feel that it is the discovery of science which is responsible for what Dr. J. H. Plumb has called the 'Idea of Progress';[58] and indeed it is true that science, as a method of thinking and acting as well as a cumulative body of knowledge, has, like so many other social phenomena, acquired a momentum of its own, independent of any original material base. This does not mean that we should abandon our solid foundations for an idealism based on science as the demiurge of modern civilization; on the contrary, the original power of science depended directly on the fact that it acted on the material base, and that today, perhaps, it *is* the material base.

You may remember the classic phrase I quoted earlier: if the hand mill gives us feudalism and the steam mill gives us industrial capitalism, then the atomic reactor and our science-oriented industry, must be among the determinants of present-day society. Further, there is no doubt that science was sent on its march of conquest, not because of the sudden miraculous arrival of 'scientists', but because men were crying out for its aid in the business of gaining a livelihood. And their number has increased since, in geometric progression, not because we breed men of greater brain-power than heretofore, but because the demand for them has also expanded in geometric progression. And the demand will increase, as long as the logic of progress of our Western economy requires it. Sooner or later, it may become a fetter or a danger, and then society will find a way of controlling it.

Some there are who think that the moment for control is already here. Its advent may, indeed, be held responsible for the astonishing assimilation of all modern societies, from that of the United States right across the spectrum to that of the Soviet Union, in spite of their superficially centrifugal political systems. It is this striking similarity of development which offers hope for our own survival as an advanced civilization. It needs hardly to be stressed that the social control demanded by today's powers of production presupposes a high degree of historical self-consciousness and that this, in turn, explains the rise and the timing of the historical doctrines I have been propounding to you.

Man is now more aware than ever before of the extent of his powers to control his own destiny. Marc Bloch thought that history was diverting, 'otherwise' he reasoned, why should any historian have chosen his profession?'.[59] I would rather think with E. H. Carr, if I may quote him to you for the last time, that the function of history was 'to enable man to understand the society of the past and to increase his mastery over the society of the present', and it is this, rather than its internal logical context, which ultimately gives history its scientifically objective standard.[60]

You may wonder, you may have wondered all along, how it is that I defend so fervently one side in what is still a live controversy. Is it not my duty, in a University, to do justice to all respectable views, and above all, not to abuse the privileges of an inaugural lecture by making partisan statements?

I would agree that within my teaching, I must present to my students all the doctrines, no matter how distasteful to me, which have in the past, or may in the future, contribute to their enlightenment and understanding. But in the present issue I have no choice. If I did not search for reason in history, I should have no subject to teach. In entering upon the occupation of this new chair, I do not propose to profess an anarchy of facts. I intend to send young men and women on a quest for a science, a quest which cannot ever be easy, but which must be possible. We can agree at least to this extent with Fustel de Coulanges, that

'History is not the accumulation of all sorts of events which have occurred in the past. It is the science of human societies'.[61]

I do not, in fact, believe that all attempts made hitherto to derive laws and draw lessons from the study of history have been entirely fruitless, but even if they could be shown to have failed, this would be no reason for abandoning the search, but rather for improving our work, and, in paritcular, for becoming more proficient in calling to our aid the methods and results of the other social sciences. It is this search which also provides historians with their teleology. To seek after perfection, to learn by acting, and to act with knowledge with the whole of society as your hunting ground, are no mean aims. Some may have other, perhaps higher guiding stars in their life; but this is a challenge none of us can ignore.

Basically, all social sciences seek their purpose and find their logic in active intervention in social life, in social melioration. At some point or other, Psychology seeks to integrate man's personality, Sociology seeks to adapt organizations to their purpose, Political Science seeks to reduce the human cost of the exercise of power, and Economics seeks to lessen that part of human misery which arises from want. These are all partial solutions.

I will not conceal from you that there are many economic historians whose sole equipment is a hand lens, and that there is a micro-Economic History, as we have seen that there is a micro-Economics, and, we know, a micro-Sociology, because its imprint appears weekly on the news-stands. Yet they all contribute to a fundamental understanding of Society, which is the understanding of how Society as a whole changes, transforming all its subordinate relationships in the process. It is there that all paths meet, and it is there that the Economic Historian has his post, seeking, listening and learning, and attempting to collect into his feeble hands what little there is of knowledge about the destiny of mankind.

It is a post of great, of frightening, responsibility.

NOTES

1   Professor M. M. Postan, at the Annual Conference of the Economic History Society, held in Sheffield in 1962.
2   George Unwin, *Studies in Economic History* (London, 1927), p. 18.

3 'Que pourrions-nous gagner à recueillir des opinions absurdes, des doctrines décriés et qui méritent de l'être? . . . Les erreurs ne sont pas ce qu'il s'agit d'apprendre, mais ce qu'il foudrait oublier'. J. B. Say, *Cours complet d'economie politique pratique* (Paris, 3rd ed. 1852) p. 537.

4 Karl Knies, *Die politische Oekonomei vom geschichtlichen Standpuncte* (Brauschweig, 1883, ed., First ed. 1853), pp. 24, 376, also footnote on p. 23.

5 J. E. Thorold Rogers, *The Economic Interpretation of History* (7th ed. 1909, 1st ed. 1888) pp. *vi–vii*; J. K. Ingram, *A History of Political Economy* (Edinburgh, 1893), pp. 221–235.

6 Carl Menger, *Die Irrthümer des Historismus in der deutschen Nationalökonomie* (Vienna, 1884), pp. 18–19, and *Problems of Economics and Sociology* (Urbana, Ill., 1963, first publ. 1882), p. 58.

7 Arthur Spiethoff, 'The "Historical" Character of Economic Theories', *J. Econ. Hist.* XII, 2 (Spring 1952).

8 Alfred Marshall, *Principles of Economics* (London, 8th ed. 1946; 1st ed. 1890); F. W. Taussig, *Principles of Economics* (New York, 3rd ed. 1911) I, 14; E. Cannan, *Elementary Political Economy* (Oxford 1888, 2nd ed. 1897) p. 1; Lionel Robbins, *An Essay on the Nature and Significance of Economic Science* (London, 1932), p. 15.

9 Eli F. Heckscher, 'A Plea for Theory in Economic History', *Economic History*, I, (1926–8), 528–9.

10 Gunnar Myrdal, *The Political Element in the Development of Economic Theory* (1929, Engl. ed. 1953), p. 5.

11 'and, of course', the author goes on, 'why all prices, wages, incomes, interest rates and other economic quantities are what they are'. Kenneth E. Boulding, *Economic Analysis* (London, 3rd ed. 1955. 1st ed. 1941). p. 7.

12 J. H. Clapham, 'Of empty economic boxes', *Economic Journal*, XXXII (1922), 305–314.

13 William N. Parker, Introduction to N.B.E.R. Conference on Research in Income and Wealth: *Trends in the American Economy in the Nineteenth Century* (Princeton, 1960), p. 5.

14 H. A. L. Fisher, *A History of Europe* (London, 1946 ed.) p. V.

15 Sidney Hook, *The Hero in History* (New York, 1943), pp. 144–5.

16 Albert Camus, *The Rebel* (L'homme révolté) (London, 1953), p. 215. It is only fair to add that Camus thought little better of the Marxist solution: 'the former', he goes on, 'never dreamed of liberating all men, but only of liberating a few by subjecting the rest. The latter, in its most profound principle, aims at liberating all men by provisionally enslaving them. . . . It must be granted the grandeur of its intentions', *Ibid.*

17 Ludwig von Mises, *Theory and History* (London, 1958), pp. 74, 177–8.

18 Karl Popper, *The Logic of Scientific Discovery* (London, 1959), p. 248.

19 In Patrick Gardiner (ed.), *Theories of History* (London, 1959), p. 299.

20 Edwin R. A. Seligman, *The Economic Interpretation of History* (New York, 1902).

21 J. H. Clapham, *The Study of Economic History, An Inaugural Lecture* (Cambridge 1929), p. 24. [and above p.64.].

22 Quoted in Dennis Chapman, 'William Brown of Dundee, 1791–1864: Management in a Scottish Flax Mill', *Explorations in Entrepreneurial History*, IV, 3 (February, 1952), p. 124.

23 Karl Marx, *Der Achtzehnte Brumaire des Louis Bonaparte* (Berlin, 1946), p. 40.

24 Heinrich Rickert, *Science and History* (Princeton, 1962, 1st ed. 1898), p. 114. Also see Gardiner, *op. cit.*, p. 126.

25 T. B. Bottomore and Maximilian Rubel (eds.) Karl Marx, *Selected Writings* (London, 1960), pp. 53–6.

26 Werner Sombart, *Der Moderne Kapitalismus* (6th ed. Munich and Leipzig, 1924 and 1927), I, p. 7.

27 E. H. Carr, *What is History?* (London, 1961), p. 25.

28 Quotation from New Preface to the *Critique of Political Economy* (Chicago, 1904), pp. 11 and 13. Also see the discussion in G. V. Plekhanov, *In Defence of Materialism* (London, 1947), pp.148, 196 ff., and *The Material Conception of History* (London, 1940).

29 Marx, *La misère de la philosophie* (Paris & Brussels, 1847), p. 100.

30 *Marx-Engels Selected Correspondence* (London, 1934), Engels to Conrad Schmidt, 27 October, 1890.

31 S. G. Checkland, 'Scottish Economic History: Recent Work', *Economica*, N.S., XXXI, 123, August, 1964, p. 305.

32 See esp. E. H. Carr, *What is History?* (London, 1961); Isaiah Berlin, *Historical Inevitability* (Oxford, 1954); and the controversy in the *Listener*, April-June, 1961.

33 Ludwig von Mises, *Theory and History* (London, 1958), p. 5.

34 Jakob Burckhardt, *Reflections on History* (London, 1943), p. 186.

35 G. V. Plekhanov, *The Role of the Individual in History*, pp. 37–8.

36 Sidney Hook, *The Hero in History* (New York, 1943), esp. Ch. 10; also cf. p. 176.

37 J. Witt-Hansen, *Historical Materialism: The Method, The Theories* (Copenhagen, 1960), Book I, p. 36. Italics in original.

38 See esp. his *The Poverty of Historicism* (London, 1957), and 'Prediction and Prophecy in the Social Sciences', in Gardiner, *op. cit.*

39 *Loc. cit.*, p. 113, also p. 174.

40 Isaiah Berlin, *op. cit.*, pp. 1, 25–6.

41 Plekhanov, *Individual in History*, pp. 11–12; Sidney Hook, *op. cit.*, p. 13.

42 William Dray, *Laws and Explanation in History* (Oxford, 1957), p. 18.

43 O. R. Frisch, 'Causality', *Listener*, 16th July, 1964, p. 83.

44 C. G. Hempel, 'The Function of General Laws in History', *Journal of Philosophy*, XXXIX (1942), 37.

45 Cf. E. H. Carr, *op. cit.*, pp. 43, 50 ff; Ernest Cuneo, *Science and History* (London, 1963), pp. 16–17.

46 W. W. Rostow. 'Leading Sectors and the Take-Off' in *The Economics of Take-Off into Sustained Growth* (London, 1963), p. 2. Cf. also Plekhanov's example of the bursting shell, *In Defence of Materialism*, p. 217.

47 Cf. Dray, pp. 62–3.

48 *Op. cit.*, pp. 98, 102.

49 E.g. Owen Lattimore, *Studies in Frontier History* (Oxford, 1962), Preface, pp. 24–6, and 'The Mainspring of Asiatic Migration', pp. 86 ff. Gordon Childe, *The Dawn of European Civilisation* (London, 3rd ed. 1939), pp. 14. ff.

50 Marx and Engels, *Manifesto of the Communist Party* (1848; Lawrence & Wishart ed., 1939) pp. 12–14.

51 E. H. Carr, *op. cit.*, pp. 57–59.

52 J. S. Mill, *A System of Logic*, in Gardiner, *op. cit.*, p. 88. Also, J. B. Bury, *The Idea of Progress* (London, 1921), pp. 308–9.

53 J. G. A. Pocock, 'History and Theory', *Comparative Studies in Society and History* IV (1961–2), p. 527. Also Hempel, *loc. cit.*, and Dray, p. 7.

54 See Gardiner, *op. cit.*, pp. 79, 85.

55 Not necessarily absolute, cf. *Wage Labour and Capital* (Glasgow, n.d.), p. 22.

56 Eric Williams, *Capitalism and Slavery* (London, 1964), p. 7.

57   W. W. Rostow, *op. cit.*, p. xxiii.
58   J. H. Plumb, 'The Historian's Dilemma', in *idem* (ed.), *Crisis in the Humanities* (Harmondsworth, 1964).
59   Marc Bloch, *Apologie pour l'histoire, ou Métier d'historien* (Paris, 1949), pp. X–XI.
60   Carr, *op. cit.*, pp. 49, 117, 132; Maurice Mandelbaum, *The Problem of Historical Knowledge,* (New York, 1938), p. 200.
61   Quoted by Riemersma in F. C. Lane and J. C. Riemersma (ed.), *Enterprise and Secular Change* (London, 1953), p. 490.

18

Ralph Davis

HISTORY AND THE SOCIAL SCIENCES
(Leicester, 1965)

This inaugural lecture was delivered at the University of Leicester on the 2nd March 1965.

z

HISTORY AND THE SOCIAL SCIENCES

'HISTORY' says the distinguished French historian, Frédéric Mauro, 'is the projection of the social sciences into the past'. Few historians, I think, will wholeheartedly accept such a declaration; but this view of history ought not to be dismissed out of hand without some consideration of what elements of value it contains. The economist and the sociologist attempt for their own reasons to interpret certain aspects of the life of present-day societies. They consider facts, they develop theories and apply them to data—strictly speaking to *historical* data, though very often relating to the immediate past. There is no reason in principle why the theories they develop and test adequately should not be applied usefully to the data of the more remote past—and sometimes they are—but historians often suspect this application. They do so chiefly because these are fairly new sciences, much of their theory as yet extremely tentative, imprecisely worked out, inadequately tested and frequently revised. If the social sciences could claim the precision of the physical sciences—of, say, chemistry —most historians would feel obliged to attempt some understanding of their methods and their application to historical problems. Moreover, as a rule the historian has plenty of facts; and confronted with an economist's or a sociologist's or a psychologist's attempt to fit some aspect of history into a theoretical framework, he can usually dredge up a few facts which appear to discredit the result. He can do this the more easily, the less he understands of the purposes, methods and unexpressed assumptions of the branch of social science concerned; the less, that is to say, he is ready to think himself sympathetically into the intentions of those he is criticising, and to consider whether his information really makes their propositions quite untenable, or merely throws light on ambiguities of formulation or ways in which the social scientists theory may usefully be remodelled.

Another reason why some historians are uninterested in theory lies in the nature of the things historians study. Many of them are concerned essentially with personal relations, with situations in which, it is thought, the personality of individuals has effects overriding material circumstances and habits of thought derived from the material environment. A good deal of political history, and especially much diplomatic history, has traditionally been treated more or less in isolation from the social context. The social sciences can offer very little to this kind of history; even psychology, which should have something to say in the field of personal relationships, has been unconvincing in its few applications to long-dead men whose personalities have to be judged from their writings and speeches and from their contemporaries' comments on them. But if this kind of history is in a sense too narrow for the social sciences, much history is too broad for them as they now stand. And this is particularly true of the subject we label economic and social history. The economic historian, if he is not merely an economist *manqué*, is constantly faced with the complexities of situations in the past, which he must try to see whole; situations in which the play of personality of outstanding individuals is not overwhelmingly important; situations which the social sciences should in principle be capable of analysing, but whose many-sidedness defeats the resources of any one of them. The economist or the sociologist is entitled to argue he is interested only in this or that aspect of a situation; the historian, though he may handle it in pieces, has sooner or later to explain it as a whole. Each of the social sciences is admirably equipped to deal with problems of certain types, and is naturally reluctant to venture outside the territories in which it is competent. Indeed, this is the sense in which they are sciences. Each has selected, abstracted if you like, a series of related problems for analysis. The rigour of this selection is the key to their progress. They are interested in recurring phenomena, offering predictable patterns of behaviour. The historian by contrast has continually to make the effort to comprehend a social situation as a whole and in its uniqueness.

Consider this situation. In 1936 Japanese shoppers found themselves buying matches in boxes labelled 'Down with Japan'. Police enquiries showed that these were matches made in Japan; their enterprising manufacturer had labelled them for the Chinese market, to appeal to customers who hated Japan and all its works. Unfortunately, the Chinese government, entering at this moment on one of its phases of conciliatoriness towards Japan, had banned the dissemination of inflammatory anti-Japanese propaganda in China; so the consignment of matches was shipped back from Shanghai to Yokohama, and the manufacturer had to try and dispose of them in the only place where their slogan would not give rise to protests by the Japanese Foreign Office—that is, in Japan itself.

This is a piece of reality; and it cannot be explained just by supply curves, or by studies of social roles or the aggressive instinct, or the steps permissible to states in a condition of undeclared war, or location of industry theories. Each throws its light; none gives all-round illumination.

It would be misleading to suggest that in this country any social science except economics has as yet contributed very much to history. Many historians today, and not merely among those calling themselves economic historians, have a quite substantial training in economics; only a handful of the youngest have acquired, in any formal way, more than a smattering of sociology, political theory or psychology. If there *is* a field in which we may look at the effect of projecting even a single one of the social sciences into the past, therefore, it is that of economic history.

I must remind you what a young subject economic history is. Young, in a double sense, for it has already gone through two quite distinct phases. The earliest writers were generally concerned to write descriptive histories, not to discover cause and effect or to reveal regularities or general laws; and their work promoted the view that state policy and state intervention in economic affairs were the main interests of the subject. These attitudes are enshrined in the two great general works of English economic history; Cunningham's *Growth of English Industry and Commerce*, first published in 1882, and Lipson's *Economic History of England*, published between 1915 and 1931. Nobody has since written general textbooks on this scale, and Lipson still holds the field, in some places, as the standard advanced textbook of economic history. Yet, great as the conception was, it was dead before the work was completed. For the real beginning of economic history as we know it today came when Unwin, Clapham and Ashton recognised that in the growing analytical power of Marshallian economics lay a tool for the much more fruitful dissection of our economic past. Their work showed what could be done with this tool; and their example was followed not only by historians but also by economists—in particular by those economists who wanted to go beyond the analysis of static conditions to a fuller understanding of the forces of growth and change operating over time. Consequently, universities came to teach this kind of history first of all in Economics Departments, to Economic students—as it was here for many years.

Two generations of work of this kind have shown how much economic history has to gain from the application of economic theory; but they have shown very clearly that economics is not enough. Having explored the uses of economics as applied to history, we have discovered that it does not explain everything of importance even in the economic field; and more than this, we can see that much of what it cannot explain falls within the sphere of others of the social sciences. It may be said that this is going beyond economic history. Of course it is possible to define economic history in such a way as to exclude problems which cannot in principle be handled by economic analysis; but few people do define it in this way, and to do so is to remove all interest from it for anyone but the economist, to make it a backyard in which economists endlessly count their own chickens. The demand curve which traces its smooth path over the pages of textbooks of economics is a beautiful thing; but the shape and position of any demand curve depend largely on non-economic factors of taste and habit, and these are likely to be the most interesting and also the most important things that affect it. The rather clumsy label of 'economic and social history' describes more adequately the ground covered by economic historians; formal definitions are legion and I shall not add to them.

Consider, for example, a foreigner's view of alehouses in England in 1659:

'There is within this city, and in all the towns of England, so prodigious a number of houses where they sell a certain drink called ale, that I think a good half of the inhabitants may be denominated ale-house keepers. . . . But what is most deplorable, where the gentlemen sit, and spend much of their time drinking of a muddy kind of beverage, and tobacco, which has universally besotted this nation, and at which, I hear, they have consumed many noble estates . . . and that nothing may be wanting to the height of luxury and impiety of this abomination, they have translated the organs out of the churches to set them up in taverns, chanting their dithyrambics and bestial bacchanalias to the tune of those instruments which were wont to assist them in the celebration of God's praises, and regulate the voices of the worst singers in the world, which are the English in their churches'.

He is clearly telling us about something which has important implications for labour productivity and for capital accumulation; what he has to say (if supported by other evidence) is of the utmost importance to economic history even in its strictest and narrowest definition, affecting the shape of supply, demand, and capital efficiency curves. But the economist cannot *alone* explain the patterns of demand which are here described.

I shall illustrate some of the difficulties which arise from projecting economics alone into the past, by looking at one of the topics which today engrosses the attention of economic historians; economic growth, economic development, economic progress—the terms are used more or less synonymously.

A great many economic historians have in the past two decades been examining the problems which come under this heading; that is, the history of countries which *have* achieved economic progress. The economists, too, have looked at history with a view to discerning within it the secret of development, to learning from the past how other countries may make economic progress in the future, and they have proceeded to create theoretical models of economic development—a Schumpeter model, a Gerschenkron model, a Domar/ Harrod model, a Leibenstein model, a Rostow model and a whole series of others. From the one side, numbers of economists have applied the latest economic tools to economic history to see how well they fitted and what they could explain; from the other side, many economic historians have tailored their own researches to the presentation of material in forms suitable for testing by means of modern economic ideas.

Of course all these models have offered wide scope for criticism; a theory which will embrace many aspects of the dynamics of economic life is far more difficult to formulate and justify than short-term particular models. But what has emerged is not merely the difficulty of devising formulae to fit the facts and plausibly interpret their suptle and complex interrelations. It has become clear to everyone—economists as much as any—in the course of these debates that economic development is not wholly, indeed, not even mainly, an economic matter; it is equally a social one, social in the sense that sociologists and psychologists deal with, concerned with effecting the changes in social structure which will enable economic forces to work more nearly in accordance with the expectations of pure theory.

This not merely a matter of rediscovering that that ancient and lonely inhabitant of the economic jungle, Economic Man, does not exist. Economic Man has been dead a very long time. Nor is it any philosophical difficulty about 'what is progress' or 'what is development', for we can find a definition of 'economic progress' even though an agreed definition of plain 'progress' may defy all the philosophers. Economic growth is usually defined in narrow, strictly material terms, as increasing real national income per head of population. Of course, a definition of economic growth by income per head of population has only a limited value; we may feel that *economic* growth, defined in this way, is so narrow a conception and so little related to our vague notions about general progress as to be of little interest. For example, the long argument about whether the Industrial Revolution in England, in its early decades, improved or worsened the condition of the working class, has now settled down to a rather dreary swapping of statistics of food prices and money wages, as though the index of the real wages of a man in regular employment, even if accurately determinable, could truly represent the complicated changes in the whole structure of working class society, its habits, attitudes, opportunities and perils over half a century or more of upheaval. Again, the last thirty years have seen in England a marked rise in real income per head; it has brought with it new social problems associated with the ease of getting employment, with the extension of leisure, with the attitude of the individual to society, which are difficult to resolve; and again there are apparently many people who deprecate the material progress because they believe too great a price has been paid in social dislocation.

In spite of these reservations, most people will surely agree that a country in which people are materially a great deal better off, in which they eat chocolate cake, battery-reared chickens and iced lollies quite often, instead of living on a diet of bread and cheese and a little bacon as most Englishmen did two hundred years ago, is at least likely to be in other respects a better one to live in. It *is* reasonable to suppose that a higher income per head of population is a good thing; that economic growth in economic terms is at any rate one of the desirable ends of human endeavour.

We may, then lay aside these rather obvious qualifications and accept real income per head of population as a useful measurement of the growth we seek to analyse; but we are still left with the question, can economics alone explain how this growth occurs? It is plain today that it cannot; that even this strictly material, narrowly defined, measurable growth cannot be wholly—perhaps not even mainly— explained in terms of the working of economic forces. Population growth, for example, is usually seen as one of the necessary conditions for economic growth—that is, for raising real income *per head*, since it makes possible new efficiency in specialisation and division of labour. Yet what causes population growth? Economic influences on it can be very important, for increasing prosperity may result in the enlargement of the family and the lengthening of life, as Malthus saw 160 years ago. But other influences which powerfully affect population growth are entirely non-economic—indeed even non-human— such as changes in the behaviour of viruses and of their animal hosts which affect the course of epidemic and endemic disease. Moreover, when we contemplate the enlargement of the family in certain circumstances of relative prosperity around 1800, we are reminded of the reduction of the family in circumstances of prosperity in this century; economic growth is neither the sole influence upon population growth, nor one that influences it in ways which are clearly predictable.

But the discussion of economic development which has been carried on in the last two decades has in fact given special attention to two things. One is the accumulation of capital in the hands of people who are likely to put it to productive uses; the other is the rise of a spirit of enterprise, of capacity for business leadership, within a society.

Capital accumulation has the attraction of being quantifiable; the road to economic development has been seen by some writers as essentially a matter of raising the level of investment, as a percentage of national income, above some stated rate. Economics even has something to tell us about how it is done in capitalist societies. Generally speaking, people with larger incomes save a larger proportion of them than people with smaller incomes—not simply a larger amount, but a larger *proportion*. Make the rich richer, therefore, (even at the cost of making the poor poorer for a generation or two) and economic development can be set going which will benefit everyone—except, of course, that unfortunate generation or two of the poor. Historical examples can be adduced which suggest this has actually happened.

Enriching the rich is a way that may lead to capital accumulation and economic progress; but it is not a sure way. The history of mankind, from the agricultural revolution of neolithic times until two centuries ago, has been basically one of the production, by a peasantry constituting the majority of the people, of a good deal more than its bare subsistence needs; and the appropriation of the excess over peasant subsistence by other, smaller classes, usually wealthy landowners or privileged tribute receivers of some kind. We know of many societies in which the surplus that was siphoned off amounted to nearly half the peasant's production. If its receivers had lived at peasant standards or anything like them, there would have been a vast annual capital accumulation; but of course they did not. They lived well and accumulated only moderately or not at all. The real problem of capital accumulation has never been simply a matter of creating large incomes, but of putting large incomes into the hands of people without habits of large expenditure—or alternatively into the hands of governing institutions—and finding channels into which the capital so accumulated might be productively directed. The first problem is one largely of social habits; the second of technology and all the attitudes to enquiry and change that are connected with it.

Typical rent- and tribute-receivers, in other words the majority of the rich in Britain and elsewhere until quite recent times, have not generally been savers of their income; they have firmly-rooted habits of lavish expenditure associated with the social roles they play. The aristocrat or the squire was not normally induced to transfer his efforts to the arena of commerce simply because there was money to be made there. In seventeenth-century Britain the landowner was at the pinnacle of society, and it was the complaint of contemporary economic writers that as soon as an English merchant had built up a fortune he wanted to buy land, to set his eldest son up as a squire, and his other children in ladylike marriages and gentlemanly pursuits with corresponding patterns of expenditure. Most trading businesses were strictly single-generation, or at most two-generation affairs; each generation of merchants had to build up its own fortunes, its own capital, more or less from scratch.

By contrast, in nineteenth-century England trade and industry had a growing prestige; much more often son followed father in the family business; it came to be a source of pride to an old man that he left son, grandson and great-grandson to carry the family name on in a great firm. This is not to say they might not add landed estates to their assets, withdraw some resources from industry; but the complete withdrawal from commercial money-making, as from something unclean, which was normal in those who had made enough to do it in the seventeenth century, was now very much rarer. In these new circumstances of the nineteenth century, expenditure was likely to be kept within moderate bounds and capital to accumulate within the firm. This change in English attitudes was not in any important sense a reflection of economic possibilities; the son, well-trained in trade, of the merchant of 1700, could reasonably have expected to make far more money by carrying on his father's business than he would if he abandoned it. He turned his back on trade because he had been brought up by his father to do so. The industrialist's son of 1900 was much more likely to have been reared with expectations of entering the family business and of living and accumulating in something like his father's style. But of course the social status of the country gentleman was far from unchallenged in 1900; by 1965 it has nearly gone, and if business men go back to the land today, it is for a plain economic reason—to acquire the special taxation advantages that go with agricultural occupations.

Capital accumulation, then—or the propensity to save from which it derives—is determined only to a very limited extent by things economics deals with. The biggest part in determining what is saved is played by the social setting, by the roles, the customary modes of life, of those with incomes beyond bare subsistence. The price which will be paid for capital in capitalist societies, the price which sets the demand curve for saving, cuts a supply curve about whose position the economists, as economists, can say very little, and the sociologists and psychologists should be able to say a great deal.

In any case, is capital accumulation, however brought about, really the master key to the problem of increasing national income? Have we not also to consider in what forms new capital is embodied —what kinds of new machines, buildings, vehicles are provided? Even if a society has no *net* saving at all, its income will still rise if the depreciation allowances set aside to replace existing capital equipment as it wears out are in fact used to instal newer, more efficient machines, the products of an advancing technology. Moreover, the advance in productivity which is given by a new invention need bear no particular relation to the capital investment it requires. Some inventions, like the Bessemer converter for steel-making, transform whole industries by bringing down costs many-fold; other, equally costly innovations produce quite small gains, only marginally worth while. The main function of capital accumulation is to provide for the creation of better equipment as soon as this is technically feasible and economically desirable; not to put into the refrigerator-making factory of 1965 more of the kind of machines which were installed there in 1955, but to bring in new and better types. It is true that without capital this cannot be done very fast; but without technical innovation there will be simply a growing quantity of machines designed long ago, and only a slow growth of incomes. It has been estimated recently that only a quarter of the growth in income per head in this country since 1945 can be attributed to the increase in capital employed; all the rest results from the introduction of new techniques, and from such intangible things as better management and a generally higher level of education.

Can invention, then—this essential factor in economic progress—be wholly accounted for by economic influences? Certainly invention is closely related to matters of demand, or bottlenecks of supply, and it can be argued that different systems of rewarding inventors in the past might have encouraged invention, and even more the dissemination of new methods. Few things did more to hasten the decisive advance of the English Industrial Revolution, which was the turning of cotton spinning into a factory industry, than the breaking of Richard Arkwright's patents in 1785. But, if necessity is the mother of invention—and necessity may plausibly be put in economic terms—we are entitled to ask, who is the father? There are clearly limits to the extent to which technical advance can be explained purely in economic terms, and fostered by appropriately adjusted mechanism of incentive and penalty. Economic influence is not so precisely directed that it determines in every case an invention shall be made here rather than there, this year rather than next. The play of accident is quite important in this field. Cunningham tells us of 'Mr. William Lee, of St. John's College, Cambridge, who in 1589 constructed a stocking knitting frame, and this gave rise to a new and important branch of industry. He is said to have been much put out, when paying his addresses to a young lady, by the sedulous interest she gave to her knitting, and he determined to find a mechanical means of doing such work'. At a deeper level, of course, the distribution of inventive ability and of willingness to excerise it is set by the character of society, just as is the extent of the habit of saving. Consider this seventeenth-century ordinance on the French cloth industry:

'If a cloth weaver intends to process a piece according to his own invention, he must not set it to the loom but should obtain permission from the judges of the town . . . after the question has been considered by four of the oldest merchants and four of the oldest weavers of the guild'.

This, typical of its age and of long ages before it, is not the kind of thing that encourages change. We usually assert that the change in scientific attitudes which is associated with the seventeenth century, the development of the spirit of rational and more or less unrestricted enquiry, provided the basis for much invention which came to have practical application, and the material success of invention in the late eighteenth century certainly gave change the prestige which tradition had had, and helped the snowballing of invention down to our own time. What would have been the point of high capital accumulation in all the ages of opposition to change, of lack of interest in finding new ways of doing things?

Thus both the accumulation of capital, and the physical forms which accumulated capital takes, are to an important extent socially determined in ways the economist can say little about.

The other subject that has flourished in the discussion of economic growth in society is the role of the man of enterprise, the risk-taker, the entrepreneur. He is a most ambiguous figure in economic theory. Some nineteenth-century economists defined him as the man who supplied the risk capital, and took the reward of risking his capital in the form of profit. He was not necessarily a figure of great vigour, competence and drive; the fourth-generation owner of a family business might be lazy and incompetent, but as the bearer of risk, he was still on this view the entrepreneur. But the conception has changed as theories of profit have become less coherent. In modern terminology the entrepreneur is really, as his title implies, the enterprising man, the man who will see new opportunities in finance, in marketing, in the application of inventions, and will organise the combinations of capital and labour needed to bring these possibilities to maturity. His role is much wider than that of the inventor of new productive techniques, and he is not a new figure; two hundred years ago Dr. Johnson remarked:

'The man who first took advantage of the general curiosity that was excited by a siege or battle to betray the readers of news into the knowledge of the shop where the best puffs and powder were to be sold, was undoubtedly a man of great sagacity, and profound skill in the nature of man. . . .'

The appearance in society of a constant stream of these innovators—Nuffields, Leverhulmes, Charles Clores, Isaac Wolfsons—is a major requirement for continued economic progress; economic development depends not only on people who will save, and on people who will invent, but also on people who will use their resources and organise the acquisition of other people's resources to put new ideas to useful effect. Great efforts have been made in recent years to discover, on the one hand, precisely what are the qualities which make the successful entrepreneur, and on the other, what conditions of society are most likely to bring forward large numbers of good entrepreneurs. This again seems a field in which the economist can give less guidance than other kinds of social scientist. There is, indeed, a school of thought which contends that one of the characteristics of the entrepreneur is that he is ready to behave in ways which contradict the economic rationality of his time. The psychologists have been busy trying to measure the strength, in different societies, of men's ambition for achievement, or studying the effect of childhood upbringing or a membership of minority groups on the production in individuals of entrepreneurial characteristics. If the working out of these ideas has been unconvincing, a haunting feeling is left with the reader that something important is being discussed which better techniques may one day see defined more clearly and measured more precisely.

Economic historians, then, no longer attempt to explain the past simply with what they can muster of historical insight, or with little economic tool-boxes of demand curves and capital efficiency schedules. Or if, to be honest, most of us still do, the inadequacy of this approach is now widely recognised, and particularly in America much valuable work has been done by economic historians using sociological tools. If this application has been largely in the field of modern economic growth, it is being extended to earlier times and their problems. Yesterday morning what must surely be 1965's largest contribution to economic history arrived on my desk: Lawrence Stone's *The Crisis of the Aristocracy 1558–1641*. Opening it at an early page I read 'I am now persuaded that the upheavals of the mid-seventeenth century cannot be explained in terms of any single factor but only as a product of a great variety of forces, some of which historians have hitherto been content to leave to sociologists and the anthropologist'.

We might put the task of economic history in a nutshell by saying it is concerned, not with tracing the rigid operation of economic laws in the past, but with understanding the pressure of *economic* forces to overcome the *social* obstacles to change. Economic forces are at work in every society; powerful, blind, morally neutral. They operate amidst all the conservative strengths, all the great capacities for cohesion and tradition and inertia which human societies, great and small, savage or sophisticated, *must* have if they are to survive. Social forces damp down economic forces in an untold number of ways; they thwart and divert and delay them so that change can be assimilated without utterly disrupting society. This immensely subtle and complex and continually changing interplay of economic and social forces which nevertheless allows for change and growth constitutes a field of study that we are only just beginning to see the size of. It is a field in which the economic historian must be one of the busiest workers. He cannot dispense with some understanding of what the social sciences are about, what kinds of problems they are equipped to deal with today; with a knowledge of when and where to look for help in his enquiries, just as he looks to the ancillary disciplines of history, to palaeography, numismatics, archaeology and the others.

All this, let me hasten to say, is very far indeed from suggesting that the social sciences are merely the running dogs of history, to be patted on the head when they shuffle up with particularly succulent theoretical conceptions that fit a mass of factual information into an acceptable pattern; or to be driven away with curses when their theories suggest that some firmly established historical notion contains hidden flaws requiring extensive reconsideration of the evidence. The purpose of the social sciences is to explain the *modern* world; if social scientists look to the past, it is to throw light on the validity of the methods they use for effecting that purpose. Nor of course is economic and social history simply the slave of the social sciences. The production of examples from the recent economic history of Canada or Costa Rica to indicate how Cambodia or Cameroon may be developed in the future is only an incidental use of the subject. Economic history is first and foremost a part of history, giving its special attention to historical problems of particular kinds and contributing its solutions to the sum of historical understanding. We have worked with the economists for a long time, yet even they may tire of us presently; already their economic simulation models can with the aid of computers produce extensive sample economic histories of hypothetical countries, introducing progress and decline, stability and upheaval; reproducing the economic impact of plague, mass suicide, invasion from outer space or anything else that looks interesting. Perhaps they will come to prefer these clearly expressed, unambiguous, infinitely manipulable and totally explained hypothetical histories to struggling with the facts—with the dubious, incomplete and doubtfully relevant evidence about the real life of real societies.

To come back, then, to my starting point. In saying 'History is the projection of the social sciences into the past' Mauro suggested— in my view rightly—that the theoretical conceptions, the presuppositions and assumptions which all historians bring to history, should *in principle* be drawn from the social sciences. In practice the social sciences, even economics, the most firmly established of them, are very far indeed from being able to fill the required role, but they have much to offer the historian even now.

The dangers, such as they are, in the use of the social sciences by historians, lie in another direction; in threatening to deprive history, and especially economic history, of its audience. Much of historical writing has always been descriptive rather than analytical, and this is not to be despised. In large measure it is the admixture of description with explanation, of analysis with illustration, of theory with example, that provides history with its non-specialist audience. And for history, this is the principal audience. The greater part of the historian's audience is made up not by social scientists, trained and equipped with their specialised language, but by a vast educated public which looks to the past for aid in understanding the present, and includes the school-teachers responsible for imparting a view of history to millions of school-children. The historian's main function is to present what he believes to be a true picture and a supportable explanation of the past to those vast numbers of people whose attitudes to the great questions of our time, to politics and society, will be in important ways shaped by what they believe about the past, if only by what they have learned of it at school. If the historian does not explain the past, his place will be filled by the myth-makers, the propagandists, inventing and distorting the past for their own purposes.

The economic historian is anxious that his special view of history, which emphasises the importance in shaping the course of events of the myriad decisions of great numbers of people in the course of earning their livelihood or spending it, and which tries to set the actions of outstanding individuals within this context rather than above it, should have a secure place in historical writing and teaching. While most historians today show a willingness to take this view of society into account, there is a serious, and I suspect growing difficulty of communication. The very fact that the economic historian's preoccupations are particularly susceptible to economic or sociological analysis, and to statistical handling, can easily lead him to write solely for an audience of his fellow specialists. It is sometimes desirable, and often convenient, to use a technical vocabulary and a mathematical formulation; but the taste grows insidiously and it is easy to slip into a habitual and quite unnecessary use of them.

In consequence, there is a risk that some of the most valuable work of economic historians may be cut off from the main stream of history, left unread by the general historians, by the teachers and by the writers of textbooks, who will pick up their ideas of economic history from outdated or discredited works which have the single virtue of being written in language they can understand. On the other hand, since economic historians do usually struggle to eliminate obscurities of expression, we ask for the indulgence of our audience towards the traces of them that remain; we may reasonably point out that it is less easy to attain literary elegance and to dispense with the use of statistics in the exposition of the terms of trade of Louis XV's France than it is in depicting the life-story of Madame de Pompadour.

If I had another hour I should devote it to the important topic of the unity of history which I have momentarily touched. But I have made my choice and I have had my hour. Let me briefly illustrate the unity of history by referring to the career of an early teacher at this University, who will shortly be returning to us—W. G. Hoskins. Hoskins came here thirty years ago, at first as an 'Assistant Lecturer in Commerce'. In that post he taught economics, and he laid the foundations in this university of the study of economic history. It cannot have been easy, in those short-staffed days, for anyone to raise his nose far above the grindstone of perpetual teaching, but within a few years Hoskins was making his mark, with works on the history of Devon and of Leicestershire which were seen to provide major contributions towards general problems of economic history. By 1948, when he was appointed Reader in English Local History here, he had a national reputation; he was lured away to Oxford four years later to be its Reader in Economic History; and though he returns here later this year to head the Department of English Local History which has added so much to the reputation of this University, the chair he fills will be that of Hatton Professor of English History. Few local historians can claim they have brought so much as Hoskins to the study of English local history; few economic historians that they have contributed more to economic history; and the study of English history as a whole will bear for generations to come the impress of his scholarship. His work has embraced many specialised branches of history, but it is sufficient to say of him that we shall be welcoming back a historian next October; and a historian of great distinction.

19

A. W. Coats

ECONOMIC GROWTH: THE ECONOMIC AND SOCIAL HISTORIAN'S DILEMMA
(Nottingham, 1966)

This inaugural lecture was delivered at the University of Nottingham on the 18th March 1966.

ECONOMIC GROWTH: THE ECONOMIC
AND SOCIAL HISTORIAN'S DILEMMA

I

ECONOMIC and social history came of age in this university six years ago when Professor Chambers delivered his inaugural lecture from this platform.[1] He then described the inaugural occasion as a privileged one, because the lecturer could, if he chose, throw his academic cap over the windmill knowing that his chair would not be required to follow. But although this may be a privileged occasion, it can also be a painful one for the audience as well as the lecturer, and there is something to be said for Professor Chambers' dictum that the object of the exercise should be to bait the cognoscendi without boring the laity. Too often the lecturer spends his time exposing the errors of his fellow specialists, or explaining how grossly neglected and financially under-nourished is that supremely important field of research to which he has devoted his life. Another besetting sin of inaugurals is the preoccupation with methodology; but in the present case I must plead extenuating circumstances, for the practitioner of a hybrid discipline like economic history is, as it were, thrice-tempted—he is tempted not only to pontificate on the nature and methods of economic history, but on those of economics and history as well.

Tonight, I propose neither to bore you by discussing the details of my own research, nor to entertain you by belabouring my professional colleagues. Instead, I shall compromise by considering the subject of economic growth, and some of the general problems that economic historians encounter in dealing with it.

II

Economic growth is essentially an economist's concept: strictly speaking, it means a rise in real income per capita, or, in other words, a rise in average purchasing power per head of population, and it is obviously important because the welfare of any community is directly affected by the size and the trend of its output of goods and services. Needless to say, this is not everything: prosperity does not ensure happiness (though it surely helps); rapid economic growth may be accompanied by great economic, social, and political instability; and the distribution of wealth is almost as important as its size. Moreover, an undue preoccupation with economic growth can lead to a neglect of some aspects and periods of economic history and a distortion of others, even if we extend the mathematical range to include zero and negative growth and recognize that economic and social conditions interact upon each other. Yet whatever its dangers,[2] the study of economic growth is a central theme in economic history, and I shall use it as a peg on which to hang some illustrations of the present condition of the subject and its current and prospective connections with economics and history. In what follows, for the sake of brevity, I shall speak of economic history rather than economic *and social* history; but at a later stage I shall comment on the relations between the social and economic aspects of the subject.

In a sense, the economic historian's dilemma is a by-product of current efforts to promote economic growth, both in advanced and so-called underdeveloped countries. It is often suggested that historians can shed light on the problems of the present by disclosing the secrets of the past, and as most of the underdeveloped countries are in a pre-industrial stage of development, and anxious to have an industrial revolution of their very own, an added stimulus has been given to the study of the first or 'classic' industrial revolution which occurred in eighteenth century England. This interest can, of course, be gratifying, even flattering to the scholar; but it has its disadvantages. Those who study history in the hope of relieving present discontents are apt to distort the past; and if the economic historian tries to provide answers to the questions posed by his academic colleagues, or by the general public, he immediately encounters serious difficulties—difficulties of communication, of method, and of substance—all of which stem from the endless subtlety and complexity of the process of economic and social change. Here, as elsewhere, as knowledge advances it becomes more precise and technical, more difficult to communicate to the layman; yet if the economic historian wishes to be heard he must be prepared to make simple straightforward statements about complex historical processes which he may not fully understand. This problem arises not only in addressing a popular audience but also in communicating with his indispensable academic colleagues, the economists and historians, though the difficulties are not the same in each case. It is his duty to warn the economists whenever they seem over-eager to apply the 'lessons' of the past to the problems of the present; but in order to command a respectful hearing the economic historian must not only acquire some command of the economists' peculiar language, he may also be called on to make broad generalizations about the results of his researches in a way that troubles his historical conscience. His dealings with the historians, on the other hand, are less exacting, and they should be mutually beneficial provided that the economic historian displays a due regard to the limitations of his evidence, and an awareness of the dangers of a deterministic economic interpretation of history. The historians ought to sympathize with the economic historian's desire to communicate, for the original meaning of the word history was: to inquire, to know, to tell what one has learned; but in approaching his fellow historians, the economic historian often senses that he must overcome certain barriers of scepticism, tradition, and indifference. Whenever this is so, he must restrain his impatience, remembering that he is a comparative newcomer to Clio's circle, a dealer in parts rather than wholes; and he must recall J. H. Clapham's well-known remark that while economic history is the most 'fundamental' type of history, it is not the most 'important', for 'foundations exist to carry better things'.[3]

Above all, the economic historian knows that he cannot live off his own; he is cultivating a hybrid, planted in the fertile borderlands between the Arts and the Social Sciences; but he can derive some satisfaction from the knowledge that this zone is now being cultivated much more effectively than it was a few years ago.

In studying economic growth—the rise of real income per capita— the economic historian faces certain technical problems, especially in connection with the theory of economic growth and the use of historical statistics, and I shall make a few preliminary remarks on each of these matters.

Economic historians have always regarded the study of long term economic change as an integral part of their work, if not its *raison d'être*, and they sustained their interest in this subject throughout the period when economists were concentrating on the analysis of static equilibrium conditions and short term fluctuations. Admittedly the economic historians have usually employed somewhat casual and unsystematic methods, partly because, like other historians, they have been suspicious of abstract generalized theories. However in recent years there has been an increasing desire for a more systematic treatment of long term economic development, and as there has been a marked revival of interest in the theory of economic growth on the part of economists during the past two or three decades, it is natural to ask whether the results of their researchers are of any value to economic historians.

Unfortunately, as the economists themselves admit, the outcome has been distinctly disappointing. Late in 1964, two leading British economists published an authoritative survey of economic growth theories in which they pointed out that literally thousands of theoretical 'growth models' could be constructed, none of which was inherently unreasonable, simply by combining a few key variables of acknowledged importance in the process of economic change—such as the supply of labour, savings, investment, output, technical progress, etc.,[4]. However, once the models became complex (e.g. by introducing additional variables, uncertainty, or non-homogeneity conditions) they either became mathematically unmanageable, lacked determinate solutions, or failed to make economic sense. Moreover, economic growth theorists have concentrated on a narrow segment of the conceivable range of relevant models while seriously neglecting certain of the weaker links in the causal chain; consequently very little analytical work has been done on some of the problems of greatest interest to economic historians.

Of course, the economic historian views the economists' failure to develop a satisfactory theory of economic growth with mixed feelings: he is sorry to learn that there are no simple solutions to his problems, but he is hardly surprised by this state of affairs, and he is greatly relieved to hear that he need not plunge into the technicalities of a subject in which, for example, production functions range from the 'well behaved' through the 'polyhedral' to the 'disaggregated', even to the 'decomposed'. It may amuse him to retain a smattering of terminology with which to impress his colleagues at economic history conferences—such as the 'Bastard Golden Age' model, the 'sausage machine' model, the 'knife-edge' problem, and the 'ratchet' effect; but in more sober moments he realizes only too well that he has no cause for complacency about his attempts to describe the process or to explain the causes of economic growth. The construction of economic models is, I believe, indispensable to the student of economic growth in any period, because they force him to define his problem clearly, to identify the key variables, and to specify their interrelationships. These 'models' fall somewhere between the magnificent generalized 'laws' of history propounded by 19th century philosophers of history like Comte and Marx—towards which most professional historians are nowadays quite properly sceptical, and the looser, more conventional types of historical explanation—which have been termed 'distillations of generalized sagacity'. Something more precise than this generalized common sense is needed to explain economic growth. Too often one encounters such statements as: 'it is difficult to over-emphasize the importance of "x",' or 'the significance of "y" must not be underestimated'—statements which are difficult to interpret or check, and which can serve as a cover for gross inconsistencies or gaps in the explanation. As far as possible, implicit assumptions must be explicated; and to the extent that the data permit, the historian must endeavour to construct a logically watertight 'model' of economic change in which the magnitude, direction, and interaction of the key variables are specified in precise and unambiguous terms. This is, of course, a counsel of perfection: the economic historian cannot expect to succeed where a generation of economic theorists has failed; but in the present state of our knowledge the effort must be made if we are to make significant advances in our understanding of the historical process of economic growth.

Economic growth is, in essence, a statistical concept, and although the more esoteric growth theories need not occupy the economic historian's mind, the problems of historical statistics cannot be so readily dismissed—indeed, they have never occupied so prominent a place in his subject as they do now. Here, too, he is confronted with a choice between evils: he cannot do without historical statistics, but he is often puzzled to know what to do with them. It is obviously true (but not very helpful) to say that statistics must be the historian's servant, not his master—that he must become 'numerate' without becoming a 'metrophile'—for he faces problems of statistical inference that can easily lead even a cautious scholar from the paths of historical righteousness, to say nothing of those who are blithely prepared to interpolate or extrapolate on the basis of one or two dubious figures. In the United States a so called 'new,' statistical species of economic history has recently arisen which, though brash, is nevertheless technically brilliant, and its devotees are not without humour in calling their approach 'cliometrics'. We in this country are more sober, and of course more conservative; we are neither as adventuresome nor as fashion-conscious, and, what is more to the point, we are not tempted by lavish research grants of the kind available to those willing to study the nature and causes of American economic growth—resources which have been provided partly as a result of American concern with the current and prospective economic growth race between the U.S.A. and the U.S.S.R. Nevertheless, the quantitative study of economic growth has leapt ahead in this country too during the past decade or so. We now have a comprehensive *Abstract of British Historical Statistics*, and a general statistical survey of *British Economic Growth 1688–1959*;[6] and the interest in quantification has recently spilled over into social history, especially with the study of population statistics, which Mr. Laslett is busily inflating into a 'numerical study of English society'.[7] Nowadays the social historian, as well as the economic historian, must needs be 'numerate'; and it is no longer true, as C. R. Fay once remarked, that 'social history is economic history with the hard parts left out'.

Later this evening I shall comment on some recent developments in social history; but I have not yet disposed of the problem of historical statistics. In recent years, especially in the U.S.A., there has been a rapprochement between the economic historian and that most fashionable and pyrotechnical species of economist, the econometrician; and this is no mere fad. As a leading econometrician has observed,

> econometrics is a way of studying history—a very systematic way.... The econometrician tries to piece together the fundamental aspects of economic behaviour by looking at the interrelationships of the quantitative magnitudes generated historically, and then tries further to extrapolate past behaviour into the unknown future. . . . A sensible method of extrapolation is not naive or mechanical, and the econometrician is no less flexible than any other historian who tries to evaluate the future on the basis of the past.[8]

The use of this technique involves a much closer collaboration between econometricians and economic historians than the obvious and trivial fact that all statistics refer to the past, and are therefore historical data. The economic historian, as historian, is not interested in predicting the future; yet, in a technical sense, he is interested in predicting the past, and some of the work of the 'new' economic historians in the U.S.A. demonstrates that a scholarly deployment of econometric techniques can shed valuable new light on the past. Moreover, the collaboration between economic historians and econometricians is more of a two-way process than is generally recognized by either group.

> To every explanatory economic model there corresponds a set of more or less definite background or external conditions that must be fulfilled in a given period of economic history if observations for that period are to be deemed appropriate for predictive testing of that model . . . [and] the conceptualization of relevant background conditions is a task for which the economic historian *qua* historian is equipped by training, experience and general point of view.[9]

Thus the economic historian can serve not only by restraining the economic theorists who too readily draw conclusions from the experience of the past, but also by constantly insisting upon the relevance of the historical situation in which the econometrician's quantitative magnitudes were generated. In this respect he will be doing his duty as an historian rather than as a social scientist, and in return he can borrow from the economist, the econometrician, and other social scientists, concepts and techniques that will enable him to pose new questions of the past and perhaps to derive new answers.

Econometric history—this 'act of inter-disciplinary miscegenation' as it has been called, must of course remain a subordinate part of economic history, if only because of the woeful inadequacy of the available statistical data.[10] There is, unfortunately, a kind of alchemy about figures which transforms the most dubious materials into something pure and precious; hence the price of working with historical statistics is eternal vigilance. Writers of economic history textbooks repeatedly warn that 'many things went unrecorded or falsely recorded, sometimes because nobody asked about them at the time, sometimes because those making the returns were interested in evading taxation, sometimes because the recording of accurate information appeared too troublesome or genuinely impossible';[11] and many 'howlers' have been perpetrated by incautious quantifiers. Nevertheless, statistical data are indispensible to the economic historian, for, like the economist, he finds that much of his information is automatically presented to him in statistical form (e.g. prices, outputs, costs, tax revenues, population data) and the more authoritarian and inquisitorial the government at any time the richer the community is liable to be in statistical information. It is no coincidence that the present age of economic and social planning is experiencing a statistical deluge; but it was more than 40 years ago that J. H. Clapham asserted that the questions of primary concern to the economic historian were: 'How large? How long? How often? How representative?'[12]—all of which are essentially statistical questions.

Of course, much of the economic historian's material does not lend itself to quantitative presentation, and some of his most delicate exercises in historical judgement arise from the need to weigh statistical evidence against the (strictly non-commensurable) qualitative influences at work, such as human psychology, custom, political power, etc. As one literate American economic historian has observed, historical statistics are 'embarrassingly explicit', their use 'requires figures, as the Minotaur required maidens, it requires them exactly and on time', and it is difficult to hide their limitations.[13] Whenever statistical results cannot be expressed in terms of aggregates, percentages, rates of growth, etc., with precisely defined 'confidence limits', the statistical historian cannot fall back on the time-honoured devices employed by the literary historian. On one occasion Edward Freeman, the 19th century English historian, confided to a correspondent that the volume he was currently working on would be very bad, but added, 'when I don't know a thing I believe I generally know that I don't know it, and so manage to wrap it up in some vague phrase which, if not right, may at least not be wrong'[14]—and this is but an unusually frank exposure of a procedure familiar to every historian. This is not the place to enter into the time-honoured debate about the 'science' versus the 'art' of history—though that debate is now undergoing a vigorous and potentially fruitful revival.[15] The essential point is that the economic historian has a foot in both worlds: like the scientist, he must use precise and standardized terms wherever possible, and expose his techniques to other scholars who wish to check his findings; but when these procedures are inapplicable or unattainable, he must inevitably follow his fellow historians into realms where qualitative judgements abound and language is governed partly by aesthetic considerations —even though this leaves him with an irreducible residue of ambiguity.

III

Turning from this methodological prolegomenon, let me now try to illustrate some of the problems of current research in economic history by commenting on the process of economic growth in eighteenth century England, a topic to which my professional colleagues have devoted considerable attention in recent years.

In school textbooks, (and still in some university lectures), the course of modern British economic history is usually explained in terms of a loose, overlapping sequence of 'revolutions', from the geographical discoveries of the 15th century; the 'price revolution' of the 16th; the 'scientific' and 'commercial' revolutions of the 17th; the 'agricultural', 'demographic', and 'industrial' revolutions of the 18th and early 19th centuries; to the 'transport', 'communications', 'financial', and 'organizational' revolutions of more recent times. Most of these revolutionary concepts have been a downright nuisance, for there has been endless controversy as to how they should be defined and dated; and most economic historians prefer to emphasize the continuity rather than the discontinuities of the past. But it has not been easy to emancipate ourselves from our terminological inheritance, especially since Professor Rostow recently redefined the industrial revolution as a 'take-off into self-sustained growth', a metaphor which at least had the virtue of precision, since its author claimed that the 'take-off' occurred in any given country when the proportion of its national income devoted to capital formation rose from below 5% to over 10%.[16] The concept of the 'take-off' has caught on and will doubtless haunt the textbooks for many years to come; yet, once let loose in the cynical world of scholars its virtue quickly proved to be its undoing, since neither capital formation nor national income could be accurately measured during the relevant period (1783–1803 in the British case), and the most careful statistical studies of British economic growth do not disclose any marked *overall* acceleration during the 1780's, as Rostow claimed. Admittedly there are significant increases in some statistical series, especially raw cotton imports and textile exports; but this is partly attributable to the recovery of trade after the end of the American war of independence, and although cotton led the way in mechanization and in the extension of the factory system, this 'leading sector' was not by itself of sufficient importance to lift the entire economy off the ground. If, indeed, a turning point or 'critical threshold' of economic growth must be sought in 18th century Britain it now seems that the 1740's or 1750's have a stronger claim than the 1780's, though any judgment on this point is subject to considerable margins of error owing to the limitations of the statistical evidence.

Professor Rostow's hypothesis admirably illustrates the dilemma posed by 'models' of economic growth, for in his effort to introduce some order into the 'disorganized complexity' of existing views of economic growth he came under heavy cross-fire from economists and economic historians. The latter have, on the whole, argued that the evidence does not support his claim that a 'take-off' occurred in late 18th century Britain, whereas the economists have protested: 'How can one translate all this fuzzy talk about take-off into something which an economic theorist can understand and grapple with; what are the initial conditions, parameters, and changes in rules of behaviour which distinguish a take-off from earlier periods?'[17] The demands of the economists and the historians are by no means incompatible; but in the present stage of our knowledge it is exceedingly difficult to satisfy both simultaneously. Rostow's 'take-off' concept has been the subject of intense debate during the past decade, and he may well be the most widely known economic historian since Karl Marx; but his contribution has not, unfortunately, significantly advanced our understanding of the problem.

So far economic historians have made no serious efforts to construct explicit 'models' of English economic growth in the first three quarters of the eighteenth century. Nevertheless provisional constructs of this type are often implicit in their writings, and if a substantial body of research can be summarized in a few words without undue distortion, the currently fashionable explanation runs in terms of a three-variable model, in which the three variables are population, agricultural output, and prices.[18] Other influences are not ignored, but are relegated to a subordinate place. For example, such institutional and social factors as political stability, respect for property rights, social mobility, the availability of entrepreneurial talent, and a climate of opinion favourable to economic freedom, are regarded as pre-conditions for economic growth rather than indispensable components of the growth mechanism itself; while more familiar economic elements, such as the supply of capital, transport, technological innovation, and foreign trade, are regarded as dependent variables. It is generally accepted that early 18th century England was a comparatively wealthy community —much more so than most mid-twentieth century underdeveloped countries—and that she possessed an adequate supply of currency and funds available for investment. The development of transport and the introduction of new techniques in manufacturing, hitherto occasionally regarded as independent causes of economic growth, nowadays tend to be treated as *responses* rather than initiating *causes*; but the case of foreign trade cannot be so curtly dismissed. It is now accepted that rapid growth of foreign trade, virtually amounting to a 'commercial revolution', occurred between the Restoration and the Glorious Revolution of 1688; but exports of manufactures, especially to Europe, grew comparatively slowly thereafter until the mid-eighteenth century, and as exports of manufactures probably constituted no more than 20% or 25% of the total output of any major commodity the growth of total output must have been mainly due to the *home* rather than to the overseas market. Admittedly trade with the American colonies grew apace; but our sales of manufactured goods to the colonies were dependent on the growth of colonial incomes, which were, in their turn, dependent on the sales of colonial raw materials in the home market; hence, the home market appears to have been the main determinant, and the colonial market the dependent variable[19]. Notwithstanding Adam Smith's incisive attack on the 'mercantile system' in the *Wealth of Nations*, most economic historians now agree that the system facilitated British economic growth, for without the protected colonial market, the expansion of our home industrial sector would have been less rapid, and an industrial revolution might have been postponed. Yet only a bold scholar would argue, in the present state of our knowledge, that but for the colonial market the 'critical threshold' would not have been crossed in the eighteenth century.

Having sketched part of the background, let me now return to the three-variable model, comprising population growth, agricultural output, and prices. Agriculture was by far the most important single branch of economic activity in eighteenth century Britain and during the past two decades our conception of the so-called 'agricultural revolution' has undergone radical revision.[20] The effective beginning of the rapid expansion of agricultural productivity, which was one of the essential pre-conditions of the industrial revolution, must now be dated back to the mid-seventeenth rather than the mid-eighteenth century, and those well-known textbook heroes, Jethro Tull and Turnip Townshend, are now known to have had many precursors. Likewise, the conventional sad story of the eighteenth century Parliamentary enclosure movement, which swept away the remnants of the medieval strip system of farming, has never sounded the same since the classic article in which Professor Chambers showed that the demand for labour rose rather than fell after enclosure.[21] The sentimental echoes of Goldsmith's *Deserted Village* and the tragic tones of Marx's epic of the expropriated peasantry, now carry no conviction: much enclosure had already taken place before the mid-eighteenth century Parliamentary movement got into its stride and the growth of population did far more than the dispossession of the peasantry to swell the labour force engaged in manufacturing. Although agricultural productivity grew fast enough to feed all the hungry mouths, there were too many hands to be employed in the fields.

Economic historians disagree on matters of emphasis in accounting for the process of growth in the second and third quarters of the eighteenth century;[22] but there is a consensus of opinion that an acceleration occurred in the mid 1740's and 50's, after two or more decades of slow growth or even stagnation. This acceleration seems to have been *preceded* by a rise in population, which was facilitated by a long series of good harvests in the 1730's and 40's, and a correspondingly plentiful supply of cheap foodstuffs. This is not a sufficient explanation, for there is no exact correlation between an increase in food supply and a rise of population, either in the short or the long run. Yet it seems likely that population rose both because easy living conditions encouraged marriages, bringing a subsequent rise in birth rates, and because death rates fell owing to the diminished incidence of epidemic diseases—a point strongly emphasized by Professor Chambers. In this region, the period of low prices brought agricultural depression in the 1730's and 40's, and a fall in the incomes of farmers and landlords, who responded in part by converting their arable land to grass; but it is unlikely that the fall in farm incomes was general, for depression on the heavy soils of the Vale of Trent was offset by prosperity on the light soils, especially in East Anglia, where costs of production had fallen with the extension of crop rotation and turnip husbandry. The labourer benefitted from the period of low food prices, for as the cost of living fell, money wage rates apparently remained constant, while larger crops meant more employment and higher family earnings in harvest time. It is uncertain how far the labourers took out their higher real income in the form of manufactured goods rather than additional leisure or gin—for this was the so called gin age; but there seems to have been a general stimulus to the sales of manufactured goods. Moreover, low agricultural prices also meant lower costs for the many branches of industry using agricultural raw materials—such as soap making, brewing, starch making, milling, etc., and the growing exports of surplus grain, which reached unprecedented levels in the 1740's and early 50's, led to increased export earnings, a more favourable balance of payments, and possibly increased capital available for home investment. Although food prices rose from the mid 50's, population continued to increase and the demand for manufactured goods expanded further, aided by a spurt of exports. Under the pressure of this expansion, critical shortages began to appear in certain branches of textile manufacturing, and consequently there was an added inducement to employ labour-saving devices. The recovery of agricultural prices raised the incomes of the farming community, providing both the means and the incentives to further Parliamentary enclosures, improved farming methods, and turnpike construction; and by the 60's, the pressure on transport facilities, especially with the rising demand for coal, brought the beginnings of the canal age and the first water-powered cotton factories.

In this brief sketch of the process of mid-eighteenth century English economic growth I have deliberately concentrated on the bare essentials because I wish to devote the rest of my time to the population variable. Historical demography—the statistical study of population change in past societies—is nowadays the most fascinating and exciting field of historical research pertaining to economic growth, and it exemplifies the need for conscious and systematic collaboration between historians and social scientists. Of course, the current preoccupation with population change can have unfortunate consequences; as Professor Habbakuk remarked some years ago:

> For those who care for the overmastering pattern, the elements are evidently there for a heroically simplified version of English history before the nineteenth century in which the long-term movements in prices, in income distribution, in investment, in real wages, and in migration, are dominated by changes in the growth of real population . . . [and as] our knowledge of population movements is partly inferred from economic evidence . . . there is therefore no rigorous control on the natural temptation to turn 'population growth' on and off as the occasion requires and to treat it sometimes as independent of economic change and sometimes as a response to economic change.[23]

Nevertheless, despite the dangers, the population variable is important, not only because it looms so large in current explanations of economic growth, but also because it illustrates the economic and social historian's crucial dilemma, which stems from the conflicting demands of theory and fact.

No man can be a historian unless he has at least a touch of the antiquarian about him, unless he derives some simple-minded satisfaction from knowing how things really were in a part of the past . . . [and yet] in accepting economic growth as a central problem we shall, from one perspective, be forced to become general theorists of whole societies; for the motives of men and the human institutions which bear directly and technically on the rate of increase of output per capita are not narrowly limited. And our loyalty should be to the problem of economic growth, wherever it may take us, not to the bureaucratic confines of economic history or of economics as they are presently consecrated in our graduate schools.[24]

These are Professor Rostow's bold words, not mine, and they may be somewhat over-ambitious. But the dilemma posed for the economic and social historian is a real one, and I believe the study of population change gives some idea of the way it might be resolved. It involves two distinct elements: first, the systematic analysis of the *mechanism* of population change, especially through the statistical study of such variables as birth rates, death rates, marriage rates, ages of marriage, fertility, and their interrelationships; second, the search for the *causes* of population change. Both these enquiries must necessarily be conducted at the local and regional rather than the national level, since the raw data in parish registers and census reports are essentially local data; and in recognizing that the *causes* are not merely economic, we are forced to study the interactions between economic motives and opportunities and the social context. Students of underdeveloped countries now acknowledge the importance of the social and cultural dimensions of economic growth; economic growth, it might be said, is too interesting and important to be left to the economists; it calls for systematic collaboration between historians, economists, sociologists, demographers, anthropologists, and medical historians—and the list is by no means exhaustive. While offering glimpses of the broader patterns of change in entire societies it takes us into the most intimate matters of daily life, such as the organization and functions of marriage, the mechanism of conception and contraception, and the effects of nutrition on health and fertility. Though the statistical deluge continues it need not follow, as one scholar has complained, that the reader of economic history books must continue to encounter every conceivable figure except the human figure; on the contrary, we may at last obtain some reliable knowledge of the life of typical members of the poor in pre-industrial society—those virtually anonymous persons whom we encounter only through their baptismal, marriage and burial entries in the parish registers. Research of this type demands a combination of clear reasoning, statistical skill, and historical insight; its exponents include amateurs as well as a variety of specialist scholars; and sometimes its collaborators include the dead as well as the living, as in the case of the Vicar of Linton, Cambridgeshire, in 1780, who noted in his register:

> It has not been usual for many years past to register the sickly children who are named at home, till they are brought to Church to be incorporated. Consequently all that die and are never incorporated come into the List of Burials but not of Baptisms. This circumstance should be known to the curious who may be inclined to form their ideas of population from these lists.[25]

This is not the place to consider the complexities of the parish registers, or the laborious and painstaking process of family reconstitution by which British and European scholars are endeavouring to reconstruct the social structure of entire communities. Research of this kind reveals important elements of stability, as well as patterns of social and economic change, and the relevance of this to the process of economic growth has been admirably suggested by Professor Chambers' pioneer regional study of the *Vale of Trent*.

I have already referred to the interaction of population, agricultural output, and prices in mid-eighteenth century English economic growth, and stressed the importance of the home market for manufactured goods. Unfortunately, we know far too little about pre-industrial revolution patterns of work, leisure, and consumption, and no one has yet obtained detailed evidence of the responses of the labouring poor to the rise in real income during the 1730's and 1740's. Did they relax and drink more gin as the cost of living fell, as many contemporaries claimed; or did they spend a significant proportion of their additional purchasing power on manufactured goods?[26] We may never get a precise answer to this question; but Professor Chambers' study of the demographic differences between the agricultural and the industrial villages in the East Midlands may give us a clue—though what I should like to suggest goes well beyond the limits of his cautious conclusions. He discovered that in the industrial villages—those whose inhabitants were mainly engaged in domestic manufacturing, mining, or other non-agricultural pursuits—the marriage rate and the balance of baptisms over burials were higher than in the agricultural villages,[27] and these demographic differences may well represent the tip of a large iceberg of social change accompanying the shift from full or part time agricultural work to full time non-agricultural employment. Increased employment opportunities removed obstacles to early marriage[28] and permitted higher birth rates; and it may have been accompanied by a change of social attitudes which included a rise in the propensity to consume manufactured goods and a more positive response to economic incentives—a trend that some perceptive contemporaries like Adam Smith regarded as a natural consequence of economic growth.[29] Contrary to the majority of earlier writers, Smith and some of his contemporaries in the 1760's and 70's argued that when money wages rose those employed in manufacturing worked more, not less—and this suggests that with the extension of the market an earlier, more traditional, pattern of consumption had broken down. The relative shift of the occupied population from agriculture to manufacturing clearly facilitated the continuous rise in the birth rate; broadly speaking, the occupational changes also represented movements into demographically more productive sectors of the population; and as the cost of living rose from the mid 1750's it is conceivable that many labourers worked harder to maintain their enlarged families at the higher standard of living to which they had become accustomed during the period of low food prices. Thus a change in the attitude of the labouring classes towards manufactured goods—an attitude that shrewd employers like Richard Arkwright recognized and endeavoured to exploit—may have reinforced the growth of population in bringing about a growth of home demand sufficient to warrant the introduction and widespread diffusion of output-increasing mechanical innovations.

As this speculation indicates, the study of economic growth takes us far from the narrower economic issues of prices, costs, and outputs, into the more obscure corners of social life. In calling for a more systematic approach to economic and social history I would not go as far as E. H. Carr, who declared a few years ago that 'the more sociological history becomes, and the more historical sociology becomes, the better for both',[30] for that assertion is too sweeping and too easily misconstrued. But there *is* an urgent need for closer collaboration between historians and social scientists, and lest this be misinterpreted as an over-enthusiastic response to Mr. Laslett's current publicity campaign let me recall that R. H. Tawney, in his 1933 inaugural lecture on 'The Study of Economic History' emphasized his conviction that 'the future of history, and, in particular, of economic history, depends on its ability to acquire a more consciously sociological outlook'.[31] In making conscious and systematic use of the concepts and methods employed by social scientists the economic and social historian will not only discover fresh insights and new ways of investigating the past; he will also be less likely to adopt a crude form of 'reductionism' according to which the complexities of any historical situation are regarded as reducible to some key element or prime mover—a view that often produces a watered down Marxist type explanation of the past.

Fortunately, at long last, there are many indications of renewed activity across the conventional frontiers of history and economic history, for example in such recent works as Laurence Stone's *The Crisis of the Aristocracy*, Asa Briggs' *Victorian Cities* (the herald of a new era of urban history), and Edward Thompson's magnificent polemic, *The Making of the English Working Class*. Some of Thompson's strictures upon the narrower, more conventional 'economic' type of economic history are fully justified; but the outlook is hopeful, for the theme of economic growth, if treated broadly, can provide the basis for a synthesis of the two main traditions in the literature of our discipline—namely, the narrower, more analytical and economic work of Clapham, Ashton, and Rostow, on the one hand, and the more narrative, humanistic approach of Tawney, the Hammonds, and the Webbs.

IV

One of the inescapable duties of an inaugural lecturer is to pay his respects to his predecessor, and I have deliberately set aside this task until the end, for there can have been few occasions when its performance has given such unalloyed pleasure. Professor Chambers is now appropriately enough, among the emeriti; but he has not gone out to grass—fitting though that might be for an agricultural historian—for he is enjoying an extremely vigorous and productive retirement. As a man, he has long enjoyed the warm affection and respect of members of this University; but he is so modest and unassuming that I doubt whether his colleagues have realized how important his contributions to scholarship have been, or how distinguished is his reputation in the world of learning. While I have the honour to occupy his chair, I shall do my utmost to maintain and strengthen the tradition he inaugurated, and to minimise the irreparable loss the university has suffered by his retirement.

NOTES

1 J. D. Chambers, *The Place of Economic History in Historical Studies* (1960). [and above pp. 231–251].
2 See Barry E. Supple, 'Economic History and Economic Growth', *Journal of Economic History* Vol. 20. (1960) pp. 548–556; and M. M. Postan,

'Function and Dialectic in Economic History', *Economic History Review* 2nd. Ser. Vol. 14 (1962) pp. 397–407, for some general comments on this problem.

3   J. H. Clapham, *Concise Economic History of Britain* (1949) p. xvii.

4   F. H. Hahn & R. C. O. Matthews, 'The Theory of Economic Growth: A Survey', *Economic Journal* Vol. 74. (1964) pp. 779–902. For an earlier survey see Moses Abramovitz, 'Economics of Growth' in Bernard F. Haley (ed.) *A Survey of Contemporary Economics* (1952) pp. 132–182.

5   Cf. L. E. Davis, J. R. T. Hughes, & S. Reiter, 'Aspects of Quantitative Research in Economic History', *Journal of Economic History* Vol. 20. (1960) p. 540. For useful surveys of work of this type see R. Fogel, 'The Reunification of Economic History with Economic Theory', *American Economic Review* Vol. 55, pp. 92–9.; S. B. Saul, 'The New Economic History', *Bulletin of the British Association for American Studies* N.S. No. 11. (1966) pp. 24–34; and the critique by J. R. T. Hughes, 'Fact and Theory in Economic History', *Explorations in Entrepreneurial History* 2nd Ser. Vol. 3 (1966) pp. 75–100.

6   B. R. Mitchell & Phyllis Deane, *Abstract of British Historical Statistics* (1962); Phyllis Deane & W. A. Cole, *British Economic Growth 1688–1959*; *Trends and Structure* (1962).

7   See E. A. Wrigley (ed.) *An Introduction to English Historical Demography* (1965); also Peter Laslett, *The World We Have Lost* (1965) and his series of B.B.C. Third Programme talks in January and February 1966 entitled 'The Numerical Study of English Society'.

8   Lawrence R. Klein, *A Textbook of Econometrics* (1956) p. 2.

9   R. L. Bassman, 'The Role of the Economic Historian in Predictive Testing of Proffered "Economic Laws"', *Explorations in Entrepreneurial History* 2nd Ser. Vol. 2. (1965.) p. 173. Cf. Hughes, 'Fact and Theory in Economic History', *op. cit.*

10   However, exponents of the 'new' economic history argue, with some cogency, that it is precisely where the statistical data are limited and suspect that highly refined techniques (and, of course, good historical judgment) are needed to extract such valuable ore as they contain.

11   W. Ashworth, *An Economic History of England, 1870–1939* (1960) p. 4.

12   J. H. Clapham, 'Economic History as a Discipline', *Encyclopaedia of the Social Sciences* Vol. 5. (1930) p. 328.

13   W. N. Parker (ed), *Trends in the American Economy in the Nineteenth Century* (1960) pp. 9–10.

14   Quoted by Mrs. Humphrey Ward, *A Writer's Recollections* (1918) pp. 148–9.

15   For example, in the pages of *History and Theory*, a journal published triennially since 1960.

16   Cf. H. J. Habakkuk and P. Deane, 'The Take-off in Britain', in W. W. Rostow (ed.), *The Economics of Take-off into Sustained Growth* (1963) pp. 63–82. Rostow's take-off concept was originally published in the *Economic Journal* in 1956 and subsequently in *The Stages of Economic Growth* (1960).

17   Robert Solow, as cited by Rostow in *The Economics of Take-off*, p. xxiv. For Rostow's concept of 'disorganized complexity', *ibid*; p. 2.

18   See, for example, Deane and Cole, *op. cit*, Chap. 11, and, more recently, the brilliant survey of the literature by David Landes, in M. M. Postan and H. J. Habakkuk (eds.), *The Cambridge Economic History of Europe, Vol. VI:, The Industrial Revolutions and After* (1965) pp. 274–352.

19   This bald summary largely follows Deane and Cole, *op. cit.*, and David Eversley, 'In Pudding Time: The Early Stages of Industrialization in England, 1730–1780', an unpublished University of Birmingham Faculty of

Commerce Discussion Paper (1962). For a somewhat different emphasis see Landes, *op. cit.*, p. 288, and the authoritative article by Ralph Davis, 'English Foreign Trade, 1700–1774', *Econ. Hist. Rev.* 2nd Ser. Vol. 15 (1962) especially p. 290.

20   For a recent general survey see J. D. Chambers and G. E. Mingay, *The Agricultural Revolution* (1965).

21   J. D. Chambers, 'Enclosure and Labour Supply in the Industrial Revolution', *Econ. Hist. Rev.* 2nd Ser. Vol. 5 (1953).

22   The following paragraph is based on the works cited in the four preceding footnotes and: T. S. Ashton, *An Economic History of England: The Eighteenth Century* (1955); Ashton, *Economic Fluctuations in England, 1700–1800* (1959); Chambers, *The Vale of Trent 1670–1800: A Regional Study of Economic Change, Econ. Hist. Rev.* Supplement (1957); M. W. Flinn 'Agricultural Productivity and Economic Growth in England, 1700–1760: A Comment', *Jour. Econ. Hist.* Vol. 26 (1966); A. H. John 'Aspects of English Economic Growth in the First Half of the Eighteenth Century', *Economica* N.S. Vol. 28 (1961); John, 'Agricultural Productivity and Economic Growth in England, 1700–1760', *Jour. Econ. Hist.* Vol. 25 (1965); E. L. Jones, 'Agriculture and Economic Growth in England, 1660-1750: Agricultural Change', *ibid.*; G. E. Mingay 'The Agricultural Depression, 1730–1750', *Econ. Hist. Rev.* 2nd. Ser. Vol. 8 (1956); Charles Wilson, *England's Apprenticeship* 1603–1763 (1965) Part 3.

23   H. J. Habakkuk, 'The Economic History of Modern Britain', *Jour. Econ. Hist.* Vol. 18 (1958), reprinted in a valuable collection of papers edited by D. V. Glass and D. E. C. Eversley, *Population in History: Essays in Historical Demography* (1965) pp. 150–1.

24   W. W. Rostow, 'The Interrelation of Theory and Economic History', *Jour. Econ. Hist.* Vol. 17 (1957) pp. 513, 522–3.

25   Cited by Wrigley, *op. cit.*, p. 156.

26   Cf. the discussion of this point by A. H. John, 'Agricultural Productivity and Economic Growth', *op. cit.*, pp. 182–7.

27   Chambers, *Vale of Trent, op. cit.*, pp. 51–5.

28   Professor Chambers did not specifically commit himself to the view that the age of marriage fell, and the point is still disputed by experts. For an important recent study of the flexibility of the age of brides and the size of families see E. A. Wrigley, 'Family Limitation in Pre-Industrial England', *Econ. Hist. Rev.* 2nd Ser. Vol. 19 (1966) pp. 82–109.

29   For evidence of contemporary opinion see my article 'Changing Attitudes to Labour in the Mid Eighteenth Century', *Econ. Hist. Rev.* 2nd Ser. Vol.11 (1958). Cf. Eversley, 'In Pudding Time', *op. cit.*, pp. 28–30.

30   E. H. Carr, *What is History?* (1961) p. 60.

31   R. H. Tawney, 'The Study of Economic History', *Economica* N.S. Vol. 13 (1933) p. 19 [and above p. 105.].

20

W. A. Cole

ECONOMIC HISTORY AS A SOCIAL SCIENCE
(Swansea, 1967)

This inaugural lecture was delivered at the University College of Swansea on the 24th October 1967.

ECONOMIC HISTORY AS A SOCIAL SCIENCE

I HOPE I may be forgiven if I begin this evening by counting my blessings. Anyone in my position, who is called upon publicly to justify his subject, and in a measure at least himself, to an audience of his colleagues and peers, must, I suppose, regard the assignment with rather mixed feelings. But whatever misgivings I may have on this occasion—and I will not pretend that they do not exist—they cannot conceal the sense of pride which I also feel at being asked to occupy the first chair of Economic History in this University College, and, indeed, in the University of Wales. In a sense, I must confess that it seems a little inappropriate that this honour should have fallen on me as an Englishman, for as many of you will know, Wales has a proud record of endeavour in the field of economic history of its own. Quite apart from the distinguished contributions which have been made to the subject by Professor Brinley Thomas and others here in Wales, we should not forget that the occupants of the chairs at both Oxford and Cambridge, and one of the professors at the London School of Economics, all have very close connections with this part of the world. But for my own part I am particularly happy that I should have been invited to occupy a chair here in Swansea, in such delightful surroundings, in such congenial company, and with so many signs of growth and vitality around me.

I have a further reason for gratification this evening, namely that I should have the good fortune to address you on behalf of a discipline that has made such rapid advances in recent years. Indeed, I think it is fair to say that in the past few years there has been a revolution in the status of economic history. The subject itself is not, of course, new, though it is certainly much younger than most other branches of historical study. Most of the great classical economists, from Adam Smith to Karl Marx, drew freely on historical experience to illustrate their theories, and some of them, such as Marx, were as much historians as economic theorists. Moreover, in the late eighteenth and early nineteenth centuries, there were a number of specialized studies of the history of trade, industry and prices which in fact, if not in name, must rank as works of economic history. By the beginning of the twentieth century, thanks to the labours of men like Thorold Rogers, Archdeacon Cunningham and

Sir William Ashley in this country, and Max Weber and Werner Sombart on the Continent, the subject had clearly begun to take shape as a field of study in its own right; and since the 1920's this fact has been underlined by the regular appearance of learned journals devoted to it, *Economic History*, a supplement to the *Economic Journal*, and only a little later, the *Economic History Review*. But until recently economic history had scarcely begun to gain recognition as a legitimate subject for specialised study at the undergraduate level. Twenty years ago nearly all economic historians were trained either as historians or economists, and there were only two chairs in the subject in British universities outside London, Oxford and Cambridge, Moreover, even where chairs existed, the subject usually continued to occupy a strictly subordinate place within the established disciplines of history or economics; and at both the ancient universities, especially Oxford, this remains true even today. But in many of the newer universities there has been a remarkable change: new chairs have been created, separate Departments of Economic History have been established, and about half of Britain's university institutions now offer some kind of economic history degree. Belfast, Exeter, Kent, Leeds, Nottingham and Sheffield all provide single-subject courses, and in many other institutions, including, of course, this University College, it is possible to 'major' in economic history in one or more combined-subject courses.

There are several reasons for this transformation. To a large extent, the emergence of the new discipline is simply the result of the increasing specialization which accompanies the growth of human knowledge. For the study of economic history cannot readily be undertaken by one who has received a conventional training in either general historical studies or economic theory. If the historian is to make sense of the past he often needs to make use of the analytical tools developed by other social scientists. But it is clearly impossible for any historian to keep up with the relevant developments in all the social sciences, and at the same time to master our ever-increasing knowledge of the whole of the past. Unless he confines his energies to the understanding of one aspect of human experience, and to the theoretical developments most relevant to his own particular field of study, there is a real danger that he will become a 'Jack of all trades and master of none'. And in the same way, the professional economist is not likely to get far in economic history unless he has acquired some of the historian's skill in analysing historical evidence, his understanding of the multifarious influences, geographic, social, political and cultural, as well as the purely economic, which help to produce economic changes; and unless, above all, he has acquired that highly developed 'historical sense' which comes from constant study and reflection about the past. Hence the need to produce a peculiar breed of historian who is prepared to devote his attention to the problems of man's economic development, and who is equipped with the necessary theoretical and statistical tools to aid him in this task.

But why, you may ask, should the process of specialisation have gone so much further in economic history than in most other branches of historical study? For many years historians have tended to specialize in a particular period or branch of history, but this development has not usually resulted in the emergence of distinctive disciplines or the creation of separate university departments for their advancement. Clearly, part of the explanation must lie in the fact that the links between history and theory are very much closer in the analysis of economic changes than they are in some other branches of historical study. Indeed, many historians, particularly those concerned with the narration and explanation of political events, would deny that any elaborately articulated body of theory can be of assistance to them in their work. For the student of economic and social changes, on the other hand, the need for theory is much more pressing, and the economic historian who, for example, tried to explain the rise in prices in sixteenth-century England without some understanding of the quantity theory of money and the laws of supply and demand would soon find himself in rather deep waters. But it is also true that the progress of economic history as an independent discipline would hardly have been so rapid in recent years if there had not been significant developments in both its parent disciplines of history and economics.

On the historical side, much the most important development has been the influence of Marxism, which has enormously heightened our understanding of the importance of economic factors in shaping the process of historical change. This does not mean, of course, that the study of economic history itself implies a commitment to an economic *interpretation* of history. For economic history is concerned with the factors which determine the course of economic development, not with the influence of economic changes in other spheres of human activity. And although, like other historians, students of economic development may have views about the importance of the economic factor, they are very far from being united by a belief in its primacy in human affairs. Yet it is undoubtedly true that the recognition by most twentieth-century historians, including non-Marxists, that economic development is important, both in itself, and because of its repercussions on art and religion, politics and social institutions, has greatly stimulated research into the causes of economic change.

No less significant have been the changes in the outlook of economists, changes which have both strengthened the interest of economists in historical developments and, at the same time, heightened the awareness by economic historians of the contribution which economic theory can make to the progress of their own subject. We have seen that, in its earliest years, economic history was closely associated with the rise of the great classical school of political economy. In the course of the nineteenth century, however, the links between history and theory weakened: gradually political economy turned into economics, as economists, in their search for universal economic laws, tended to contract their area of interest, to isolate economic phenomena from their historical context, and to concentrate attention on those relationships which could be readily expressed in mathematical terms. Moreover, partly for this reason, and perhaps partly because in the Victorian era economic progress could almost be taken for granted, orthodox economists ceased to display that interest in the conditions of economic growth which had informed both Adam Smith's celebrated *Inquiry into the Nature and Causes of the Wealth of Nations* and most of the other major works of the classical school. Hence it is scarcely surprising that the new economics often appeared to have little relevance for the minority of scholars who retained an interest in the problems of economic history. Certainly, any layman who has witnessed the frequently violent disagreements between economists on matters of current economic policy may understand the feeling of many economic historians that, for all its dazzling intellectual achievements, the isolation of economic problems from their social context has not greatly increased the ability of economics to elucidate the problems of the real world.

In the twentieth century, this process of refinement in economic studies has continued, but in certain respects there has been a significant change. In the first place, historical developments have encouraged economists to modify many of their traditional ideas: the theory of imperfect competition, for example, involves some recognition of the fact that many of the laws which applied in the relatively free market conditions of the nineteenth century no longer operate in the same way in the different conditions of the twentieth. Secondly, and perhaps even more important, the experience of the inter-war years destroyed men's faith in the inevitability of steady economic progress; and since the Second World War, the competition between East and West and the efforts of underdeveloped countries to set their feet on the industrial ladder, have once again stimulated interest in the problems of economic development. Today, the manufacture of theories of economic growth has become a flourishing industry, and just as economists are beginning to show a renewed interest in the historical facts against which they can test their theoretical models, so, too, the economic historian is being equipped with a whole new range of tools which he can bring to bear in his efforts to explain and interpret the course of economic change.

Yet curiously enough this blossoming of economic history is taking place at a time when the faith of many in the value of historical studies as a whole has been seriously undermined. A generation or so ago it was commonly believed that the study of the past would provide us with the key which would help us to solve the problems of the present and even to unlock the secrets of the future. Today we are not so sure. The more we learn, the more we realize how little we do or can know. It is not simply that many of the relevant facts about the past can never be ascertained, although the violence of the seemingly endless controversies over apparently simple questions of historical fact, which once appeared to have been settled, must make us conscious of the limits and frailty of the historian's art. Many have even doubted whether any objective knowledge of the past is possible, since the historian cannot directly observe historical events but must perforce rely on what contemporaries thought, or professed to believe, about their world, or on those scattered and often fragmentary historical records which have been deemed worthy of preservation. But there is also the much more fundamental difficulty that even the facts which can be established are not self-explanatory. And as soon as we move from the mundane task of trying to describe what happened in history to explaining *why* it happened, we rapidly become aware of certain difficulties which have led many to suppose that an historical explanation is radically different in character, and much more restricted in its application, than the laws of the natural sciences. For it is evident that the course of human history is continually being influenced, to a greater or lesser extent, by the vagaries of the weather, the accidents of human personality and the multitude of other phenomena which together constitute the element of chance in human affairs. It is true that what we call chance is not necessarily incapable of rational explanation. When a historian attributes a particular event to chance, all that he means is that its cause lies outside the historian's province. But the fact that history is, in this sense, an 'incomplete causal system' necessarily means that it cannot have the same predictive value as the exact sciences. Nor does the difference between historical and scientific explanation end there. Indeed some writers have claimed that even in what may properly be regarded as the historian's province, there are no such things as historical laws: 'Historical laws are not just more or less difficult to find—the very concept of historical law carries an inner contradiction'.[1] Or as Karl Popper puts it: 'Generalization belongs simply to a different line of interest, sharply to be distinguished from that interest in specific events and their causal explanation which is the business of history'.[2] The reason usually advanced for this is that every past event is in a sense unique. History never repeats itself in exactly the same way, if only because everything that happens necessarily influences the course of all subsequent development, nor can it be artificially reproduced in an historical laboratory. The historian cannot, therefore, test his theories by experiment: he can only attempt to formulate hypotheses which appear to fit all the facts as he knows them. And more important, his explanation of specific events can never have a universal validity. Indeed, the scientist might be forgiven if he concluded that they are rather pointless: certainly there would be little value in trying to explain why water boils when it is heated if it could only be heated once.

Anyone with even the slightest acquaintance with history can scarcely ignore such formidable difficulties. Yet the historian who claims a scientific status for his subject clearly cannot admit that they are insurmountable without forfeiting his claim; and it may well be that one reason why economic history, alone among the different branches of historical study, is today establishing its position in the Social Science Faculties of British universities, is that economic historians have been rather less inclined than some of their colleagues to indulge in the pessimism of the 'history teaches us that history teaches us nothing' school. Nor is it evident that they are wrong. For although it is true that the study of history presents us with peculiarly difficult problems, I certainly do not believe that it is pointless or that the methodology and aims of the historian need be fundamentally different from those of other scientists.

But we must begin at the beginning. Scientific study of any kind, whether it be in the realm of nature or society, depends on the availability of adequate objective information. The difficulty of obtaining the necessary information presents problems for most of the social sciences and in history these problems are more difficult to solve than elsewhere. Since the historian cannot directly observe past events he is dependent for his knowledge on what he can learn from those records which have survived, and it is certainly true that the records are frequently biassed, fragmentary and misleading. All this is true. But it does not follow that objective knowledge of the past is impossible. This point cannot be emphasised too strongly, and I am glad to learn that it has recently been re-affirmed by no less an historian than Professor G. R. Elton,[3] a scholar whose interests and general approach to history could hardly be more different from my own. For the first requirement for any historian is that he should learn how to handle the evidence which is available to him. He must learn to assess the credibility of his witnesses, test the internal consistency of their testimony, and wherever possible check it against other types of evidence. Only then, when the evidence *obliges* him to believe it, can he be said to know something about the past. Sometimes the evidence available may be too fragmentary to enable him to conclude that a particular event in fact occurred, and in that case he must confess his ignorance. But at others he may be able to *infer* that something took place even when no direct evidence of it is available, or indirectly to confirm a supposition which may have been suggested by the fragments of evidence which have survived.

Here perhaps I may be permitted to cite an example from my own experience. Some years ago, as a young research worker, I was confronted with the problem of trying to measure the amount of smuggling in eighteenth-century Britain, in order to assess its possible effect on the official statistics of overseas trade. At first this problem seemed insoluble, since, in the nature of the case, the smugglers had not been obliging enough to leave us any records of their activities. There were, it is true, a few conflicting, and far from disinterested, contemporary estimates of the extent of the illicit traffic; but although I suspected that the truth might lie somewhere between the extremes which they suggested, there appeared to be no way of testing the the accuracy of my guess. Fortunately, however, the legal imports of one of the more important smuggled commodities, tea, were monopolized by the East India Company, and we have records of the quantity and price of all tea sold at the Company's sales. By analysing the fluctuations in the demand for legally imported tea, and in particular the effects of the major changes in duty which were likely to affect the illicit traffic, I was able to make my own estimates of the quantity of tea smuggled. As it happened, these estimates confirmed my original guess that the illicit traffic was rather less widespread than the contemporary advocates of freer trade professed to believe, but more extensive than the government officials of the day cared to admit. And since other evidence was available which suggested that the smuggling of other contraband goods varied in much the same way as the traffic in tea, I was able to deduce the probable trends in the smuggling trade as a whole.

It is true, of course, that however scrupulous the historian may be in his handling of the evidence, and however diligent in his search for clues which will enable him to interpret more fully the scraps of information available to him, he can never achieve final certainty: it is always possible that some new piece of evidence may come to light which will compel him to change his mind. But this is also the case in any other branch of science, and the fact that the historian cannot directly observe the past does not alter the position. I understand that no geneticist has ever seen a gene; nor can protons or neutrons be directly observed by the nuclear physicist, although an image of them may be projected on to a screen. But so far as I am aware, no-one has therefore suggested that the study of genetics and nuclear physics should be transferred to the Faculty of Arts.

If, then, the special nature of past events does not in itself prevent the historian from achieving objective knowledge of them, how far can he provide a rational explanation of the facts which he can discover? As we have seen there are two principal reasons which have been advanced for the belief that scientific and historical explanation are fundamentally incompatible, which are connected with the importance of chance in human affairs and the alleged uniqueness of historical events. The first of these objections need not detain us long, for it appears to rest on a real but somewhat exaggerated distinction between the nature of the events which historians and other types of scientist try to explain. When a scientist explains a particular event he does so in terms of a given set of initial conditions and some causal law or generalization. Now it is true that at various times, such phenomena as Cleopatra's nose, the survival of Lenin in 1917, or even the Russian winter, have exerted a significant influence on the course of history, and that these phenomena cannot be readily explained in terms of the particular conjuncture of historical forces which historians frequently adduce to explain the events with which they are concerned. But in many other fields of study, including, I understand, that of atomic physics, there are likewise areas of uncertainty, random occurrences which cannot be explained at least in terms of the ordinary causal laws pertaining to that branch of science. We may freely admit that in history such random occurrences are more frequent than elsewhere. But it does not follow that there is a distinction in principle between historical and other types of explanation, unless, of course, we are prepared to assert that the random variables always dominate the course of events. To be sure, some historians have appeared to do just that. Thus, H. A. L. Fisher, in an unguarded and rather over-quoted passage, professed to see in history 'only one great emergency following upon another as wave follows wave, only one great fact with respect to which, since it is unique, there can be no generalizations, only one safe rule for the historian: that he should recognize in the development of human destinies the play of the contingent and the unforeseen'.[4] If this statement is accepted at its face value, it would appear that any rational explanation of historical events is impossible, and we should have to conclude with E. M. Forster that history is simply a mess, or more precisely, 'a series of messes'.[5] But very few historians, including Fisher himself, have in practice adopted such an extreme view, however much they may disagree amongst themselves about the role of chance in general or in particular historical situations. Thus some historians may be prepared to argue that if Princip had not murdered the Austrian Archduke Franz Ferdinand at Sarajevo in 1914, the First World War might never have occurred. But most would probably agree that given the state of international relations at the time any spark might have set Europe ablaze. And this is as it should be. For the historian, like many other scientists, cannot insist on rigid determination. Rather his task must be to narrow the range of alternative possibilities and to predict the most likely outcome, given a set of initial conditions and the causal law appropriate to his own field of enquiry.[6]

This brings me to the wider question of the role of universal laws in history. I do not wish to pursue here at length that rather hoary old will-o'-the-wisp of so-called universal historical laws. For it is clear that, in formal terms, such a universal historical law, or body of laws, is no more than a tautology, since history as a whole is a unique sequence of events. Nevertheless, there is a variety of more or less meta-historical theories which claim to discern in history the working of some universal law which would ultimately explain all historical changes. All through the ages there have been those who believed that the hand of Providence was at work, guiding and controlling the destinies of men: sometimes this has taken the form of a belief in direct supernatural intervention in human affairs, and at others a belief in a universal moral law against which men rebel at their peril. Each of us is at liberty to have such a belief, and I, for one, having spent my years as a research student, studying the lives and thought of the early Quakers, certainly learned to respect and admire, if not entirely to share, the sublime and unshakeable faith of those simple men of the seventeenth century, a faith which enabled them to withstand persecution and death, and at last to win for themselves and others that measure of toleration for the individual conscience which today we regard as one of the essential characteristics of a liberal state. Yet it must, I think, be clear that the belief in such a universal moral law is a matter of faith, not reason, and as such it is not a question on which the historian can pronounce. For when we ask if it is true that in history individuals and societies have committed crimes and got away with it, the answer must be that sometimes they have done so and sometimes not. This does not necessarily mean, of course, that the Providential view of history is wrong, but merely that in common with all such meta-historical theories, it finds its *ultimate* justification not *in* history, but beyond or outside it.

Similar considerations apply—although rather less obviously—to the Marxist interpretation of history to which I referred earlier. If the Marxist asserted that all historical changes are the direct result of economic developments, it would be easy to prove him wrong. But he does not. In the course of his efforts to satisfy his material needs, the Marxist will tell us, man enters into certain social relationships, and from these ultimately arise all those ideas and institutions which go to make up the 'superstructure' of society. And once again the key word is 'ultimately'. For the Marxist does not deny that once it has come into existence the superstructure has a life of its own and acts and reacts on the material base. But if so, how are we to prove or disprove the frequent Marxist assertion that economic changes are ultimately decisive? The word 'ultimately' here cannot mean 'initially', for in that case we should have to assume that all great economic changes are in some sense self-motivating. But that is clearly not what the Marxist means. For he sometimes argues that economic changes initially stem from technological advances. But this only brings us back to the superstructure again, and so the circle is complete. Of course, the Marxist is quite right in claiming that economic changes frequently do have profound repercussions, and as I suggested earlier his point of view has had a pronounced influence on modern historical writing. At its best it may suggest a number of useful questions which we may put to historical data; but, like all other such theories, it cannot possibly provide us with an empirically verifiable law which would explain all observable historical changes.

But if the concept of an all-embracing historical law or laws must be regarded as illusory, it does not necessarily follow that we must also reject the view that in history there are no historical laws in the more limited sense in which the term is employed in other sciences. Of course, if all historical events are unique, clearly there could be no historical laws. But is this really so? For although it is true that no two historical events are ever identical, it is absurd to pretend that they never have anything in common. History is littered with examples of wars, revolutions, and innumerable other phenomena, each of which is in a sense unique, but each of which has certain characteristics in common with others of its kind. And if this is so, we may reasonably ask why it should be impossible to generalize about them. The answer sometimes given is that although somewhat similar events do occur in history, they are not sufficiently alike for us to be able to frame laws about them. Historians can, and sometimes do, make rough and ready generalizations which may provide a useful guide to the understanding of particular events. But such generalizations do not have the status of laws, for they are usually so loosely formulated that they cannot be tested and often do not pretend to universal application.

Now we may freely admit that in history the task of formulating verifiable laws presents us with peculiar problems. But are they as insoluble as many philosophers and historians profess to believe? For if historical data are so unamenable to quantification and generalization as this position implies, should we not have to conclude that no social science is possible? In this connection it is interesting to note that Professor Popper, whom we quoted earlier on the subject of historical laws or generalizations, does not deny the existence of *sociological* laws; and in *The Poverty of Historicism* he specifies a number of them, such as Plato's law of revolutions and Lord Acton's well-known law of corruption, which he quite rightly says social scientists may discuss and attempt to substantiate.[7] But several of the laws which he cites could just as well be described as historical, since they are either general propositions about certain relationships obtaining in given historical situations, or generalizations about particular types of historical change. Nevertheless, Popper argues that from his point of view historical laws do not exist because historians are not interested in framing or testing them. This is because the historian is concerned with the explanation of specific events, and although he must make use of general laws, most of the rather 'trivial' laws he needs may be taken for granted. Hence the historian consumes theories but does not produce them.[8]

Now this somewhat surprising conclusion is important, for similar views have been expressed by many historians. The historian, it is said, is interested in historical events in all their richness and variety, and does not seek to subsume them under general laws. He is interested in the causes of *this* war, not of wars in general. He may seek to explain a particular situation in which he is interested in terms of some general hypothesis, but regards this more as an 'explanation sketch' which requires filling in, rather than as a case of a general law. Nor is he interested in proving or disproving the general law which his hypothesis implies, but only in ascertaining whether it can be applied to the particular situation with which he is concerned. And he will probably regard the man who does seek in history the validation of general laws, not as an historian, but as something else.[9]

But this position cannot, I think, be adopted by an *economic* historian. For unlike some of his colleagues who may be able to assume Popper's 'trivial universal laws' in seeking for explanations of the events with which he is concerned, the economic historian is engaged in the task of trying to explain man's economic development, a highly complex process governed by laws which as yet are only

2c

dimly perceived. To be sure, as I mentioned at the beginning, he can turn to his economist colleagues for many of the general laws of economic behaviour which he may need in his work, though he will sometimes find that they are not always applicable as they stand to all historical situations. But when it is a question of laws of economic development the position is rather different. The economist may be able to offer him a variety of useful and sometimes highly sophisticated theoretical models, but in the nature of the case few of these will have much empirical foundation. For the economic historian alone is in a position by his observation of the past to frame the relevant hypotheses, to test them against the available data and then to try to establish the empirical laws which he needs. And in recent years economic historians have, particularly in the United States, begun to elaborate a number of schema which are designed to conceptualize and elucidate the course of development. As yet, it must be confessed, their success has been limited. The schemes offered have tended to be taxonomic rather than fully explanatory in character, sometimes their formulation has not made them susceptible to ready verification, and usually they have been based on a limited sample of historical experience. This is hardly surprising, for the problems involved are formidable, and as we saw at the beginning, economic history as a fully-fledged discipline is still in its infancy. But at least a start has been made and hypotheses have been put forward which humbler scholars may be able to test and amplify as they dig deeper into the past.

Thus it appears that most of the objections which have been raised against regarding historical studies as a branch of science can be answered, and if history as a whole has not achieved that status this is in part because most of its practitioners have not sought to develop it in that way. Today, however, it seems that we are witnessing the growth of a new discipline which unites the traditions of historical and economic enquiry, and which in embryo at least may justifiably be regarded as a genuine social science. But if this is so we may perhaps enquire how much bearing this new branch of knowledge has on man's contemporary concerns. Most sciences derive their social justification, if not their academic rationale, from the fact that by increasing our understanding they help man to master his world. How far can the same be said of economic history?

The answer I should give to this question would, I think, be threefold. In the first place, since most contemporary economic problems have their roots in the past, the study of the historical record should enable us to achieve a fuller diagnosis of these problems even though it cannot in itself provide us with the solutions. Secondly, as in any other branch of history, the study of the past enables us to evaluate our own society and thought in the light of the standards and aspirations of another age. And thirdly, we may sometimes find in the rich storehouse of historical experience examples which, if judiciously interpreted, may have particular applications to the problems of today. When we enquire, for example, how far Soviet experience in the process of industrialisation can be regarded as a model for underdeveloped countries today, we are asking a question of the most urgent practical importance to millions of people throughout the world. Yet we cannot begin to answer such a question unless we first know why Soviet industrialization took the form which it did. Of course it is true that no amount of historical understanding will enable us to give a precise and complete answer to our initial question. But the more we know, not only about the Soviet case, but also about the experience of other industrial countries in different historical conditions, the more likely we are to be able to make an informed estimate of the possibilities open to underdeveloped countries today.

I say 'possibilities' rather than 'probabilities' because we can only say what *may* happen, not what is *likely* to happen, Or, to put the point another way, we can only say what is likely to happen on certain unverifiable assumptions. This is not primarily because any prediction we may make may be upset by the intervention of chance: indeed, it can be argued that, in principle at least, the problem of the chance element has been exaggerated. In some types of economic prediction the chance element may be small, and in others it may be possible to estimate both the statistical probability of many types of random occurrence and their likely effect. But there is also the much more fundamental difficulty that the course of human history is influenced, sometimes decisively, by the growth of human knowledge. An increase in knowledge cannot be regarded as a chance element in the sense that we defined it earlier, that is to say as an event outside the realm of historical explanation; but as Popper has pointed out, it is nevertheless largely indeterminate in that we cannot know today what we shall only know tomorrow.[10]

Perhaps we may illustrate this point by reference to one of the most famous of all historical predictions, Marx's prophecy of the impending end of the capitalist system. A crucial element in the Marxian diagnosis of the 'laws of motion of capitalist society' was the supposed law of the falling rate of profit. According to Marx, it was an outstanding feature of the process of capital accumulation that outlays on fixed capital and raw materials would tend to increase in relation to wages. This was because, in the nineteenth century, most innovations were labour- rather than capital-saving in their effect; and in consequence as new and more powerful machines were invented to do the work of men capital costs per unit of output necessarily tended to increase. Hence it followed that if the shares of the total product obtained by capital, on the one hand, in the form of rent, interest and profit, and of labour, on the other, were to remain constant, the rate of profit must fall. It should be stressed that Marx did not assert that the rate of profit would fall in all circumstances, but that it would *tend* to fall. Capitalists might, for example, try to increase their share of the total product at the expense of labour, although in that case the system would be on the other horn of its dilemma, the contradiction between the impoverishment of the mass of the population and the wealth they had created. But since Marx regarded the tendency of the rate of profit to fall as a law which would ensure that economic crises would recur and become progressively deeper, he presumably believed that in the long run the various counter-vailing tendencies which he noted could not be of decisive importance.

Now and interesting attempt[11] to test this analysis in the light of the historical record, suggests that in the United States, despite some increase in what Marx termed the rate of exploitation of the working population, the rate of profit did reveal a long-term tendency to fall in the period before 1914. But since the First World War this has not been the case, largely because many new technical innovations have tended to economize capital as well as labour. In other words, changes in human knowledge which Marx might have foreseen, but could not confidently predict, have rendered his celebrated law inoperative.

This does not mean, of course, that all Marx's predictions have been completely falsified by events. It is possible, though perhaps unlikely, that the long-term tendency of the rate of profit to fall may yet reassert itself. It can be argued that the effect of capital saving innovations in a society geared to a high rate of savings and investment created new problems which partially help to explain the unprecedented crash of 1929; and anyone who has read Professor J. K. Galbraith may suspect that the problems of an 'affluent society' will ultimately prove as formidable as any which Marx anticipated. And finally, of course, although proletarian revolutions have not taken place in the advanced capitalist countries as Marx predicted, his expectation that economic processes would be subjected to a greater measure of social control is being progressively fulfilled in all modern industrial countries. Nevertheless, a hunch is not the same thing as a scientific prediction, and it certainly cannot be maintained that Marx's expectations have so far been fulfilled in quite the way he anticipated. But even if it could be shown that all his prophecies were completely false, it would not follow that

Marx's labours were in vain. For it remains true that the Marxian analysis provides us with a profound insight into the workings of nineteenth-century capitalism and it does not take much perspicacity to see that an intelligent opponent of Marx might have learned from him what needed to be done to invalidate the master's 'laws'. Such an understanding would not and could not have given our imaginary upholder of capitalism any guarantee of success, any more than Marx would have been justified in assuming that he was bound to fail. But at least it would have told him the direction in which he should try to move.

In short, then, because men are not merely the slaves of their past, it is not given to the historian to predict the future. As Alexander Gerschenkron, one of the greatest living exponents of economic history has put it, 'No past experience, however rich, and no historical research, however thorough, can save the living generation the creative task of finding their own answers and shaping their own future'.[12] But if we are not the slaves of the past, we are its children. It must be the historian's ultimate aim, by deepening our understanding of the past, to help us to catch a fuller glimpse of the possibilities of the present, so that we may decide how best to shape our own future. And that, perhaps, is justification enough.

NOTES

1 Heinrich Rickert, *Die Grenzen der naturwissenschaftlichen Begriffsbildung*, quoted in A. H. Conrad and J. R. Meyer, *Studies in Econometric History* (London, 1965), p. 6
2 K. R. Popper, *The Open Society and its Enemies* (London, 1957), Vol. II, p. 264
3 G. R. Elton, *The Practice of History* (Sydney, 1967).
4 H. A. L. Fisher, *A History of Europe* (London, 1952), p. vi.
5 Quoted in Patrick Gardiner, *The Nature of Historical Explanation* (London, 1952), p. 51
6 Conrad and Meyer, *Studies in Econometric History*, p. 13.
7 K. R. Popper, *The Poverty of Historicism* (London, 1957), pp. 62–3
8 *The Open Society and its Enemies*, Vol. II, pp. 261–5
9 Cf. Patrick Gardiner, *The Nature of Historical Explanation*, pp. 80–99
10 *The Poverty of Historicism*, pp. ix–x.
11 Joseph M. Gillman, *The Falling Rate of Profit* (London, 1957).
12 Alexander Gerschenkron, *Economic Backwardness in Historical Perspective* (New York, 1965), p. 6

21

Peter Mathias

LIVING WITH THE NEIGHBOURS: THE ROLE OF ECONOMIC HISTORY
(Oxford, 1970)

This inaugural lecture was delivered at the Hall of All Souls College, Oxford on the 24th November 1970.

LIVING WITH THE NEIGHBOURS:
THE ROLE OF ECONOMIC HISTORY

SMALL countries are more influenced by their neighbours than large; small countries without defensible linear frontiers, over whose territories all neighbours enjoy grazing rights, may be hard put to it to maintain their identity at all. Economic history, as its hybrid name acknowledges, occupies such a role between the major powers of history and economics, at once its neighbours and its parent disciplines, but has been subject to periodic incursions from more distant quarters, such as anthropology, law, and theology and now, increasingly, from sociology. Every invasion has left its mark; even if no colonies survive, genetical influences are absorbed. Being a small, relatively new subject (at least in institutionalized ways with special university degrees, posts, and examination papers), most established scholars have come into it from adjacent disciplines in history and economics. In Britain history has been the principal progenitor; in the United States economics—at least for modern economic history. In Oxford and Cambridge, as elsewhere, it lives without a freehold of its own, with lodgings in both history and social studies, enjoying a presence on the menu in both establishments, but never a solid meal in either, with a double ration of committees and half the number of students. And the economic historian, caught between history and economics, never knowing where booksellers may choose to locate the wares he wants, commonly having to change his faculty whenever he crosses the Atlantic, is for ever a historian among economists; an economist among historians. As Housman said in another college hall when professor of latin: 'Here stand I, a better poet than Porson, a better scholar than Wordsworth, betwixt and between.' These trivia of uncertainty are to be seen as the symbols of deeper gulfs, just as profound theological incompatibilities once broke surface to astonished villagers as controversies about altar clothes and tables, candles and images.

The institutional consequences of eclecticism have reinforced the intellectual. On one side of him, the economic historian sees historians complaining that those things which are patently unequal—the unreality of necessarily restrictive assumptions—rob the theoretical models of economists, however immutably their conclusions must follow from the assumptions in their internal logic, of operational value in explaining the broader problems of change within a specific context, which historians customarily encounter. Economists, standing on the other side of him—even those who have written economic history—lament that the data served up by historians are unsystematic to the point of futility for testing theory and that, in any case, the hypotheses of historians are usually so naïve, or so unconsciously adopted, that their data is bound to be indiscriminate. Even worse, the number of variables brought into the explanation of change by historians is so thoughtlessly large, and their nature so tediously heterogeneous, as to defy mathematical formulation in principle, let alone regression analysis in practice. Economic history may be fun: it can never be useful.

Nor, alas, can these problems be resolved definitively by economists relaxing their assumptions and increasing their variables, or by historians collecting data more systematically—although all these can help. Controversies will doubtless continue over the assumptions required to make exact theorizing possible, while historical controversies customarily collapse under the weight of semantic confusion amid pleas for more systematic research.

Economic historians themselves range across the spectrum, like their subject. Some are general historians in *mufti* applying the conventions of study current in writing history, customarily with a very low degree of theorizing, to economic data of various kinds. Others see themselves as straight economists putting a time dimension to economic theory and econometrics. The proselytizing zeal of these 'new' economic historians is now giving the subject a seachange. Trained as economists, established among economists and econometricians, they remain true disciples and, as missionaries carrying the gospel into strange lands, proclaim the message that economic history is newly united to economic theory.[1] Only the rare scholars in economic history can escape the condescension of economists or historians. Happily, in Oxford, such eminence has been always present, not least with my predecessor in this chair, equating the application of theory with critical evaluation of evidence which customarily polarize the professional skills of economist and historian.

II

In reality, of course, all historical work relates to adjacent disciplines; medieval political history to theology and law no less than economic history to the social sciences. But the ideas, theoretical assumptions and techniques of study prevailing in neighbouring social sciences have given economic history a greater theoretical impetus and a greater commitment to quantitative evidence (with the techniques for manipulating this) than other branches of history. It has thus become the main testing ground, or battlefield, for these incursions into history as a whole, and been cast, by some historians, in the role of a Trojan horse, infiltrating subversive forces of theory into the historical camp.

Conflicts over the relationships between history and theory will not cease but, although expressed in the same general terms, they will be continuously shifting their ground. Facts for their own sake have never taken a subject very far, however deceived its practitioners may have been about the values and assumptions brought to the search for facts. Hypotheses and generalizations can emerge from a study of the facts, tested in accordance with the rules of evidence of the historian, without benefit of prior assumptions. But a wide gap exists between such inductively produced generalizations, growing out of the data, and hypotheses which descend from more *a priori* theorizing. Even if much work in economic history remains, and will remain, that of adding to the stock of knowledge—simply finding out more about the past—the direction in which this extension of knowledge takes place, even without any more precise influences of theory, is everywhere governed by prevailing ideas about what is relevant to economic relationships and processes of change. From an infinite population of facts some conceptual filter is required for selection. Economic history developed as a specialized branch of study in the late nineteenth century with strong orientations towards current problems, be they those of free trade versus tariffs or socialist versus free-market desiderata in urbanization and industrialization. It was never the case that the business of economic history lay in just painting in the economic strokes on a general descriptive historian canvas—to describe the oven used by Alfred when he burned the cakes. Social history has only just emerged from the servitude of collecting facts to supply such a 'background'. Problems have always determined the main advances in economic history, which is one reason, doubtless, for the fact that economists have contributed some of its most important literature. As M. M. Postan said long ago: 'Economic history ends at the point at which the facts cease to answer questions . . . and the more completely the problems dominate the search for facts, the nearer is the study to the true function of history in social science.'[2]

Influence from the neighbours impinges at very different levels. At the least theoretical—on the surface comes that of contemporary problems. With headlines about the gold reserves appearing monthly, and the full armoury of economic policy periodically deployed to curb imports, raise exports, and inhibit foreign spending, it is little wonder that economic historians should question the interpretation, cast in the shadow of free trade and classical economics, that mercantilist policies in the seventeenth century were only to be explained as the result of simple intellectual confusion or a conspiracy of vested interests. Nor is it surprising, given the population and low-income 'traps' in which so many present-day developing countries are so plainly seen to be struggling, that the role of demographic change in past sequences of economic development (or stagnation) should have become a major topic of research. The same is true of agricultural development, education and a host of newly fashionable themes. What afflicts the world of today inspires research in the economic history of tomorrow.

A mode of research current in neighbouring disciplines can be as influential as the topics upon which it focuses. The search for quantity is changing the face of economic history more than any other single influence, not least because it is the vehicle for a more intensified application of theory. Economic history, of its nature and from its beginning, has been more concerned with quantities than have other kinds of history, even where the object of the inquiry has been the simple narration of change and where statistical series were pieces of narrative in a different notation rather than new intellectual exercises. But figures, no less than facts, are by themselves unstructured and uncritical; as analytically disorientated as opinions without evidence. Indeed the prehistory of writings in the subject is cluttered with work of little value other than as a piecemeal quarry for subsequent research, simply because it consists of haphazard jackdaw collections of quantities, or quantities quite uncritically assembled to prove a case. There is no defence in numbers alone.

Quantification is now becoming so different in degree that the results become changed in nature. The new level of quantification, adopted from contemporary techniques in social sciences, has brought the most noticeable consequences, with labour-intensive and machine-intensive research. At its most extensive, the use of computers, or at least machine sorting, has become a precondition for calculation on this scale (with many thousands of entries required, for example, to perform a 'family reconstitution' on the registers of a single parish, or to compose the many price and quantity series for an accurate index of the current values of English overseas trade in the eighteenth century). Only the computer allows a mass assault on the great data-banks of census records, wills, trade statistics, prices, and the like. The hallmarks of this tradition of research are systematic data upon which to base rigorous statistical analysis. On many issues, piecemeal or literary evidence, supported by contemporary observations and opinions, however well informed or perceptive they might have been, cannot yield objective truth. Where contemporaries could not, or did not, base opinions on systematic data, or use correct sampling methods, their conclusions must be suspect. Their opinions could have been widespread, and not uninfluential in formulating policy, of course, but this does not mean that they were true. Historical demographers are now only too clear that Juliet's marriage at the age of thirteen sets off a completely false trail about the age of first marriage of women in Shakespeare's England, or Verona. Quantification, based on systematic primary sources, here gives the possibility of a definitive assessment for the first time—and many unresolved questions in economic history are such that the only intellectually satisfying answers are, by definition, quantitative.

New-style quantification demands more rigorous critical evaluation of sources—the hallmark of traditional historical skills—rather than less. The greater the degree of mathematical processing being applied to data the greater the premium upon knowing the reliability of the sources and the potential degree of error built into them. The new techniques thus rest more heavily than some of their practitioners acknowledge upon the traditional expertise of the professional historian. The skills of both neighbours need to be combined, as complementary to each other, rather than used as mutual substitutes. Quite apart from problems of reliability in the original data, however, the longer the time-span over which a series runs, the greater the effect of qualitative change upon its constituent parts and the more cumulative the changes in the institutional contest. When statisticians speak of 'index-number' problems in series measuring accurately only quantitative changes in homogeneous data, they are acknowledging the historian's dilemma in assessing qualitative change.

Quantification, needing support by only a very low level of theorizing beyond the technical expertise for producing the series, has also been opening up quite new horizons for comparative economic history. Led by the magisterial initiative of Professor Kuznets, the broad statistical profiles of most of the advanced industrial nations have taken shape, so that we can compare their rates of change over time and their changing economic and financial structures.[3] Some sort of rough-hewn typology is becoming known, viewing these case-histories by their results in quantitative terms. Upon this bedrock of quantities (despite doubts about the sources, which increase as they retreat in time) can be based comparisons of structures and relationships in different economies at different phases of their evolution with greater assurance than with earlier empty hypothesizing about 'stage' theories of history. But statistical similarities (or identities) in structure and rates of change do not, of themselves, imply similarity or identity in the processes of change in different countries, Imputing causation from correlation is as injudicious in economic history as guilt by association in law. What to the economist is seen as a new 'identification problem' is revealed for the historian as a version of an old warning against the temptation of assuming *post hoc ergo propter hoc*. Again, the traditional discipline of one neighbour should complement the newer techniques of the other.

III

Exact measurement is being pressed upon the economic historian from his neighbours, not for its own sake as much as for a new commitment to theory. A 'model' expressing in verbal, geometric, or algebraic form the relationships posited between variables in a sequence is one thing: but filling the boxes with data can then allow correlations to test the relative importance of each element, reveal the ways in which the different variables interact, or measure the relative contribution of each to the final result. Equations and regression analysis march hand in hand.

Certain of the technical assumptions necessary for these mathematical exercises have been challenged by economists and econometricians; but, for historians, the general methodological issue which has brought the new economic history most specifically to their attention has been the 'counter-factual': not accidentally, for at first sight it challenges one of the most widely accepted assumptions of the methodology of history as a discipline; that history can never be scientific in its demonstrations of proof and causation, because no exact repetition of any sequence is possible, and therefore no control experiment to test what would have happened if one variable in a sequence had been different and all others held constant.[4] The 'cliometricians' now claim that, in certain instances, a counter-factual position can be constructed which will allow the gap between what actually happened and what would have happened had one variable been different to be measured and hence the quantitative effect of that variable to be identified. Professor Fogel's construct of the American economy in 1890 *sans* railways is deservedly assured of its place in the annals of economic history as a methodological exercise of the first importance, quite independently of the arithmetical significance of his conclusion.[5]

Discounting arguments over the assumptions used in the model and the operational problems of finding data to fit it, which will continue, he can claim that he is seeking to do no more than test, in a measured way, judgements perforce made by the most empirical historian. When any assessment is put forward that railways were 'important' or that tariffs had a 'major effect' upon the growth of American industry or that slavery was 'economically inefficient', then a counterfactual is implied. The claim is that things would have been significantly different had that particular variable been changed in an American economy without railways, or tariffs, or slavery. Whether explicit or unconscious, whether taken instinctively from common sense and wide reading in the field, on the basis of piecemeal evidence, or by unspecified 'historical judgement', such assertions nevertheless contain assumptions about the interrelationship and order of importance of different variables. If the job of the economic historian, or any other kind of historian, is seeking to understand processes of change the issue is unavoidable. The new techniques of analysis and measurement make assumptions explicit and set up models to allow them to be measured and tested—a procedure in the tradition of Bacon, following a noble line of scientific endeavour concerned to measure, to test, and to prove. The search for quantity in the interests of more exact analysis and testing will be one of the more rapidly advancing frontiers of economic history in the next years. Now the hunt for systematic data is on we shall doubtless all be surprised about how much has been waiting to be discovered.

The more ambitious claims of the new methodology, however, are likely to be fulfilled only within more restricted research inquiries, where evidence allows. The narrower the time-span, the less extensive the range of change under analysis, the more limited the number of potential variables involved, the more stable the institutional context, then the more legitimately can mathematical analysis be applied. But the potential degree of error multiplies as each of these qualifications is relaxed. And more general doubts surround assumptions used in interpreting the price data upon which so much of this analysis rests—whether the necessary partial equilibrium assumptions are legitimate; whether (for Fogel) freight rates were equal to marginal costs and that marginal costs were constant; whether the pricing of the mythical alternative canal transport was realistic; whether—more generally—the income of a social group or an economic sector accurately measures its net contribution to the total product. Here again, for each piece of research, empirical testing will be required to assess these tolerances.

IV

The reorientation of economic theory since 1945 away from short-run equilibrium analysis towards processes of long-term growth, spurred by the problems of engineering economic development in the poorer countries of the world and more local worries

about lagging rates of growth in some 'maturing' industrial economies, has wrought a further major change in economic history.
Clearly, development economics plus a time dimension is analytical
economic history by another name—in intention if not by result.
With Britain and other advanced economies having achieved
industrial development in the past, which it has now become the
great object of policy for other countries to promote in the present,
historical experiences of industrialization became of new interest as
case-histories of growth. By providing a new focus of interest, with
a new fund of ideas and theory, the deployment of such powerful
new resources in the field was bound to make economic historians
rework their conceptions of the subject.

To argue in economists' terms meant a search to measure the
national income, production, trade, population, the labour force,
capital formation, demand, the balance of payments, and a host of
other relationships, for the ultimate pay-off of the infinitely complex
process of change was to be expressed as a group of aggregate
statistics and a percentage rate of growth. Discovering the data for
many such inquiries creates problems enough before 1900, and a
bewildered historian finds scarcely a hypothesis or theoretical
formulation unchallenged amongst his neighbours, which he can
use in the hope that it represents a highest common factor of an
agreed body of theory. But more recent advances in development
theory have robbed him even of the assurance that these disagreements were confined to one principal area.

Most of these early theories of growth centred upon exclusively
economic hypotheses and relationships—capital, labour, resources.
Non-economic variables were acknowledged to come into the act
with population growth, changing tastes, or the entrepreneur but
they scarcely entered into the analysis—apart from Schumpeterian
theory. This was exceptional, both in its dating and in its eventual
direct impact upon economic history. Schumpeter's book *The Theory
of Economic Development*, which set up the entrepreneur as the
'unmoved mover' of economic growth, the active agent of change
which took an economy out of a 'circular flow', was first published
in German in 1911, with a second edition in 1926 and in an English
translation in 1934, after French and Italian versions. It is still true
that its main influence amongst economic historians dated from
after 1945, when Professor A. H. Cole developed an active research
centre in 'entrepreneurial history' at Harvard, inspired by Schumpeter.
The Centre institutionalized this body of theoretical ideas in economic history and spread interest in them very widely through its
journal *Explorations in Entrepreneurial History*. Business history has
been much stimulated by such a focus of interest, based upon a

corpus of theoretical assumptions which gave it coherence, the surface symbol of which has been the popularization of the term 'entrepreneur'.

Schumpeter's ideas, none the less, remained outside the main stream of theorizing about economic growth. Like political or institutional change, non-economic factors were assumed to be responses to economic change as dependent variables (even if allowed feed-backs) or outside the terms of theory altogether as 'exogenous' factors. But, as some economists declared that the main constraints upon the advance of economically backward nations were non-economic[6] and others, seeking to measure the contributions to total growth from different sources in advanced economies, concluded that only a modest fraction of the growth rate achieved could be directly identified with increasing inputs of capital, labour, and resources,[7] so the range of potential analysis became widened. The measure of such 'residual' contributions as technical change, economies of scale, improved organization, the growth of knowledge and education needed to be taken. With this front door being opened for them by economists disillusioned by the analysis of growth in terms of economic variables alone (even if the results were measurable in economic terms), political scientists, demographers, education theorists, psychologists, and sociologists have crowded on to the stage. Economic development had become too important to be left to the economists.

Long before such recent happenings, the terms of reference of economic history at British universities had traditionally included the words 'and social'. Often this meant little more than studying poverty (particularly the legislation and public response evoked by poverty), the standard of living, the institutional development of the labour movement, and the impact of commercial, industrial, and urban life upon the human condition. At the back of such intellectual concern was often a moral imperative, which lay behind the study of economic history more widely. 'What thoughtful rich people call the problem of poverty', wrote R. H. Tawney, 'thoughtful poor people call the problem of riches.'[8] Tawney declined the offer to be the first holder of this chair in 1931.

Social changes were then studied in the main as the consequences of economic change. No longer. New orientations in development theory have been supported by sociologists, armed with new interests and new skills, identifying social and cultural relationships as a dynamic in the process of economic growth in a causative way, whether as forces for inertia or for change. Research is now coming in a flood of 'growth-orientated' studies into such topics as demography, social structure and attitudes, family and kinship, entre-

2D

preneurship, education, law, motivational analysis, the growth and structure of demand in relation to social determinants and cultural traits. Such themes enjoy high priority on the list of fashionable explanations for growth (or absence of growth). With new psychological theories propounding achievement motivation and status attainment through economic success by disprivileged social groups, different ways of bringing up children, as well as the knowledge and motivations imparted by particular styles of education, have become relevant things for economic historians to unearth.[9] When studied intensively, and where possible, quantitatively, such themes will put more specific content into generalizations about the role of social and cultural relationships in the economic matrix. If economic historians have taken most of their new ideas in the past generation from economic theory, it is a reasonable prediction that they will be looking more closely at their other rapidly expanding neighbour, sociology, in the next.

The sort of evidence required for rigorous sociological analysis, which usually comes from the questionnaire and detailed interview in contemporary research, may well prove to be more intractable to discover than economic data but, even so, greater precision will no doubt come to the business of testing the influence of social and psychological phenomena. But these modes of analysis will still remain very different from the treatment of economic variables, and the intractable problem remains that of constructing unitary analytical schemes which can embrace economic and non-economic phenomena as operative variables.

V

To demand that a theory or hypothesis be true before it can be useful is to impose a misleading standard of relevance—even for the most exacting of sciences. Old-style ideal types, like new-style paradigms and models, pose new questions, formulate new puzzles for solution, suggest relationships and mechanisms to be explored and tested.[10] They should also raise the quality of analysis. When hidden assumptions are made explicit, new standards of precision can be imposed upon arguments. When an unchallengeable internal logic has been formulated, much greater critical assessment will need to be applied to the original assumptions if the conclusions drawn from a model are unacceptable. Quantification can challenge opiate generalizations resting upon piecemeal evidence, which were substitutes for systematic analysis. Above all, such theorizing can widen the range of awareness of the historian in seeking to understand change and heighten the critical standards brought to its analysis. Hypotheses stand to be qualified or rejected, of course, in the light of the evidence and from the challenge of other hypotheses and the data brought forward in association with them. Clapham's question 'how representative?' is the first inquiry that an historian will make to the data produced in support of a theory.

Acceptance of the need for theory—indeed its inevitability in one form or another—says little about the style of theorizing which is acceptable. The search for an all-embracing theory of economic growth, for example, may be judged as unoperational for economic history as a wilderness of individual instances, unstructured by paradigms. Only relevant typologies can span the gap between an infinity of facts and the general theory or the single-cause explanation. To decline to accept a single typology of industrialization is not to disparage the search for scheduling such ideal types, merely to prefer that the typologies established should be chosen according to the range of variables we seek to identify and assess, and the degree of difference between the case histories to which they have to be fitted. A typology appropriate for scheduling similarities and contrasts in the process of industrialization between Britain and Russia or Spain and Japan will probably prove too blunt an instrument to probe the differences between these processes in Sweden and Denmark. In other words we should not treat our typologies like old friends and stick by them through thick and thin: when they have ceased to be useful they should be dropped without compunction.

In more limited investigations the full rigour of exact analysis will be increasingly deployed but on the larger historical canvas social science techniques are being held at bay as much by methodological difficulties as by the operational problems of applying theory and finding data. Economic history, I suspect, will remain a largely synthesizing discipline at this level. Scientific in its intentions, necessarily conceptual in its explanatory apparatus, drawing sustenance from new ideas produced by social sciences, the limitations of data and the multiplicity of influences upon change in a non-mechanistic universe nevertheless condemn it to remain a depressingly inexact science. But it will be economic history with a difference. The incursions of theory will not be self-neutralizing, allowing the subject to go untouched upon its way. Battles will be fought, not over the head of old-style economic history but over its dead body.

The easy escape hatches offered by changing the semantic code lead back to the same conclusion by another route. Direct tautological assumptions that economic history is what economic historians do—their practice or their discipline (whatever that word implies)— give no guidance at all to the criteria upon which these activities can be assessed. To suppose that an economic historian can retreat into a world of exclusively economic variables—or those economic variables subject to quantification—slamming the door behind him on social, cultural, and all other relationships (which become, by assumption, the responsibility of other social scientists and historians), also does not solve the problem of understanding or analysing processes of economic change. The alternatives offered by such a choice lie between taking a more unbalanced view in the analysis of larger issues and tackling problems of narrowing range with ever more technical tools of analysis. The problems of relating variables in any would-be general model of development raise much wider methodological issues than just a critical evaluation of the raw data inputs and the logical consistency of its algebra.

VI

To conclude. As the range of relationships now seen to be relevant to the processes of economic change has widened, as new theories are flung out from the social sciences with which historians must grapple (to understand, if only to reject), so—paradoxically it may be felt— the position of the economic historian as historian is being strengthened. A historian tries to see things in the round, being concerned to take into account all relevant facts when making an assessment about the process of change in a specific context, even though much of the data cannot be quantified and even if the analysis of the interaction of variables becomes impressionistic rather than specific. In contemporary social theory concerned with economic growth, such a multiplicity of variables has no hope of being fitted into a single formula. That hope, if ever hope it was, recedes as each year passes and the activities of social scientists increase. No general theory of growth, no unified 'field theory', is remotely tenable. Social scientists who think that they can fashion data produced, or producible, by historians into such universal explanatory conceptual schemes do as much harm to the intellectual status of their own discipline as they do to that of the historians. So also do those who assume that it is the job of the historian simply to collect data to fill the empty boxes held out to him by the social scientist. In this particular purgatory beggars get overwhelmed with useless riches. The bounty of the past provides individual instances in plenty to support virtually any general proposition. It is only too easy to beat history over the head with the blunt instrument of a hypothesis and leave an impression. But that does not begin to face the issues of whether the discovered instances which fit the hypothesis are representative of their appropriate 'populations' of data; whether they can be explained more efficiently by some other proposition or belong to some other causal relationship altogether.

In the absolute sense, abstracted from specificity of context, little can be said about the effect of any main variable in the process of economic change. No single theoretical relationship has a universal or 'autonomous'—hence predictable—effect. A rising population may be a stimulus, in other circumstances it may be a drag; equivalent alternatives can be posed for a stagnant population. Wars can be favourable or unfavourable. Foreign investment can help to maximize growth or inhibit it. Commercial and merchant strength can lead forward into industrial development or block other forces which might have induced such an impetus. The 'demonstration effect' of alien patterns of demand or institutions, favourable to economic growth in their original societies, can have a disastrous effect when exported. Educational systems can promote new forces for change or consolidate traditional values opposed to it. Social discrimination can energize minority groups into the enterprise roles of a society; other minority groups remain as a *lumpenproletariat*. The same equivocal judgement applies to the economic effects of tariffs or patents or particular tax structures—or any other attribute, perhaps, of economic policy. The contribution of inputs, whether they be of labour, capital investment, research, education, cannot be measured simply as quantities of resources, without regard to their content, values, and qualitative effects; as the contrast in results judged against the quantitative inputs of these things in different advanced industrial countries makes plainer year by year. And even quantitatively and qualitatively identical inputs will vary in their effects according to the context upon which they impinge. The organic difficulties of such transplants between contexts, of course, raise as fundamental questions for comparative history as they do for the quest for universality in social theory.

The conclusions are inescapable. Significance depends upon context. Universality in a theory or a typology can be bought only at the price of abstraction in a function which seems to operate in strictly linear terms: complete universality brings total abstraction, with theory removed from significance in time and place; universalized but, at the same stroke, robbed of all means of identification; of all relevance as an analytical guide to any particular situation; without utility as a diagnosis upon which to base a policy. For the abstract sciences this may be a fate not beyond redemption: for the social sciences it is difficult to see life after such a death. Inside every social scientist there should be a historian struggling to get out. The methodological claims of economic history as one of the social sciences are modest but they can challenge over-ambitious method-

ologies amongst the neighbours. Not least important is this awareness that hypotheses are subordinate to specificity of context in time
and society; that particular relationships potentially interact in such
a multiplicity of ways according to their juxtaposition in a specific
context; that each main attribute of societies can be part cause, part
effect, at the same time a dependent attribute and a creative part of
change; that identical external pressures can induce dramatically
different external responses in a society. More generally, the historian
can argue that the conceptual, even though the source of all analytical significance about the past, must be brought to the stubborn
test of the empirical. And this may prove to be a saving grace for
social science no less than for economic history, as much for those
social scientists unconscious of the past and its disciplines as for
empiricist historians who remain unmindful of the paternity of their
ideas amongst the social sciences. Was it not Lenin who remarked
that history is more cunning than any of us?

Mr. Vice-Chancellor, living with the neighbours is never restful.
But we may hope that the tensions will be creative and that, with
open access to each other's territories, the offspring of such cohabitation will prove vigorous. We must also seek to ensure, even
though this may be unfashionable in a permissive world, that they
remain disciplined.

NOTES

1. R. W. Fogel, 'The Reunification of Economic History with Economic
    Theory', *American Economic Review* (1957); J. R. Meyer and A. H.
    Conrad, 'Economic Theory, Statistical Inference and Economic History',
    Journal of Economic History (1957); S. Kuznets, 'The Interrelation of
    Theory and Economic History', ibid.
2. M. M. Postan, *The Historical Method in Social Science: an Inaugural
    Lecture* (1939); [and above pp. 127–141.].
3. See bibliography in the survey volume, S. Kuznets, *Modern Economic
    Growth* (1966); R. W. Goldsmith, *Financial Structure and Development*
    (1969).
4. F. Redlich, 'New and Traditional Approaches to Economic History . . .',
    Journal of Economic History (1965); R. Dacey, 'Aspects of the Counter-
    factual Controversy', IX *Purdue Conference Papers* (1969).
5. R. W. Fogel, *Railroads and American Economic Growth: Essays in Econo-
    metric History* (1964). For references to the subsequent controversy see
    P. A. David, 'Transport Innovation and Economic Growth: Professor
    Fogel on and off the Rails', *Economic History Review* (1969).
6. Amongst a long list see W. A. Lewis, *Theory of Economic Growth* (1955),
    pp. 12–17; W. W. Rostow, *The Process of Economic Growth* (1952), Ch. II;
    B. F. Hoselitz and W. E. Moore (eds.), *Industrialization and Society* (1960),
    Ch. 15; B. F. Hoselitz, *Sociological Aspects of Economic Growth* (1960).
7. M. Abramovitz, 'Economic Growth in the United States', *American
    Economic Review* (1962); 'Resources and Output Trends in the United
    States since 1870', *American Economic Review* (1960); R. W. Solow,

'Technical Change and the Aggregate Production Function', *Review of Economics and Statistics* (1957); E. F. Denison, *The Sources of Economic Growth in the United States* (1962); *Why Growth Rates Differ* (1967).

8. R. H. Tawney, *An Inaugural Lecture* (as Director of the Ratan Tata Foundation), p. 10.

9. See D. C. McClelland, *The Achieving Society* (1961); E. E. Hagen, *On the Theory of Social Change* (1962), 'British Personality and the Industrial Revolution', in T. Burns and S. B. Saul (eds.), *Social Theory and Economic Change* (1967).

10. M. Weber, *The Methodology of the Social Sciences* (Chicago, 1949); T. S. Kuhn, *The Structure of Scientific Revolutions* (1962); A. Ryan, *The Philosophy of the Social Sciences* (1970); I. Lakatos and A. Musgrave (eds.), *Criticism and the Growth of Knowledge* (1970).

INDEX

Anderson, Adam, xii, 60–61
Anthropology, 49, 106, 112, 114, 118
Antiquarianism, xx, 132, 343
Archaeology, 67, 77, 257
Archives, *see* History, Sources for
Arithmetic, Political, xi–xii, 185
Arkwright, Sir Richard, 323, 345
Ashley, Sir W. J., xiii, xvii, xix, xxii–xxiii, 25, 58, 75, 156, 352
Ashton, T. S., xxix, 237, 317
Ashworth, W., xxix, xxxviii

Bagehot, Walter, xiv, 11, 151
Banking, 33
Beales, H. L., xxxix, 178
Benthamism, xii, 84
Beresford, M. W., xxix
Berlin, Sir Isaiah, 301, 302
Biography, 138
Bloch, Marc, 239–40, 308
Booth, Charles, xvi, 11, 12
Bowley, A. L., 171
Bright, John, 248, 249
Buckle, T. H., 279
Bury, J. B., 279

Capital Formation, 321–4, 363–4
Capitalism, problems in concept of, 178, 187; history of, 65, 93, 302, 363, 365; extension of, 306; spirit of, 116, 122, 124; medieval pre-capitalism, 116–117. *See also* Marxism
Carr, E. H., 301, 304, 308, 345
Carus Wilson, E. M., xxxviii
Causation, nature of, 30–1, 51, 277, 297, 300, 355–6
Chambers, J. D., viii, xxix, xxxviii, 331, 344, 346
Change, occupational, 228–9
Change, technological, *see* Invention

Chapman, Sir S. J., xxv, 22, 163–4
Chartism, 247, 248, 286–7
Checkland, S. G., xxix, 300
China, Tawney on, 156
Chronicon Preciosum, 59, 70
Clapham, Sir J. H., xxv, xxvii, xxviii, 81, 95, 129, 153, 168, 171, 207, 235, 255, 298, 317, 333, 337
Clark, Sir G. N., xxviii, 145
Class in Russia, 50; power of, 53; working class, 168–9, 247, 319
Cliometrics, 335, 374. *See also* History, Econometric and under History, Economc
Coats, A. W., xxx
Collingwood, R. G., 283
Communist Manifesto, 305–6
Comte, Auguste, 15, 334
Consumption, significance of, 175; changes in, 189, 345
Coulton, G. G., 114
Court, W. H. B., xxix, xxxviii
Credit, history of, 174
Cunningham, William, xix, xx–xxii, xxiv–xxv, xxvi, 25, 39, 57, 75, 115, 129, 221, 223, 317, 351

Demography, historical, 81, 335, 342, 373; and Hume, 60; and Malthus, 62
Depression, Great, xv, 168–9
De Tocqueville, A., 92
Dicey, A. V., 76

Econometrics, 224, 227, 336
Economics, Robbinsian definition of, 147, 294; method of, 29, 113, 132, 133, 170–1, 177; observation of real life in, 6, 22, 25, 28, 62, 131, 204, 294; control over forces of, xvii, 85, 309, 362; abstract, 32, 67,

84, 103, 133, 209, 295; mathematical, 31, 68, 74; Marshallian, 317;
language of, 332; origins of, 27;
progress of, 150; recognition as
subject, 21–2, 34; academic posts
in, 22, 58; its relations with economic history, xii–xvii, xx, 14, 30–
32, 51, 65, 67–8, 70, 83, 101, 113,
114, 136, 146, 147–8, 149, 170–6,
204, 206–7, 214, 222, 227, 234,
295, 296, 317, 325–6, 336, 370–382,
see also Economists; Growth,
Economic; History, Economic;
Laws, Economic; Man, Economic;
Motivation; Policy, Economic;
Theory, Economic
Economies, underdeveloped, 200,
234, 237, 249, 332, 343
Economists, defined, 66; tolerance
among, 3, 7–8, 17, 67, 75; *Methodenstreit* among, xiv–xvi, xxi, 4–6,
29, 84, 113, 177, 293; not understanding each other, 9
Economists, Classical School of, xii–
xvi, 74, 84, 94, 246, 248, 292, 354
Economists, Historical School of,
xiii, 4, 5, 6–8, 24, 28–9, 46–7, 66,
84, 92, 112–3, 130, 137, 166, 207,
292–4
Economy, English in Middle Ages,
119–123; in sixteenth and seven-
teenth centuries, 188–200; in
eighteenth century, 338–345
Eden, Sir Frederick, xii, 62, 74
Elton, G. R., 356–7
Empiricism, 130–1, 134, 136, 280,
292, 306, 382
Employment, theory of, 135
Enclosures, 81, 341
Engels, Friedrich, 64, 306
Entrepreneurs, 199, 322, 324–5
Evelyn, John, 58
Evolution, concept of, xvii, 49, 102,
282
Extension, University, xxi, xxiv

Facts, 132, 146, 280, *see also* under
History, Economic
Fay, C. R., xxv, 224, 335
Feudalism, 242
Firth, Raymond, 100, 151, 152–3
Fisher, H. A. L., 296, 358

Fisher, F. J., xxix
Fleetwood, William, 59
Fogel, R. W., 374
Free Trade, 65

Generalisation, xxvii, 103, 137–8,
171, 177, 306, 360–1, 371
Gentry, 196, 243
Geography, 57, 204
George, Henry, 16
Gerschenkron, A., 365
Gibbins, H. de B., xxiii
Gilds, 51–3, 255
Gneist, R. von, 52
Green, J. R., xix, 35
Growth, economic, 188, 190, 206,
208, 209, 235, 248, 318–325, 331–5,
338–346, 354–5, 376–380

Habakkuk, H. J., xxxviii, 370
Hammond, J. L. and Barbara, xxxix,
95, 178
Hancock, Sir W. K., xxix
Heckscher, Eli, 148
Hewins, W. A. S., xv, xxiv–xxv
Hicks, Sir J. R., 146
Hildebrand, Bruno, 93, 167
History, nature and aims of, 48,
96–8, 132, 138, 139–140, 153, 199,
233–4, 282–3, 327, 365, 370–1;
method of, 105, 115, 137–9, 153,
170, 283, 303, 337–8, 355–6; appeal
of, 89, 106–7, 164–5, 286, 308, 327;
origins of, 275–8, 333; growth of,
158, 278–280; revolution in, xviii,
280; generalisations of, 98–9, 103,
138–9; concepts in, 105, 115, 282;
concern of with particular, 104–5,
136, 138, 139, 306, 359–360; concern of with problems, 112, 125,
132, 316, 371; lessons of, xxii, 136,
137, 285, 296–7, 332, 358–9; stages
in, 99, 166–7, 378; prediction in,
363–4; laws of, 359–360; science
of, 279, 280, 301, 356; teaching
of, 286, 308; examinations in, xviii,
90; bias in, 154, 308; objectivity in,
284, 300; change in, 105, 287; and
voluntary associations, 49–51;
growth in, 68, 164; literary, 107,
130, 158; its relations with econ-

omic history, xviii–xix, 14, 26, 30–32, 47–9, 58, 64, 65, 68, 69–70, 76, 83, 85, 98, 153, 157–8, 165–6, 170–1, 176–7, 206, 222, 226, 233–5, 249–250, 296, 326, 369–370, 380

History, Business, 77–9, 179, 376–7

History, Contemporary, 284

History, Econometric, 336, 337, see also under History, Economic

History, Economic, defined (or nearly), 30, 42, 83, 146, 147–8, 169–70, 199, 222, 235, 249–50, 256; questions and problems of, 12–13, 113, 114, 115, 139, 153, 183, 213, 216, 227, 229, 316, 326, 332, 362; its use, 15–16, 85, 139; its appeal, 68; its philosophy, 47, 164, 223; its method, 206, 208; as discipline, 57, 93, 250, 362, 379; unity of, 43, 53; in nutshell, 325–6; as bone business, 70; as help-study, 70; as parvenu, 95; as companion study, 111; as progress, 223–4; visual things and, 256; concerned with groups, 51; concerned with individuals, 226, 227; of common man, 62, 74; and social problems, 130; and scientists, 145–6, 281–2, 303–4, 308; value judgements in, 155; quantification in, 60, 67, 68, 91, 119, 171, 184, 209–10, 214–5, 224–6, 335–7, 372–82; facts in, 152, 165, 199, 226, 371; counterfactuals in, 374; as fact collector, 115, 146–7; as distinct from collections of facts, 115, 132; institutional side of, 102; comparative economic history, 83, 106, 125, 157, 212; general economic history, 82; specialisation within, xxxix, 76, 95, 256; 'new economic history', xxx, 335, 336, 370, 374–5; computers in, xxx, 372; antecedents of, xi–xii, 24, 25, 58–63, 65, 73–4, 90–1, 221, 317, 351–2; growth of, xiv, 159, 291; controversies and, xxx, 29, 32, 33, 49, 205, 371; origins of Germanic nations and, 49, 121; Germans and, xiii, xviii, xxii, 66, 75, 92, 94, 207; French and, 92; recognition as subject, xi, xii, xxi, xxiii, xxvii, 25–6, 48, 73, 94, 129, 317, 351–2, 369; academic posts in,

xxv–xxvii, xxviii–xxx, 22, 57, 159, 203, 255–6, 291, 317, 352–3; textbooks in, xxi, 25, 100; monographs on, xxvii, 33, 95, 174, 184; journals in, 57, 352; Economic History Review, xi, xxvii, 158; Economic History Society, xi, xxvii; research in, xxvii, 26, 100; examinations in, xviii–xix, xxiii–xxiv, xxv–xxvi; at Harvard, xxii, 8, 15, 76; at LSE, xxiv, 33, 57; at Manchester, xxv, xxvi, 76, 164; at Cambridge, xviii–xix, 129; at Oxford, xxvi, 158; at Edinburgh, xxxvi, 39–40, 221; at Nottingham, 233, 331; teaching of, 154, 156–7, 203, 215–6, 233, 291; two traditions in, 346; its position betwixt and between other subjects, xxx, 11, 30, 146, 147, 153, 165, 177, 203, 221–2, 236–7, 291, 309, 326, 331, 333, 338, 352–3, 369, 379; for its relations with other subjects, see under Anthropology, Archaeology, Economics, Geography, History, Mathematics, Psychology, Sociology, Statistics

History, Economic Interpretation of, 27–8, 31, 63–4, 223, 298, 304–5, 353

History, Entrepreneurial, 213, 376

History, Industrial, xii, 63, 77

History, Legal, xix, 32, 48–9, 76, 94, 106, 130, 137

History, Local, xxxix, 191, 257, 328

History, Political, xxvi, 106, 315–6

History, Price, importance of, 59; Thorold Rogers and, xx, 13, 60, 68–9, 75, 77–8; Fleetwood and, 59–60, 63; Beveridge and, 94, 119, 172, 176; Keynesians and, 175; Prices of Corn in Oxford, 74; war and, 172

History, Social, 12, 13, 112, 114, 116, 118, 124–5, 184, 205, 213, 214, 335, 371, 377

History, Sources for, use of, 12, 60, 78–9, 105, 170, 189, 226, 373; limitations of, 79–80, 184–5, 215–6, 357; bulk of, 155; publication of, xviii; foreign records, 82–3; business records, 78, 87, 178–9; legal documents, 79; manorial

documents, 78; blue-books, 79; pamphlets, 80-1, 184; price records, 69; Port Books, 69, 79, 82
History, Urban, 346
Hoskins, W. G., 328
Huet, Bishop, P. D., 59

Ideas, History of, 81, 106
Income, National, 237
India, study of, 156
Industrialisation, in China, 124; in Soviet Union, 363; comparative, 100, 379; see also Revolution, Industrial
Inflation, 59
Ingram, J. K., xiv, 4
Interest, Rates of, 172-3
Invention, 190, 211-2, 228-9, 245, 323, 364

Jevons, W. S., xvi
Johnson, Arthur, 76
Jones, Richard, xiv, 12
Joslin, D. M., xxxviii

Keynes, J. M., 131, 175, 296
Knapp, G. F., 7
Knies, Karl, 92, 293
Knowles, Lilian, xxv, 57, 89

Laissez-Faire, 44, 45, 79, 84
Lancashire, 169
Landlords, 242-3, 244, 321-322
Laslett, Peter, 335, 345
Law, Common, 241; see also History, Legal
Laws, Economic, xiv, 4, 7, 29, 103, 113, 114, 118, 167
Lectures, Inaugural, themes of, xxviii-xxix, xxx; function of, 21, 89, 183, 331; horrors of, 89, 163, 221, 351
Leeds, 257-266
Lenin, V. I., 218, 301
Leslie, T. E. Cliffe, xiv, xxvi, 3, 4, 24, 28, 29
Liberty in Europe, 240, 298; in Russia, 50; in Smith, 246; voluntary associations and, 41-2, 50

Lipson, E., xxxix, 317
List, Friedrich, 46-7, 52, 65-6, 92, 150
Lloyd, W. F., 74
London, growth of, 191-2

Macaulay, T. B., 33, 94
Macdonald, D. F., xxix
Maine, Sir Henry, 84
Maitland, F. W., xix, 271
Malthus, Thomas, 24-5, 62
Man, Economic, xv, 28-9, 53, 85, 319; see also Motivation
Marshall, Alfred, xvi-xvii, xxii, 5, 29, 58, 131, 146, 148, 154, 156, 206, 222
Marx, Karl, 28, 63-5, 93, 207, 218, 221, 249, 299, 306-7, 334, 351, 363-5
Marxism, xiii-xiv, 64-5, 93, 118-9, 187, 247, 279, 346, 353, 360
Mathematics, its relation to economic history, 31, 67, 140, 327, 374
Mathias, P., xxx
McCulloch, J. R., 206, 248
Menger, Carl, 7, 14, 293
Mercantilism, 47, 49, 52, 148, 340
Meredith, H. O., xxv
Middle Ages, 119-124, 125, 138, 186, 238, 241, 281; towns in, 263-271
Mill, John Stuart, xiii, xxi, 9, 248
Models, 319, 334, 336, 339, 362, 374
Money, 167, 172-3
Motivation, economic and/or non-economic, 40, 42, 46, 51, 53, 61, 101, 123-4, 134, 149, 151-2, 213, 229, 245, 318, 376-7, 380
Multiplier, 177
Myrdal, Gunnar, 148, 249, 294

Nationality, 52, 99, 157
Nexus, Universal Cash, 41
Nicholson, J. S., 39

Peers, Robert, 223
Periodisation, 183, 186, 214, 215, 338
Pigou, A. C., xxv, 84
Pilgrim's Progress, 74
Pirenne, H., 95, 122

Policy, Economic, 95, 151, 166, 354; an illusion, 80; History of, 115, 173
Popper, Sir Karl, 297, 306, 361
Population, growth of, 62, 100, 188, 191, 320, 341–5
Porter, G. R., xii, 66
Postan, M. M., xxviii
Poverty, 169, 189–90, 247
Power, Eileen, xxviii, 164, 167
Price, L. L., xvi, xxvi, 76
Prices, History of, *see* History, Price
Primogeniture, 241
Profit, 298, 363–4
Progress, 41, 52, 53, 188, 223, 228, 307, 319
Psychology and history, 283, 306, 309, 316, 319; and social history, 205

Quakers, 359

Race, 148–9
Redford, Arthur, xxix
Religion, 238–9, 300
Revolution, search for explanations of, 90, 92; economic causes of, 74; economic history and, 218; superabundance of, 239, 277, 338
Revolution, Agricultural, 340–1
Revolution, Industrial, xx, 23, 91, 166, 167, 214, 217, 237, 244, 248, 319, 323, 332, 338
Revolution, Scientific, 238
Ricardo, David, xiii, 24, 28, 292
Robbins, Lord, 147, 171, 293–4
Rogers, Thorold, xix-xx, 13, 16, 23–4, 75, 77–8, 84, 94, 293, 351
Roscher, Wilhelm, xiii, 66, 92
Rostow, W. W., 303, 307, 338, 339, 343
Russia, economic development of, 223, 224, 363

St Simon, C. H., 63, 92
Savigny, 137
Schmoller, Gustav, xiii, xxvi, 6, 7, 66, 94
Schumpeter, J., 169, 376
Science, object of, 130; nature of, compared to the social sciences, 301, 303–4, 358; and progress, 307
Science, History of, 256

Science, Political, 131, 153
Sciences, The Social, xvii, 85, 96, 111, 114, 119, 296, 303–4, 306, 309, 315–6, 326, 352, 382; historical method in, 136–7, 139, 177, 306, 327; role of economic history in, 116, 124–5, 130, 132, 139, 140, 216–7, 315, 337, 345
Scotland, and dictionary-makers, 61; economic history of, 221, 227
Scott, W. R., 78
Seebohm, F., xix, 11, 13
Seeley, Sir John, 28, 69
Servants, Domestic, 229
Slavery, 307
Smiles, Samuel, 246
Smith, Adam, xii, 24, 34, 39, 43, 45–6, 48, 52, 58, 61, 73–4, 91, 130, 171, 221, 222, 223, 237, 245, 292, 340, 345, 354
Smith, John, xii, 60
Smuggling, 357
Socialism, 247
Sociology, concern of, 104–5, 118, 119, 130, 309; husks of, 16; relations with economic history, 105, 111–2, 114, 136–7, 138, 199, 207–8, 212, 319, 325, 345, 377
Sombart, Werner, 65, 66, 95, 116–7, 206, 352
State, regulation of industry by, 44–5, 236, 243; inhibiting economic progress, 45–7, 52, 94–5; and capital formation, 228; Roman idea of, 48, 49; individual and, 49, 240; restraints on, 49–50; and Society, 47, 52–3; Unwin's distrust of, xxvi, 84
Statistics, supply of, 67, 119, 335; need for an economic history, 171, 208–11, 214–5, 224–5, 227, 335–7, 343–4, 357, 372–3; difficulties of, 184–6
Steuart, Sir James, 61
Stone, Lawrence, 325, 346
Stubbs, W., xviii, xix
Subjects, Academic, 90

Take-off, 338–9
Tariff Reform Campaign, xxiii, xxv
Tawney, R. H., xxviii, xxx, 64, 156, 173, 178, 200, 248, 278, 345, 377

Taxation, 243–4
Technology, History of, 77, 256
Temple, Sir William, 58
Theory, Economic, 9–10, 67, 131, 134, 146, 177, 206, 295, 315, 375; its use to the historian, 10–12, 40–1, 83, 100–102, 104, 115, 148, 149–50, 153, 170–1, 210, 214, 317–8, 378; relativity of, xiv, xxi, 150–1, 152, 293; general, 100, 149–50, 170, 222, 371, 378–9
Thomas, Brinley, 351
Thompson, E. P., 346
Towns, origin of, 263–271; historical function of, 50–1, 242
Toynbee, Arnold, xvi, xix, xx, xxii, 14, 23–4, 75
Toynbee Trust, xvi, 23
Trade Cycle, 153, 169, 257–8
Trade, Terms of, 174
Types, Ideal, 116–7, 208, 378

Underemployment, 190

Unemployment, 168, 169, 174, 258
Unwin, George, xxvi–xxvii, xxviii, 57, 68, 76, 80, 84, 89, 163–4, 166, 221, 223, 229, 242, 317

Vinogradoff, Sir Paul, xix, 76, 115

Warfare, history of, 82, 137–8, 140, 155, 166
Warner, G. Townsend, xxiii, 30
Wealth of Nations, 24, 39, 43–4, 61, 67, 91, 94
Webb, Sidney and/or Beatrice, xvii, xxiv–xxv, 89, 112, 168
Weber, Max, 101, 116, 124, 352
White, Gilbert, 74
Work, medieval concept of, 239

Young, Allyn, 114, 171
Youngson, A. J., xxix